Nontoxic & Natural

Nontoxic 1: not being poisonous. **2:** incapable of carcinogenic, mutagenic, or teratogenic effects, and having no generally recognized specific toxicity symptoms associated with exposure. **3:** produced in a manner that does not include the use of toxic substances. **4:** having had toxic contaminants removed from it. **5:** not producing volatile toxic fumes during use or leaving volatile toxic residues.

Natural 1: existing in or formed by nature; not artificial. **2:** in conformity with the ordinary course of nature; not unusual or exceptional.

NONTOXIC & NATURAL
How to Avoid Dangerous Everyday Products and Buy or Make Safe Ones

Over 1200 Brand-Name Items including

>Additive-free Foods
>Unscented Cosmetics
>Odorless Office Supplies
>Formaldehyde-free Building Materials
>Effective Air and Water Filters
>Natural-Fiber Items
>Safe Cleaning Products
>Nonpoisonous Pesticides
>And Much, Much More

Over 500 Mail Order Sources
Over 400 Inexpensive, Do-It-Yourself Formulas for Everyday Products

DEBRA LYNN DADD

JEREMY P. TARCHER, INC.
Los Angeles
Distributed by St. Martin's Press
New York

Library of Congress Cataloging in Publication Data

Dadd, Debra Lynn.
  Nontoxic & natural.

  Bibliography: p. 286
  l. Toxicology—Popular works.   2. Product safety.
3. Consumer education.   I. Title.
RA1213.D33   1984   602'.94'73   .84-16176
ISBN 0-87477-330-X (pbk.)

Jeremy P. Tarcher, Inc.
9110 Sunset Blvd.
Los Angeles, CA 90069

Design by Tanya Maiboroda

Manufactured in the United States of America
s   10   9

To be healthy ourselves we must heal the Earth and create an environment in which the nurture of that which sustains life is a constant goal.

From *Well Body, Well Earth:*
The Sierra Club Environmental Health Sourcebook
by Mike Samuels, M.D. and Hal Zina Bennett

CONTENTS

ACKNOWLEDGMENTS

First I must correct an oversight in the acknowledgments of the first book I ever wrote and thank my brother Bradley for lending me his electric typewriter so I could begin my career as an author.

Regarding this book, Mark J. Mendell must be mentioned first because, next to me, he has contributed the most. Since practically the beginning of this project he has functioned as research assistant, manuscript reviewer, moral supporter, and friend. While struggling with me through countless early drafts, he improved my writing ability immeasurably and helped to solidify many of the ideas expressed in this book.

Without Martha Sternberg's vision and understanding, this book would never have found a publisher. And once Janice Gallagher accepted the proposed manuscript, she was the ideal editor, helping me to be concise and selective and to express clearly exactly what I wanted to say in a well-organized, streamlined manner.

Gratitude also must be extended to the following people for being supportive, sharing information, or for just being there when I needed them: Robert C. Dadd; Arthur Naiman; Michael Rosenbaum, M.D.; Jeffery Anderson, M.D.; Dean Learned; Denis Dumont; Jim Nigra; Steven O'Malley; Gar Smith; Guy Harris, C. Chem. F.R.S.C.; Alan Levin, M.D.; Merla Zellerbach; Imelda Santos; Regina Reyerson; June Embury; Sterling Johnson, Esq.; Michael Wall; and Kate Zentall. I must also express my appreciation to the 3M company for making Post-It notes with a nontoxic adhesive, and to the entire computer industry for developing word processors.

And a special thank-you to Sara K. for her endless friendship and magic.

PREFACE

Four years ago I didn't know a toxic chemical from a natural substance, I took aspirin for headaches, and I thought that pollution was something caused by industries the government was controlling.

That all changed in January of 1980, when I finally discovered that the swollen eyes, sore throats, skin problems, headaches, insomnia, fatigue, depression, lack of self-confidence and motivation, and compulsive eating I had been suffering from for a good part of my twenty-four years were all being caused by certain toxic chemicals I was exposed to in my everyday environment.

To find relief from my almost constant symptoms, I began to look for common products I could use that did not contain these chemicals. As I experimented with countless different alternatives, I made many mistakes because I knew nothing of labeling laws. I didn't know that chemicals could be hidden in products or that they could take on different names. As I found and incorporated nontoxic and natural products into my life, I began shedding my physical and psychological problems, as well as forty pounds of excess weight. For the first time, I experienced what it was like to feel good. Today I lead a creative, energetic life, am virtually symptom free, and am in control of my wellness instead of being a helpless victim.

Before I began my research, I thought I was alone in reacting to so many things that seemed to be safe for everyone else—things such as tap water, gas heat, acrylic sweaters, perfume. But then I found they weren't so safe for everyone else either, because they contained substances that have been scientifically studied and tested and are known to cause cancer, birth defects, and changes in genetic structure, as well as a multitude of common symptoms and diseases that can range from irritation to disability. Once I knew what to look for, I saw that many other people around me were also being affected, even if they hadn't yet made the connection. Even though many prevalent man-made substances currently appear to be harmless, scientists are concerned about the unknown long-range effects of our low-dose exposure.

In addition, I became more interested in the environment beyond my own and began to consider the effect my actions as a consumer had on the living ecosystem of this planet. I realized that living here is a privilege, and that we have a responsibility to use our technology wisely to work with nature's gifts and not to abuse them.

We as consumers generally incorrectly assume that a product must be safe and nonpolluting or else it wouldn't be on the market. In fact, a good many products are unsafe for a large segment of the population, and most pollution is caused by the manufacture, use, and disposal of consumer products in the home or workplace. Although some regulations do exist for consumer products, such as those limiting the use of coal-tar colors in foods and cosmetics, or the amount of pollutants that can be dumped into our air and water, there are still many products for which there are no government policies. No agency is regulating the levels of toluene diisocyanate that are being emitted from your polyurethane-foam-stuffed, polyester-covered, fireproofed mattress; the phenol in your perfume; or the xylene in your felt-tipped marker. There are no warning labels on toothpaste tubes, bedsheets, cereal boxes, gas appliances, or water faucets. Neither are there any laws that govern the word *natural* on consumer products.

This book is an update and revision of what began as a survival manual for people who have adverse reactions to chemicals in our environment. *A Consumer Guide for the Chemically Sensitive*, self-published on a duplicating machine and bound with staples, met with more success than I had ever imagined would be possible. Not only did it become an essential book for those with chemical sensitivities, it was also purchased by many who were not ill but wanted to preserve their health, use nonpolluting products, and limit their use of products made from nonrenewable resources. Faultless Starch/Bon Ami Corporation was so pleased that their Bon Ami Polishing Cleanser and Cleaning Powder were included that they sent me on a national tour as a spokesperson for nontoxic cleaning products. From the letters, book orders, and positive media response I received, it became clear that a revised and expanded version was needed for the general public.

I wanted to write this book to show that there really are safe alternatives available to those people who want to be healthy and protect our environment; I wanted also to give positive, constructive solutions, instead of just restating the problems. This book will help you choose products that are truly natural and will show you how to stay away from the most toxic of man-made chemicals. It contains something for everyone: instructions for do-it-yourselfers, brand-name products to look for in your local stores, and many wonderful things to order by mail. I have included the most nontoxic and natural alternatives possible and some that are not so natural and not so nontoxic but are less expensive, more readily available, and probably better than what you are using now. Please don't feel you need to throw out all your everyday products and buy new ones. Substitute gradually, and you won't be overwhelmed.

I am not a fanatic, and I didn't write this book to make you one, either. In fact, I am writing these words with a plastic pen. I couldn't live without my plastic telephone answering machine. And I even occasionally eat sugar, but only when I choose, not because it's hidden in my ketchup or my soup mix. And when I do eat it, it is in small amounts, in products with no other harmful additives.

Living nontoxically and naturally is as important a preventive measure as getting proper nutrition and enough exercise, and minimizing stress. And while it is impossible in today's world to be completely free of all contaminants, we have much more control over the amount of toxic chemicals we are exposed to than we think. Even in the urban environment around me, I have significantly reduced my exposure to improve my life 1000 percent; you can, too.

After I finished writing this book, I read it through and felt satisfied with the information it contained, but also felt detached from that information because I had said nothing about how it related to life. I see this book as a tool for transformation; it can go beyond simply recommending the right brand of soap and be applied to every phase of life. It is my hope that after reading this book you will realize that you don't have to be victim to the stresses of environmental assaults, and that the possibilities are endless for creating a nontoxic and natural style of work and pleasure that can help you achieve your full potential.

Nontoxic and natural living is definitely a trend. In 1984, I was able to find easily more than twice the number of products and dealers than I had collected after diligent searching in 1982. As John Naisbitt says in *Megatrends*, "The new source of power is not money in the hands of a few, but information in the hands of many." And as we use the information that this book contains, we can show with our buying dollars that we, the American public, are concerned about the toxins we are often unknowingly exposed to, and that we want to do something about it.

HOW TO USE THIS BOOK

The purpose of this book is to act as a guide to the many products available that do not contain harmful substances. Products are listed alphabetically and use the following format:

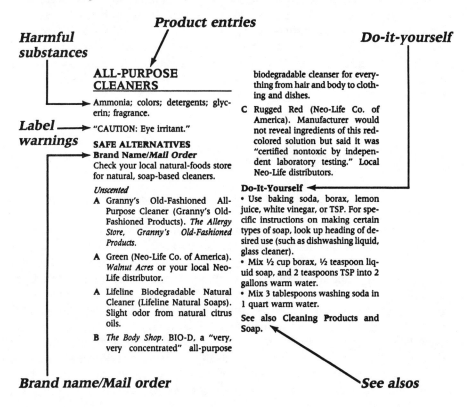

Product entries

Harmful substances

Do-it-yourself

Label warnings

ALL-PURPOSE CLEANERS

Ammonia; colors; detergents; glycerin; fragrance.

"CAUTION: Eye irritant."

SAFE ALTERNATIVES

Brand Name/*Mail Order*

Check your local natural-foods store for natural, soap-based cleaners.

Unscented

A Granny's Old-Fashioned All-Purpose Cleaner (Granny's Old-Fashioned Products). *The Allergy Store, Granny's Old-Fashioned Products.*

A Green (Neo-Life Co. of America). *Walnut Acres* or your local Neo-Life distributor.

A Lifeline Biodegradable Natural Cleaner (Lifeline Natural Soaps). Slight odor from natural citrus oils.

B *The Body Shop.* BIO-D, a "very, very concentrated" all-purpose biodegradable cleanser for everything from hair and body to clothing and dishes.

C Rugged Red (Neo-Life Co. of America). Manufacturer would not reveal ingredients of this red-colored solution but said it was "certified nontoxic by independent laboratory testing." Local Neo-Life distributors.

Do-It-Yourself

• Use baking soda, borax, lemon juice, white vinegar, or TSP. For specific instructions on making certain types of soap, look up heading of desired use (such as dishwashing liquid, glass cleaner).
• Mix ½ cup borax, ½ teaspoon liquid soap, and 2 teaspoons TSP into 2 gallons warm water.
• Mix 3 tablespoons washing soda in 1 quart warm water.

See also **Cleaning Products** and **Soap**.

Brand name/Mail order

See alsos

PRODUCT ENTRIES

Many consumer products commonly used in your home and office are included, but to list every possible type of product would have made this book prohibitively long. Therefore, I have not included entries about which whole books have already been written (for example, drugs, pet-care products, or organic gardening), but instead have concentrated on a broad range of everyday products (mostly necessities, a few luxuries) that would be commonly used by most people. Also not included are such things as cotton dishcloths or wooden clothespins that are so commonplace they are easy to find.

When looking for a particular product, keep in mind that the logic behind this book's layout is to present safe alternatives to everyday products. So look under the heading of the product itself, and not the alternative. For example, if you are interested in finding out about water filters, look up Water, and filters will be a safe alternative, along with bottled water. If you want to know about honey, look it up as the alternative to Sugar. Also, keep in mind that similar items are grouped together under general headings; to find examples of eyeshadow and condoms, look up Cosmetics and Contraceptives.

HARMFUL SUBSTANCES

At the beginning of each entry are listed some of the undesirable substances often found in many brands of the product. These lists are not complete because most products have very complex chemical formulas and may contain hundreds of different chemical compounds, many of which do not appear on labels. For your own reference, the health effects of the basic, undesirable substances are listed in Appendix 1, so that you can decide for yourself if you are willing to be exposed to them. Harmful substances peculiar to a particular product are mentioned in the descriptive text of the main entry. Although all substances have been thoroughly researched and the facts pertaining to them have been double checked, I have not footnoted the text of this book. The danger of toxins constitutes a book in itself, and we are concerned here, after all, with *alternatives*. Nevertheless, for those readers so interested, I have provided references to Appendix 1, as well as a complete bibliography at the end of the book.

Note: Some products, particularly foods, are combinations of other products. Ice cream, for example, is comprised of milk, eggs, and sugar. Under Ice Cream are listed harmful substances added to the basic recipe only, and not the harmful components of the milk, eggs, or sugar, which the ice cream would, of course, also contain. In this case, you might also want to look up Milk, Eggs, and Sugar.

LABEL WARNINGS

Warnings commonly appearing on commercial products that contain toxic chemicals are included here in quotation marks to emphasize just how many products in general use are considered so toxic that they by law require label cautions. Conversely, the absence of such warnings on some products may point out that they, too, should be so labeled.

BRAND NAME/*MAIL ORDER*

Listed here are products you can buy that are relatively safe and for the most part free from the harmful substances listed, or else contain fewer of them than do other products.

Brand-name products generally available in consumer retail outlets come first; following the brand name, the manufacturer is mentioned (in parenthesis) plus pertinent information about the product; last come the *mail-order sources*, in italics. When all products under a particular brand name have been found to be acceptable, they are all combined together (for example, Bickford Flavors). When only some products are acceptable or when products of the same brand are different enough to warrant particular mention, they will be listed after the brand, separated by a slash (for example, Pilot Fineliner/Precise Ball Liner/Razorpoint Pens, or Mother's Oat Bran/Whole Wheat/Quick-Cooking Barley). The addresses of manufacturers and mail-order businesses are listed in the two directories at the end of the book.

Included are as many products as space would allow; an effort has been made to choose brand names that could have national distribution and to eliminate those products available only locally. All research for this book was conducted in the San Francisco area, so there may be many other products available in your local area that also are nontoxic and natural. If not, ask local stores to carry products mentioned in this book. Their managers will most likely be willing to stock specific items if you make it clear you will buy them. Even more effective would be to get together with your friends and all speak to the manager. People who run stores are always happy to stock what will sell but often have a difficult time guessing what their customers want.

Mail-order businesses are followed by a description of the items they sell, if they produce their own goods and sell them primarily by mail order. An effort has been made to itemize listings in their catalogs for easy reference, but to be really complete would have meant several hundred more pages to this book. Therefore, when you order catalogs, you will probably be delighted to find other nontoxic and natural products that were not listed here. The reverse is also true, so do not assume that everything in the catalogs will be acceptable. Be sure to read descriptions carefully and to ask questions before you order.

If you have never shopped by mail, you are in for a pleasant surprise. Reading the mail-order catalogs was the most enjoyable part of writing this book. Every day my mailbox would contain new catalogs selling things I never even imagined existed, things I had never seen in stores even in the major metropolitan city in which I live. These products are often sold at very competitive prices, and are delivered right to your door. Text descriptions of these products that appear within quotation marks are taken from the catalogs themselves, or from letters from the mail-order merchants.

To help you decide which products are most suited to your needs, product ratings of "A," "B," and "C" for nontoxicity and naturalness are given in each listing. These ratings are based on information taken from labels and advertisements, or from manufacturers and retail dealers. Many of the products are used regularly by people who are hypersensitive to toxic chemicals and their derivatives. *These product ratings are based solely on my experience and evaluation. None of these products has been evaluated by independent laboratory tests.*

A—Products of Choice

These products contain none of the harmful substances listed at the beginning of the entry. They are grown, raised, manufactured, packaged, and processed without any toxic or man-made ingredients, materials, or chemicals added in any phase of production. Prepared foods contain at least one organic ingredient and many contain honey, rice syrup, barley malt syrup, or date sugar as a sweetener. A-rated products are truly nontoxic and natural; they are not merely the most nontoxic or natural that happen to be available. For many entries, no brand names are rated A.

B—Better Than Average; Relatively Nontoxic and Commonly Available

These products are basically made up of nontoxic materials and ingredients, but may contain residues of toxic chemicals (such as pesticides or dyes), may be made from relatively harmless derivatives of man-made chemicals, may release a slight toxic odor when wet but be odorless and nontoxic when dry, or have some unavoidable plastic parts.

C—Use With Caution

A C-rated product is included only when it has a particular advantage, even though it normally would be excluded because it contains one or more of the harmful substances listed (an unscented beauty product that contains synthetic glycerin, for example, or an additive-free but sugar-sweetened chocolate bar).

Products rated C may contain sucrose, hydrogenated oil, synthetic glycerin, or some plastic if those are on the harmful substances list. In addition,

C-rated cosmetics may contain artificial colors, mineral oil, talc, paraffin, or EDTA. These products are not really recommended, but are better than others. If you *must* have a chocolate bar, select a C-rated one rather than another containing more artificial additives.

Please do not take these ratings too literally; they are provided simply as a rough guideline to help direct you to products or catalogs that will meet your needs so you do not waste your time or money. *Always investigate the products for yourself.*

Note: The listings of mail-order businesses are accurate as of January 1984. Write for a catalog before ordering anything, and be specific about what you are interested in. What you want may not be in the current catalog, but may still be available. Other items may be discontinued by the time you read this, or else companies may have moved or gone out of business.

DO-IT-YOURSELF

Making products for yourself is the only way to guarantee what's in them. Because of limited space, I had to draw the line somewhere, and so you will not find instructions for many things that need long, detailed explanations (such as knitting a sweater, making soap, or dyeing your own yarn with natural dyestuffs), or any food recipes. Books with these instructions are readily available. And I don't prompt you to do it yourself if it's obvious that you could do something like bake your own bread or sew your own clothing.

What you will find are short, simple formulas for things like cleaning, beauty, and pest-control products that could be hard to locate elsewhere. Under some entries, quite a few different formulas are listed, either because they have different purposes or because different ingredients are called for. I tried to include formulas with varying ingredients for people who are allergic.

The primary criteria for selecting ingredients used in formulas were that they be readily available natural substances, and generally recognized as being safe and effective. Many of the ingredients are common foods that can be purchased at any supermarket. No petroleum derivatives are used. Some natural substances are included that are biodegradable and safe when inhaled but that must be used with caution as they might cause skin irritation or be harmful if swallowed. If any of the ingredients are unfamiliar to you, look in Appendix 2 for more information about them and where they can be purchased.

SEE ALSOS

Mentioned at the end of each listing are other headings to look under for related information—either more detailed information on the same subject, or more information on other subjects mentioned in the text.

AUTHOR'S NOTE

Included in this book are brand-name products and mail-order businesses to help you recognize and choose the many natural and nontoxic products that exist in today's marketplace. Buying these products yourself, encouraging your friends and family members to buy them, and asking for them by name at your local stores will help guarantee their continued and increased availability. No advertising or promotional fees were accepted here, and inclusion of any product or business is not intended to be an endorsement.

This book was written by a consumer for other consumers, in good faith. But to be an effective user or consumer of products means to take responsibility for the choices you make. Be no more quick to blindly accept the information presented here than to blindly accept the fact that all products on the market are safe. Despite heroic efforts on my and the publisher's part for accuracy, any notation of ingredients, chemical components, and the like in a product listing may end up being inaccurate due to typographical error, incorrect information from producers, or other unknown factors. Always, *always* inquire for yourself. Use this book as a hiker would use a detailed map: Choose your course with confidence as to the general terrain, but when you walk, be vigilant for boulders, the weather, and other aspects of the adventure that the map cannot necessarily portray or prepare you for. Remember: You are responsible for the choices you make!

Neither the publisher nor I can guarantee *everything* in this book to be absolutely correct, though we both have worked hard toward that standard. Specifically, we can make no representations about, and therefore cannot be responsible for:

incorrect or incomplete information regarding products;

changes in product ingredients;

substances or processes with toxicity as yet undiscovered;

continued availability of any item;

the effectiveness of any product listed;

hypoallergenicity or lack of toxicity of any product listed;

any adverse health effects caused by using any product or formula.

Assessment of products was made according to information available to all consumers. As with any available product, these particular selections may contain as yet undisclosed harmful substances. Nevertheless, we can be fairly certain that these products are safer than those revealing dangerous contents. It is my belief that products produced and sold by conscientious people truly are purer than those produced and sold by manufacturers unconcerned with this issue.

Throughout the book, many suggestions are made for using products in ways other than those for which they were originally intended. Because government regulations do not allow manufacturers to claim their products to be applicable for certain uses without laboratory proof that they are indeed safe and effective for such uses (and then procuring government approval of the results), these alternate uses are not necessarily approved by the manufacturer. Not all of the formulas are necessarily tried and true, but all have been found by some people to work for them.

If environmental changes are recommended by your doctor, they may be tax deductible as medical expenses with proper documentation and prescriptions. According to Revenue Ruling 55-261, 1955-1 CB307 and in the Tax Court case of T. G. Randolph 67TC481, Dec. 34, 152, one-half of all expenses for pure water and organic food were allowed as a tax deduction to the taxpayer. In addition, air filters, home remodeling, cotton beds, and even moving—if your doctor feels it is necessary—also may be deductible. Consult your own tax advisor to see how this might apply to you.

PRODUCT LISTINGS

Afghans
Air
Air Filters (see Air)
Air Fresheners
Alcoholic Beverages
All-Purpose Cleaners
Aluminum Polish (see Metal
    Polishes)
Ammonia
Antiperspirants & Deodorants
Applesauce
Appliances
Aprons
Astringents

Baby-Care Products
Baby Carriers
Baby Cream (see Baby-Care Prod-
    ucts)
Baby Food
Baby Oil (see Baby-Care Products)
Baby Powder (see Baby-Care
    Products)
Baking Mixes
Baking Powder
Bandages
Barbecue Sauce
Barley Malt Sweeteners (see Sugar)
Barrier Cloth
Basin, Tub & Tile Cleaners
Bath Products
Bathmats
Batting
Beauty Products
Beans

Bed Linens
Beds
Bedspreads
Beer (see Alcoholic Beverages)
Blankets
Bleach
Blusher (see Cosmetics)
Body Powders
Brass Polish (see Metal Polishes)
Bread
Bumper Pads
Butter
Buttons

Cabinets
Cake
Candles
Candy
Carob (see Chocolate)
Carpets (see Rugs & Carpets)
Carpet Shampoo (see Rug, Carpet &
    Upholstery Shampoo)
Caulking Compounds
Cellophane (see Food Storage)
Cereal
Charcoal Lighter Fluid
Cheese
Chewing Gum
Chips
Chocolate
Chrome Cleaners (see Metal
    Polishes)
Cigarettes (see The No-Smoking
    Section)
Cleaning Products

Cleansing Grains
Clothes Washers & Dryers (see Appliances)
Clothing
Coconut
Coffee
Coffee Filters (see Coffee)
Coffee Substitutes (see Coffee)
Combs (see Hairbrushes & Combs)
Comforters & Quilts
Computers
Condoms (see Contraceptives)
Contact Lenses
Contraceptive Jelly (see Contraceptives)
Contraceptives
Cookies
Cookware
Copper Polish (see Metal Polishes)
Copy Machines
Cosmetic Clays (see Cosmetics)
Cosmetics
Cotton Balls
Crackers
Cream (see Lotions, Creams & Moisturizers)
Curtains (see Window Coverings)

Date Sugar (see Sugar)
Denture Cleaners
Deodorant (see Antiperspirants & Deodorants)
Diapers
Dishwasher Detergent
Dishwashers (see Appliances)
Dishwashing Liquid
Disinfectants
Douches
Drain Cleaners
Dried Fruits
Dry Cleaners
Dyes

Eggnog
Eggs
Elastic

English Muffins
Essential Oils (see Fragrances)
Eyedrops
Eyeglasses
Eyeshadow (see Cosmetics)
Fabric
Fabric Softeners
Face Powder (see Cosmetics)
Facials
Featherbeds (see Beds)
Feminine Hygiene Sprays
Feminine Protection
Fireplace Cleaners
Fish & Seafood
Flavoring Extracts
Floor Polish (see Furniture & Floor Polish)
Flooring
Flour
Food
Food Coloring
Food Processors
Food Storage
Foundation (see Cosmetics)
Fragrances
Freezers (see Appliances)
Fruit Butter (see Jams, Jellies & Preserves)
Fruitcake
Fruit Spreads (see Jams, Jellies & Preserves)
Furniture
Furniture & Floor Polish
Futons (see Beds)

Gelatin Desserts
Glass Cleaners
Glue & Tape
Gold Cleaner (see Metal Polishes)
Grains
Granola and Granola Bars
Gravy

Hairbrushes & Combs
Hair Color
Hair Conditioners

Hair-Removal Products
Hair-Setting Lotion
Hairspray
Hammocks (see Beds)
Heaters (see Appliances)
Heat Exchangers (see Air)
Herbs & Spices
Honey (see Sugar)

Ice Cream
Ice Cream Cones
Insulation
Ironing Board Covers

Jams, Jellies, & Preserves
Juices & Fruit Drinks

Kefir (see Yogurt & Kefir)
Kefir Cheese
Ketchup

Laundry Agents
Laundry Starch
Lip Gloss & Lipsticks (see Cosmetics)
Loofas (see Sponges)
Lotions, Creams & Moisturizers
Lubricating Oil
Luggage

Maple Syrup (see Sugar)
Margarine
Markers (see Pens & Markers)
Mascara (see Cosmetics)
Mattress Pads
Mattresses & Box Springs (see Beds)
Mayonnaise
Meat & Poultry
Metal Polishes
Milk
Moisturizers (see Lotions, Creams & Moisturizers)
Mold & Mildew Cleaners
Mosquito Netting
Mouthwash
Mustard

Nail Polish
Napkins (see Paper Napkins & Towels and Table Linens)
Nut Butters (see Peanut Butter & Nut Butters)
Nuts & Seeds

Oils
Olives
Oven Cleaners

Paint
Paint Removers
Paint Thinners
Paper Napkins & Towels
Pasta
Peanut Butter & Nut Butters
Pens & Markers
Perfume (see Fragrances)
Permanent Waves
Pesticides
Petroleum Jelly
Pickles
Pies
Pillows
Placemats (see Table Linens)
Popsicles
Potholders
Poultry (see Meat & Poultry)
Preserves (see Jams, Jellies, & Preserves)
Pretzels
Printer's Ink
Produce
Pudding

Quilts (see Comforters & Quilts)

Ranges (see Appliances)
Reading Boxes (see Printer's Ink)
Refrigerators (see Appliances)
Rice Syrup (see Sugar)
Roofing
Rug, Carpet & Upholstery Shampoo
Rugs & Carpets

Salad Dressing
Salsa
Sanitary Napkins (see Feminine
   Protection)
Sauces
Sauerkraut
Scouring Pads
Scouring Powders
Seafood (see Fish & Seafood)
Seasonings (see Herbs & Spices)
Seeds (see Produce and Nuts &
   Seeds)
Seeds & Plants
Shampoo
Shaving Creams
Shelf Paper
Shoe Polish
Shoes
Shortening
Shower Caps
Shower Curtains
Silver Polish (see Metal Polishes)
Skin Cleansers
Sleeping Bags
Slippers
Soap
Socks & Stockings (see Clothing)
Sodas
Soup Mixes
Soy Sauce
Spices (see Herbs & Spices)
Sponges
Spot Removers
Sprouts (see Produce)
Sugar
Suntan Lotion

Tablecloths (see Table Linens)
Table Linens

Tampons (see Feminine Protection)
Tape (see Glue & Tape)
Tea
Telephones
Textiles
Thread
Tissues
Tofu (see Cheese)
Toilet Paper
Tomato Sauce/Paste
Toothbrushes
Toothpaste
Towels
Toys
Typewriter Correction Fluid

Umbrellas
Undergarments (see Clothing)
Upholstery Shampoo (see Rug, Car-
   pet & Upholstery Shampoo)

Vapor Barrier
Vinegar
Vitamins & Minerals

Wall Cleaners
Wallpaper Cleaners
Water
Water Filters (see Water)
Water Heaters (see Appliances)
Water Softeners
Window Coverings
Wine (see Alcoholic Beverages)
Wood
Wood Finishes
Wood Stoves (see Appliances)
Worcestershire Sauce

Yarn
Yogurt & Kefir

AFGHANS

Dyes; pesticides (mothproofing); plastics (acrylic, nylon, polyester).

SAFE ALTERNATIVES
Brand Name/*Mail Order*
Look for afghans made from natural fibers at fine linen shops, or order by mail.

Cotton
A *Agatha's Cozy Corner, Buffalo Shirt Co., The Cotton Co., The Cotton Place, David Morgan, Erlander's Natural Products, Garnet Hill, Good Things Collective, Homespun Crafts, Norm Thompson, Powers' Country Store, Vermont Country Store, Visions.*

See also Textiles and Yarn.

AIR

Asbestos; formaldehyde; lead; pesticides; plastics.

Air is composed of bits of all substances. As it envelops us and our world, it picks up volatile pollutants and tiny specks of solid particles, moving them around to destinations sometimes far from their original source. Air in an enclosed space can also build up high concentrations of pollutants if they are not sufficiently diluted in our ocean of air.

Air pollution affects our health by damaging tissue of the respiratory system, by poisoning the blood, and by altering DNA within the cells. It can cause emphysema, bronchitis, asthma, cancer, birth defects, and increased incidence of upper respiratory disease and heart disease. Some estimates by health officials attribute up to 20,000 deaths per year in the United States to pollutants in the air.

On a more subtle level, air pollution can cause watery eyes, breathing difficulties, headaches, cough, frequent upper respiratory problems, aggravation of chronic heart and lung disease, shortened life spans, and general poor health.

The quality of outdoor air is regulated by the federal Clean Air Act. Since its passage in 1963, outdoor air has become significantly cleaner in many polluted areas. In 1981, however, the act came up for renewal, and since then industry has been working to weaken the regulations in their favor.

Toxic chemicals in the air are not only outside your window, subject to government regulation; they're in your own home and workplace, under your own control. Americans spend 90 to 95 percent of their time indoors, breathing toxic fumes. In fact, the level of toxic pollutants inside many modern buildings is often higher than that of the air outside—sometimes even higher than the maximum allowable outdoor standards. A 1984 preliminary report made by the Consumer Product Safety Commission estimates that indoor air pollution may be up to *ten times* worse than outdoor pollution.

Indoor air pollution has become a problem in the past decade because of the significant decrease in ventilation in energy-efficient buildings coupled with a tremendous increase in the number of indoor pollution sources: synthetic materials, plastics, and synthetic fibers used in constructing and furnishing modern buildings; scented items; cleaning products; pesticides; gas appliances and heaters; and many other common items made from synthetic substances.

At present, there are no laws that regulate pollutant levels indoors, although the California State Department of Consumer Affairs has compiled a 700-page document, *Clean Your Room!,* that examines the issue in depth and makes recommendations to lawmakers for legislation.

SAFE ALTERNATIVES

Spend as much time as possible in "clean air" locations, away from major metropolitan centers, industrial areas, and freeways: at the beach, in the mountains, around the countryside.

In addition, lower your contribution and reduce exposure to auto emission pollutants:

Use unleaded gas in your car.

Live near your job and walk or bicycle to work on less-trafficked streets.

Travel during noncommute hours and avoid traffic jams.

Use public transportation (especially electric buses, cable cars, and horse-drawn carriages) or carpools.

Live on a street with little traffic.

Avoid living in houses or apartments that have attached garages, unless no one parks in them. A number of cases have been reported of poisoning from combustion by-products that enter the living space from such garages. Pollutants can enter due to improper location of air-conditioning intakes or heater vents, leaky or poorly maintained ducting in the garage, or inadequate seals between the garage and the living space. Especially dangerous is to leave your car engine running to "warm it up" in a basement garage during cold weather, when the heated house would draw the cold polluted air right into it and distribute pollutants from the garage throughout. Air within apartment houses and office buildings can become polluted from basement garages through stairwells and elevator shafts.

To reduce indoor pollution, start by increasing ventilation. Open the window (the air is probably less polluted outside) or, if necessary, use an air-to-air heat exchanger to effectively ventilate a closed house, with only 20- to 30-percent heat loss. Especially necessary in the winter when windows are kept tightly closed and pollutants build up quickly, such a machine functions by blowing stale indoor air out of the house while bringing that air into close contact with fresh outdoor air that it is simultaneously pulling in. This contact, occurring in many small, thin-walled tubes or channels, allows much of the indoor air's heat to be transferred to the incoming cold air so that warmth is retained.

Air is blown through a heat exchanger core that is made of metal, plastic, or treated paper. Tests at the Lawrence Berkeley Lab in California have found the metal core to work best at transferring heat. Metal cores also would release the fewest pollutants to the incoming air.

Heat exchangers are available in several sizes, from a window unit to full house systems that may require installation of ducting. Depending on the amount of pollution being produced, it could take five or six small units to adequately ventilate an average house, or one or two for a small house kept free of pollution sources.

Less ventilation is necessary if pollutant emissions are reduced at their source, by cutting down on consumer products that pollute:

scented beauty and hygiene products

cleaning products made from synthetic chemicals

pesticides

synthetic fibers and fabric finishes

office supplies

furnishings made from synthetic materials

gas appliances and heaters

building materials made with formaldehyde

If you cannot avoid plastics altogether, use only items made from hard plastics, as they are less volatile. To test plastic, try to bend it; use only those kinds you cannot bend or that would break if you applied enough pressure. If a plastic substance is at all pliable, don't use it.

Avoid smokers and indoor areas where smokers are present, and do not allow smoking in your own home or workplace.

In indoor environments and automobiles, use an air purifier if neces-sary. Air-cleaning devices use one or more of four types of cleaning methods: activated carbon; mechanical filtration (HEPA); electrostatic (precipitators, electret); and negative-ion generation. Each method works in a different way and each removes different pollutants. Examine the different methods incorporated into each device before choosing which best suits your personal needs.

Activated Carbon

Activated carbon used in filters work by adsorption, a process by which the pollutant gasses are attracted by and stick to the carbon. There are four types of activated carbon: coconut shell carbon (highest quality); lignite (wood coal); wood carbon; and bituminous (a petrochemical product).

Some coconut shell carbon is impregnated to increase efficiency in removing formaldehyde. CI-impregnated carbon, also known as Formaldezorb, uses a copper/nickel salt; Formaldepure uses nonmetal salts. These special carbons can increase formaldehyde adsorption to up to 90 percent and beyond.

The small air cleaners found in most department, drug, and discount stores are inexpensive and convenient, but do not contain sufficient carbon to effectively clean the amount of air that passes through. Most carbon manufacturers recommend a minimum of one-inch-thick carbon beds; anything less than that is practically useless.

When choosing a carbon filter, take into consideration the placement of the motor, which can produce objectionable fumes of its own. Some filters have the motor placed on top; others

COMPARISON OF POLLUTANTS REMOVED BY AIR FILTERS

	Activated carbon	Mechanical filtration (HEPA)	Negative-ion generation	Electrostatic
Particles (larger than .01 microns) e.g., asbestos, dust, pollen, mold, animal hair, tobacco-smoke particles	No	Yes	No	Yes
Gases (smaller than .001 micron)				
Ammonia	Some	No	No	No
Carbon monoxide	No	No	No	No
Formaldehyde	Some	No	No	No
Lead	Yes	No	No	No
Nitrogen oxide	Some	No	No	No
Pesticides	Yes	No	No	No
Phenol	Yes	No	No	No
Plastic emissions	Yes	No	No	No
Sulfur dioxide	Some	No	No	No
Tobacco-smoke gasses	Yes	No	No	No
Other organic chemicals	Yes	No	No	No

are inside, sandwiched between the filter. Motors can be lubricated, if necessary, with jojoba oil, available in natural food stores.

In some activated carbon units, the carbon is combined with Purafil, a nontoxic odoroxidant made of activated alumina impregnated with potassium permanganate. Purafil works by both absorbing and adsorbing gasses and then destroying them by oxidation. This combination is more effective than carbon alone, but not as effective as the new impregnated carbons.

Activated carbon must be changed regularly. Frequency depends on how many hours a day the filter is used and how polluted the air is. Manufacturers estimate that activated carbon will last about 2000 hours, or twelve hours per day for six months. Under normal use, the carbon should last six to nine months.

Mechanical
These filters work by trapping particles. High-Efficiency Particulate Arrestance (HEPA) filters are rated at 99.99-percent efficiency at .3 microns (dust, pollen, plant and mold spores). Developed by the Atomic Energy Commission during World War II to remove radioactive dust from plant exhausts, they are paperlike filters made of randomly positioned fibers that create narrow passages with many twists and turns. As the air passes through, particles are trapped, making the filter even more efficient with use. One disadvantage is that HEPA filters are generally bonded with polyvinyl acetate plastic, although nonpetrochemical HEPA filters are also available.

HEPA filters need to be changed every twelve to eighteen months.

Electrostatic
These filters attract particles by electricity. This is accomplished either by way of an electronic air cleaner (electrostatic precipitator) or with electret ("Filtret"), electronically charged plastic fibers.

Generally, neither type is recommended. Electrostatic precipitators are rarely more than 80-percent efficient and can quickly drop to 20-percent efficiency. They also produce ozone and positive ions, and must be cleaned often with volatile petrochemical solvents. Electret, on the other hand, is extremely efficient for removing particles, but is a petrochemical product that gives off a strong odor.

Negative-Ion Generators and Ionizers
These machines simply produce negative ions. The biological advantages of negative ions are well known, but because these machines cannot be sold to promote these health effects, they are often advertised as "air cleaners."

As air cleaners, however, they are quite limited. The negative ions produced by the generator will precipitate only certain small particles. While practically useless for dust or pollen, these generators are very effective on the particles found in cigarette smoke and smog, cleaning the air so that it becomes clear and odorless. What they cannot remove from the air are the toxic gasses that are not seen or smelled which are also present in cigarette smoke and smog.

Negative-ion generators and ionizers should be purchased for their health benefits or for use with activated carbon filters for removal of cigarette smoke, but not as broad-spectrum air cleaners. One problem with ion generators in the past has been a buildup of black particles on the walls and furniture around the generator. The newer ionizers have built-in collection systems to trap these particles.

For personal pollution protection when going out in public places, wear a long scarf around your neck of well-washed cotton or raw silk noil that can quickly be placed over your nose to filter unexpected fumes. Otherwise, carry a pipe filled with activated carbon instead of tobacco and breathe through it when necessary.

Brand Name/*Mail Order*

Activated Carbon Air Filters

A Aireox Clean Aire (Aireox Research Corp.). Carbon in a stainless-steel housing for room or auto. *Aireox Research Corp., The Allergy Store, Nigra Enterprises.*

A Klean Air (E. L. Foust Co.) Carbon in a stainless-steel housing for desk top, room, or auto. *E. L. Foust Co., Environmental Purification Systems, Nigra Enterprises.*

A Martinaire F-400A and VH300 (AllerMed Corp.). Carbon and nonpetrochemical HEPA with Formaldepure in a stainless-steel housing. *AllerMed Corp.*

Heat Exchangers

A E-Z-Vent Air-to-Air Energy Recovery Unit (Des Champs Laboratories). *Des Champs Laboratories.*

A Model "DM" Air-to-Air Heat Exchanger (ACS-Hoval). *ACS-Hoval.*

A Q-Pipe Modular Thermal Recovery Unit (Q-Dot Corp.). *Q-Dot Corp.*

B Aldes-Riehs Ventilation System with Heat Exchanger (Riehs & Riehs). *Riehs & Riehs.*

B Berner Economini Rotary Air-to-Air Heat Exchanger (Berner International Corp.). *Berner International Corp.*

B Echo Changer Air-to-Air Heat Exchanger (Memphremagog Heat Exchangers). *Memphremagog Heat Exchangers.*

B Lossnay Air-to-Air Heat Exchange Ventilators (Mitsubishi Electric Industrial Products). *Mitsubishi Electric Sales America, Nigra Enterprises.*

Do-It-Yourself

Plans for making your own heat exchanger can be ordered by sending $2 to Division of Extension, University of Saskatchewan, Saskatoon, Saskatchewan, Canada S7N OWO.

AIR FILTERS

See Air.

AIR FRESHENERS

Aerosol propellants; colors; cresol; ethanol; formaldehyde; fragrances; isopropyl alcohol; napthalene; phenol; xylene.

Air "fresheners" work in one of several ways: interfering by way of a nerve-deadening agent with your ability to smell; coating the nasal passages with an undetectable oil film; deactivating the offensive odor; or covering up the odor with another. Most air fresheners do nothing to freshen the air—they only add more pollutants.

SAFE ALTERNATIVES

Eliminate the need for air fresheners by keeping things clean. Putting an air freshener in a moldy closet, for example, will do nothing to solve the problem; the space must be kept dry and warm to prevent mold growth.

Also, ventilate frequently. Open the windows throughout the house for at least a short period every day. This will not only keep the air smelling fresh, but will help reduce any buildup of toxic fumes that may be emitting from items in your home.

Empty the garbage frequently and clean the can when needed. One-half cup borax sprinkled in the bottom of the garbage can will help inhibit the growth of odor-producing molds and bacteria.

Keep damp kitchen and bathroom towels from mildewing by hanging them so they can dry thoroughly.

Brand Name/*Mail Order*

Instead of commercial air fresheners, buy herbal mixtures or use scented citrus pomanders available at herb stores and bath shops.

A Aura Cacia Natural Air Fresheners (Aura Cacia). Oriental coin baskets filled with air-freshening herbs, spices, and flowers. *Aura Cacia.*

A *Bear Meadow Farm.* Ready-made and kit pomanders.

A *Capriland's Herb Farm.* Ready-made and kit pomanders.

A *Caswell-Massey.* Ready-made pomanders.

Do-It-Yourself

• Distribute partially filled bowls of baking soda or white vinegar discreetly around the room to absorb odors.

• Put herb mixtures in boiling water and continue to boil to release the natural scent.

• Make citrus pomanders: Pierce a thin-skinned orange, lemon, or lime with cloves (if the cloves break while trying to pierce the skin, make small holes with a toothpick first). When the entire fruit is covered, roll in a mixture of 1½ teaspoons orris root powder and 1½ teaspoons ground cinnamon. Wrap in tissue and store in a closed drawer, cabinet, or closet.

See also **Air** and **Herbs & Spices.**

ALCOHOLIC BEVERAGES

Ammonia; asbestos residues; colors; EDTA; flavors; glycerin; hydrogen peroxide; lead residues; methylene chloride; mineral oil; pesticide residues; plastic (PVP); sulfur compounds. (These additives have not been tested for safety in the presence of alcohol or on animals whose detoxification systems have been weakened by long-term alcohol consumption.)

Alcoholic beverages are regulated by the Bureau of Alcohol, Tobacco, and Firearms (BATF), not the FDA. Although the Food, Drug, and Cosmetic Act of 1938 does not exempt alcoholic beverages, no agency is enforcing the law, and ingredients are not listed on the labels.

One or two drinks a day actually can be good for you. Studies of long-lived peoples reveal that small amounts of alcohol are often regularly consumed. Yale University has verified this with studies indicating that two drinks a day provide optimum health.

Once the two-drink-per-day limit is passed, however, problems begin. Alcoholism can cause heart disease, hepatitis, cirrhosis of the liver, decreased resistance to disease, shortened life span, nutrient deficiencies, cancer, fetal alcohol syndrome, brain damage, stroke, phlebitis, varicose veins, and a reduced testosterone level that in males causes sexual impotence, loss of libido, breast enlargement, and loss of facial hair. A bill currently in the House of Representatives suggests that labels on alcoholic beverages contain a warning: "*Caution:* The Surgeon General has determined that consumption of alcoholic beverages during pregnancy can cause serious birth defects. Alcohol can also impair driving ability, create dependency or addiction, and can contribute to other major health hazards."

The harmful effects of alcohol unfortunately do not stop with harming the body of the drinker. Alcohol is responsible for many needless deaths caused by drunk drivers and is a factor in more than half of all the homicides, rapes, and sexually aggressive acts in this nation. Many alcoholics also die from falling, inability to escape during a fire, drowning, and suicide.

SAFE ALTERNATIVES

If you wish to avoid alcoholic beverages entirely, try one of the nonalcoholic beers listed below or a nonalcoholic varietal grape juice. Sparkling apple juice is a good substitute for champagne; sparkling "wine" can be made by mixing varietal grape juice with carbonated mineral water. Beware of the popular new "dealcoholized wines." Many still contain the same additives as alcoholized wines (some even declare them on the labels). Those who are hypersensitive to petrochemical derivatives should avoid *all* alcoholic beverages.

Brand Name/*Mail Order*

Since the law does not require ingredients of alcohol beverages to be listed, look for the brands listed below, or brands that state on their labels that no chemicals or additives have been added. Natural beers and wines can be found wherever alcoholic beverages are sold, as well as in natural-foods stores.

Beer

B All brands of German beer are protected by a law called the *Reinheitsgebot* ("law of purity"), making it a crime to brew beer with ingredients other than hops, malt, and water.

B Budweiser Beer (Anheuser-Busch).

B Busch Beer (Anheuser-Busch).

B Cold Spring Brewing Beer (Cold Spring Brewing Co.).

B Coors Beer (Adolph Coors Co.).

B Genesee (Genesee). "No preservatives or chemicals."

B Jacob Linenkugel (Jacob Linenkugel Brewing).

B Pabst (Pabst Brewing Co.).

B Pearl Brewing (Pearl Brewing Co.).

B Rolling Rock Premium Beer (Latrobe Brewing Co.).

B Sierra Nevada Stout/Old Chico Brewery Commemerative Beer/ Pale Ale (Sierra Nevada Brewing Co.). "Handmade with purest ingredients. No additives."

B Stroh Beer (The Stroh Brewing Co.).

B Thos. Cooper & Sons (Boles & Co.). Imported from Australia. "Naturally fermented in wooden casks. . . . No chemicals or preservatives are added."

Nonalcoholic Beer

B Birell Premium Light (Swiss Gold). "All natural ingredients. The largest-selling light brew in Europe."

B Kingsbury Brew Near Beer (G. Herleman Brewing Co.).

B Near Beer (Pearl Brewing Co.).

B Texas Select (Pearl Brewing Co.).

Wine

A Domaine de la Bousquette French Red Wine (Veronique Raskin).

A *Four Chimneys*. A varied selection of red and white wines including a Catawba grape wine and "Eye of the Bee," a Concord grape wine made with honey.

A Frey Grey Riesling/Cabernet Sauvignon (Frey Vineyards).

B Canandaigua Wines (Canandaigua Wine Co.).

B Coturri Wines (H. Coturri & Sons).

B Gallo Wines (E & J Gallo Winery). Naturally fermented juice of the finest-quality wine grapes. No sugar or water is ever added; no artificial coloring, flavoring, sulfur dioxide, or additives of any types are used.

B Las Montañas Wines(Las Montañas Winery).

Do-It-Yourself

The Country Store & Farm, Life Tools Co-op, Milan Laboratory and *Nichols Garden Nursery* all carry instructions and supplies for making additive-free beer or wine at home.

See also Juices & Fruit Drinks.

ALL-PURPOSE CLEANERS

Ammonia; colors; detergents; glycerin; fragrance.

"CAUTION: Eye irritant."

SAFE ALTERNATIVES
Brand Name/*Mail Order*
Check your local natural-foods store for natural, soap-based cleaners.

Unscented

A Granny's Old-Fashioned All-Purpose Cleaner (Granny's Old-Fashioned Products). *The Allergy Store, Granny's Old-Fashioned Products.*

A Green (Neo-Life Co. of America). *Walnut Acres* or your local Neo-Life distributor.

A Lifeline Biodegradable Natural Cleaner (Lifeline Natural Soaps). Slight odor from natural citrus oils.

B *The Body Shop*. BIO-D, a "very, very concentrated" all-purpose biodegradable cleanser for everything from hair and body to clothing and dishes.

C Rugged Red (Neo-Life Co. of America). Manufacturer would not reveal ingredients of this red-colored solution but said it was "certified nontoxic by independent laboratory testing." Local Neo-Life distributors.

Do-It-Yourself
• Use baking soda, borax, lemon juice, white vinegar, or TSP. For specific instructions on making certain types of soap, look up heading of desired use (such as dishwashing liquid, glass cleaner).
• Mix ½ cup borax, ½ teaspoon liquid soap, and 2 teaspoons TSP into 2 gallons warm water.
• Mix 3 tablespoons washing soda in 1 quart warm water.

See also Cleaning Products and Soap.

AMMONIA

Ammonia; colors; detergents; ethanol; fragrance.

"CAUTION: Harmful if swallowed. Irritant. Avoid contact with eyes and prolonged contact with skin. Do not swallow. *Avoid inhalation of vapors. Use in a well-ventilated area.*

"POISON: May cause burns. Call a physician. Keep out of reach of children."

SAFE ALTERNATIVES
Use substances other than ammonia for cleaning.

See also All-Purpose Cleaners and Cleaning Products.

ANTIPERSPIRANTS & DEODORANTS

Aerosol propellants; colors; ammonia; ethanol; formaldehyde; fragrance; and glycerin.

In the past ten years, more than eight different ingredients have been banned by the FDA or voluntarily removed from antiperspirants and deodorants because they posed a hazard to users.

The most common symptom from use is skin irritation, often severe enough to require medical attention. This is caused by the mixing of the antisweat compound (aluminum chlorohydrate or, in nonaerosol products, zirconium compounds) with perspiration.

Nonantiperspirant deodorants may contain the bactericide triclosan, which can cause liver damage when absorbed through the skin.

SAFE ALTERNATIVES
Brand Name/*Mail Order*
Look for aluminum/zirconium–free antiperspirants and deodorants in natural-foods stores and drugstores.

Unscented
A Tom's Unscented Roll-On Deodorant (Tom's of Maine). *Kennedy's Natural Foods.*

Natural Scent
A Aubrey Organics Natural Roll-On Deodorants (Aubrey Organics).

A *The Body Shop (England).* Herbal roll-on deodorant with antiperspirant properties.

A Nature de France French Clay Deodorants (Nature de France). *Erewhon Mail Order, Nature de France, The Soap Opera.*

A *New Age Creations.* Herbal Deodorant Powder.

A Weleda Natural Deodorant with Sage (Weleda). Nonaerosol pump spray bottle. *Weleda, Wholesome Paks.*

B Mill Creek Roll-On Herbal Deodorant (Mill Creek Natural Products).

B Tom's Natural Deodorants (Tom's of Maine). *Erewhon Mail Order, Kennedy's Natural Foods, Penn Herb Co., The Soap Opera, Walnut Acres.*

Do-It-Yourself

Antiperspirant
• Mix ½ cup vodka, 2½ cups pure water, 1 tablespoon alum, and 1 tablespoon powdered zinc oxide in a blender or food processor. Place in spray bottle. Shake before using.

Deodorants
• Apply pure, dry baking soda or white clay directly to underarm.
• Mix baking soda with cornstarch, wheat starch, rice starch, or white clay. Apply to underarm.
• Mix 2 teaspoons alum into 1 pint warm pure water. Place in spray bottle.

See also Beauty Products.

APPLESAUCE

Pesticide residues; sucrose.

SAFE ALTERNATIVES
Brand Name/*Mail Order*
Applesauce is generally additive free, but may contain sugar and be sold in a lead-soldered can. Choose an unsweetened brand in a glass jar.

A Erewhon Applesauce (Erewhon). *Erewhon Mail Order.*

A Walnut Acres Applesauce (Walnut Acres). *Walnut Acres.*

B Apple Time Applesauce (Sebastopol Co-operative Cannery).

B Barbara Jo Applesauce (Barbara Jo Ranch Products).

B The Cherry Tree Applesauce (The Cherry Tree). *The Cherry Tree.*

B Gathering Winds Applesauce (Gathering Winds Natural Foods).

B L & A Applesauce (L & A Juice Co.). *Kennedy's Natural Foods.*

B Seneca Applesauce (Seneca Foods Corp.).

B Westbrae Applesauce (Westbrae Natural Foods).

See also Food and Produce.

APPLIANCES

Plastics (phenol-formaldehyde resin; PVC/vinyl chloride).

Study of the health effects of combustion by-products from gas appliances was begun only recently, when energy conservation led us to closing our windows and tightening our homes. Even at this point, the health implications of tightly sealed buildings are just beginning to be known. No one knows what the long-term effects might be.

There is an increasing scientific awareness of the subtle effects of low-level concentrations of combustion by-products. Because these effects are so subtle, you may not be able to easily associate symptoms with exposure.

By-products of gas appliances include formaldehyde, nitrogen dioxide and other oxides, sulfur dioxide and other oxides, various particles, carbon monoxide and dioxide, hydrogen cyanide, nitric oxide, and vapors from various organic chemicals.

Possible symptoms are headaches,

dizziness, fatigue, decreased hearing, slight impairment of vision or brain functioning, personality changes, seizures, psychosis, heart palpitations, loss of appetite, nausea and vomiting, bronchitis, asthma attacks, and respiratory problems. At high levels, exposure may be fatal. Those with emphyzema, asthma, angina, or sensitivities to petrochemicals should be particularly careful about exposure to combustion by-products.

SAFE ALTERNATIVES

Use electric appliances—clothes washers and dryers, dishwashers, heaters, freezers, refrigerators, ranges, and water heaters. Studies show that all-electric homes have lower concentrations of combustion by-products than do homes with gas appliances, and they are almost always lower than corresponding outdoor concentrations. Natural gas should not be used for any other purposes either, such as in a gas fireplace. Ideally, gas pipes should not enter the house at all.

If you are altering a house with existing gas appliances, have the gas supply pipe disconnected and plugged outside the house. Either remove gas pipes within the house or seal all openings tightly.

Converting a house to all-electric utilities often necessitates rewiring for 220 volts and increasing the amperage to 150 or more, depending on the appliances. This should be done by a licensed electrician, although once installed, internal wiring can often be done yourself.

When installing new wiring, electricians use a spray lubricant to ease pulling wires through small holes in the framing material. This is a strong-smelling and highly scented petrochemical that will pool generously within your walls. Provide your electrician with an unscented liquid soap spray instead.

If installing additional wiring through the walls would require much repainting, there are several alternatives. Wiremold, a metal casing that mounts on the wall, may be used to add electric outlets, switches, or lighting fixtures. Heavier wiring, such as for heaters or an electric stove, may also be run outside the wall in BX (flexible metal) cable. Alternately, wiring can be run outside the building in metal conduit.

When using a number of electric appliances, care must be taken not to blow the fuses, especially if you live in an older building that is wired for only 110 volts. To do this, it is necessary to know the wattage of your appliances. On the back or underside of each will be a small metal plate indicating the number of watts the appliance uses (like the number of watts used by a light bulb). A house circuit wired for 110 volts, 15 amps, has 1650 available watts, so the number of watts used when appliances are running cannot exceed 1650. Wattage increases additively, so if, for example, you have a 1000-watt hotplate and a 1500-watt toaster oven, they could not be operated at the same time on the same circuit without the 2500 watts blowing the fuse on that circuit. Many older houses have four 15-amp circuits, two for lights and two for the outlets. If there are two separate circuits in your kitchen, the hotplate could be plugged into one and the toaster oven into the other with no problem. To test the circuits, plug one light into each electrical outlet and unscrew one fuse to see which light goes out.

Electric appliances are currently more expensive to run than are gas appliances. Be sure to inform your local electric company that you have an all-electric house, mentioning specifically your stove, water heating, and space heating. They will give you a special rate to allow you much more electricity at the lowest rate.

You can make your electricity expenditure two to three times more efficient by installing heat pumps into your central heating system and hot-water heater. Ask a local heating and cooling contractor about heat pumps (which function both as heaters and air conditioners) and choose an all-metal unit with a minimum of materials that might release fumes when heated (such as insulation or sealers). Units with a 2.5–3.5 coefficient of performance and an 8–11 EER (energy:efficiency ratio) produce adequate heat for most home needs.

Refrigerators, freezers, dishwashers, washing machines, and clothes dryers should all have interiors of porcelain enamel or stainless steel, not plastic. When purchasing, consider buying reconditioned used appliances; new appliances today all contain significant amounts of plastic, while older appliances have much less plastic, what there is having been outgassed. Also, new appliances with metal interiors are the top of their line and quite expensive; older models provide high-quality nontoxic materials at significant savings. For used appliances, look in newspaper ads, or check in the Yellow Pages under "Electric Appliances—Major."

Most electric ranges are perfectly acceptable. Do not use self-cleaning ovens because they produce carcinogenic polynuclear aromatics (on the EPA list of priority pollutants). Ceramic cooktops are also available with heating elements hidden beneath a smooth ceramic slab. They are as nontoxic as regular electric ranges but have many disadvantages—slow cooling time (up to an hour later they are still hot enough to burn); vulnerability to scratches as well as permanent stains from pots and pans, and other discoloration; and difficulty in cleaning.

If the wiring in your home cannot handle an electric range, either rewire or use small, portable electric appliances: broiler ovens, coffee makers, convection ovens, crockpots, electric frying pans, electric woks, hotplates, rice cookers, toaster ovens, and toaster oven/broilers. These appliances should be made with a minimum of plastic parts and should not have no-stick finishes.

Avoid microwave ovens, since emissions from them have been observed to cause headaches, fatigue, irritability, sleep disturbances, weakness, slow heart rates, changes in EEGs, and increased thyroid functions. Microwaves also affect the blood-brain barrier that prevents particular chemicals from permeating the brain through the bloodstream. An altered blood-brain barrier may allow chemicals to cross the barrier and enter the brain, with unforeseeable results.

Electric space heaters are best for heating. With energy costs continuing to rise, it is better to heat only one room at a time, anyway. Most people find these heaters acceptable, although occasionally an individual may be sensitive to fumes from heated aluminum, heated plastic parts, or heated paint. If paint is a problem, leave the heater on in a separate room for several days or a week to additionally dry the paint. If the problem persists, have the heater sandblasted (this is very inexpensive; look in the Yellow Pages under "Sandblasting"). Currently, unpainted electric heaters are not on the market.

Electric space heaters are available in three types: radiant, convection, or a combination of the two. Radiant heaters "warm people, not air," and are primarily designed for fast spot-heating. Heat is produced by exposed quartz tubes in a metal frame. Convection heaters, on the other hand, slowly warm the air in the whole room by heating a metal case with an enclosed heating element. The element can be a tube filled with either heatable water or oil. These heaters are available in several shapes and sizes, including upright rectangular boxes; long, low "baseboard" models; and modern replicas of old steam radiators. Radiant/convection heaters have quartz tubes for the heating element as well as a fan to help distribute the warmed air.

When using electric heaters, take these safety precautions:

Use a low setting to keep the heater itself from getting too hot.

Keep drapes, bedding, shag rugs, and other combustible objects away from heaters.

Keep electric cords away from heaters.

Clean heaters frequently.

Keep infants and children away from heaters.

Conserve heated air inside with effective insulation, double-pane glass, storm windows, shades or heavy natural-fiber drapes, and internal or external shutters. Do not "tighten" your house with weatherstripping, caulking, or by otherwise sealing all cracks to prevent loss of heated air and the entry of cold outside air. It is precisely this tightening of houses, combined with the increase in indoor pollution sources, that has caused the current indoor pollution problem. If you need more ventilation, use an air-to-air heat exchanger to ventilate without the tremendous heat loss of an open window.

Many people are now turning to wood stoves and fireplaces for heat. Even though the burning of wood produces toxic by-products (such as carcinogenic benzo-a-pyrene), you will know if they are present in your living space because they are extremely irritating to eyes, nose, and respiratory system. Little research has been done on the effects of wood combustion by-products on indoor pollution, so take precautions to make sure there is adequate ventilation. In addition, be particularly vigilant about the following: Make sure wood stoves and fireplaces are installed and fitted properly. Fix cracks or leaks in the stovepipe and keep a regular maintenance schedule to keep the chimney and stovepipe clean and unblocked. Finally, guard against negative air pressure indoors, watch for downdrafts, and avoid such accidents as logs rolling out of the fireplace. Choose wood stoves with doors as airtight as possible, preferably with an outside air source, ensuring a good draft up the flue.

Fragrant softwoods such as pine and cedar may give off odors that can be troublesome for some people. Use dry, well-seasoned wood only, because it will smoke less. Do not use the pressed-sawdust logs or paper-wrapped, easy-to-light logs sold in grocery stores; they may have been treated with toxic chemicals.

Research is just beginning on the effects of wood burning on outdoor air quality. The state of Oregon has recognized it as a problem and is working to set standards for emissions, with enforcement by 1986. Washington and Colorado are also considering regulations, and the EPA is working on federal standards. The problem seems to be greatest in areas where there is little air movement or during certain weather conditions such as might cause a buildup of other forms of pollution as well.

If you are considering buying or renting, look for places already equipped with—or plan to install yourself—electric, solar, or steam heat.

Do not use unvented gas and kerosene heaters or central forced-air gas heat; these processes emit combustion by-products directly into the living space. If you currently have central forced-air gas heat and are hypersensitive to petrochemicals, it is imperative that you turn off the furnace and substitute a nonpolluting source of heat. In a multiunit building where turning off the central furnace is impossible, close the vents and seal off the ducts in your living space very securely with a foil vapor barrier and foil tape. Vapors still may permeate your unit from adjacent units.

If you must use gas appliances, take steps to reduce pollutant exposure:

Catch pollutants at the source and dilute them with ventilation—through flues, fans, vents. Combustion by-product gases concentrate initially in the area around the appliance and then spread to other areas of the house. Cross-ventilation (two open windows) is significantly more effective than a hood fan after buildup. During cooking, however, a hood fan can remove up to 70 percent of emissions.

Open windows.

Check frequently to make sure equipment is functioning properly and is not sending pollutants back into the house instead of venting them outside. Clean clogged stove burners and blocked flues, fix cracks and leaks in pipes, and perform regular maintenance. A poorly adjusted gas stove can give off carbon monoxide thirty times the rate of a well-adjusted stove.

Make sure you are using the appliance properly.

Put your gas appliances in a space outside of the living area, venting the fumes to the outside and placing a tight seal between the appliances and the living space.

Use a new-model gas stove with low-heat-input gas pilot lights and nongas ignition systems. These stoves produce significantly fewer pollutants than do older stoves with pilot lights.

Brand Name/*Mail Order*
Brand-name appliances are not listed here because electric appliances are available in most stores.

See also Air, Vapor Barrier, and Tape.

APRONS

Dyes; formaldehyde; plastics (polyester).

SAFE ALTERNATIVES
Brand Name/*Mail Order*
Art supply, cookware, and fine linen stores often sell cotton or linen aprons.

A   *Cotton Brokers.* Restaurant-type white aprons.

A   *Hearthsong.* White linen/cotton aprons decorated with handmade lace and embroidery.

AB   *Port Canvas Co.* Simple cotton canvas aprons in natural shade or solid bright colors.

B   *Charette.* Blue denim drafting apron.

B   *Clothcrafters.* White cotton restaurant aprons and a 100% cotton blue hickory-stripe denim apron "made to last all your life."

B   *Erlander's Natural Products.* Several styles of cotton aprons.

B   *Limericks Linens.* Striped cotton aprons from England.

B   *Williams-Sonoma.* Inexpensive cotton kitchen aprons.

See also Fabric, Textiles, and Thread.

ASTRINGENTS

Colors; ethanol; fragrance; glycerin.

SAFE ALTERNATIVES
Brand Name/*Mail Order*
Check your local natural-foods store for natural astringents.

Unscented
B   *Lotions & Potions.* Naturally fermented, alcohol-based astringents.

B   *Denis Dumont.* Non-alcohol Elastin-Aloe Balancing Skin Toner.

C   Basic Formula Pure Toner (Dorothy Gray).

Natural Scent
A   Aubrey Organics Herbal Facial Astringent (Aubrey Organics).

A   *The Body Shop (England).* A variety of toners for all skin types.

A   *Heavenly Soap.* Facial Astringent.

A   *New Age Creations.* Herbal astringents.

C   Rachel Perry Lemon Mint Astringent (Rachel Perry).

Do-It-Yourself
Instead of bottled astringent, try using the following:
• Vodka.
• Club soda.
• White vinegar.
• Buttermilk, applied to skin and allowed to dry for 10 minutes before rinsing.

Following are a number of simple, homemade "potions"; after processing ingredients, pour into a glass spray bottle and store under refrigeration.
• Boil dark-leaved lettuce leaves for 10 minutes in enough water to cover. Let cool and strain.
• Brew strong chamomile or mint tea.
• Mix 1 part vodka with 9 parts strong chamomile or mint tea.

• Combine ⅔ cup pure water, 2 tablespoons vodka, and ¾ cup borax in a blender until borax is dissolved.

• Soak 4 ounces herbs in 2 cups vodka or distilled white vinegar for 2 weeks.

• Blend 2 ounces lemon juice, 2 ounces lime juice, 2 ounces pure water, and 1 ounce vodka.

See also Beauty Products.

B

BABY-CARE PRODUCTS

Ammonia; BHA/BHT; color; fragrance; glycerin; mineral oil; paraffin; talc.

SAFE ALTERNATIVES
Brand Name/*Mail Order*
Look for natural baby-care products at your local natural-foods store.

Baby Cream: Natural Scent
A Country Comfort Baby Cream (Country Comfort).

A *Fluir Herbals.* Baby Balm.

A Lindos Chamomile Baby Cream (Meadowbrook Herbs & Things). *Meadowbrook Herbs & Things.*

A Weleda Calendula Baby Cream (Weleda). *The Allergy Store, Meadowbrook Herbs & Things, Moonflower Birthing Supply, Weleda, Wholesome Paks.*

Baby Oil: Natural Scent
A Baby Oil (Oak Valley Herb Farm).

A Country Comfort Baby Oil (Country Comfort).

A Earthchild Baby Oil (Autumn-Harp). *The Herb Patch, Wholesome Paks.*

A Lindos Chamomile Baby Oil (Meadowbrook Herbs & Things). *Meadowbrook Herbs & Things.*

A Tom's Honeysuckle Baby Oil (Tom's of Maine). *Erewhon Mail Order, Kennedy's Natural Foods, Wholesome Paks.*

A Weleda Calendula Baby Oil (Weleda). *The Allergy Store, Meadowbrook Herbs & Things, Moonflower Birthing Supply, Weleda.*

Baby Powder (talc free): Natural Scent
A Country Comfort Baby Powder (Country Comfort). *After the Stork.*

A Earthchild Baby Powder (Autumn-Harp). Made from powdered herbs. *The Herb Patch, Wholesome Paks.*

A *Fluir Herbals.* Body Powder made with arrowroot and white clay.

A Lindos Chamomile Baby Powder (Meadowbrook Herbs & Things). *Meadowbrook Herbs & Things.*

A Nature de France Natural Baby Powder (Nature de France). *Nature de France.*

Do-It-Yourself
• For baby powder, use cornstarch, wheat starch, or rice starch.
• For baby oil, use any vegetable oil.

See also Baby Carriers; Baby Food; Beauty Products; Beds; Body

Powders; Bumper Pads; Clothing; Diapers; Lotions, Creams & Moisturizers; and Petroleum Jelly.

BABY CARRIERS

Dyes; formaldehyde; plastic (polyester).

SAFE ALTERNATIVES
Brand Name/*Mail Order*
Order cotton baby bundlers by mail, as they are not usually available in local stores.

B *After the Stork.* Cotton corduroy bundlers.

B *Kangaroo Kits.* Carrier kits of cotton corduroy. Also a "Tie Chair" kit that transforms any chair into a highchair.

B *Life Tools Co-op.* Cotton Carriers.

B *Moonflower Birthing Supply.* Cotton denim with calico lining.

B *Poppy Singer-Sayada.* Cotton "snuggly."

B *Whole Earth Access.* Cotton Snug Baby Carrier "handmade by the people of the Dunkard faith who follow lifestyles similar to the Amish in farming communities of Ohio and Indiana."

Do-It-Yourself
Make your own baby carriers from kits offered by *After the Stork* and *Whole Earth Access.*

See also Fabric and Textiles.

BABY CREAM

See Baby-Care Products.

BABY FOOD

Pesticide residues.

SAFE ALTERNATIVES
Brand Name/*Mail Order*
Baby food seems to be an area that natural-food suppliers have overlooked; your local supermarket is the only place that sells baby food.

A *Weleda.* Holle Wholegrain Baby Food imported from Switzerland. Made from biodynamically grown stone-ground, partially sprouted whole grains.

BC Gerber Baby Foods (Gerber Products Co.). Labels on individual food products state, "Prepared without added preservatives . . . artificial colors or flavors." Some varieties contain added salt or sugar.

Do-It-Yourself
Puree small amounts of food in a blender or food processor.

Breast feed. Talk with your physician or contact La Leche League (Franklin Park, IL 60131). Even though mother's milk has yielded high levels of pesticides in tested samples, it is still nutritionally far superior to cow's milk or artificial infant formulas (which are also contaminated). To produce the purest breast milk, mothers should eat a vegetarian diet and drink pure water. Two studies by the FDA revealed that nonmeat-eating nursing mothers had significantly lower levels of pesticides in their breast milk than did mothers who ate meat. Ideally, minimizing toxic chemicals of all kinds should be practiced by every woman of childbearing age, as many toxic substances are stored in the body fat and can be released during pregnancy.

See also Food.

BABY OIL

See Baby-Care Products.

BABY POWDER

See Baby-Care Products.

BAKING MIXES

BHA/BHT; hydrogenated oil; pesticide residues; sucrose.

SAFE ALTERNATIVES
Brand Name/*Mail Order*
Choose a whole-grain, sugar-free baking mix, available at natural-foods stores and supermarkets.

A   *Diamond K Enterprises.* Barley, buckwheat, corn, and whole-wheat pancake mixes.

A   *Paul's Grains.* Whole-grain pancake mixes.

A   Shiloh Farms Pancake Mixes (Shiloh Farms). *Shiloh Farms.*

AB   *Walnut Acres.* Muffin, bread, and pancake mixes made with aluminum-free baking powder.

B   Arrowhead Mills Whole Grain Baking Mixes (Arrowhead Mills). *Erewhon Mail Order.*

B   Barbara's 100% Whole Wheat & Buttermilk All-Purpose Baking Mix (Barbara's Bakery).

B   *Butte Creek Mill.* Stone-ground baking mixes.

B   Elam's Stone Ground Baking Mixes (Elam's).

B   Ener-G Wheat-Free Baking Mixes (Ener-g Foods). *Kennedy's Natural Foods.*

B   Fearn Baking Mixes (Fearn Soya Foods/Richard Foods Corp.)

B   *Old Mill of Guilford.* Baking mixes made from stone-ground and water-ground whole grains. "All natural ingredients, no preservatives."

B   Willamette Valley Mills: The Original 100% Whole Wheat Biscuit Mix (Willamette Mills).

C   Fisher All-Purpose Buttermilk Biskit Mix (Continental Mills).

C   Goldrush Instant San Francisco Style Sourdough Pancake and Waffle Mix (Goldrush Enterprises).

C   *Heartymix.* Large selection of "healthful gourmet" baking mixes made with unbleached and stone-ground flours, but all contain sugar.

C   Roman Meal Natural Foods Whole Grain Complete Baking Mix (Roman Meal Co.).

See also **Baking Powder, Flour, and Food.**

BAKING POWDER

Most baking powders contain aluminum salts. While little research has been done on the actual amounts of these salts we are exposed to from this source, we do know that aluminum salts are toxic. A letter to the *New England Journal of Medicine* points out the connection between aluminum and such brain disorders as dementia, Alzheimer's disease, behavior abnormalities, poor memory, and impaired visual-motor coordination.

SAFE ALTERNATIVES
Brand Name/*Mail Order*

Check your local natural-foods stores for baking powder that does not contain aluminum salts.

A *Special Foods*. Baking powders made from baking soda, calcium phosphate, and white sweet potato, malanga, yam, or cassava flour.

B *Butte Creek Mill*. Aluminum-free double-action baking powder.

B Featherweight Baking Powder (Chicago Dietetic Supply). *Chicago Dietetic Supply, Kennedy's Natural Foods.*

B Rumford's Baking Powder (The Rumford Co.). Double-acting. *Deer Valley Farm, Diamond K Enterprises, Earthsong Herb Shop.*

B *Walnut Acres*. Double-acting, cereal-free, aluminum-free baking powders.

Do-It-Yourself

Eat unleavened baked goods, use recipes that call for baking soda, or make your own baking powder:

• Combine 2 parts cream of tartar, 1 part baking soda, and 1 part cornstarch or 2 parts arrowroot powder (optional). Thoroughly mix ingredients by stirring and sifting several times. If cornstarch is omitted, use immediately after making. For low-sodium baking powder, substitute potassium bicarbonate for baking soda.

• Alternately, substitute the following for 1 teaspoon baking powder: $\frac{1}{4}$ teaspoon baking soda plus $\frac{5}{8}$ teaspoon cream of tartar OR $\frac{1}{4}$ teaspoon baking soda plus $\frac{1}{2}$ cup buttermilk or yogurt.

BANDAGES

Plastic.

SAFE ALTERNATIVES
Brand Name/*Mail Order*

Nonadhesive cotton gauze bandages and cloth adhesive strips are available wherever bandages are sold.

A Johnson & Johnson Cotton Gauze Bandage (Johnson & Johnson). Pure cotton gauze without adhesive.

B Band-Aid Flexible Fabric Bandages (Johnson & Johnson).

B Band-Aid Tricot Mesh Bandages (Johnson & Johnson).

B Curity Curad Flexible Fabric Bandages (Colgate-Palmolive).

B Johnson & Johnson Dermicel Rayon First Aid Tape (Johnson & Johnson).

B Johnson & Johnson Dermilite Paper First Aid Tape (Johnson & Johnson).

BARBECUE SAUCE

Benzyl alcohol/sodium benzoate; flavors; sucrose.

SAFE ALTERNATIVES
Brand Name/*Mail Order*

Choose an additive-free barbecue sauce from your supermarket.

A Walnut Acres Barbeque Sauce (Walnut Acres). *Walnut Acres.*

B Hain Natural Bar-B-Que Sauce (Hain Pure Food Co.).

B Lifespice Hot Shot Barbeque Sauce (SanSel).

B Robbie's "Award Winning" Barbeque Sauce (Robbie's).

B Soken Natural Barbeque Sauce (Soken Trading Co.).

C Cowboy Marinade Barbecue Sauce (Market Square Food Co.).

C Everett & Jones Barbeque Super Q Sauce (Tastebud Delight Co.).

C Floyd & Ila's Oklahoma Style Hickory Bar-B-Q and All-Purpose Sauce (Floyd & Ila).

C Heinz Barbeque Sauce (H. J. Heinz Co.).

C Hunt's All Natural Barbecue Sauce (Hunt-Wesson Foods).

C Island Style Barbeque Sauce (Hawaiian Plantations).

C Oakland Style Barbeque (New Oakland Food Co.).

C Ol' Hired Hands Barbeque Sauce (Far West Trail Cooks Assn.). "No (ugh) preservatives."

C San Francisco's Original Fire-house Bar-B-Que Bar-B-Que Sauce (Firehouse No. 1 Bar-b-que Restaurant).

C Texas Best Barbecue Sauce (Texas Best).

C Trader Vic's Barbecue Glaze/Sauce (Trader Vic's Food Products).

See also Food.

BARLEY MALT SWEETENERS

See Sugar.

BARRIER CLOTH

Barrier cloth, a special type of fabric made from cotton, is reputed to act as a shield through which petrochemical vapors cannot penetrate. Many people who are sensitive to petrochemicals use this tightly woven fabric with 300 threads per inch for mattress covers, auto seat covers, furniture upholstery, and to cover any other item that may be giving off undesirable fumes. Barrier cloth is quite expensive, and though it may be helpful to many, it may not provide sufficient protection for some. It can also serve to make either unbleached cotton batting or down and feathers more tolerable for those who are allergic to these natural materials.

Wash thoroughly before using, as barrier cloth has a very strong odor when new.

Brand Name/*Mail Order*

Order barrier cloth by mail; if you ask the salespeople at your local fabric store, they probably will not have heard of it.

A *The Cotton Place.* By the yard or in ready-made zippered mattress covers, ironing board covers, garment bags, sweater bags, and blanket bags.

A *Janice Corp.* By the yard.

See also Textiles.

BASIN, TUB & TILE CLEANERS

Aerosol propellants; ammonia; detergents; ethanol; fragrance.

SAFE ALTERNATIVES
Do-It-Yourself
• Rub area to be cleaned with half a lemon dipped in borax. Rinse and dry with a soft cloth.
• Scour area to be cleaned with TSP or baking soda sprinkled on a wet cloth.

• Dissolve ¼ cup soapflakes in 1 cup boiling water. When cool, stir in 1 cup whiting.

• Combine 24 ounces TSP, 2½ ounce borax, and 1 ounce powdered soap. Mix thoroughly by shaking in a box or bag. When ready to use, make a paste of the powder and water.

• Dissolve 1 teaspoon sodium hexametaphosphate in 1 gallon water.

See also Cleaning Products.

BATH PRODUCTS

Colors; detergents; ethanol; fragrance; glycerin; mineral oil.

Bubble-bath preparations present the greatest hazard of all bath products. The FDA receives many complaints about urinary-tract, bladder, and kidney infections, as well as genital injuries, skin rashes, and irritations that seem to have been caused by these products.

SAFE ALTERNATIVES
Brand Name/Mail Order
Various herbs, salts, and other natural products to add to your bath can be purchased from natural-foods, drug, and bath stores.

Unscented

A Abracadabra Mineral Bath Salts (Abracadabra). *Erewhon Mail Order, The Herb Patch.*

A Aveeno Colloidal Oatmeal (Cooper Laboratories).

A Batherapy (Para Laboratories). *Common Scents, Penn Herb Co., The Soap Opera.*

A *The Body Shop (England).* Foaming and nonfoaming bath oils.

A Little's Epsom Salt (Little Chemical Co.).

BC *Homebody.* Bath oils and foaming gels.

C *Denis Dumont.* Bubble bath and bath oil.

Natural Scent

A Abracadabra Mineral Bath Salts (Abracadabra). *Common Scents, Erewhon Mail Order, The Herb Patch.*

A Bath Herbs (Country House).

A *Bear Meadow Farm.* Herbal bath blends.

A Dr. Hauschka Baths (Dr. Hauschka Cosmetics). *Meadowbrook Herbs & Things, Weleda.*

A *Fluir Herbals.* Herbal Bath Sachets in cotton chintz bags.

A *Hartenthaler's.* Liquid herb bath formulas.

A *Misty Morning Farm.* Herb-filled bath bags.

A *New Age Creations.* Herbal bath blends.

A Olbas Bath (Penn Herb Co.). *Hartenthaler's, Penn Herb Co.*

A O'Natural Saisons (O'Natural).

A Pre de Provence Bain Moussant Huile d'Olive (Justin Matthew).

A *Ram Island Farm Herbs.* Muslin bath bags filled with sweet-smelling herbs.

A *Richter's.* Herbal bath blends.

A Sand Castle Bath Crystals (Aura Cacia). Ocean and desert minerals. *Aura Cacia.*

A Scarborough Fair Herbal Bath Saque (Scarborough Fair). *Sunnybrook Farms.*

A   *The Soap Opera.* Herb-filled bath bags.

A   Weleda Baths (Weleda). *The Soap Opera, Weleda, Wholesome Paks.*

Do-It-Yourself
• Add one of the following to a tubful of warm bath-water:
   ½ cup or more baking soda
   1 quart of whole or skim milk
   slices and juice of several lemons
   ¼ cup white vinegar
   juice of 1 large grapefruit
• Place 5 to 10 chamomile, mint, or other type of tea bags in very hot water in the bathtub. Steep 5 to 10 minutes and add the rest of the bath water at normal temperature.
• While standing in the bathtub, rub your entire body with your favorite warm oil. Scrape it off with a damp loofa sponge. Follow with a hot bath.
• Dissolve 1 cup honey in 1 cup boiling water. Add 2 cups milk. Dissolve ½ cup sea salt and 2 tablespoons baking soda in warm bath-water and add honey/milk mixture.
• Dissolve 4 tablespoons of sodium hexametaphosphate under warm running water as the tub is filling. After washing with your favorite soap there will be no soap film left on your skin or in the bathtub.

See also Beauty Products and Sponges.

BATHMATS

Dyes, plastics (acrylic, latex, polyester).

SAFE ALTERNATIVES
Brand Name/*Mail Order*
Choose all-cotton bathmats without latex backings, usually available only by mail. Or buy the terrycloth bathmats that come as part of terry bath-towel sets.

Cotton
AB   *Collins Designers, The Cotton Co., The Cotton Place, Erlander's Natural Products, Essential Alternatives, J. Schachter, RAS Distributors.*

Do-It-Yourself
Fold a large white cotton bath-towel in half and sew the edges together.

See also Textiles and Towels.

BATTING

Plastic (polyester); pesticides.

SAFE ALTERNATIVES
Use cotton or wool batting. Choose cotton batting carefully, because it may contain contaminants.

A petrochemical oil is the most common contaminant, used on most batting to reduce cotton dust produced by the batting machines. It is not removed during later processing. The Occupational Safety and Health Administration (OSHA) has set strict standards for cotton dust, as excess amounts cause lung disease in factory workers. Some manufacturers say that applying oil to the batting is the only way to comply with this regulation; nevertheless, batting is available that is made without the oil.

Bleach is sometimes used to whiten the batting. It also removes the natural cotton smell. Unbleached batting is light brown, flecked with cotton seeds, and can smell strongly of the cotton itself. Because the bleach is washed out after it has removed objectionable natural and chemical odors, some people may prefer the bleached batting.

Pesticides are used heavily on cotton. The batting process is purely mechanical and does not cleanse the fibers of these chemicals.

Choose cotton batting that is free from pesticides, oil, and bleach. The characteristics of a particular cotton batting are not usually noticed in cotton clothing, but individuals with chemical sensitivities should give batting careful tests before use in futons, mattresses, pillows, or quilts.

Brand Name/*Mail Order*

Look for natural-fiber batting in fabric stores.

Cotton

A *Dona Shrier*. Batting made from unbleached, organically grown, glandless cotton, free from all pesticides, herbicides, and other chemicals. Available in bulk for stuffing, or felted for upholstery, quilts, or pillows.

A *Erlander's Natural Products*. Batting "not treated with mineral oil, boric acid, or any other fire retardant. Pure cotton, milled from freshly cleaned machines."

A *Janice Corp.* Made "without oil, pesticide, or any additive."

B Mountain Mist Cotton Batting for Quilts (Stearns & Foster Co.). Bleached of all natural oils in a harsh chemical bath, then processed through other solutions that remove the chemicals. Finished with "glazene," a natural aqueous starch solution. Not treated with boric acid for fire retardancy. *Gohn Bros., Norton Candle & Handiwork House, Sears*.

B Mountain Mist Gold (Stearns & Foster Co.). Unbleached long-staple cotton fibers, machine combed and finished with glazene. No cleaning or bleaching is done. Not treated with boric acid.

B *Vermont Country Store.* "Real 100% cotton batting."

Wool

A *Erlander's Natural Products, Life Tools Co-op.*

See also Textiles.

BEAUTY PRODUCTS

Aerosol propellants; ammonia; benzyl alcohol/sodium benzoate; BHA/BHT; colors; cresol; detergents; EDTA; ethanol (alcohol); flavors; fluoride; formaldehyde; fragrance; glycerin; hexane; hydrogen peroxide; isopropyl alcohol; lead; mineral oil; paraffin; phenol; plastics (actylonitrile, nylon, polyester, PVC/VC, PVP); saccharin; talc; toluene; xylene.

Thousands of different ingredients are used in the manufacture of beauty and hygiene products. They are derived from either petrochemicals or natural animal, vegetable, or mineral sources.

Many beauty products for sale are unsafe because cosmetics are not legally required to be tested for safety. The FDA can take action only after a cosmetic is on the market and after enough evidence exists to prove in court that it is hazardous, after which the FDA may halt its production and sale.

Natural beauty and hygiene products are becoming big business, yet there is no official legal definition of the term *natural* as it relates to these items. Even though the FDA requires a complete listing of ingredients on all domestic cosmetics packaged after 15 April 1977, itemized in decreasing order and using standardized language, there are still some problems with the system.

Some items commonly considered by consumers to be cosmetics do not need to have their ingredients listed at all, because they are actually considered to be over-the-counter drugs. According to the FDA's definition, a cosmetic is anything that can be "rubbed, poured, sprinkled or sprayed on, introduced into, or otherwise applied to the human body . . . for cleansing, beautifying, promoting attractiveness, or altering the appearance without affecting the body's structure or functions." If a product claims to affect the body's structure or function (such as fighting tooth decay), it is considered an over-the-counter drug. Hygiene items *not* covered by the cosmetics labeling requirements include deodorant soaps, fluoridated toothpastes, antiperspirants, sunscreens, and antidandruff shampoos.

And on those cosmetic items that do list their ingredients, everything is not necessarily revealed on the label. "Trade secrets" such as fragrance or flavor formulas are not divulged, and hide behind their standardized terms. Nor do the labels tell you whether or not the ingredients in "natural" beauty products are actually derived from natural sources. Some clever manufacturers create "natural" formulas by adding natural-sounding ingredients such as honey or herbs or jojoba oil, instead of actually making a more natural formula by removing unnecessary artificial colors, fragrances, and preservatives.

If you have allergies, beware of products labeled "hypoallergenic." No one product can be truly "hypoallergenic" to everyone. "Hypoallergenic" simply means that some of the most *common* allergens have been removed (fragrance, lanolin, cocoa butter, cornstarch, cottonseed oils). These products still contain ingredients to which you may be allergic, especially if you are sensitive to petrochemicals.

SAFE ALTERNATIVES

Use unscented products. A study by the FDA in conjunction with the American Academy of Dermatologists showed that people with skin irritations should avoid any scented products, regardless of the source of the fragrance. If you are allergic or sensitive to scents, not only should you not use any scented products, but other people in your immediate environment should not, either. Moreover, no scented product should be so much as stored in your medicine cabinet, under the sink, in dresser drawers, or anywhere else in your house.

If you are not sensitive to fragrances, buy unscented products and scent them delicately with natural essential oils, or else buy products with a natural scent, rather than using harsh synthetic fragrances.

Try to use beauty and hygiene products made primarily from naturally derived ingredients. Commonly used petrochemical ingredients that you may want to avoid include: aerosol propellants, alcohol, ammonia, artificial colors and flavors, BHA/-

BHT, EDTA, ethanol, fluoride, formaldehyde, fragrance, glycerol, glyceryl, hexachlorophene, hydrogen peroxide, isopropyl alcohol, methyl ethyl ketone, mineral oil, nylon, paraffin, phenol, anything that begins with PEG- or PPG-, PVP, quaternium 15 (releases formaldehyde), saccharin, and talc.

In addition, you may want to avoid products that contain 2-bromo-2-nitroprone-1, 3-diol (BNPD)—a nitrosating agent that occasionally reacts chemically to form carcinogenic nitrosamines when combined in the bottle with triethanolamine (TEA) or diethanolamine (DEA), or with amines on the skin and in the body. This occurs unpredictably at random; one bottle may become contaminated while another bottle of the same brand sitting right next to it may be safe. Nitrosamines are absorbed through the skin, and you may get a higher level of exposure from beauty products applied to your skin than you would by eating nitrite-cured meats.

Two petrochemical derivatives that are almost inescapable in beauty products are methylparaben and propylparaben. Laboratory tests have proved these common preservatives to be safe; nevertheless, they may cause reactions in those who are very sensitive. Products in this book that do *not* contain methylparaben and propylparaben are rated "A"; those rated "B" or "C" probably do to some extent.

If you wish to make your own beauty products at home, this book contains formulas for items from astringents to toothpastes that are simple and produce results that are much less expensive than buying commercial preparations would be; you won't have to pay for labeling, advertising, or aerosol spray cans. Other books that contain additional formulas for natural beauty products can be found in your local natural-foods store.

Note: Products that contain natural preservatives and those you make at home will not keep indefinitely. Buy or make only enough to last for six months or less, as bacteria grow in these products much more quickly than in those containing synthetic preservatives.

See also Antiperspirants & Deodorants; Astringents; Baby-Care Products; Bath Products; Body Powders; Cleansing Grains; Cosmetics; Cotton Balls; Denture Cleaners; Douches; Eyedrops; Facials; Feminine Hygiene Sprays; Fragrances; Hairbrushes & Combs; Hair Color; Hair Conditioners; Hair-Removal Products; Hair-Setting Lotion; Hair-spray; Lotions, Creams & Moisturizers; Mouthwash; Nail Polish; Permanent Waves; Petroleum Jelly; Shampoo; Shaving Creams; Skin Cleansers; Sponges; Suntan Lotion; Toothbrushes; and Toothpaste.

BEANS

Pesticide residues; sucrose.

SAFE ALTERNATIVES
Brand Name/*Mail Order*
Dried and plain cooked beans are generally additive free, but baked beans, chili beans, or pork 'n' beans may contain sugar; in addition, beans are generally sold in lead-soldered cans. Choose plain beans in glass jars or lead-free cans.

A Eden Organically Grown Pre-Cooked Beans (Eden Foods).

A Walnut Acres Garbanzo Beans/Kidney Beans (Walnut Acres). *Walnut Acres.*

Do-It-Yourself
Buy dried beans at your supermarket or natural-foods store, or order organically grown beans by mail from *Diamond K Enterprises, Erewhon Mail Order, Jaffe Bros., Kennedy's Natural Foods, Shiloh Farms,* or *Walnut Acres* and cook them yourself.

See also Food.

BED LINENS

Dyes; formaldehyde finishes; plastic (polyester).

SAFE ALTERNATIVES
Brand Name/*Mail Order*
Choose all-cotton, linen, or silk bed-linens, which most department stores and linen shops carry. Cotton bed-linens are available in both smooth cotton percale and warm cotton flannel. Some department stores now import cotton flannel varieties from Portugal under their own house brand. Beware of 100-percent cotton sheets labeled "Easy Care" or "No-Iron," as these owe their convenience to formaldehyde.

A *The Cotton Place.* White cotton knit crib sheets and imported linen sheet sets.

A *Homespun Crafts.* Cotton flannel bed-linens.

A *Janice Corp.* Extra-thick English cotton flannel sheets. Also 100% cotton knit crib sheets.

AB *Agatha's Cozy Corner.* "The widest selection of 100% cotton flannel sheets in the country." Can be monogrammed.

AB *The Blue Ribbon Bedding Co.* Nearly two dozen cotton fabrics to choose from for crib size, including percales and flannels, solid colors and prints.

AB *Cuddledown.* Cotton flannel from Europe in solid colors and patterns, crib to king sizes. Also French cotton percale varieties that can be monogrammed.

AB *Day Break.* English cotton flannel sheets.

AB *Erlander's Natural Products.* Extra-heavy cotton flannel bed-linens from Belgium. Also crib size.

AB *Essential Alternatives.* Cotton flannel, from England.

AB *The Futon Shop.* English cotton flannel sheets.

AB *Garnet Hill.* Two types of cotton flannel, in many colors and patterns. Their Line 2 sheets have a higher thread count and are cut longer than any others, and are still priced competitively. Will monogram.

AB *Good Things Collective.* Cotton flannel sheets in several patterns.

AB *J. Schachter.* Cotton flannel bed-linens.

AB *L. L. Bean.* Cotton flannel bed-linens in several solid colors.

AB *Land's End.* Well-priced cotton flannel sheets and pillowcases in out-of-the-ordinary colors and patterns.

AB *Life Tools Co-op.* White cotton flannel sheet sets with seams and "untreated" cotton flannel sheets, imported from England.

AB *Limericks Linens.* Cotton percale and flannel, as well as linen, in solid colors and patterns.

AB *New Moon.* Cotton flannel sheets in solid colors and patterns.

AB *Orvis.* English cotton flannel, in solid colors and patterns.

AB Wamsutta Supercale (Wamsutta). A 200-thread-count percale, "with no chemical processes, but a natural finish." *Collins Designers, The Cotton Place, E. Braun & Co., Erlander's Natural Products, Essential Alternatives, Eugene Trading Co., The Futon Shop, Garnet Hill, Janice Corp., New Moon, RAS Distributors, Vermont Country Store.*

B *Clothcrafters.* Good prices on seamed cotton flannel; flat sheets only, limited colors.

B *Essential Alternatives.* Cotton flannel, from England.

B *Eugene Trading Company.* Pinstripe cotton flannel sheets.

B *Feathered Friends.* Cotton flannel in solid color, stripe, and unusual Belgian floral patterns.

B *Frette.* Expensive, fine-cotton bed-linens with lace, embroidery, and other decoration.

B *Gokeys.* Cotton flannel, with a unique grid check.

B *J. Jill.* Posy-print cotton flannel sheets, and cotton percale trimmed with a calico print.

B *Laura Furlong Designs.* Cotton flannel crib-size sheets, fitted top and bottom.

B Perry Ellis Linen Sheets (Martex).

B Pratesi (Pratesi). High-quality, expensive cotton or silk bed-linens. *Pratesi.*

B *Sleep & Dream.* Cotton flannel, in solid colors and a pastel stripe.

B *Wee Care.* Fitted and flat cradle/crib sizes in white cotton flannel with rosebud print. Also, a sheet set sewn like a pillowcase that can be reversed when soiled.

B *The White House.* High-quality, expensive cotton or silk, embroidered and appliquéd.

B *Vermont Country Store.* Cotton flannel, from Belgium and Germany.

Do-It-Yourself

Sew your own from extra-wide natural-fiber fabrics. *Gohn Bros.* has the best price on heavy-weight, unbleached 100-percent cotton sheeting; *Testfabrics* carries untreated "cotton supercale"; and *Limericks Linens* sells both unbleached and dyed cotton sheeting and linen sheeting.

See also Beds and Textiles.

BEDS

Dyes; flame retardants; plastics (polyester, polyurethane).

SAFE ALTERNATIVES

Nontoxic beds can be made by combining different components made of natural materials.

Cotton Box-Springs

These can be purchased to match from the same companies that make cotton mattresses. Or, if you already own a synthetic bed and box spring that you will be discarding, you may want to strip off the synthetic materials and have the springs recovered, or else use the bare springs. Local mattress companies or used-bed stores are often willing to order new bare springs or to salvage old ones and recover them with fabric of your choice.

Cotton Mattresses

These are stuffed with cotton batting and covered with cotton ticking. Well-made cotton innerspring mattresses are very comfortable and can last for twenty years.

Cotton Thermal Blankets

A stack of at least eight blankets can serve as a mattress.

Featherbeds

These are large pillows the size of a mattress, filled with feathers and covered with 100-percent cotton down-proof ticking. Not thick enough to be used alone as a mattress, featherbeds are usually placed on top of a mattress or futon for added softness and warmth.

Futons

These Japanese folding mattresses made of cotton batting covered with cotton ticking have become quite popular in recent years. They are available in several thicknesses. Local futon stores are often willing to custom make futons with your preferred materials.

Because futons cannot be washed, it is best to use a protective futon cover. Flip the futon frequently when making the bed and puff it up, as the cotton compresses as you sleep. In Japan, futons are rolled up and stored during the day, then unrolled for sleep at night. They should be aired outdoors in the sun at least four times a year.

Hammocks

Completely washable, portable, and inexpensive, hammocks make you feel as if you are floating on a cloud.

Rollaway Bed Frames
Wooden Slat Beds

The above components can be combined in many ways to provide you with a bed that suits your need for height, thickness, firmness/softness, as well as budget. You might try a futon on the metal springs from your old bed, and possibly a featherbed on top of that. The most nontoxic bed would be made of washed cotton blankets on a metal frame.

Be very careful when choosing a cotton mattress or futon. It can be a big investment (a mattress/box-spring set is slightly more expensive than a high-quality synthetic mattress) and will usually not be returnable, so you'll want to make sure it is as free from chemicals as possible. Even the simplest mattress or futon made of 100-percent cotton may contain petrochemical additives; most cotton ticking, for instance, is finished with a sizing to give the fabric stiffness. Moreover, most brands of cotton batting are sprayed with a petrochemical oil during processing, to keep cotton dust levels down; other brands are bleached.

If you are hypersensitive to petrochemicals, it is especially important that the materials used in making your bed be acceptable to you. Ask for samples of ticking and batting before ordering a bed. Put them in your cotton pillowcase and sleep on them to see if you are comfortable with the materials. Wash the ticking as many times as is necessary (for your level of sensitivity) to remove the sizing, and then make sure the ticking used on your bed is washed (in a manner that is acceptable to you) that many times before the bed is constructed.

Less desirable but still somewhat effective is to enclose your synthetic mattress in a barrier-cloth cover. Barrier cloth is a tightly woven 100-percent cotton fabric (300 threads per inch) that is reputed to act as a barrier to petrochemical vapors. Although not as effective for some people as are other methods for reducing the petrochemical exposures in their mattresses, barrier-cloth mattress covers do decrease the level of chemical exposure to some degree, and may be adequate for your needs. They can also be very useful for blocking the slight natural odor of cotton batting or other residue odors that some people may find objectionable in their natural-fiber beds.

One problem you will run into when attempting to buy a totally untreated bed will be the federal flammability laws for mattresses and futons in accordance with the Flammable Fabrics Act of 1953. The most natural fire retardant used is boric acid, a mild skin irritant made from borax and sulfuric acid (derived from petroleum or natural gas). According to the law, all mattresses and futons must be fire resistant except "one-of-a-kind mattress[es] . . . manufactured in accordance with a physician's written prescription . . . to be used in connection with the treatment or management of a named individual's physical illness or injury." The law requires only that the mattress meet the specifications, not that certain specific materials be used, so if you can't get your doctor to write a prescription, having an untreated natural-fiber mattress custom made with a layer of polyester or naturally flame retardant wool might be satisfactory for you and still comply with the law.

Brand Name/*Mail Order*

Those companies designated as offering "custom" mattresses or futons are able to make untreated beds upon request. You might also approach a local mattress manufacturer or futon shop to custom make your bed.

Featherbeds

B *Dreamy Down Fashions, Feathered Friends, Scandia Down Shops, St. Patrick's Down.*

Futons

A *Dona Shrier.* Custom cotton futons made with organic cotton batting, covered with bleached white cotton muslin prewashed in baking soda.

A *Erlander's Natural Products.* "Custom cotton futons made from heavy 100% cotton duck covering that has been washed with soda ash. . . . Cotton batting has *not* been treated with mineral oil, boric acid, or any other chemical and is not fire-proofed."

A *Jantz Design & Manufacturing.* Instruction manual for the traditional technique for making futons and easy slatted-frame designs. Also carries necessary materials and equipment.

A *Peach Blossom Futon.* "Custom cotton futons made from pure, white, odorless long-staple fibre cotton. . . . Free of all linters, seeds, dust, and allergy-producing oils." Crib to king sizes. Also futon covers.

A *Simple Pleasures.* Custom cotton futons with "no flame-retardant-treated materials."

B *Arise Futon Mattress Co.* Futons from "100% fancy blend cotton. . . encased in a heavy mattress ticking . . . manufactured to meet federal regulations regarding fire retardancy."

B *Blue Heron Futons.* Futons from 10-ounce cotton canvas and 8 layers of extra-thick "untreated" cotton batting. Natural or solid-color canvas covers.

B *Bright Future Futon Co.* "Five-inch-thick futons made from 100% cotton batting encased in strong, unbleached cotton muslin."

B *Essential Alternatives.* Six-inch-thick futons made with thick cotton batting in a "heavy cotton muslin shell." Also futon kits.

B *Eugene Trading Co.* Cotton futons. Solid color or patterned covers.

B *The Futon Co.* Made from 8 layers of "cleaned, combed, felted cotton, encased in unbleached muslin." Covers available in muslin, polished cotton, and duck.

B *The Futon Shop.* "Cleaned, combed cotton batting . . . encased in a heavy unbleached cotton drill." Also available with a "slightly springier" wool/cotton filling. Also futon covers.

B *Great Lakes Futons.* Seven-inch-thick cotton futons with unbleached cotton muslin covers.

B *Life Tools Co-op.* "Cotton batting tufted to a muslin cover." Also futon covers.

B *Moonflower Birthing Supply.* Cotton futons, crib and bed sizes, covered with heavy-duty duck.

B *New Moon.* "High-grade cleaned and combed 100% cotton batting with a durable unbleached fire-retardant cotton duck shell. . . . Uses flame-retardant batting and fabric, and meets the bedding and fire law regulations of every state." Also futon covers.

B *Northwest Futon Co.* Futons made of 7-ounce cotton duck filled with "raw" cotton. Solid-color covers.

B *Sleep & Dream.* Futons made of heavy cotton muslin filled with "pure" cotton. Kits also available. Solid-color covers.

B *Xhaxhi.* Cotton treated with boric acid.

Hammocks

A *L. L. Bean.* Natural-color cotton hammocks.

A *Vermont Country Store.* Hand-made cotton rope hammock.

AB *House of Hammocks.* Hammocks in natural white or colors.

B *Heavenly Hammocks.* Uniquely designed cotton hammocks in rainbow colors.

Mattresses & Box-Springs

A *Adams Mattress Co.* Custom innerspring mattresses and box springs made with organic cotton batting and cotton ticking; no dyes or chemical treatments. Ticking can be prewashed according to customer's wishes.

A *Erlander's Natural Products.* Custom innerspring mattresses, crib to king sizes, and for roll-away beds. "Not fireproofed . . . cover is washed with pure washing soda. . . untreated 100% cotton batting . . . unpainted steel springs . . . unfinished hardwood."

A *Janice Corp.* Custom innerspring and solid cotton mattresses and box springs made from "the purest 100% cotton filling and the best 100% cotton ticking which contains no known irritants." Ticking prewashed with vinegar and baking soda. "Tested and approved by ecology patients and doctors." Crib sizes available.

A *Santa Cruz Mattress & Upholstery Co.* Custom innerspring mattress and box springs with "all-cotton cover and padding." No fire retardant used. Will also rebuild your mattress and box spring in all cotton for less than half the price of buying a new one.

B *Scope Natural Fibers.* "All fabrics made of natural cotton. . . . Chemical tests show that hydrocarbons present in materials used to manufacture Scope mattresses do not exceed 10 parts per billion. . . . Products are as pure as possible under current law. . . . Boric acid is used as a fire retardant."

Wooden Slat Beds
B *Essential Alternatives, Eugene Trading Co., The Futon Co., Great Lakes*

Futons, New Moon, Northwest Futon Co., Simple Pleasures, Sleep & Dream, Xhaxhi.

See also Barrier Cloth, Batting, Bed Linens, Blankets, Mattress Pads, and Pillows.

BEDSPREADS

Dyes; plastics (nylon, polyester).

SAFE ALTERNATIVES
Brand Name/*Mail Order*
Cotton bedspreads can be found in most department stores; bedspreads made of cotton and other natural fibers are also available by mail.

A *Annie Cole.* Cotton bedspreads, handknit in England from traditional heirloom patterns.

A *Garnet Hill.* Cotton and cotton/linen blanket covers with cotton dust-ruffles.

A *Homespun Fabrics & Draperies.* Fringed bedspreads made of "raw" or bleached cotton.

A *Janice Corp.* Fringed cotton bedspread.

A *Pembroke Squares.* Hand-crocheted cotton or wool bedspreads copied or adapted from old designs that have been collected from all over Britain.

AB *Agatha's Cozy Corner.* Cotton and cotton chenille bedspreads imported from England.

AB *Avoca Handweavers.* Irish handwoven and handknit wool bedspreads.

AB Bates Bedspreads (Bates). Cotton bedspreads in colonial patterns. *The Cotton Place, Erlander's*

Natural Products, Sears, Vermont Country Store.

AB *E. Braun & Co.* Monogrammed cotton seersucker bedspreads.

AB *East Wind.* Handwoven wool bedspread with a painted floral-wreath design.

AB *Homespun Crafts.* Good selection of cotton bedspreads in colonial patterns.

AB *Laura Copenhaver Industries.* Cotton or cotton/wool "coverlets" and cotton blanket covers in colonial designs. Also hand-knotted cotton fishnet canopy covers.

AB *Limericks Linens.* Fringed cotton bedspreads made in England.

B *Blowing Rock Crafts.* Cotton or cotton/wool "coverlets" and cotton blanket covers in colonial designs. Also hand-knotted cotton fishnet canopy covers.

B *The Cotton Place.* Cotton bedspreads in several styles.

B *Gill Imports.* Bedspreads made of natural handloomed cotton, hand embroidered in Kashmir with dyed wool.

B *Gurian's.* Bedspreads made of natural handloomed cotton, hand embroidered in Kashmir with dyed wool.

B *Shama Imports.* Bedspreads made of natural handloomed cotton, hand embroidered in Kashmir with dyed wool.

B *Trefriw Woolen Mills.* Wool tapestry bedspreads from Wales.

See also Beds, Fabric, Textiles, Thread, and Yarn.

BEER

See Alcoholic Beverages.

BLANKETS

Dyes; pesticides (mothproofing); plastics (acrylic, nylon, polyester).

SAFE ALTERNATIVES
Brand Name/*Mail Order*

Buy blankets made of natural fibers: cotton, cotton/wool blends, unmothproofed alpaca, unmothproofed wool, cashmere, and unmothproofed, undyed Icelandic wool. Preferably, blankets should be white or a natural, undyed color. Cotton thermal blankets can be found in department stores; other fibers will probably have to be ordered by mail.

A *Alice in Wonderland Creations.* Full-size blankets, hand knit with natural-color wool from healthy lambs raised on the company's farm.

A *Cotton Brokers.* Cotton thermal blankets.

A *Hearthsong.* Untreated raw-wool baby blankets.

A *Icemart.* Icelandic wool blankets with plaid and traditional Icelandic designs in natural shades of white, gray, black, and brown.

A *Orvis.* Chinese camel's-hair blanket with silk binding.

A *The Peruvian Connection.* Alpaca blankets in natural alpaca colors.

A *Rammagerdin of Reykjavik.* Blankets made of Icelandic wool in natural shades of brown, gray, and white. Stripes, plaids, and traditional Icelandic motifs.

A   *S. & C. Huber, Accoutrements.* White and indigo (blue) or cochineal (red) windowpane-design 100% wool blanket. Will do custom work.

AB   *Agatha's Cozy Corner.* Cotton thermal blankets.

AB   *The Cotton Place.* Cotton thermal blankets.

AB   *Daybreak.* Cotton thermal blankets.

AB   *Erlander's Natural Products.* Wool and cotton blankets.

AB   *Garnet Hill.* The largest selection of natural-fiber blankets: cotton, llama/alpaca, Merino wool, cashmere/wool, silk, cashmere, cotton/silk, and mohair.

AB   *Gohn Bros.* Cotton thermal blankets.

AB   *Homespun Crafts.* Cotton thermal blankets.

AB   *J. Schachter.* Cotton thermal blankets.

AB   *Janice Corp.* Cotton thermal blankets.

AB   *Landau.* Icelandic-sheep wool blankets in natural and dyed colors.

AB   *Limericks Linens.* Cotton thermal blankets.

AB   *Natural Child.* Wool and cotton thermal crib-size blankets.

AB   *New Moon.* Cotton thermal blankets.

AB   *Vermont Country Store.* Commercial-grade cotton thermal blankets.

B   Cannon Four Seasons Cotton Thermal Blanket (Cannon). *After the Stork, RAS Distributors.*

B   Fieldcrest Cotton Comfort Thermal Blanket (Fieldcrest Mills).

B   *The Scottish Lion.* Wool and wool/cashmere blankets made in Scotland in traditional tartan plaids.

B   *The White House.* Expensive cashmere and cashmere/wool blankets.

See also Textiles and Yarn.

BLEACH

Chlorine; colors; detergents; dyes (fluorescent brighteners); fragrance; hydrogen peroxide.

"CAUTION: Keep out of reach of children. May be harmful if swallowed or may cause severe eye irritation. *Never* mix chlorine bleach with cleaning products containing ammonia, or with vinegar. *The resulting chloramine fumes are deadly.* It also should not be used on silk, wool, mohair, leather, spandex or on any natural fiber that is not colorfast as it can damage or discolor the fabric, and cause colors to run."

Some people may have reactions to the fumes from chlorine bleach, both from the open bottle and from residues left on clothes washed with it, even after the clothes have been dried.

SAFE ALTERNATIVES
Brand Name/*Mail Order*
All commercial brands of bleach con-

tain either chlorine or synthetic scent, so none have been listed.

Do-It-Yourself
Make your whites "whiter" and your brights "brighter" by using sodium hexametaphosphate to remove mineral deposits and soap scum that make fabrics dull and dingy. Sodium perborate and borax are the active ingredients in most "nonchlorine" bleaches, but sodium hexametaphosphate works even better.

Use ¼ cup to 1 cup sodium hexametaphosphate per 5 gallons of water, depending on water hardness, to prevent dulling film from forming. If you don't know how hard your water is, start with ⅛ cup sodium hexametaphosphate and keep adding until water feels slippery between your fingers. Add your soap after the sodium hexametaphosphate, and use only half as much as you normally would.

The first time you use sodium hexametaphosphate, remove old washing film first: Run the laundry through the whole cycle and wash with twice as much sodium hexametaphosphate as you would normally use, and no soap or detergent. You will see a visible difference.

See also Cleaning Products.

BLUSHER

See Cosmetics.

BODY POWDERS

Fragrance; talc.

SAFE ALTERNATIVES
Brand Name/*Mail Order*
Look for body powders at your natural-foods store.

Natural Scent
A Aura Cacia Natural Body Powders (Aura Cacia). Cornstarch-colored, and scented with ground botanicals and essential oils. *Aura Cacia.*

A Dr. Hauschka Body Powder (Dr. R. Hauschka Cosmetics). *Meadowbrook Herbs & Things, Weleda.*

A *Fluir Herbals.* Body Powder made with arrowroot and white clay.

A Nature de France French White Clay Dusting Powder (Nature de France). *Nature de France.*

A *New Age Creations.* Herbal Body Powder made from ground herbs in an eggshell base.

A *Winter Creek Farms.* Sweet Body Powder made from 12 different hand-ground herbs.

Do-It-Yourself
• Use cornstarch or oat powder.
• Mix 10 ounces corn or rice starch with 1 ounce borax.
• Mix 3 ounces French white clay, ⅔ teaspoon magnesium carbonate, and 1 teaspoon calcium carbonate.
• Rinse and dry eggshells thoroughly, then crush to a fine powder in a blender or food processor.

See also Beauty Products.

BRASS POLISH

See Metal Polishes.

BREAD

BHA/BHT; colors; flavors; hydrogenated shortening; mineral oil; MSG; pesticide residues.

Food standards allow more than eighty ingredients to be included in a loaf of bread without their being listed on the label.

SAFE ALTERNATIVES
Brand Name/*Mail Order*

Since many breads are available only locally, only mail-order varieties are listed here. Check labels carefully for breads that are made with organic, unbleached, or whole-grain flour, and that do not contain additives. Most French breads are acceptable. Your natural-foods store will carry whole-grain, additive-free breads and can perhaps recommend a local bakery where you can purchase fresh-baked bread.

A   *Baldwin Hill Bakery.* Traditional European sourdough bread made from stone-ground wheat flour, pure well water, and natural sourdough, baked over a wood fire in a brick oven.

A   Shiloh Farms Breads (Shiloh Farms). Made from stone-ground flours, aluminum-free baking powder, and honey. Some contain sucrose. *Shiloh Farms.*

A   *Walnut Acres.* Nine varieties of bread made with organic ingredients, but containing sucrose.

AB *Deer Vally Farm.* Stone-milled whole-grain breads.

AB *Kennedy's Natural Foods.* Additive-free wheat and wheat-free breads.

See also Baking Mixes, Crackers, English Muffins, Flour, Food, and Grains.

BUMPER PADS

Plastics (polyester, polyurethane).

SAFE ALTERNATIVES
Brand Name/*Mail Order*

Buy cotton bumper pads for cradles and cribs by mail.

B   *Kangaroo Kits.* Kits for bumper pads with precut cotton pieces and polyester batting (replace with cotton batting).

B   *Wee Care.* Cotton flannel bumper pads in cradle and crib sizes. White and rosebud print.

Do-It-Yourself

Roll up double-bed-size cotton blankets and attach them to the crib with six or more cotton muslin ties.

See also Batting, Blankets, Fabric, Thread, and Textiles.

BUTTER

BHA/BHT; colors; hydrogen peroxide; pesticide residues.

Many brands of domestic butter are colored seasonally in order to maintain a consistent color year round. Dairies may use artificial colors or the "natural" colors annatto and carotene (which may be preserved with BHA/BHT) without listing them on the label as ingredients. It is therefore nearly impossible to tell whether any particular brand of domestic butter at any particular time may contain artificial additives.

Pesticide residues (including DDT) are higher in butter than in other milk products because the pesticides in the milk get stored in the fat. Butter also contains residues of antibiotics, hormones, and tranquilizers used in milk production.

SAFE ALTERNATIVES

Use natural vegetable oils instead, or butter without added color.

Brand Name/*Mail Order*

Buy sweet (unsalted) butter from France or a domestic sweet butter sold in bulk in specialty gourmet shops, or in the frozen-food department of your supermarket or natural-foods store. These usually do not contain added color.

B   Alta-Dena Country Churned Butter (Alta-Dena). "No color or preservatives added." *Kennedy's Natural Foods.*

B   Shiloh Farms Lightly Salted Sour Cream Butter (Shiloh Farms). "No colorings of any kind are used." *Shiloh Farms.*

Do-It-Yourself

• Make your own butter: Put 2 cups well-chilled heavy cream (do not use the ultrapasteurized kind) into a food processor or electric mixer and process or beat at high speed until the cream separates into solids and liquid. Pour off the liquid and add 2 to 3 crushed ice cubes and cover before continuing to process or beat. Run until the butter forms a mass on the top of the blade, or until the ice melts. Put into a sieve to drain. Transfer the butter to a bowl and knead to remove traces of milk. Continue kneading, adding small amounts of ice water until the liquid is clear. Press out all liquid and refrigerate for 48 hours before using. Some food processors have a butter-making blade. If you use that, follow manufacturer's instructions.

New England Cheesemaking Supply

and *Sparks Enterprises* carry electric and hand-crank butter churns.

See also Food, Milk, and Oils.

BUTTONS

Plastics (PVC/vinyl chloride).

SAFE ALTERNATIVES
Brand Name/*Mail Order*

Fabric stores generally carry buttons made from wood, metal, cloisonné, ceramic, pewter, shell, leather, horn, or stone, as well as Chinese silk frogs.

A   *Natural Fiber Fabric Club.* "Natural buttons."

A   *Romni Wools and Fibres.* Buttons made of abalone and yew, rosewood, bubinga, tulio, and zebra woods.

C

CABINETS

Formaldehyde.

SAFE ALTERNATIVES

Use cabinets made of solid wood or metal. Solid wood cabinets can be custom made of pine for not much more than good commercial cabinets would cost. The pine can be sealed with water-base paint or other wood finish.

If your existing cabinets are up to ten years old, they probably contain particle board, often covered with a wood, paper, or vinyl veneer. Check carefully. Older cabinets are generally plywood, often veneered. If you suspect that the particle board in your cabinets is releasing formaldehyde, you can seal it in several different ways. Most formaldehyde builds up on the inside of the cabinets, because the cabinets are usually closed and cannot air out. Simply lining the cabinets entirely with foil vapor barrier and aluminum-foil tape frequently will solve the problem. If significant amounts of formaldehyde are outgassing from the outside of the cabinets, try sealing the cabinet doors with a nontoxic wood finish.

Brand Name/*Mail Order*

A *Sears.* Heavy-duty steel cabinets.

See also Glue & Tape, Paint, Vapor Barrier, and Wood Finishes.

CAKE

BHA/BHT; colors; flavors; glycerin, hydrogenated oil; pesticide residues; sucrose.

SAFE ALTERNATIVES
Brand Name/*Mail Order*
Look for additive-free cakes and mixes in your natural-foods store.

A *Deer Valley Farm.* Stone-milled whole-grain cakes, including an organic, wheat-free nut-flour cake.

B Arrowhead Mills Carob Cake Mix (Arrowhead Mills).

B Elf Liberty Natural Cake Mix (L-Tec).

B Holland Unsalted Honey Cakes (Holland Honey Co.). *Kennedy's Natural Foods.*

BC *Fearn Cake Mixes* (Fearn Soya Foods/Richard Foods Corp.). *Walnut Acres.*

C *Elisabeth the Chef.* Traditional British sugar-sweetened cakes from England produced from "only the best natural ingredients . . . free from preservatives and hand baked to a high standard."

See also Eggs, Flour, Food, Fruitcake, and Sugar.

CANDLES

Colors; fragrance; paraffin.

SAFE ALTERNATIVES
Brand Name/*Mail Order*
Buy beeswax candles at a candle shop or natural-foods store.

Beeswax Candles
A *Hearthsong, Erlander's Natural Products, General Wax and Candle Co., Kennedy's Natural Foods, Leon R. Horsted, Norm Thompson, S. & C. Huber Accoutrements, Thousand Island Apiaries.*

CANDY

BHA/BHT; colors; flavors; hydrogenated oil; pesticide residues; sucrose.

SAFE ALTERNATIVES
Eat fresh or dried fruit instead.

Brand Name/*Mail Order*
Natural-foods stores carry additive-free, nonsucrose-sweetened candies. Brands listed below are sweetened with carob, dried fruits, honey, barley malt, grape extract, date sugar, grape extract, plum extract, or rice syrup.

A Chico-San Carob Coated Rice Cakes/Golden Rice Nuggets (Chico-San). *Chico-San.*

A Ricola Swiss Herb Candy (Ricola). Made from organically grown herbs, but containing sucrose. *Kennedy's Natural Foods.*

AB *Jaffe Bros.* Organic date/coconut and unsweetened carob/nut confections.

B Barbara's Delicious Sesame Crunch/Peanut Brittle (Barbara's Bakery).

B Barton's Natural Carob Bars (Barton's Candy Corp.).

B Brazil Sun Bar (Trinity Sun Bars).

B Carafections (Tree of Life). *Erewhon Mail Order, Kennedy's Natural Foods.*

B Carob Rice Wheel (Nellson Candies).

B Coconut Delite (Robinson Foods).

B Crackerballs! (Edward & Sons).

B Date-a-Mints After Dinner Breath Mints (House of Quality Herbs).

B *Deer Valley Farm.* Carob confections and honey drops.

B Eden Carob Covered Clusters (Eden Foods).

B Glenny's Bee Pollen Sunrise/ 100% Natural Nookies (Glenn Foods).

B Good Karmal (Natural Nectar Products Corp.).

B Herb-a-Mints After Dinner Breath Mints (House of Quality Herbs).

B 100% High Protein Energy Bars (Natural Nectar Products Corp.).

B Joan's Natural Carob Bars (The Estee Corp.).

B Katreen's Love Nut/Hula Bar (Katreen Foods).

B Nellson 14 Karat Bar/Fruit & Nut Bar (Nellson Candies).

B Nik's Sweets (Erewhon). *Erewhon Mail Order.*

B *Penn Herb Co.* An assortment of honey and carob candies.

B Protein-Aide Sesame Chew (International Protein Industries). *Shiloh Farms.*

B *Queen Bee Gardens.* Fudge, taffy, and other candies made with "no sugar, food coloring or preservatives. . . . The only sweetener is pure natural honey."

B Robinson's Celebration (Robinson Foods).

B Soken Plum Candy/Seaweed Candy (Soken Trading Co.). *Erewhon Mail Order.*

B Sorbee Sugarless Hard Candy/ Lollipops (Sorbee International). *Kennedy's Natural Foods, Penn Herb Co.*

B Sunspire Sensation (Sunspire Natural Foods).

B *U.S. Health Club.* Honey candy drops.

B Wayfarers Food Bars (Edner Corp.).

B Westbrae Brown Rice Taffy/ Sour Plum Drops/Miso Drops (Westbrae Natural Foods).

B Wizard Baldour's Power Pak Bars/Zapple (Linden's Elf Works). *Shiloh Farms.*

B   Yinnies All Natural Caramel/ Taffy (Chico-San). *Chico-San, Erewhon Mail Order.*

BC *Walnut Acres.* Naturally sweet carob candies and sesame candy.

C   Brigittine Monks Fudge (Brigittine Monks).

C   Caracoa Carob Bars (El Molino Mills).

C   Jack LaLanne Bars (Natural Protein Products).

C   *Milton York.* Traditional candies "naturally fresh, made without any preservatives, just as they were almost 100 years ago."

C   Munch Bar (M & M Mars/ Mars).

C   Natural Nectar Nectar Nuggets (Natural Nectar Products Corp.).

C   Old Colony Pure Maple Sugar Candy (American Maple Products Corp.). *Mrs. Appleyard's Kitchen.*

C   Old Fashioned Natural Licorice Bar (American Licorice Co.).

C   Panda All Natural Licorice Bar (Panda).

C   Peter Paul Almond Joy/ Mounds/York Peppermint Pattie (Peter Paul/Cadbury).

C   *Sugarbush Farm.* Maple sugar candy.

C   Yogonut Bars (Natural Protein Products).

See also Chocolate, Dried Fruits, Produce, and Sugar.

CAROB

See Chocolate.

CARPETS

See Rugs & Carpets.

CARPET SHAMPOO

See Rug, Carpet, & Upholstery Shampoo.

CAULKING COMPOUNDS

Asbestos; colors; glycerin; kerosene; lead; phenol; talc; xylene.

SAFE ALTERNATIVES
Brand Name/*Mail Order*
The following brands, found in most hardware stores and lumberyards, seem to smell the least and dry the quickest.

C   Dap Kwik Seal Tub and Tile All Purpose Caulk (Dap).

C   Phenoseal Adhesive Caulking (Gloucester). Polyvinyl acetate plastic adhesive caulk; will seal cracks, bond most materials together. Waterproof. Does not contain phenolic resin.

CELLOPHANE

See Food Storage.

CEREAL

BHA/BHT; colors; pesticide residues; sucrose.

SAFE ALTERNATIVES
Eat cooked whole grains for hot cereal: barley, buckwheat (kasha), corn grits or cornmeal, millet, oats or oatmeal, brown rice, rye, or wheat (bulgur).

Brand Name/*Mail Order*

Additive-free cereals can be found in natural-foods stores and supermarkets.

A   Arrowhead Mills Cereals (Arrowhead Mills). *Kennedy's Natural Foods, Shiloh Farms.*

A   *Diamond K Enterprises.* Brown rice, steel-cut oats, and a 7-grain cereal.

A   Eden Cereals (Eden Foods).

A   Erewhon Cereals (Erewhon). *Erewhon Mail Order, Kennedy's Natural Foods.*

A   *Jaffe Bros.* Cornmeal, rolled oats, and a multigrain stone-ground cereal.

A   *Paul's Grains.* Cornmeal, oatmeal, cracked wheat, rye cereal, soy grits, wheat bran, and a 7-grain cereal.

A   Shiloh Farms Cereals (Shiloh Farms). *Shiloh Farms.*

AB   *Deer Valley Farm.* Complete selection of stone-milled, flaked, and rolled grains, and an assortment of meals.

AB   *Erewhon Mail Order.* Brown rice flakes, cornmeal, wheat (bran, flakes, and germ), rolled and steel-cut oats, and rye flakes.

AB   *Walnut Acres.* Complete selection of single- and mixed-grain hot cereals.

B   Albers Quick Grits (Carnation Co.).

B   Alpen Natural Cereal (Weetabix of Canada).

B   Aunt Jemima Grits (Quaker Oats Co.).

B   Back to Nature Red Bird Germade Farina Hot Cereal (Organic Milling Co.).

B   *Butte Creek Mill.* Stone-ground corn and rye meals; 10-grain cereal; cracked wheat and rye; rolled and steel-cut oats; rolled barley, rye, wheat, and triticale.

B   Conagra Cream of Rye (Conagra).

B   Crawford's Toasted Bran (Shaffer, Clarke & Co.).

B   Cream of Rice/Cream of Wheat (Grocery Store Products).

B   Elam's Cereals (Elam's). *Kennedy's Natural Foods.*

B   El Molino Puffed Cereals/Unprocessed Millers Bran Flakes (El Molino Mills). *Deer Valley Farm, Erewhon Mail Order, Kennedy's Natural Foods.*

B   Fisher Wheat Germ (Continental Mills).

B   Hadley's Natural Nutrition Puffed Cereals (Nutritional Food Products).

B   Health Valley Cereals (Health Valley Natural Foods). *Erewhon Mail Order.*

B   Kretschmer Wheat Germ (International Multifoods).

B   Loma Linda Ruskets (Loma Linda Foods).

B   Malt-O-Meal Puffed Rice/Wheat. (Malt-O-Meal Co.).

B   McCann's Irish Oatmeal (Odlum).

B   Miller's Bran (Escondido Mills).

B   Mother's Oat Bran/Whole Wheat/Quick Cooking Barley

(Quaker Oats Co.). *Kennedy's Natural Foods.*

B Mrs. Wright's Hominy Grits (Safeway Stores).

B Nabisco Cream of Wheat (Nabisco).

B Nature's Cuisine Unprocessed Miller's Bran (Nature's Best).

B New Morning Cereals (NEOPC).

B Niblack Toasted Wheat Germ (Niblack Foods).

B Nutri-Grain Flaked Whole Grain Cereals (Kellogg Co.).

B Oroweat Hot Cereal 7 Grain Recipe (Oroweat Foods Co.).

B Post Grape Nuts (General Foods).

B Pure and Simple Puffed Cereals (Pure Sales).

B Quaker Grits/Hot & Creamy Farina/Instant Oatmeal/Oats/ Puffed Cereals/Unprocessed Bran (Quaker Oats Co.).

B Quick Malt-O-Meal (Malt-O-Meal Co.).

B Roman Meal Natural Foods Whole Grain Wheat Hot Cereal (Roman Meal Co.).

B Roman Meal 5 Minute Cereal (Roman Meal Co.).

B Scott's Porrage Oats (A & R Scott).

B Stone-Buhr Cereals (Stone Buhr Milling Co.).

B Uncle Sam Cereal (Uncle Ben's). *Deer Valley Farm.*

B Wheatena Cereal (Standard Milling Co.).

B Wheat Hearts (General Mills).

B Zoom (Continental Mills).

C Buckwheats (General Mills).

C C. W. Post Cereal (General Foods).

C Cheerios (General Mills).

C Familia Cereal (Bio-Familia).

C Honey Nut Cheerios (General Mills).

C Kellogg's Bran Buds Natural High Fiber Cereal/Cracklin' Oat Bran Natural High Fiber Cereal/ Fruitful Bran/Honey & Nut Corn Flakes/Honey Smacks/Product 19 (Kellogg Co.).

C Nabisco 100% Bran (Nabisco).

C Post Raisin Bran (General Foods).

C Quaker 100% Natural Cereal (Quaker Oats Co.).

C Roman Meal Natural Foods Bran & Raisin Ready-to-Eat Cereal (Roman Meal Co.).

C Skinner's Raisin Bran (U.S. Mills).

See also Food, Grains, and Granola.

CHARCOAL LIGHTER FLUID

Fragrance; napthalene.

SAFE ALTERNATIVES
Do-It-Yourself

• Use paper or dry twigs to start fires.
• Make a "fire chimney" from a large tin can. Simply remove both ends from the can and punch some holes around the bottom for air vents. Place can in barbecue, crumple up paper in the bottom, add charcoal, and light.

• When coals are glowing, remove the fire chimney with a coat hanger.

CHEESE

Aerosol propellants; BHA/BHT; colors; flavors.

Labels on cheeses need state only the presence of benzoyl peroxide, a petrochemical-derived bleaching agent that is generally considered to be safe as a food additive, but is toxic by inhalation.

Pesticide residues (including DDT) are greater in high-fat cheeses than in other milk products because pesticides in the milk get stored in the fat. Cheeses also contain residues of antibiotics, hormones, and tranquilizers used in milk production.

SAFE ALTERNATIVES

Avoid "processed" cheeses, flavored specialty cheeses, and cheeses in aerosol cans. Choose fresh, natural cheeses instead. "Raw milk" cheeses usually do not contain any additives.

To minimize pesticide concentrations, choose cheeses made from organic milk. Or eat lowfat, undyed cheese: Mini-chol, Heidi Ann, farmer cheese, Gouda, Swiss Lorraine, New Holland, Swiss-Chris, St. Otho, Fromage à la pie, some Gruyères, Mozzarella, Sapsago, some Edams, Neufchâtel, Parmesan, and Pont-l'Evêque. Some varieties of cheese are made with whole milk or skimmed milk. Ask at your local cheese shop for undyed cheeses made from skimmed milk.

Brand Name/*Mail Order*

Buy cheese from a cheese shop or delicatessen instead of a supermarket. There your questions about how the cheese was produced can be answered and your cheese can be cut fresh. Request that it not be wrapped in the standard polyethylene plastic film, but wrapped in paper instead. Or bring your own cellophane bags or foil from home. Less expensive natural cheeses can be purchased at your supermarket, but these have been sitting for long periods in plastic wrappers.

Mail-order cheeses made from organic milk are often less expensive than cheeses you buy in your local store. Buy them five or ten pounds at a time and freeze them or wrap them tightly in aluminum foil and store in the refrigerator. Brushing all surfaces of the cheese with white vinegar or apple cider vinegar will help retard mold growth without changing the texture or flavor.

A *Cresset Farms Cheese.* Four varieties of Gouda made on a biodynamic farm in upstate New York. "No preservatives, coloring or flavorings are added. Recent laboratory test of our cheese for the acutely toxic pesticides and herbicides show no chemical residues up to <.005."

A *Hawthorne Valley Farm.* Raw-milk cheese "compared to Emmentaler, Gruyère, and Cheddar," produced on a farm operated according to biodynamic methods "without the use of pesticides, herbicides, or chemical fertilizers."

A *Leon R. Horsted.* His semisoft Colby is "produced from milk that comes from a naturally run Wisconsin farm."

A *Morningland Dairy.* Nine varieties of raw milk cheese made with vegetable rennet on a biodynamic farm.

A *Shelburne Farms.* "Estate produced cheddar cheese" made from "absolutely fresh and pure" milk from their own purebred Brown Swiss cows. Grazed only on their own grass and legume pastures maintained by "avoiding the use of pesticide sprays." No preservatives are added.

A *Walnut Acres.* "Made entirely from milk from naturally-raised-and-fed cows . . . no preservatives, inhibitors, artificial flavorings or colorings." Also goat milk cheese and cheese spreads.

AB *Deer Valley Farm.* Organic Romano cheese and other raw milk and natural cheeses.

AB *Eiler's Cheese Market.* "Organic" semisoft and Cheddar cheeses, plus other cheeses.

AB *Kennedy's Natural Foods.* Organic, rennetless raw goat-cheese "tested . . . for pesticide residues by gas chromatographic analysis," as well as other natural cheeses.

B *Calef's Country Store.* Cheddar cheese made in New Hampshire by "the same ancient process employed by its discoverer."

B *Cheese Junction.* "More than 100 varieties of gourmet cheese from around the world." Selection includes raw milk, salt-free, and skim milk cheeses.

B *Crowley Cheese.* Cheddar cheese made by hand, employing the same methods used for over 100 years. "We guarantee that every wheel of Crowley Cheese is made from fresh, whole milk without additives, preservatives, or other artificial substances."

B *Eichten's Hidden Acres Cheese Farm.* Raw whole-milk cheeses made on the farm from unpasteurized milk "without additives, preservatives, artificial flavoring or coloring." Also, Gouda cheese spreads made with all-natural flavorings, as well as natural cheeses from other producers.

B *Maytag Dairy Farms.* Blue cheese made on their own farm.

B *Nauvoo Cheese Co.* Blue cheese made in Nauvoo, Illinois, in caves similar to those where blue cheese is made in Roquefort, France.

B *Sugarbush Farms.* Cheddar and sage raw-milk cheeses. "None of our cheeses contain any preservatives, or chemicals, or colorings."

Do-It-Yourself

New England Cheesemaking Supply Co. carries everything you need to make your own cheese, including how-to books and the bimonthly *Cheesemaker's Journal.*

See also Food, Food Storage, Milk, and Tofu.

CHEWING GUM

BHA/BHT; colors; flavors; paraffin; plastic (polyethylene); saccharin; and talc.

SAFE ALTERNATIVES
Chew bits of honeycomb, available at your natural-foods store.

CHIPS

BHA/BHT; colors; hydrogenated oil; MSG; pesticide residues.

SAFE ALTERNATIVES
Brand Name/*Mail Order*
Additive-free chips can be purchased at natural-foods stores and supermarkets.

Carrot
B R. W. Knudsen Carrot Chips (R. W. Knudsen & Sons). *Kennedy's Natural Foods.*

B Soken Natural Carrot Snack (Soken Trading Co.).

Corn
A Erewhon Aztec Corn Chips/Tortilla Chips (Erewhon). *Erewhon Mail Order.*

A Garden of Eatin' Corn Chips (Garden of Eatin').

A Mother Earth Tortilla Chips (Mother Earth Enterprises/Pure Sales).

B Ananda Seasoned Corn Chips (Ananda Products).

B Barbara's Corn Chips/Chili & Cheese Chips (Barbara's Bakery). *Deer Valley Farm.*

B Corn Cheaps (Alfalfa-Omega Express).

B Dr. Bronner's Corn Chips/Snack (All-One-God-Faith).

B Granny Goose Corn Chips/Native American Style Corn Chips/Corn Tortillos (Granny Goose Foods). *Kennedy's Natural Foods.*

B Health Valley Corn Chips (Health Valley Natural Foods). *Kennedy's Natural Foods.*

B Nature's Snacks 100% Natural Tortilla Chips (Mexi-Snax).

C Doritos Tortilla Chips (Frito-Lay).

C Fritos Corn Chips (Frito-Lay).

C Laura Scudders Corn/Tortilla Chips. (Pet Snack Foods).

C Tostitos Corn Chips. (Frito-Lay).

Mushroom
B Soken Mushroom Chips (Soken Trading Co.).

Potato
B Barbara's Potato Chips/Texas Style Barbeque Potato Chips/ Yogurt & Green Onion Potato Chips (Barbara's Bakery).

B Bonnie Hubbard Potato Chips (United Grocers Ltd.).

B Erewhon Potato Chips (Erewhon). *Erewhon Mail Order.*

B Granny Goose Dip Chips/ Hawaiian Style Potato Chips/ 100% Natural Dip Chips/100% Natural Potato Chips/Potato Chips/Unsalted 100% Natural Potato Chips (Granny Goose Foods). *Kennedy's Natural Foods.*

B Hain Natural Chips (Hain Pure Food Co.).

B Health Valley Potato Chips (Health Valley Natural Foods). *Deer Valley Farm, Kennedy's Natural Foods.*

B Kettle Chips (NS Khalsa Co.)

B R. W. Knudsen Hawaiian Style Potato Chips (R. W. Knudsen & Sons).

C Laura Scudders Potato Chips (Pet Snack Foods).

C Lay's Potato Chips (Frito-Lay).

C Ruffles Potato Chips (Frito-Lay).

Rice

B Amsnack Rice Chips (Amsnack).

Seven-Grain

B Hain Seven Grain Chips (Hain Pure Food Co.).

Vegetable

B Soken Vegetable Chips (Soken Trading Co.). *Erewhon Mail Order, Kennedy's Natural Foods.*

See also Food, Oils, and Tortillas.

CHOCOLATE

Flavors; pesticide residues; sucrose.

All chocolate is grown in foreign countries which often use pesticides that have been banned in the United States. In addition, all chocolate is fumigated before entering this country.

Chocolate also contains caffeine. Although little research has been done on the effect of caffeine ingested while eating chocolate, the caffeine in coffee is known to cause increased incidence of heart attacks, headaches, addiction, indigestion and ulcers, insomnia, anxiety, and depression. Pregnant women should limit their intake of caffeine, since it has been known to cause miscarriages, premature births, and birth defects.

White chocolate does not contain chocolate at all; it is a totally artificial concoction of fats, color, and flavors.

SAFE ALTERNATIVES

Eat carob, a naturally sweet food similar in taste, texture and appearance to chocolate. It is far healthier because it has 97 percent less fat than chocolate, *no* caffeine, and does not require the addition of sugar to make it taste good.

Unsweetened carob powder can be used in the same manner as cocoa powder in cakes, candies, cookies, brownies, and whenever else you would use chocolate. For every ounce of chocolate, substitute 3 tablespoons carob powder mixed with 2 tablespoons water; for powdered cocoa, substitute with equal amounts of carob powder. Use less sugar because carob is sweeter.

Brand Name/*Mail Order*

Ask for carob powder in your natural-foods store. There you will also find ready-to-eat carob products that are either unsweetened or sweetened with date sugar or barley malt syrup.

Carob

B Carob Powder. *Deer Valley Farm, Earthsong Herb Shop, Erewhon Mail Order, Jaffe Bros., Kennedy's Natural Foods, U.S. Health Club, Walnut Acres.*

B Carob Syrup (Teva Natural Foods).

B Superb Instant Carob Syrup (Sona Food Products Co.).

Chocolate

B Baker's Unsweetened Chocolate (General Foods).

B Droste Unsweetened Cocoa (Droste/H. Hamstra & Co.).

B Ghirardelli Unsweetened Chocolate (Ghirardelli Chocolate Co.).

B Guittard Unsweetened Baking Chocolate (Guittard Chocolate Co.).

B Hershey's All Natural Unsweetened Baking Chocolate (Hershey's Chocolate Co.).

B Honey Chocolates (Deer Garden Foods).

C Baker's German Sweet Chocolate/ Semi-Sweet All Natural Chocolate (General Foods).

C Bendicks' Sporting & Military Chocolate (Bendicks).

C Corné de la Toison d'Or (H. Corné Chocolatier).

C Droste Pastilles (Droste/H. Hamstra & Co.).

C Feodora Edel-Bitter Chocolate/ Milk Chocolate (Zuckerraffinerie Tangermunde/Bahlsen of North America).

C Ghirardelli Eagle Brand Premium Quality Bittersweet Chocolate/ Semi-Sweet Chocolate (Ghirardelli Chocolate Co.)

C Godiva Chocolates (Godiva Chocolatier). *Godiva Chocolatier.*

C Guittard Gourmet Touch Semi-Sweet Chocolate Chips (Guittard Chocolate Co.).

C Hershey's Real Chocolate Semi-Sweet Chips (Hershey's Chocolate Co.).

C *Krön Chocolatier.* Chocolates "made by hand from only the finest natural ingredients and . . . based on traditional European recipes."

C *Li-Lac Chocolates.* Handmade, using only the finest ingredients from recipes used since 1923.

C Lindt Bittersweet Chocolate/Bittersweet Chocolate with Whole Hazelnuts (Lindt & Sprungli).

C Michel Guerard Chocolates (Gourmet Resources International).

C Poulain Chocolates (Chocolat Poulain S.A.).

C *Teuscher Chocolates of Switzerland.* Handmade Swiss chocolates flown in weekly from Zurich. Uses "only pure natural ingredients containing no preservatives, additives, or artificial food coloring." Also chocolates sweetened with sorbitol.

C *Valentine's Cosmopolitan Confections.* "Freshly made . . . with raw ingredients of the highest quality. . . . No preservatives added. Chocolate is refined in the old way."

Do-It-Yourself
Melt together 1 ounce unsweetened chocolate with 1 tablespoon honey.

See also Food and Sugar.

CHROME CLEANERS

See Metal Polishes.

CIGARETTES

See the No-Smoking Section.

CLEANING PRODUCTS

Aerosol propellants; ammonia; benzene; chlorine; colors; cresol; detergents; ethanol; formaldehyde; fragrance; glycerin; isopropyl alcohol; hydrogen peroxide; napthalene; nitrobenzene; paraffin; pentachlorophenol; perchloroethylene; petroleum distillates; phenol; plastic; sulfur compounds; talc; toluene; trichloroethylene; xylene.

Household cleaning products are among the most toxic substances encountered in one's everyday environment, causing health problems ranging from rashes to death. A study of Oregon housewives over a fifteen-year period showed that women who stayed in their homes all day had a 54-percent higher death rate from cancer than did women who had jobs away from the home during the day. The study suggested that this higher rate might be attributed to chemicals in household products.

Accidental poisonings from household cleaning products occur far too frequently, especially among infants and children who cannot read the label warnings. In addition to being harmful if accidently swallowed, many of these products also give off volatile fumes. Not only is one exposed to these hazardous fumes during use, but one continues to be exposed to them until they are ventilated out through an open window. During the winter, when windows are opened infrequently, fumes can accumulate undetected over a long period of time to create a dangerously high level of pollutants.

The safety of most household products is determined by its effects *if the product is swallowed.* Since most cleaning products are clearly labeled as hazardous if swallowed and are still considered safe enough to be on the market, it is obvious that no consideration is given to the toxic effects of the fumes inhaled or absorbed through the skin.

Since 1977, cleaning products have been regulated by the Consumer Product Safety Commission (CPSC) according to the Hazardous Sub-stances Act. This regulation requires them to be labeled with certain terms:

Toxic/Highly Toxic (poisonous if eaten, inhaled, or absorbed through the skin);

Extremely Flammable/Flammable/Combustible (can catch fire when exposed to flame or an electric spark);

Corrosive (will eat away your skin);

Irritant (can cause redness or rashes on skin, or inflammation of mucous membranes); and

Strong Sensitizer (may provoke an allergic reaction).

Despite these warnings and our almost constant exposure, cleaning products are *not* required by law to have full-disclosure labels revealing their noxious ingredients. Nor does any government regulatory agency require product formulation information on cleaning products to be approved before products are put on the market. Even the CPSC cannot gain access to these closely guarded "trade secrets." The CPSC requires only that the label contain: the name and address of the manufacturer or distributor; a list of any major "hazardous" ingredients (and the words *danger, caution,* or *warning* where applicable); a phrase describing the danger of the product, if any; and special instructions for handling or storage.

SAFE ALTERNATIVES

Make your own cleaning products at home, as this book suggests in the Do-It-Yourself sections of the "see also" headings below. Not only are homemade products safe to use, they are much less expensive, since you do not have to pay for labeling, advertising, or aerosol spray cans.

Many formulas that this book gives for cleaning products require only substances you probably already have in your kitchen. Some other substances may need to be handled with special care. If you are unfamiliar with an ingredient used in a formula, look in Appendix 2 to find out what it is and where it can be purchased.

Remove all toxic and scented cleaning products from your home—even those in closed containers that are stored in closed cabinets. Remember, children can't read the warning labels. And if you think cleaning products don't smell through the containers, take a good sniff next time you walk down the cleaning-supplies aisle at the supermarket.

See also Air Fresheners; All-Purpose Cleaners; Basin, Tub, & Tile Cleaners; Bleach; Dishwasher Detergent; Dishwashing Liquid; Disinfectants; Drain Cleaners; Dry Cleaners; Fabric Softeners; Furniture & Floor Polish; Glass Cleaners; Laundry Agents; Laundry Starch; Metal Polishes; Mold & Mildew Cleaners; Oven Cleaners; Rug, Carpet & Upholstery Shampoo; Scouring Pads; Scouring Powders; Shoe Polish; Soap; Sponges; Spot Removers; and Water Softeners.

CLEANSING GRAINS

Colors; fragrance; glycerin; mineral oil.

SAFE ALTERNATIVES
Brand Name/*Mail Order*

Unscented

A Amazing Grains (Body Love). *The Herb Patch, Wholesome Paks.*

A *The Body Shop.* Beauty grains made from ground azuki beans.

A *Heavenly Soap.* Facial Scrub.

A Scarborough Fair Facial Meal Scrub (Scarborough Fair). *Sunnybrook Farms.*

A *The Body Shop (England).* Cleansing grains made from dried azuki beans.

C Aapri Apricot Facial Scrub (Aapri Cosmetics).

Natural Scent

B Mill Creek Wild Oats (Mill Creek Natural Products). *Common Scents.*

B Jason Apricot Scrubble (Jason Natural Cosmetics). *Jason Natural Products.*

Do-It-Yourself
• Rub granulated sugar or ground sea salt onto wet skin, *or* combine sugar/salt with oil, *or* combine sugar/salt with liquid soap, *or* rub sugar/salt onto soaped skin. Rinse.
• Grind almonds to a fine powder. Splash water on face and rub with a handful of almond powder. (Store powder in an airtight container.)
• Grind 2 tablespoons almonds in a blender or coffee grinder until crunchy. Add 1 or 2 teaspoons whole milk and ½ teaspoon flour. Mix until a thick paste is formed. Rub into skin for a few minutes, then rinse. Also try adding ½ teaspoon honey.
• Mix equal parts baking soda and water in the palm of your hand and apply to face, rubbing gently for 3 minutes. Rinse with warm water.

See also Beauty Products.

CLOTHES WASHERS & DRYERS

See Appliances.

CLOTHING

Dyes; formaldehyde finishes; pesticides (mothproofing); plastics (acrylic, nylon, polyester, PVC/vinyl chloride, spandex).

SAFE ALTERNATIVES
Brand Name/*Mail Order*

Purchase clothing made from natural fibers and wash them before wearing to remove excess finishes and dyes. Switching to natural fibers will be a gradual process; as much as you might like to, you probably won't be able to discard your entire wardrobe and buy all new clothes. Start by sorting through your existing clothing to determine which of the pieces you already own are made from natural fibers. Wear these most often and next time you buy new clothes, look for natural fibers.

Since natural fibers are again in vogue, you should be able to find clothing made from them in better stores in metropolitan areas. If you can't, plenty of natural-fiber clothing of all types and sizes is available by mail.

About children's sleepwear: Federal law requires garments sold as "sleepwear" for infants and children to be flameproof. In the past, cotton sleepwear was simply flameproofed with TRIS. When TRIS was found to be carcinogenic, other chemicals were used (which have unknown health effects), or else the sleepwear was made from nonflammable synthetic fibers. Be creative. Many cotton garments can be used for sleepwear even though they cannot by law be described or recommended as sleepwear. If you are concerned about combustibility, make your own sleepwear from naturally flame resistant wool.

All businesses listed here carry items made from 100-percent natural fibers, but not all their garments will necessarily be made from natural fibers. Check descriptions carefully. In addition, fabrics may contain finishes and dyes or be sewn with polyester thread or be finished with polyester zippers, elastic, trim, linings, or interfacings.

Abbreviations used: (M)—men's clothing; (W)—women's clothing; (C)—children's and infants' clothing.

A *A Child's Garden.* (C) Cotton and wool clothing.

A *Alice in Wonderland Creations.* (MWC) Hand-knit sweaters of natural-color wool from healthy lambs raised on the knitters' own farm.

A *Andean Products.* (MW) Wool sweaters hand knit in South America.

A *Cotton Brokers.* (MW) White cotton terry bathrobes.

A *Eileen's Handknits.* (MW) Pure wool sweaters, hand knit in the cottages of Donegal, Ireland.

A *Helen McGroarty.* (MWC) Irish hand-knit wool sweaters.

A *Icemart.* (MWC) Knit garments from Icelandic wool in natural shades of white, gray, black, and brown. Kits also available.

A *Janice Corp.* (MWC) Cotton robes, socks, stockings, undergarments. Baby wear imported from Denmark. Some items made from untreated fabrics in the corporation's own sewing room. Will also do custom sewing.

A *Kennedy's of Ardara.* (MW) Hand-knit Irish wool sweaters, shawls, scarves, hats, and mittens.

A *Rammagerdin of Reykjavik.* (MWC) Garments of Icelandic wool in natural shades of gray, brown, and white.

A *Simply Divine Designs.* (C) Cotton clothing for infants and children dyed with "procion vegetable dyes." Made by "two sisters working together to create a business which allows room for children, family, and personal growth."

A *Una O'Neill Designs.* (MWC) Hand-knit Irish Aran sweaters in modern designs. All knit with natural "bainin" (off-white) wool or black-sheep wool.

AB *After the Stork.* (WC) A full selection of cotton and wool clothing for infants and children. Also cotton lingerie for women.

AB *Alafoss Icewool.* (MWC) Garments knit from natural and dyed Icelandic wool.

AB *Ascot Chang.* (MW) Custom and ready-made shirts from fine European cottons and silks.

AB *Avoca Handweavers.* (MW) Clothing from handwoven and hand-knit Irish wools.

AB *Babouri's Handicrafts.* (MW) Sweaters hand knit in Greece from handspun yarn in natural or dyed colors.

AB *Briar Shepard.* (W) Shawls, scarves, and sweaters hand crocheted in England from 100% pure mohair or a mohair/silk blend.

AB *Britches of Georgetown.* (MW) Natural-fiber clothing in exclusive designs based on classic styles, "from casual and rugged functional outerwear to the elegant and sophisticated business and evening wear."

AB *British Isles Collection.* (MW) Natural-fiber clothing imported from the British Isles.

AB *Brooks Brothers.* (MW) Complete selection of natural-fiber traditional clothing for men, including 100% cotton suits. A few selected dresses, suits, and blouses for women.

AB *Bullock & Jones.* (M) Complete selection of fine traditional clothing made of cotton, silk, wool, camel's hair, and cashmere, including a cotton "buffer coat" lined with thick wool melton, a 100%-cotton trenchcoat, and a pure silk raincoat.

AB *The Butterfield Co.* (C) Good selection of basic cotton clothing.

AB *Cable Car Clothiers/Robert Kirk, Ltd.* (MW) Complete selection of traditional clothing made of cotton, wool, cashmere, silk, and camel's hair for men, including sleepwear and 98% pima cotton socks. A few selected suits, dresses, and coats for women.

AB *Cambrian.* (MW) Clothing made of "100% new Welsh wool, grown, spun, woven or knitted in Wales. . . . The Cambrian Factory was established in 1918 to give employment to ex-Service men and women disabled in the First World War . . . now employs both ex-Service and other disabled persons."

AB *Carol Brown.* (W) "All sorts of clothes" made from a large selection of exquisite natural-fiber fabrics from around the world. Also hand-knit fishermen's sweaters.

AB *Castlemoor.* (MW) Clothing made of natural-fiber fabrics made entirely in the United Kingdom.

AB *Cindy-Kit.* (W) Kits for cotton clothing in Victorian styles.

AB *Cleo.* (MW) Irish country clothing made from natural-colored wool yarns and dyed tweeds.

AB *Collins Designers.* (MWC) Reasonably priced clothing, custom made from natural-fiber fabrics. Have been making clothes for people with chemical sensitivities since 1975.

AB *Cornelius Furs.* (MW) Good selection of kangaroo, mink, fox, lamb, and other fur garments from "the largest fur store in the Southern Hemisphere . . . among the top 10 fur houses in the world."

AB *Cotton Comfort.* (MW) Casual clothes made of crinkle cotton.

AB *The Cotton Co.* (MW) Cotton sportswear and undergarments. Also a reasonably priced cotton raincoat for women.

AB *Cotton Cookie Clothing Co.* (C) "High-quality cotton, sheepskin, and wool clothing at a reasonable price."

AB *Cotton Dreams.* (MWC) Large selection of cotton clothing, including sleepwear, undergarments, and socks.

AB *The Cotton Place.* (MWC) A cooperative run by people sensitive to petrochemicals; provides complete wardrobe basics made from natural fibers. Unusual items include silk stockings and silk pantyhose and a 100% cotton bikini swimsuit. Also have sizes for larger women. Discounts given to members.

AB *The Country Store & Farm.* (MWC) Cotton, silk, and wool outdoor clothing, undergarments, and sleepwear, including 100% cotton stockings. Will custom make handmade items with cotton thread and trim by request.

AB *Cuddledown.* (MW) Good selection of cotton, silk, and wool undergarments, socks, tights, and sleepwear.

AB *David Morgan.* (MW) Cotton and wool clothing based on traditional Welsh designs; natural-color cotton sweaters in many styles and a cotton bed jacket.

AB *Daybreak.* (MWC) Small collection of casual natural-fiber clothing handmade by a rural cottage industry.

AB *Deva.* (MW) Simple clothes made by a very successful cottage industry in rural Maryland from loose-weave, softly textured cotton. Also cotton sweaters and 98% cotton socks.

AB *Dublin Woolen Co.* (MWC) Irish wool clothing.

AB *East Wind.* (W) "Practical works of art" made from cotton, wool, and silk.

AB *Elizabeth James.* (C) White and brightly colored cotton "U.B. [under baby] Vests," "Spit Wipes," and hooded bath towels.

AB *Erlander's Natural Products.* (MW) Low-priced cotton clothing, sleepwear, and socks.

AB *Esprit.* (W) Bright, trendy, natural-fiber sportswear for younger women.

AB *Exactitude.* (W) Fine-tailored cotton shirts with real pearl buttons.

AB *FBS.* (W) Natural-fiber designer fashions.

AB *French Creek Sheep & Wool Co.* (MW) Stylish clothing, mostly in the original colors of the natural fibers, handmade by "America's most elegant cottage industry." Also, fine Swiss cotton undergarments and beautiful sherling coats and jackets.

AB *Funn Stockings.* (W) Classic seamed and seamless 100% silk, 100% cotton, and 100% wool stockings made in England.

AB *Garnet Hill.* (MWC) The largest selection of hard-to-find natural-fiber socks, stockings, tights, undergarments, and sleepwear, many imported from Europe.

Adult clothing is limited to sweaters and activewear, but there is a complete line for infants and children.

AB *Gohn Bros.* (MWC) Practical white cotton undergarments, cotton socks and stockings.

AB *Gokeys.* (MW) Cotton and wool outdoor clothing, including a number of cotton sweaters; silk turtlenecks, underwear, gloves, and socks; cotton blazers; cotton chamois robes and pajamas; and cotton twill belts.

AB *Good Things Collective.* (MWC) Basic clothing, sleepwear, and undergarments made of cotton and wool, including 100% wool socks and 98% cotton/2% lycra socks "corespun so that only 100% cotton touches your skin."

AB *Guernsey Knitwear.* (MW) Traditional Guernsey sweaters in natural and dyed colors.

AB *Harvie & Hudson.* (M) Exclusive cotton shirts from England.

AB *Huntington Clothiers.* (MW) Moderately priced traditional clothing, including a British cotton windbreaker.

AB *Irish Cottage Industries.* (MW) Irish wool garments and handknit sweaters in traditional Aran designs.

AB *J. Jill.* (W) Distinctive cotton, silk, wool, and mohair clothing in feminine, flowing styles based on historical and ethnic designs. Also cotton lingerie. All items made in their own workrooms, from a conviction that "synthetic fibers derived from petrochemicals are simply uncomfortable," as well as the fact that many of their "thousands of very pleased customers are people whose good health demands natural fiber fabrics."

AB *Kid Cottons.* (C) Good assortment of basic cotton clothing.

AB *Landau.* (MW) Especially stylish garments and accessories made from Icelandic sheep wool, most in natural shades.

AB *Laughing Bear Batik Co.* (MWC) Brightly colored clothing, socks, and undergarments batiked with whimsical designs.

AB *Le Tricoteur.* (MW) Traditional Guernsey sweaters knit from pure wool in the Channel Islands.

AB *Lisa Norman Lingerie Etc.* (W) Cotton and silk lingerie.

AB *Lismore Hosiery Co.* (MWC) All-cotton socks.

AB *Mairtin Standun Teo.* (MWC) Natural-fiber clothing from Ireland.

AB *Monaghans.* (MW) Irish sweaters.

AB *Muileann Beag A'Chrotail.* (MW) Scottish sweaters.

AB *Nandi Naturals.* (MW) Casual cotton clothing.

AB *Natural Child.* (C) Cotton clothing for infants and children, including 100% cotton tights from Austria.

AB *Orkney Handknits.* (MW) Pure new Shetland wool sweaters made by a Scottish cottage industry.

AB *Orvis.* (MW) Outdoor and traditional clothing made of cotton, wool, cashmere, camel's hair, and cotton/wool and silk/cashmere blends. Also, white silk undergarments, socks, and gloves, silk/wool and wool undergarments, and colored silk knit turtlenecks and t-shirts.

AB *Overland Sheepskin Co.* (MWC) Sheepskin coats and jackets and cotton sweaters.

AB *Reekie's of Grasmere.* (MW) Handwoven and hand-knit woolen garments from England.

AB *Romanes & Paterson.* (MW) Scottish wool and cashmere clothing.

AB *Shiloh Farms Cotton Collection.* (MW) Basic styles made from 100% cotton crinkle cloth, "Made in America from American-grown cotton."

AB *Sickafus Sheepskin.* (MW) Leather and sheepskin jackets, gloves, and hats.

AB *Vermont Country Store.* (MW) Small selection of cotton casual clothing, sleepwear, and undergarments, including 100% cotton stockings for women.

AB *The White Pine Co.* (MW) Silk and cotton sportswear and undergarments.

AB *Woolies.* (MW) Soft, itchless New Zealand Merino wool and long cotton underwear (sexy styles for women.)

B *Ann Taylor.* (W) Natural-fiber designer clothing.

B   *Banana Republic.* (MW) An ever-changing collection of practical cotton and wool "travel and safari clothing," including unusual natural-fiber outerwear.

B   *Beckwith Enterprises.* (C) Unusual cotton flannel kimonos and "bibshirts" for babies.

B   *Better Gooses & Garments.* (C) Cotton or wool crocheted sweaters, hats, and mittens.

B   *Bettywear.* (C) Cotton clothing.

B   *Bill Tosetti's.* (MW) Wool Pendleton sportswear.

B   *Buffalo Shirt Co.* (MW) Cotton and wool outdoor clothing.

B   *Camp Beverly Hills.* (MW) Casual cotton clothing.

B   *Charing Cross Kits.* (WC) Kits for clothing in fanciful styles, many made of cotton corduroy.

B   *Colette Modes.* (W) Coats and suits made in Ireland of 100% pure new-wool Donegal handwoven tweed.

B   *Cording of Piccadilly.* (MW) Largest selection available of outerwear made from cotton Grenfell cloth, a cotton fabric "second to none in the qualities of water resistance, windproofing, and long wear. . . . Originally made for Sir Wilfred Grenfell for protection in the arctic waste of Labrador."

B   *The Cotton Loom.* (MWC) 100% cotton clothing.

B   *Cottontails.* (C) "A cottage industry dedicated to making quality clothing for children from birth to ten years. . . . Designed and made with the finest imported and domestic natural fabrics."

B   *Cotton Togs North.* (C) Complete line of cotton and wool clothing for infants and children.

B   *Deerlick Springs.* (W) Natural-fiber maternity and nursing clothing.

B   *Deerskin Trading Post.* (MW) Leather, suede, and sheepskin clothing.

B   *Denny Andrews.* (MW) Cotton and silk clothing from India and a few Welsh wool garments.

B   *Dunham's of Maine.* (MW) Elegant traditional clothing made from natural fibers. Selection includes cotton suits for men, British Grenfell cotton raincoats, and 100% cotton socks.

B   *Elizabeth Forbes.* (W) Pure silk ties.

B   *Especially Maine.* (MW) Natural-fiber country-style clothing made in Maine.

B   *Feathered Friends.* (W) Egyptian cotton robes filled with down.

B   *Finger Prints.* (MWC) A home-centered business seeking alternatives to the commercial designs available on children's clothing. Their designs reflect a "wholesome approach to health, ecology, childbirth, peace, and self-esteem," and are screen printed by hand, using bright, nontoxic, nonplastic inks.

B *Haf-a-Jama.* (MW) Pajama tops and bottoms (sold separately) in 100% cotton.

B *Hanna Andersson.* (C) Cotton baby clothes made in Scandinavia.

B *Hartman's.* (C) Infants' and children's t-shirts in 100% cotton, decorated with lace and other pretty patterns.

B *Hayashi Kimono.* (MW) Cotton and silk kimonos, "the most comprehensive stock of this traditional garment under any one roof in Japan."

B *J. Crew Outfitters.* (MW) Good prices on basic cotton outdoor clothing in bright colors, including casual cotton dresses.

B *Jankits.* (MW) Sweater kits compiled by a sheep rancher's wife, containing wool from her husband's sheep and her own original designs.

B *Jos. A. Bank Clothiers.* (MW) Moderately priced traditional clothing made of cotton, silk, wool, cashmere, and camel. Unusual items include natural-fiber formal wear, cashmere topcoats, as well as scarves, cotton suspenders, wool surcingle belts, cotton terrycloth robes, cotton sleepwear, and a reasonably priced cotton raincoat for men.

B *The Kids Warehouse/White Creek Co.* (MWC) Country clothing in natural fabrics for the family.

B *Kinloch Anderson.* (MW) Traditional Scottish tartans (over 360 of them) and "Highland dress."

B *L. L. Bean.* (MW) A few outdoor clothing items made from cotton and wool amid a large selection of synthetic blends. Of particular interest are white Chinese-silk knit undergarments, cotton belts with dressy leather buckles, warm and fuzzy chamois cloth robes, and cotton sleepwear.

B *Lands' End.* (MWC) Large selection of outdoor and traditional clothing made from cotton, wool, cashmere, camel's hair, and cotton/wool blends. Interesting items include wool pea coats, dress-tailored cotton flannel shirts, cotton corduroy shirts, wool surcingle belts, cotton flannel sleepwear, fuzzy cotton chamois cloth robes, and reasonably priced cashmere scarves.

B *La Shack.* (W) Natural-fiber designer clothes.

B *Laura Ashley.* (WC) Romantic-style dresses, skirts, blouses, and nightclothes in natural fibers.

B *Loden Frey.* (MW) Beautiful, expensive natural-fiber clothing based on traditional German folk designs. (Catalog is in German, but company will respond to letters written in English.)

B *Mary Green Enterprises.* (MW) Silk knit undergarments and sleepwear.

B *Moffat Woolens.* (MW) Fine Scottish woolen clothing, including full-length cashmere coats for women.

B *Monarch Trading Co.* (MW) Leather, suede, shearling, and natural-fiber clothing from New Zealand.

B *Mothers Work.* (W) Professional and leisure clothing for expectant mothers; some natural fibers.

B *Motherwear.* (W) Cotton maternity clothing "made by mothers, for mothers."

B *Natural Fantasy.* (MWC) Long-johns and t-shirts, 100% cotton, dyed in bright colors or silk-screened with fantasy designs.

B *Natural Visions.* (WC) High-quality, highly utilitarian cotton clothing for infants and nursing mothers.

B *Norm Thompson.* (MW) "Escape from the ordinary," with a limited selection of surprisingly affordable clothing made from such fabrics as mink/wool, 100% camel's hair, wool/cotton, linen/cotton, Tasmanian wool, and cashmere, including Chinese-silk undergarments and sleepwear.

B *Patagonia.* (MW) Cotton outdoor clothing; cotton-web belts with leather trim.

B *The Peruvian Connection.* (MW) Alpaca sweaters and fine Peruvian pima cotton jerseys.

B *Piaffe.* (W) Natural-fiber clothing for petites only.

B *Pitlochry Knitwear Co.* (MWC) British natural-fiber clothing.

B *Pollyanna.* (C) Colorful cotton and cotton/wool clothing from England.

B *Poppy Singer-Sayada.* (WC) Maternity, nursing, and baby clothing "all handmade at home by mothers," in 100% cotton.

B *Powers' Country Store.* (MWC) Basic cotton clothing and sleepwear, including denim jeans, skirts, overalls, and overall jumpers.

B *Precious Times.* (W) Cotton clothing for the nursing mother.

B *Pure Kid.* (C) Imported, stylish natural-fiber clothing.

B *Putumayo.* (W) Original cotton and wool fashions based on South American folk art.

B *R. Watson Hogg.* (MW) "One of the largest stocks of top-quality cashmere knitwear in the United Kingdom"; also, other fine natural-fiber British clothing.

B *Richman Co.* (WC) Small selection of miscellaneous cotton clothing.

B *Royal Silk.* (W) Good prices on silk and cotton/silk separates.

B *Ruggedwear.* (MW) Active sportswear made in 41 colors from heavy-duty cotton knit.

B *Saint Laurie Ltd.* (MW) Classic tailored clothing made from fine natural fibers.

B *Sara Fermi.* (W) "Fine shirts, dresses, and nightgowns, inspired by shapes from the past and made entirely from natural fabrics."

B *The Scottish Lion.* (MW) Natural-fiber clothing made in the British Isles, including romantic nightgowns for women made of cotton, silk, or a cotton/wool blend.

B *Scottish Products.* (MW) Highland imports from Scotland.

B *Sears.* (MW) Inexpensive cotton sleepwear, undergarments, and work clothes.

B *Sermoneta.* (W) Ultrafeminine cotton clothing and sleepwear.

B *The Sheepskin Co.* (MWC) Sheepskin jackets, vests, and hats.

B *Strand Surplus Senter.* (MW) Cotton and wool surplus clothing from the armed forces of the United States, Britain, France, the Netherlands, Czechoslovakia, Germany, Italy, Switzerland, Spain, Sweden, and Canada.

B *Suzanne Pierette.* (W) Cotton sleepwear and robes made of "the best fabrics of natural fibers, in workmanship that will give you comfort, durability and style."

B *Sweater Market.* (MW) New wool, 100% pure, hand knit in Denmark.

B *Trefriw Woollen Mills.* (W) Welsh wool tweed clothing.

B *Victoria's Secret.* (MW) Cotton and silk lingerie. Silk stockings. Special silk undergarments for men.

B *Victory Shirt Co.* (MW) Cotton and silk shirts and silk ties.

B *Visions.* (W) Cotton leotards, socks, stockings, sweaters, and silk stockings.

B *Water Witch.* (W) Original clothing designs made with unusual cotton fabrics imported from the Netherlands, or a British cotton/wool blend.

B *Whole Earth Access.* (MWC) "Instead of starting with fashion we start with function." Basic cotton clothing, including denim jeans, skirts, jackets, overalls, and overall jumpers.

B *Wrap-Arounds.* (MW) A collection of unique handmade cotton garments that all "wrap around" your body, made by "a group of women working as a community cottage industry located in rural southwest Virginia."

B *Yellow Bird Crafts.* (W) Cotton clothing. "Our goods will be made from natural materials, and our standards will be the highest of which we are capable."

See also **Buttons, Elastic, Fabric, Textiles,** and **Thread.**

COCONUT

Glycerin; pesticide residues; sucrose.

SAFE ALTERNATIVES
Brand Name/*Mail Order*
Unsweetened flaked coconut can be purchased in a natural-foods store.

Unsweetened Flaked Coconut
A *Jaffe Bros.*

B *Erewhon Mail Order, Kennedy's Natural Foods, Walnut Acres.*

Do-It-Yourself
Substitute fresh coconut for packaged shredded or flaked coconut by grating

fresh coconut meat, soaking it in milk for 6 hours in the refrigerator, and draining before using. To toast grated coconut, spread it thinly on a baking sheet and warm for 10 minutes in a preheated 350° oven, stirring frequently.

See also Food.

COFFEE

Flavors; hexane; methylene chloride; pesticide residues; sucrose; trichloroethylene.

Most coffee sold in the United States is grown in foreign countries which often use pesticides so dangerous they have been banned here. A 1977 study by the FDA found that 45 percent of the coffee beans tested contained illegal residue levels of carcinogenic BHC, dieldrin, DDT, DDE, and heptachlor, as well as toxic malathion, diazinon, and lindane.

Coffee drinking may contribute to a higher incidence of cancer of the pancreas, the fourth most common cause of cancer deaths in America. Although no physiological studies have been done, scientists at the Harvard School of Public Health have made a statistical link to support this theory.

The caffeine in coffee is responsible for many ills, including increased incidence of heart attacks, headaches, indigestion and ulcers, insomnia, anxiety, and depression. Pregnant women should limit their intake of caffeine; in large quantities it has contributed to the incidence of miscarriages, premature births, and birth defects.

SAFE ALTERNATIVES
Limit your consumption of coffee and avoid instant and flavored coffees that contain many chemical additives. Instead, brew the coffee (preferably organically grown) in a nonplastic container from freshly ground beans. If you prefer decaffeinated coffee, drink steam- or water-processed varieties to avoid the hexane and methylene chloride used in the decaffeinating process.

Drink herb tea or noncaffeinated hot beverages with flavors similar to coffee (as suggested in "Coffee Substitutes," below).

Brand Name/*Mail Order*
Organic coffee can be purchased in a natural-foods store. Most specialty stores that sell coffee beans carry water-processed decaffeinated beans.

Coffee
A Cafe Altura (Terra Nova). *Earthsong Herb Shop, Kennedy's Natural Foods.*

A The Natural Coffee (Au Naturel).

B Rombouts Decaf Water-Processed Coffee (Rombouts Coffee & Coffee Filter Marketing Co.). *Kennedy's Natural Foods.*

Coffee Substitutes (made from grains unless otherwise specified)
A Inka (Adamba Imports International). Ingredients raised in Poland using "natural methods." *Kennedy's Natural Foods.*

B Bambu (Bioforce of America) *Deer Valley Farm, Kennedy's Natural Foods, Penn Herb Co., Walnut Acres.*

B Breakway (Celestial Seasonings). *Kennedy's Natural Foods, Walnut Acres.*

75

B Cafix (Richter Bros.). *Erewhon Mail Order, Kennedy's Natural Foods.*

B Da Copa (Dacopa Foods/California Natural Products). Made from dahlia flower tuber. *Kennedy's Natural Foods.*

B Duram Uncoffee (Duram Un-Coffee Co.). *Erewhon Mail Order.*

B Imperial Korona Instant (Imperial-Vienna).

B Pero (Libby, McNeil & Libby). *Deer Valley Farm, Kennedy's Natural Foods.*

B Pionier Instant Swiss Coffee Substitute (Pionier-Reformprodukte AG). *Deer Valley Farm, Kennedy's Natural Foods.*

B Roastaroma (Celestial Seasonings). *Deer Valley Farm, Walnut Acres.*

B Sipp (Modern Products).

B Walnut Acres Malted Carob Beverage (Walnut Acres). *Walnut Acres.*

B Wilson's Heritage (F. L. Wilson Co.).

C Postum (General Foods).

Coffee Filters

A *Bay Spice House.* "Gold-plated mesh permanent-filter cone filters."

A *Clothcrafters.* Cotton coffee filters.

A *The Eco-Filter* (Earthen Joys). "Premium quality 100% cotton muslin" filter will last more than one year. Comes in many sizes and "does not impart any taste to the coffee as even the best paper filters do." *The Country Store & Farm, Earthen Joys.*

See also Food and Herbs & Spices.

COFFEE FILTERS

See Coffee.

COFFEE SUBSTITUTES

See Coffee.

COMBS

See Hairbrushes & Combs.

COMFORTERS & QUILTS

Dyes; plastics (nylon, polyester).

SAFE ALTERNATIVES

Many comforters are available in today's market, priced from $25 for a polyester-filled model to $500 or more for the highest-quality white goose down encased in a fine cotton fabric.

The least expensive natural-fiber comforters are filled with cotton or wool and are made much like an old-fashioned quilt. For a little more money, you can buy a down-and-feather comforter, or one made with duck down and/or feathers instead of with pure goose down, which is more costly. (If the label says simply "down," you can assume it's duck and not goose down being referred to.)

The most expensive (and warmest) comforters are made with imported white goose down and sewn together with "baffles"—strips of fabric sewn between the top and bottom layers to prevent any cold spots caused by sewn-through seams. If you live in a very cold climate or sleep alone, it probably would be worth the extra investment to buy a comforter with baffled construction. But if you live in a moderate climate or have someone else to help generate body heat, a sewn-through comforter will keep you quite warm. Placing a cotton thermal blanket between the top sheet and the comforter can add more warmth, if needed.

Comforters should frequently be aired outside in the sunshine. A washable comforter cover (an over-sized pillowcase with zippers or snaps that also doubles as a top sheet) will help you avoid having to wash the comforter itself.

Brand Name/*Mail Order*

Purchase comforters and quilts made from cotton and stuffed with down, cotton, or wool batting in department or bedding stores, or local comforter specialty shops. All comforters listed here have 100-percent cotton covers.

Cotton-Filled Comforters

A   *Dona Shrier, Erlander's Natural Products, Janice Corp., Simple Pleasures.*

AB   *Peach Blossom Futon.*

B   *Essential Alternatives, Eugene Trading Co., New Moon, Sleep & Dream, Wee Care.*

Down-Filled Comforters

A   *Cuddledown, The Futon Shop, New Moon, Scandia Down Shops, Xhaxhi.*

AB   *The Blue Ribbon Bedding Co., Garnet Hill, J. Schachter, St. Patrick's Down.*

B   *Agatha's Cozy Corner, Down Home Comforters, Down Lite Products, Dreamy Down Fashions, Essential Alternatives, Euroquilt, Feathered Friends, Gokeys, Quilt-*

essence, Russell's Quilt & Pillow Co., Warm Things.

Wool-Filled Comforters

A   *New Moon, Xhaxhi.*

AB   *The Blue Ribbon Bedding Co.*

B   *Erlander's Natural Products, Essential Alternatives, Laura Furlong Designs, Vermont Country Store.*

Cotton Comforter Covers

A   *Janice Corp.*

B   *The Blue Ribbon Bedding Company, Cuddledown, Dreamy Down Fashions, Erlander's Natural Products, Feathered Friends, The Futon Shop, Garnet Hill, Laura Furlong Designs, Scandia Down Shops, Simple Pleasures.*

Quilts

B   *The Futon Shop.* Traditional American patchwork quilts made entirely of cotton.

See also Batting and Textiles.

COMPUTERS

Plastic.

Since 1975, over two dozen studies have concentrated on health problems associated with VDT use. For the most part, radiation, incorrect lighting and chair or desk height, screen flicker or character size, and stress of job boredom are blamed for these ills. In future studies, the plastics used in constructing the computers should also be evaluated as well as the general toxicity of the office or home where the VDT is being used.

SAFE ALTERNATIVES
Brand Name/*Mail Order*

Choose a computer and peripherals with as few plastic parts as possible.

Computers

B Columbia (Columbia Data Products). IBM-PC compatible portable computer with metal case. Has 128K memory and dual disk drives. Runs MS- or PC-DOS programs on 5¼″ floppy disks.

B Grid Compass (Grid Systems Corp.). A very small, very expensive portable computer with an "electrolumescent" screen instead of the standard VDT, a 256K memory, a 384K "bubble memory," and a built-in modem in a magnesium case. Runs IBM-PC programs. Lots of expensive peripherals are needed to increase its limited productivity.

B Kaypro II/IV/X (Non-Linear Systems). Least expensive portable computer with metal case. Has 64K memory and dual disk drives. Runs hundreds of CP/M programs on 5¼″ floppy disks or a 10 megabite hard disk.

B Sanyo Micropro MBC-550 (Sanyo). Mostly metal IBM-PC compatible computer. Comes with expandable 128K memory and one-disk drive. Runs MS-DOS programs on 5¼″ floppy disks.

Printers

B DTC Letter Quality Printers (Data Terminals & Communications). Rebuilt heavy-duty Diablo printers. *Data Terminals & Communications.*

B Okidata Dot Matrix Printers (Okidata). Full-function printers for all uses.

CONDOMS

See Contraceptives.

CONTACT LENSES

Ammonia; EDTA; glycerin; isopropyl alcohol; plastic (acrylonitrile).

SAFE ALTERNATIVES

Since all contact lenses on the market today are made from plastic, it is preferable to wear glasses. If this is impractical for you, at least alternate contact lens use with wearing glasses part of the time and choose preservative-free lens fluids.

Brand Name/*Mail Order*

B Blairex Salt Tablets (Blairex Labs). Tablets for mixing your own saline solution.

B The Blairex System (Blairex Labs).

B Unisol Preservative-Free Saline Solution (CooperVision Pharmaceuticals).

Do-It-Yourself

Mix ⅛ teaspoon baking soda and ⅛ teaspoon salt into ½ cup distilled water. Strain through a paper coffee filter to remove any undissolved grains of salt or soda.

See also Eyeglasses.

CONTRACEPTIVES

Colors; ethanol; formaldehyde; fragrance; plastic (polyurethane).

Oral Contraceptive Pills

Detailed warnings on possible side effects are required with every prescription of oral contraceptives in the United States. Symptoms can include weight gain, nausea, inflammation of the optic nerve (leading to loss of vision, double vision, eye pains and swelling, and an inability to wear contact lenses), headaches, vaginal yeast infections, depression, loss of sex drive, formation of blood clots, heart attacks, high blood pressure, stroke, gall bladder disease, liver tumors, birth defects, ectopic pregnancy, skin cancer and cancer of the reproductive organs, breast tumors, menstrual irregularities, post-pill infertility, and infections. One-third of the women who use the Pill show reduced blood levels of vitamin C, vitamins B2, B6, and B12, and folic acid.

The FDA warns that the Pill should be avoided by those women who have or have had blood clots in their legs or lungs, have pains in their heart or have had a heart attack or stroke, know or suspect they have cancer of the breast or sex organs, have unusual vaginal bleeding that has not yet been diagnosed, or know or suspect they are pregnant. If you choose to take the Pill, the FDA warns that you should be closely supervised by a doctor if you have a family history of breast cancer, have breast nodules, fibrocystic disease of the breast or an abnormal mammogram, have diabetes, have high cholesterol, get migraine headaches, have heart or kidney disease, are epileptic, have fibroid tumors of the uterus, have gall bladder disease, are frequently depressed, or if you smoke.

Intrauterine Devices (IUDs)
FDA-approved IUDs are made of polyethylene plastic infused with a small amount of barium. Some have added copper wires or synthetic progesterone. Since polyethylene is a weak carcinogen for rats, the possibility should not be ignored that IUDs may have a cancer-causing potential in humans. As of yet, no studies prove this.

Complications: increased menstrual flow coupled with heavy cramps and backaches; fatal infection; perforation of the uterus or cervix (leading to difficulty of IUD removal, requiring a possible hysterectomy); miscarriage (30- to 50-percent chance if pregnancy does occur); and ectopic (tubal) pregnancy (which usually causes sterility when IUD is surgically removed).

You should not use an IUD if you have had a recent pelvic infection or have had pelvic infections in the past, an abnormal Pap smear, an ectopic pregnancy, abnormal thickening of the uterine lining, rheumatic heart disease, diabetes, abnormal blood clotting, have taken medications that lower your resistance to infection, or do not have immediate access to emergency care.

Diaphragm
Can cause vaginal irritation, swelling, or blistering as an allergic reaction to the spermicide that must be used with it, or to the latex rubber from which it is made.

Condoms
Allergic reactions can occur from the latex rubber they are made of, or to the chemicals in the lubricants.

Vaginal Spermicides: Foam, Creams, Jellies, Suppositories, Foaming Tablets
Even though few side effects beyond irritation have been reported from the use of these kinds of contraceptives, there is a suspected correlation between the use of spermicidal contraceptives and a higher incidence of birth defects and spontaneous abortions requiring hospitalization. An

FDA advisory review panel could find only a very few out-of-date studies that evaluated the safety of spermicides. *No studies* have assessed the direct effects of active spermicides on an unborn baby carried in the womb, on future generations through genetic mutation, or of possible carcinogenic or toxic repercussions. Inactive ingredients have not been evaluated at all.

Only active ingredients need be listed on the labels of vaginal contraceptives, making it impossible for the consumer to know exactly what might be contained in the product in addition to the spermicide. Inactive ingredients may include alcohol, benzethonium chloride, boric acid, butylparaben, formaldehyde, glycerin, methylbenzethonium chloride, methylparaben, methylpolysiloxane, perfume, preservatives, and propylparaben.

Contraceptive Sponges

Approved for general use by the FDA in June 1983, the contraceptive sponge (marketed under the name "Today") is made of polyurethane plastic infused with Nonoxynol-9, the same active ingredient used in vaginal spermicides. Studies by the World Health Organization (WHO) showed a high frequency of cancerous conditions in mice given daily insertions of polyurethane sponge tampons. The Consumer Federation of America recommends that the contraceptive sponge not be used until its safety is demonstrated through further testing. After mere months of general availability, the FDA has announced that it will increase its monitoring of the sponge because of reports linking it to toxic shock syndrome.

SAFE ALTERNATIVES

Use one of the natural birth control methods. Called the Fertility Awareness Method or natural family planning, these approaches are being investigated more and more by women who want control of their bodies and the freedom to make love without chemicals of questionable safety. The Catholic church is now promoting natural family planning as a replacement for the less reliable rhythm method.

Natural birth control methods are all based on abstinence during calculated fertile times. Since it is much easier to determine when ovulation is actually occurring than it is to predict when in the future it will occur, effectiveness for all methods increases if unprotected intercourse occurs only on the days *after* ovulation.

Fertile times can be determined in several ways. The Billings (Ovulation) Method relies on vaginal mucus changes to signal hormonal changes. Monitoring these mucus changes is probably the most reliable way to determine ovulation. On some days each month there is no mucus; on others, there's a thick, sticky substance; and then for several crucial days, a thin, slippery mucus not only indicates ovulation, but is essential for conception to occur. A recent WHO study showed that over 90 percent of women can learn to recognize their mucus changes within the first month. (Some women may have difficulties with this method if they have regular vaginal discharges due to chronic yeast infection.)

Change of body temperature can also indicate fertile times. Taking your temperature each morning at the same time with a basal body thermometer and recording it on a chart will show a slight rise following ovulation. When your temperature is .4 degree higher for three days, you know ovulation has occurred. The problem is that other body changes can affect your temperature (such as infection or allergic reaction) besides this hormone change, so that change in temperature alone is not always an accurate indication that the fertile time has passed.

After several months of checking mucus and/or taking temperatures, many women notice subtle symptoms at the time of ovulation they had not previously been aware of: mood changes, skin oiliness or dryness, limp hair, weight gain. Some men notice that their partners smell or taste different or have a regular increase or decrease in interest in sex during ovulation. Natural birth control works best if you use as many indicators as possible to tell that your fertile time has passed.

A new device called the Ovutimer (Repro-Technology, Boston, MA) may soon be on the market. The small bedside machine will monitor the consistency of cervical mucous samples and flash a green light for "safe days" and a red light for days on which you should abstain.

You are urged to study and understand natural birth control methods thoroughly before trying them. It is best to read several books that answer questions on the subject; best of all, take a class.

Sterilization is another option to consider for those couples who do not want children.

Brand Name/*Mail Order*
If you need to use a contraceptive device, use condoms (unlubricated are preferable) or a diaphragm with an unscented contraceptive jelly.

Condoms
B   Trojans (Young's Rubber Corp.). Made of natural latex rubber.

Contraceptive Jelly
B   Concepterol Disposable (Ortho Pharmaceutical Corp.).

B   Gynol II (Ortho Pharmaceutical Corp.).

B   Koromex Crystal Clear Gel (Young's Drug Products Corp.). "Unscented, colorless."

COOKIES

Colors; flavors; hydrogenated oil; sucrose.

SAFE ALTERNATIVES
Brand Name/*Mail Order*
Natural-foods stores carry additive-free, nonsucrose-sweetened cookies.

A   The Best Cookie Around (The Cookie Co.). Organic, but contains sucrose.

A   *Deer Valley Farm.* Cookies made from stone-milled organic grains, fresh organic eggs, and raw honey. Some may contain maple syrup or molasses.

A   New Planet Cookies (New Planet).

A   *Walnut Acres.* Eleven varieties of cookies made with organic ingredients, but containing sucrose.

B   Barbara's the World's Best Carob Brownie/Coconut Macaroon (Barbara's Bakery). *Walnut Acres.*

B   Glenny's Real Natural Brown Rice Treat (Glenn Foods).

C Carafection Honey Grahams (Tree of Life).

C D. Lazzaroni & C. Amaretti di Saronno Cookies (D. Lazzaroni & Co. S.p.A.).

C El Molino Cookies (El Molino Mills).

C Fox's All Butter Shortbread Biscuits (Fox's Biscuits).

C Glace Fan Wafers (Gourmet France).

C Health Valley Cookies (Health Valley Natural Foods).

C *Laura Todd Cookies.* Award-winning cookies from grandmother's old-fashioned recipes.

C Marin Brand Bar Cookies (Marin Food Specialties).

C Midel 100% Whole Wheat Honey Grahams (Health Foods).

C Maggie Graham's Own Scottish Shortbread (Heather Isle Kitchen).

C Martin's Edinburgh Shortbread Fingers (Martin's Bakery).

C Moravian "Crisps" Cookies (Moravian Sugar-Crisp Co.). *Moravian Sugar-Crisp Co.*

C Paterson's Butter Shortbread (J. Paterson & Son).

C Pepperidge Farm Cookies (Pepperidge Farm).

C Sunshine Golden Fruit Raisin Biscuits/Vanilla Wafers (Sunshine Biscuits).

C Walker's Pure Butter Shortbread (Joseph Walker/Strathpey Bakery).

See also Flour, Food, Grains, and Sugar.

COOKWARE

Plastic (tetrafluoroethylene).

Copper and aluminum cookware should not be used if the cooking surface itself is made from either of these metals. Acid foods cooked in aluminum interacts with the metal to form aluminum salts. Although little research has been done on the actual amount of aluminum salts we are exposed to from food cooked in aluminum cookware or their health effects, it is known that aluminum salts are toxic. A letter to the *New England Journal of Medicine* points out the connection between aluminum and brain disorders such as dementia, Alzheimer's disease, behavior abnormalities, poor memory, and impaired visual-motor coordination. One British study shows that aluminum cookware may cause indigestion, heartburn, flatulence, constipation, and headaches, and should thus be avoided.

Pots and pans with "no-stick" finishes such as Teflon or Silverstone scratch easily and can contaminate food with bits of plastic while cooking is taking place.

SAFE ALTERNATIVES

All cookware and bakeware should be made from glass, stainless steel, cast iron, porcelain-enamel—coated cast iron, or clay. Cooking utensils, measuring cups, mixing bowls, and other kitchen gadgets should be made of glass, clay, wood, or metal.

Brand Name/*Mail Order*
Ceramic

A Marsh Industries High-Fired Ceramic Bakeware (Marsh Industries).

Glass

A Corningware (Corning Glass Works).

A Pyrex Cookware/Bakeware (Corning Glass Works).

Porcelain Enamel on Cast Iron
A Le Cruset (Z. I. Caudry).

Porcelain Enamel on Steel
A Mikasa Gourmet Color (Mikasa).

A La Cuisine Collection (Gailstyn-Sutton).

Stainless Steel
A All-Clad Ltd Cookware (All-Clad Metal Crafters).

A Cuisinart Cookware (Cuisinarts).

A Farberware (Kidde).

A Master Chef (All-Clad Metal Crafters).

A Revere Ware (Revere Copper & Brass).

A Village Baker Bakeware (C. M. Products).

The following mail-order sources offer a large variety of cookware and useful kitchen gadgets: *The Chef's Catalog, Colonial Garden Kitchens, Erewhon Mail Order, Life Tools Co-op, Sparks Enterprises, Vermont Country Store, Whole Earth Access, Williams-Sonoma, The Wooden Spoon.*

Do-It-Yourself
For a no-stick finish, "season" cast-iron cookware. Before using the pan, cover the bottom with cooking oil and place on a warm burner for one hour. Wipe out the excess oil, leaving a thin film of oil on the pan. Each time you use it (if you don't allow the food to stick), the pan will become more seasoned. To maintain the seasoning, do not apply hot water and soap, and do not scour the pan. Wipe it out with a clean towel, or rinse with water and dry immediately to prevent rust, or rub the bottom with salt.

If you don't have a seasoned pan, keep food from sticking by pouring the oil into a heated pan, allowing the oil to get hot, and then adding the food. Alternately, spread a film of liquid lecithin (available at your natural-foods store) over the cooking surface before using it. (Lecithin is the active ingredient in the greaseless-frying aerosol sprays.)

For no-stick baking, line the pan with a piece of parchment paper (available at most cookware stores).

COPPER POLISH

See Metal Polishes.

COPY MACHINES

Ammonia; ethanol; kerosene; plastics.

Most problems from copy machines come from older-model "wet copy" machines that use a variety of volatile chemical toners to produce the copy image. Copied pages continue to smell of these toners for long periods of time.

SAFE ALTERNATIVES
Use a "dry copy" copy machine that makes the copy image by electronically fusing odorless carbon powder to the paper.

Brand Name/*Mail Order*
Nearly all new copy machines on the market are dry copy; only one manufacturer still makes wet-copy machines.

COSMETICS

Ammonia; BHA/BHT; colors; flavors; fragrance; glycerin; mineral oil; paraffin; plastics (nylon, PVP); saccharin; talc.

SAFE ALTERNATIVES
To enhance and accentuate cheeks, eyes, lips, and nails, use unscented cosmetics that contain a minimum of harmful substances such as powders made from clay and minerals.

Brand Name/*Mail Order*
Unscented cosmetics containing a minimum of petrochemical derivatives are sold in natural-foods and department stores. The brands listed below are all unscented.

Blusher
A   Silken Earth (Aubrey Organics).

B   Rachel Perry Earth Blush (Rachel Perry).

C   Almay Blushing Rouge (Almay).

C   Aziza All Day Performing Cheek Color (Prince Matchabelli).

C   Clinique Young Face Powder Blusher (Clinique Labs).

C   Nutricolor Blusher (Naturade Products).

Cosmetic Clays
A   Amber Rouge (Source Naturals).

A   Bare Escentuals Down to Earth (Bare Escentuals).

A   Earthe Tones Cosmetic Clays (Earthe Tones).

A   Earth Rouge (Ida Grae/Nature's Colors). *The Allergy Store.*

A   Indian Earth Cosmetic Clay (Indian Earth). *The Cotton Place, Ere-whon Mail Order, Essential Alternatives.*

Eyeshadow
A   Bare Escentuals Glimmer Powder (Bare Escentuals).

A   Earth Eyes (Ida Grae/Nature's Colors). *The Allergy Store.*

B   *The Body Shop.* Eye Dust.

B   Earthe Tones Eye Dusters (Earthe Tones).

B   Nature Eyes (Nature Cosmetics).

C   Almay Blushing Rouge (Almay).

C   Aziza All Day Performing Eyecolor (Prince Matchabelli).

C   Clinique Soft-Pressed Eye Shadow (Clinique Labs).

C   Lancôme Maquiriche Cremepowder Eyecolor (Lancôme).

Face Powder
A   Bare Escentuals Matte Powder (Bare Escentuals).

C   Almay Sheer Finish Translucent Pressed Powder/Translucent Finish Face Powder (Almay).

C   Clinique Face Powder (Clinique Labs).

Foundation Makeup
B   Viva Vera Oil-Free Foundation (Viva Vera).

C   Almay Fresh Look Oil-Free Makeup (Almay).

C   Max Factor Unshine Oil-Free Make-Up (Max Factor).

Lip Gloss
A   Aubrey Organics Lip Silk/Lip Silk Red (Aubrey Organics). Natural flavors, colored with carmine.

A   *The Body Shop (England).* Flavored Lip Balm.

A Country Comfort Natural Lip Balm (Country Comfort). *The Soap Opera.*

A Earth Eye/Lip Creme (Ida Grae/Nature's Colors). Colored with carmine. *The Allergy Store.*

A *Fluir Herbals.* Flavored Lip Balm.

A GK Lip Moisturizer (Pure Body Creations). Flavored.

A Golden Sauve (East Earth Herb).

A Lip Aum (East Earth Herb).

A Nanak's Lip Smoothee (Golden Temple Natural Products). Flavored.

A *New Age Creations.* Flavored Lip Balm.

A *Ram Island Farm Herbs.* Flavored Lip Balm with a cocoa-butter base.

A Star & Crescent Lip Balm (Star & Crescent). Natural colors and flavors.

A Windflower Herbals Lip Balms (Windflower Herbals). Flavored.

B Aloe/Paba Lip Balm (Palm Springs Perfume & Cosmetics Laboratory).

B *The Body Shop.* Natural-flavored Lip Balm and Lip Balm with Paba.

B Lip Trip (Rocky Mountain Ocean). Flavored.

B Viva Vera Lipmender (Viva Vera).

C Clinique Lip Glosses (Clinique Labs).

C Earthe Tones Lip Gloss (Earthe Tones).

Lipsticks
C Clinique Lipsticks (Clinique Labs).

C Lily of the Desert Aloe Vera Lipsticks (Vera Products).

C Nature Lips Lipsticks (Nature Cosmetics).

C Nutricolor Lipsticks (Naturade Products).

C Orjene Lipsticks (Orgene Co.).

Mascara
B Nature Waterproof Mascara (Nature Cosmetics).

B Rimmel Cake Mascara (Caswell-Massey Co.). *Caswell-Massey.*

C Almay Mascaras (Almay).

C Aziza Mascaras (Prince Matchabelli).

C Clinique Glossy Brush-On Mascaras (Clinique Labs).

C Lancôme Maquicils Automatic Mascaras (Lancôme).

C Max Factor Maxi Extra-Long Thick Lash Mascara (Max Factor).

C Nature Thicklash Mascara (Nature Cosmetics).

C Nutricolor Dual Purpose Mascara (Naturade Products).

Do-It-Yourself

Lip Gloss Melt either of the following formulas in the top of a double boiler and mix well. Tint to desired shade with carmine, beet juice, or berry juice, or leave it clear to use alone or as a gloss over a cosmetic clay. Pour into small jars and cool.
• Melt ¼ cup beeswax; remove from heat and add ¼ cup castor oil, 2 tablespoons sesame oil, and 2 tablespoons liquid lanolin.
• Melt 1 teaspoon olive oil, 1 teaspoon beeswax, and 6 tablespoons mink oil.

Lip Color Rub a piece of raw beet over your lips and cover with a clear gloss, if desired.

Blusher Rub a piece of raw beet over skin until desired shade is reached. This works best if beet color is applied to bare skin and then powder is applied on top.

Face Powder In a dry skillet, brown oat flour, cornstarch, rice flour, or white clay to desired shade. Store in a tightly covered jar and apply with a cotton ball. Will be transparent when applied, but gives the skin a soft look and a smooth finish.

See also Beauty Products.

COTTON BALLS

Plastic (polyester).

SAFE ALTERNATIVES
Brand Name/*Mail Order*

Be sure the label says "cotton balls" and not "cosmetic puffs" (which are polyester).

A *The Body Shop (England).* "Soft and gentle high-quality cotton buds."

A Bonnie Hubbard Cotton Balls (United Grocers).

A Curity Cotton Balls (Colgate-Palmolive).

A Johnson & Johnson Cotton Balls (Johnson & Johnson).

A Q-Tips Cotton Balls (Cheesebor-ough-Ponds).

See also Textiles.

CRACKERS

Colors; flavors; hydrogenated oil; pesticide residues; sucrose.

SAFE ALTERNATIVES
Brand Name/*Mail Order*

Additive-free crackers can be found in supermarkets as well as natural-foods stores.

A Arden Organic Rice Cakes (Arden Organics). *Erewhon Mail Order, Kennedy's Natural Foods.*

A Chico-San Rice Cakes (Chico-San). *Chico-San, Deer Valley Farm, Erewhon Mail Order, Walnut Acres.*

A Erewhon Crackers (Erewhon).

A Lundberg Rice Cakes (Lundberg Farm). *Lundberg Farm.*

B Ak-Mak Crackers (A-M Bakeries). *Deer Valley Farm, Erewhon Mail Order, Kennedy's Natural Foods, Walnut Acres.*

B Chico-San Brown Rice Treats (Chico-San). *Chico-San.*

B Edward & Sons Brown Rice Snaps (Edward & Sons). *Kennedy's Natural Foods, Walnut Acres.*

B Erewhon Rice Crackers (Erewhon). *Erewhon Mail Order.*

B Finn Rye Crisp (A. V. Olsson Trading Co.). *Walnut Acres.*

B Hain Naturals Crackers (Hain Pure Food Co.).

B Harvest Moon Rice Crackers (Mitoku Co.).

B Health Valley Crackers (Health Valley Natural Foods). *Erewhon Mail Order, Kennedy's Natural Foods.*

B Jacob's Cream Crackers (W & R Jacob & Co.).

B Kavli Norwegian Flatbread (O. Kavli A/S). *Deer Valley Farm.*

B Norwegian Ideal Flatbread (Shaffer, Clarke & Co.).

B Paterson's Scotch Oatcakes (J. Paterson & Son).

B Rykrisp Natural (Ralston-Purina).

B Soken Sesame Wheels (Soken Trading Co.).

B Soken-Sha Brown Rice Crackers (Soken Trading Co.). *Kennedy's Natural Foods.*

B Wasa Crisp Bread (Wasa Ry-King). *Deer Valley Farm, Kennedy's Natural Foods.*

B Westbrae Crackers/Natural Brown Rice Wafers (Westbrae Natural Foods).

C Bremner Wafers (Bremner Biscuit Co.).

C Carr's Table Water Crackers (Carr's of Carlisle).

C Nabisco Premium Saltines (Nabisco).

C Nabisco Honey Maid Graham Crackers/Ritz Crackers/Wheat Thins/Wheatsworth Crackers/Zwieback Toast (Nabisco).

C Nature's Cupboard Crackers (Marin Food Specialties).

C Roman Meal Natural Foods Crackers (Roman Meal Co.).

C Roman Meal Wafers (Interbake Foods).

C Sailor Boy Pilot Bread Crackers (Interbake Foods).

C Sunshine Cheezits/Krispy Saltines (Sunshine Biscuits).

See also Flour, Food, and Sugar.

CURTAINS

See Window Coverings.

D

DATE SUGAR

See Sugar.

DENTURE CLEANERS

Benzyl alcohol/sodium benzoate; colors; EDTA; isopropyl alcohol; and plastic (PVP).

"DANGER: injurious to eyes. Harmful if swallowed. Keep out of reach of children."

SAFE ALTERNATIVES
Do-It-Yourself
• Soak dentures overnight in a mixture of ¼ teaspoon TSP and ½ glass water.
• Mix together thoroughly 10 ounces TSP, 5 ounces sodium perborate, and 5 ounces salt. Soak dentures overnight in ¼ teaspoon of this mixture dissolved in ½ glass of water.
• Mix 5 ounces TSP with 7 drops essential oil of cinnamon by shaking them vigorously in a bottle until thoroughly blended. Soak dentures overnight in ¼ teaspoon of this mixture dissolved in ½ glass of water. Rinse with plain water.

DEODORANT

See Antiperspirants & Deodorants.

DIAPERS

Fragrance; plastics (acrylic, polyester, polyethylene).

Disposable diapers cause more frequent and severe diaper rash than cloth diapers do. Complaints made to the Consumer Protection Agency also include chemical burns, noxious chemical and insecticide odors, reports of babies pulling the diapers apart and putting pieces of plastic into their mouths and noses, of plastic covers melting onto baby's skin, and of ink from the diaper staining the skin.

SAFE ALTERNATIVES
Use 100% cotton cloth diapers with natural-fiber diaper covers. To kill bacteria in cloth diapers, use the hottest water in your washing machine and forty minutes on the hottest dryer setting. Whenever possible, air the washed diapers outdoors in the sunlight, which acts as a natural disinfectant. Soaking soiled diapers in a mixture of ½ cup borax added to a pail of warm water will help reduce odors and staining, and will make diapers more absorbent.

Brand Name/*Mail Order*
If your local baby store doesn't carry natural-fiber diapers and covers, order them by mail.

A Biobottoms (Biobottoms). Creamy-white pure virgin wool diaper covers. *The Allergy Store, Biobottoms, The Futon Shop, Moonflower Birthing Supply, Natural Child, Whole Earth Access.*

A *Cotton Dreams.* "Soft, lightweight wool felt" diaper covers, less bulky than soakers.

A *The Cotton Place.* Hospital-quality cotton gauze diapers.

A *Erlander's Natural Products.* Cotton diapers. Also a 100% cotton diaper stacker with a hanger for attaching it to the crib.

A *Gohn Bros.* Cotton diapers.

A *Happy Baby Bunz.* Nikky no-pins wool felt diaper covers, made by a company that has specialized in diaper covers for over 60 years.

A *Janice Corp.* Heavyweight cotton diapers.

A *Janice Jacobson.* "Extra-heavyweight" double-napped 100% pure cotton flannel diapers.

A *Marni's Soakers.* Diaper covers, 100% wool jersey, with a triple-layered crotch.

A *Moonflower.* White 100% cotton double-napped flannel diapers and diaper covers, in 5 styles.

A *The Nappi Co.* White 100% cotton terrycloth superabsorbant diapers that have been used in England for more than 100 years.

A *Sears.* Cotton diapers.

B *Karess.* Fitted flannel diapers, 100% cotton, with a special 10-layer absorbant panel in the middle.

B *Laura Furlong Designs.* A special diaper/soaker made of cotton terrycloth and flannel.

B *Wee Care.* Cotton flannel diapers with extra padding for absorbancy in white with colored rosebud print.

Do-It-Yourself
Gohn Bros. and *Vermont Country Store* sell yardage for making your own cotton diapers.

See also Textiles.

DISHWASHER DETERGENT

Chlorine; colors; detergents; fragrance.

"CAUTION: Injurious to eyes. Harmful if swallowed. Avoid contact with eyes, mucous membranes and prolonged skin contact. Keep out of reach of children."

SAFE ALTERNATIVES
Brand Name/*Mail Order*
The following brands do not give off fumes of chlorine or strong fragrances but should still be used with caution as they may contain other harmful ingredients.

C Amway Automatic Dishwasher Compound (Amway Corp.).

C Electra-Sol (Economics Laboratory).

C Neo-Life Automatic Dishwashing Powder (Neo-Life Company of America).

C White Magic Dishwasher Detergent (Safeway Stores).

Do-It-Yourself
• Use 1 part borax and 1 part washing soda. If you live in a hard-water area, you will have to adjust the proportions to avoid scum forming on your dishes.

CAUTION: Never use ordinary dishwashing liquid instead, since the bubbles can inhibit the action of the water spray and can clog the drain.

See also Cleaning Products.

DISHWASHERS

See Appliances.

DISHWASHING LIQUID

Colors; detergents; ethanol; fragrance.

SAFE ALTERNATIVES
Brand Name/*Mail Order*
A Granny's Old-Fashioned Dishwashing Liquid (Granny's Old-Fashioned Products). *Granny's Old-Fashioned Products.*

Do-It-Yourself

Liquids & Powders
• Use a simple liquid soap.
• Rub your sponge with bar soap.
• Combine 24 ounces TSP, 2½ ounces borax, and 1 ounce powdered soap. Mix together thoroughly by shaking in a box or bag; add a little of the powder to dishwater.
• Use 1 teaspoon TSP in a sinkful of warm water.
• Dissolve 1 heaping tablespoon washing soda in a sinkful of water, and use about half the amount of soap you would normally use.

Special Cases
• To soften water, cut grease, and make dishes shine: Add slices of fresh lemon or lemon peels or a few tablespoons white vinegar to dishwater.
• Disinfect your dishes without soap: If you cannot use sufficiently hot water while washing, clean the food off with a sponge or brush, then pile dishes in the sink and fill it with water hotter than you can touch.
• Prevent water spotting: Dissolve 2 teaspoons sodium hexametaphosphate in a sinkful of hot water, then add about half the amount of soap you would normally use. Wash glass-

es, dishes, and silver, rinse with hot water, and dry in a dish drainer.

• Wash bottles: Put sand and water in the bottle, cover the opening with a lid or your hand, and shake vigorously.

• Clean breadboards, cutting boards, wooden salad bowls, and butcher blocks: Rub half a cut lemon or lime over the surface, rinse, dry with a cloth, and cover with salt to absorb moisture, or use a paste of baking soda and water.

• Wash fine crystal: Clean gently with warm, soapy water, then rinse in a solution of 1 part white vinegar and 3 parts warm water.

• Stains on enamel-finish cookware: Use a paste of salt and white vinegar.

• Burned-on food: Sprinkle with baking soda and moisten with water. Let set for a few hours and food should lift right out.

• Sediment from teakettles: Mix together 1½ cups apple cider vinegar, 1½ cups water, and 3 tablespoons salt in the kettle and boil for 15 minutes. Let sit overnight, then rinse with clear water.

See also Cleaning Products and Soap.

DISINFECTANTS

Aerosol propellants; ammonia; chlorine; colors; cresol; detergents; ethanol; formaldehyde; glycerin; isopropyl alcohol; phenol; pine oil (contains naturally-occurring phenolic compounds).

"CAUTION: Keep out of reach of children. Keep away from heat, sparks, and open flame. Keep out of eyes. Avoid contact with food."

SAFE ALTERNATIVES
Do-It-Yourself

• Clean regularly with plain soap and water. Even just a rinse of hot water will kill some bacteria.

• Keep things dry (bacteria, mildew, and mold cannot live without dampness).

• Use borax. Long recognized for its deodorizing properties, it is also a very effective disinfectant. One hospital experimented with using a solution of ½ cup borax to 1 gallon hot water for one year. At the end of that period, the monitoring bacteriologist reported that the borax solution satisfied all the hospital germicidal requirements.

• Use an aqueous solution of benzalkonium chloride 1:750 (brand name is Zephirin, and it is usually used for medical purposes). It can be used in the same manner as any liquid disinfectant and has far fewer fumes. Many people with sensitivities to chlorine substitute a benzalkonium chloride solution for anything they would need chlorine as a disinfectant for, including killing bacteria in hot-tubs. Some people do react to it, however, so approach use with caution.

Note: Disinfectants *reduce* germs, but do not sterilize (kill all germs present).

See also Cleaning Products and Soap.

DOUCHES

Ammonia; colors; detergents; EDTA; fragrance; glycerin; phenol.

Douching commonly causes irritation, allergic reactions, and "chemical vaginitis" from the strong chemicals often used in the douche solutions. Douches can also affect external tissues, producing swelling, inflammation, and other symptoms of dermatitis. Toxic chemicals are easily absorbed through the delicate skin inside the vagina.

SAFE ALTERNATIVES

An FDA advisory review panel says there is no need to douche and blames "tradition, ignorance, and commercial advertising" for the practice.

Do, however, rinse the vaginal area with plain water regularly when bathing. Use a mild soap externally if desired, but do not use soap inside, as it may cause irritation for you or your sexual partner.

In addition, avoid clothes and undergarments that are tight and constricting in the crotch area. Wear cotton undergarments that absorb moisture and allow perspiration to evaporate.

If unusual genital odors, itching, or discharge develops, see your doctor; it could be a sign of a medical problem.

Do-It-Yourself

• Use 1½ teaspoons vinegar mixed in 1 quart water.
• Use 1 teaspoon baking soda mixed in 1 pint water.
• To ease itching: Crush 1 garlic clove and add to 1 cup yogurt. Let set for several hours. Boil 1 cup water, add to yogurt, and shake until the yogurt dissolves. Strain through cheesecloth to remove garlic and apply.

See also Beauty Products.

DRAIN CLEANERS

Petroleum distillates; sulfur compounds. Drain cleaners also contain caustic lye.

"POISON: ☠ CALL POISON CENTER, EMERGENCY ROOM, OR PHYSICIAN AT ONCE. Causes severe eye and skin damage; may cause blindness. Harmful or fatal if swallowed."

SAFE ALTERNATIVES

Eliminate the need for a drain cleaner by preventing clogged drains:
• Use a drain strainer to trap food particles or hair that might cause a clog.
• Run lots of hot water through your drains twice a week.
• Pour 3 tablespoons washing soda down drainpipe once or twice a week, followed by lots of hot water.
• Mix 1 cup baking soda, 1 cup salt, and ¼ cup cream of tartar. Once or twice a week, pour ¼ cup down the drainpipe, followed by a cup of boiling water, then cold water.

Do-It-Yourself

For Clogged Drains

• Use a plunger or a mechanical snake (these can be rented from hardware or equipment-rental stores).
• Pour 1 handful baking soda and ½ cup white vinegar down drainpipe and cover tightly for one minute. Repeat process as needed.
• Pour ½ cup salt and ½ cup baking soda down the drain, followed by 6 cups boiling water. Let sit for several hours or overnight, then flush with water.

To Clean Garbage Disposals
- Grind used lemon in disposal.
- Pour baking soda in disposal.
- Pour 2–3 tablespoons borax in the garbage disposal, let stand for at least 15 minutes, and rinse with the disposal on.

See also Cleaning Products.

DRIED FRUITS

Methyl bromide; sulfur compounds.

SAFE ALTERNATIVES
Brand Name/Mail Order

Purchase unsulphured dried fruits at your natural-foods store. These can be easily recognized because they are usually darker in color than sulfured fruits. They are also drier and more tough, but they taste like the fruit instead of sulfur dioxide. Unsulfured fruits that are water processed or dipped in honey are softer and retain the original color of the fruit. Sulphured fruits are brightly colored.

A   *Ahlers Organic Date & Grapefruit Garden.* Four varieties of dates.

A   *Jaffe Bros.* "Organically grown, unsulphured, and unfumigated" apples, apricots, dates, figs, peaches, pears, prunes, and raisins. Also unsweetened dried pineapple, papaya, and whole bananas.

A   Shiloh Farms Dried Fruits (Shiloh Farms). *Shiloh Farms.*

A   Sonoma Dried Fruits (Timbercrest Farms). Unsulphured apples, apricots, cherries, dates, figs, peaches, pears, prunes, and raisins. *Timbercrest Farms, Walnut Acres.*

A   *Walnut Acres.* Fruits "grown and sundried in the high, cold valleys of Hunzaland. . . . No chemicals are ever used."

AB   (*Colvada Date Co.*) Eight varieties of dates grown on their own farm, plus various date confections and fancy stuffed dates. Also dried apples, apricots, currants, figs, papaya, peaches, pears, pineapple, prunes, and raisins. Gift packs available. Dates also available at natural-food stores and *Shiloh Farms.*

AB   *Deer Valley Farm.* Unsulphured apples, apricots, currants, dates, figs, papaya, peaches, pears, pineapple, prunes, and raisins.

AB   *Erewhon Mail Order.* Unsulphured apples, apricots, currants, dates, figs, peaches, pineapples, prunes, raisins.

AB   *Kennedy's Natural Foods.* Unsulphured apples, apricots, bananas, cherries, currants, dates, figs, mangos, peaches, pears, prunes, and raisins. Also dried pineapple and honey-dipped dried papaya.

B   Cinderella California Seedless Raisins (West Coast Growers & Packers).

B   Sun Giant Raisins (Tenneco West).

B   Townhouse Seedless Raisins (Safeway Stores).

See also Food and Produce.

DRY CLEANERS

Ammonia; benzene; chlorine; detergents; formaldehyde; glycerin;

naphthalene; paraffin; perchlorethylene; toluene; trichloroethylene; xylene.

Stain-repellent finishes and mothproofing may also be applied when items are dry-cleaned.

SAFE ALTERNATIVES

Make sure dry-cleaned garments are thoroughly dry before wearing; all solvents are volatile. Although solvents will dissipate in time, clothing is often returned to customers before these chemicals have completely evaporated. Remove all items from their polyethylene wrapping as soon as you get home, and air them out in a place with good ventilation so you won't breathe the fumes.

Unless garments would otherwise shrink or lose their shape, it is preferable to carefully hand wash in cold water, and then take to the cleaners for a professional pressing.

Find a local cleaner who will use naphtha as the solvent instead of perchlorethane. Even though this too is a petroleum derivative, it seems to be less odiferous and is often tolerated by those with chemical sensitivities.

See also Cleaning Products.

DYES

Dyes.

SAFE ALTERNATIVES

Available are a number of natural dyestuffs that produce a whole rainbow of beautiful colors. All types of plants, including flowers, weeds, trees, roots, and bark, as well as various foods, herbs, and spices can be used. Fennel, for example, produces a brilliant yellow, and eucalyptus, a deep red; walnut leaves a whole spectrum of earthy browns. Certain animals and insects also provide natural dyes: mollusks yield a Tyrian purple, and for centuries tiny cochineal insects were the most widely used ingredient for red dye. In ancient times, nearly one thousand different natural sources provided dyestuffs.

Some materials for dyestuffs can be gathered in their natural habitat, while other more exotic dyes can be purchased.

Brand Name/*Mail Order*

Look for natural dyestuffs in local stores that sell dyeing equipment, or order by mail.

A *C. D. Fitzhardinge-Bailey.* Natural dyestuffs from Australia.

A *Cerulean Blue.* Concentrated extracts of natural dyes from Japan, and other natural dyestuffs.

A *The Mannings Handweaving School & Supply Center.* Natural dyestuffs and books on natural dyeing.

A *The Pendelton Shop.* Books on natural dyeing.

A *Romni Wools & Fibres.* Natural dyestuffs and books on natural dyeing.

A *S. & C. Huber, Accoutrements.* Natural dyestuffs and books on natural dyeing.

A *Wide World of Herbs.* Natural dyestuffs.

Do-It-Yourself

Grow your own dye plants with seeds from *Le Jardin du Gourmet* and *Redwood City Seed Co.*

See also Fabric and Textiles.

E

EGGNOG

Colors; flavors; sucrose.

SAFE ALTERNATIVES
Brand Name/*Mail Order*
Honey-sweetened eggnogs are available seasonally at your natural-foods store.

B Alta-Dena Natural Honey Sweetened Eggnog (Alta-Dena).
B Mountain High Eggnog (Mountain High Products).

See also Eggs, Food, and Milk.

EGGS

Colors; pesticide residues.

Eggs also contain, in addition to the above, residues of antibiotics, hormones, stimulants, tranquilizers, and fumigants from feed that is given to the mother hens. And then, after the eggs are laid, they are washed with detergents and sprayed with a petrochemical oil or solvent to extend shelf life.

SAFE ALTERNATIVES
Brand Name/*Mail Order*
Buy eggs either from a local farm whose growing practices you are familiar with, or from your natural-foods store in cartons that clearly state "No Antibiotics, No Artificial Stimulants." Fertile eggs often are grown by natural methods, but the word *fertile* alone on the carton simply means that the eggs can be hatched into baby chicks; it does not mean the eggs are all-natural, unless there is also some other indication. (Brand names are not listed here because all eggs are sold locally.)

A *Kennedy's Natural Foods.* Fertile brown eggs "fed only natural foods. No antibiotics or arsenical drugs used."

See also Food and Milk.

ELASTIC

Plastics (latex, polyester).

SAFE ALTERNATIVES
Use cotton elastic.

Brand Name/*Mail Order*
Buy cotton elastic by the yard at your local fabric store, or order it by mail.
Cotton Elastic
A *Erlander's Natural Products, The Cotton Place.*

See also Textiles.

ENGLISH MUFFINS

Ammonia; hydrogenated oil; pesticide residues; sucrose.

SAFE ALTERNATIVES
Brand Name/*Mail Order*
Additive-free English muffins can be found in natural-foods stores.

A Erewhon Wholewheat English Muffins (Erewhon).
B Good Stuff Natural Whole Grain English Muffins (Good Stuff Bakery).

See also Bread, Flour, and Food.

ESSENTIAL OILS

See Fragrances.

EYEDROPS

Ammonia; EDTA; glycerin.

SAFE ALTERNATIVES
Brand Name/*Mail Order*

A Paul de Sousa's Chlorophyll Eye Drops (Paul de Sousa's Co.). *Pure Planet Products.*

Do-It-Yourself
• Apply fresh, cold cucumber slices, chilled wet teabags, or grated raw potato wrapped in cotton gauze on closed eyelids.
• Dissolve ¹⁄₁₆ teaspoon baking soda in 1 cup distilled water. Decant into glass dropper bottle.
• Dissolve ⅞ teaspoon salt in 1 pint warm water. Decant into glass dropper bottle.

See also Beauty Products.

EYEGLASSES

Plastic.

SAFE ALTERNATIVES
Brand Name/*Mail Order*
Ask your optician for eyeglasses with glass lenses and metal frames. If your prescription would make glass lenses too heavy, compromise by putting your plastic lenses in metal frames.

A *Glenn's Optiques.* Gold-plated and brass nose and ear pieces, and metal frames. Will safety-treat glass lenses with heat instead of chemicals.

See also Contact Lenses.

EYESHADOW

See Cosmetics.

FABRIC

Dyes; formaldehyde; pesticides (mothproofing); plastics (acrylic, nylon, polyester, PVC/vinyl chloride, spandex).

SAFE ALTERNATIVES
Brand Name/*Mail Order*
Better fabric stores will carry a large variety of natural-fiber fabrics. Wash all fabrics before use to remove any excess dyes and finishes.

A *Cerulean Blue.* Natural-fiber fabrics that are "bleached or white in color and have received no finish or other treatment."

A *Homespun Fabrics & Draperies.* "Raw" or bleached cotton in extrawide lengths suitable for draperies, bedspreads, and upholstery.

A *Janice Corp.* "Unbleached, untreated" cotton fabrics.

A *Testfabrics.* Untreated naturalfiber fabrics for dyeing, including 32 types of cotton.

A *Vermont Country Store.* Small selection of unusual cotton fabrics.

AB *Carol Brown.* Beautiful, highestquality natural-fiber fabrics, imported from around the world.

AB *The Cotton Place.* Many types of cotton fabrics and other natural fibers. Also cotton lace, trim, and bias tape.

AB *Erlander's Natural Products.* Many types of cotton fabric. Also cotton bias tape.

AB *Exotic Silks!* Over 80 different types of silk in many colors, including upholstery- and drapery-weight silks. Also several types of unbleached, undyed silk, and a few cottons. Good prices.

AB *Gohn Bros.* Basic cotton fabrics.

AB *Nikko Natural Fabrics.* Natural-fiber fabric club with 16 varieties of silk, plus cottons and linens. All available undyed or in 26 colors.

AB *Norton Candle & Handiwork House.* Offers "800 different cotton calicoes and solids."

AB *S. & C. Huber, Accoutrements.* Unbleached linen fabrics and cotton/linen blends in 18th- and 19th-century reproductions.

AB *Sunflower Studio.* Expensive fabrics "typical of those hand-woven in the 17th, 18th, and early 19th centuries." Wool, linen, cotton, and blends such as "linsey-woolsey."

AB *Sureway Trading Enterprises.* Good prices on nearly 70 different types of undyed silk. Many are also available dyed, including silk/wool blends for suiting.

AB *Utex Trading Enterprises.* One of the largest Chinese-silk suppliers in America; they import over 100 different varieties of silk fabric directly from China.

B *Britex-by-Mail.* Thousands of fine imported and domestic fabrics in natural fibers.

B *Castlemoor.* Pure British wool fabrics.

B *Cleo.* Wool Irish tweeds.

B *Feathered Friends.* White and solid-color. 100% Egyptian cotton.

B *Gill Imports.* Natural hand-loomed cotton, hand embroidered in Kashmir with dyed wool. Plain handloomed cotton also available.

B *Gurian's.* Natural handloomed cotton, hand embroidered with dyed wool. Also plain hand-loomed cotton.

B *Homespun Weavers.* Colonial homespun 100% cotton, in 7 colors.

B *Laura Ashley.* English country prints on regular and upholstery-weight cotton fabric. Also cotton braid and bias binding.

B *Natural Fiber Fabric Club.* Four mailings per year of swatches of natural-fiber fabrics that can be ordered at 20% discount.

B *Nizhonie Fabrics.* Authentic historical Indian designs on 100% cotton or linen fabric.

B *The Scottish Lion.* Wool or silk in over 200 traditional Scottish tartan plaids.

B *Scottish Products.* Wool Scottish tartan plaids.

B *Shama Imports.* Natural hand-loomed cotton, hand embroidered in Kashmir with dyed wool.

B *Trefriw Woolen Mills.* Welsh woolens.

See also Dyes and Textiles.

FABRIC SOFTENERS

Aerosol propellants, ammonia; colors; fragrance; glycerin.

"CAUTION: Keep out of reach of children."

SAFE ALTERNATIVES
Fabric softeners are designed to reduce static cling in synthetic fabrics and are unnecessary with natural-fiber fabrics.

Brand Name/*Mail Order*
If you must use a fabric softener, choose an unscented brand from your supermarket.

Unscented
C Bounce Unscented (Procter & Gamble). Made from unidentified "nonionic and cationic fabric softening agents" and "aluminosilicates impregnated in a rayon cloth."

Do-It-Yourself
• To make natural-fiber fabrics softer, pour 1 cup white vinegar or ¼ cup baking soda into the final rinse-water to remove any scum left from natural soap.

See also Cleaning Products, Clothing, and Textiles.

FACE POWDER

See Cosmetics.

FACIALS

Colors; ethanol; fragrance; glycerin; talc.

SAFE ALTERNATIVES
Brand Name/*Mail Order*

Herbal Mixtures for Facial Steam Baths
A Facial Steam (Country House).

A Herbal Facial Steam (Body Love). *Wholesome Paks.*

A *New Age Creations.*

A Scarborough Fair Facial Sauna Herbs (Scarborough Fair). *Sunnybrook Farms.*

Masks: Unscented
A Aubrey Organics Facial Masks (Aubrey Organics).

A *The Body Shop (England).* Several oatmeal-based facial masks.

A Dr. Hauschka Facial Steam Bath (Dr. R. Hauschka Cosmetics). *Meadowbrook Herbs & Things, Weleda.*

A *Fluir Herbals.* Almond Facial Mask.

A *The Herb Patch.*

A *New Age Creations.* Herbal Facial Masks.

A *Ram Island Farm Herbs.*

Masks: Natural Scent
A Desert Essence Jojoba Facial Mask (Desert Essence Cosmetics/Jojoba Products). *The Soap Opera.*

A Nature de France Deep Cleansing Masks (Nature de France). *Nature de France, The Soap Opera.*

Do-It-Yourself

Facial Steam Bath
• Boil 2 quarts water with 2 tablespoons fresh or dried herbs of your choice for 5 minutes. Pour into a large bowl. Drape a large towel over your head and put your face over the bowl, so that the towel forms a tent over you and the bowl. Allow the steam to penetrate your skin for 5 to 10 minutes, then rinse with very cold water to close the pores.

97

Masks

• Mix any of the following groups of ingredients, then prepare for the mask by cleansing your face and taking a facial steam bath (see above), or by moistening your face and neck with warm water. Apply mask to skin, avoiding area around eyes; allow to dry for the specified time, then rinse with warm water. Always splash the face with cold water after a mask treatment, to close the pores. Masks should be freshly made for each use; if necessary, however, larger quantities of those masks containing produce items may be made in advance, then frozen into cubes and thawed as needed.

• Soak 1 cup dried apricots in pure water until softened. Puree in a blender or food processor with 2 tablespoons skim milk powder. Leave on for 15 minutes.

• Peel and slice ½ cucumber. Place in blender or food processor and puree. Mix in 1 tablespoon yogurt. Leave on for 20 minutes.

• Puree a small piece of raw unpeeled eggplant in a blender or food processor with ½ cup plain yogurt. Leave on for 20 minutes.

• Puree ½ cup fresh mint leaves and 3 ice cubes (made from pure water) in blender. Strain liquid and apply. Leave on until dry.

• Rub a slice of papaya over clean skin. Leave on at least 30 minutes.

• Steep ½ cup fresh parsley in 1 cup pure boiling water until lukewarm. Strain. Apply in wet compress for 10 to 15 minutes.

• Crush a few strawberries and mix with 1 teaspoon honey. Leave on for 10 to 15 minutes.

• Puree 1 ripe avocado in blender or food processor. Apply as is or combine with an equal amount of sour cream or yogurt, or else ½ cup honey and 2 tablespoons peanut or olive oil, *or* 1 teaspoon honey and the juice from half a lemon. Leave on for 15 to 30 minutes.

• Mix 2 tablespoons rose clay with 3 teaspoons olive oil or 2–3 teaspoons lukewarm chamomile tea. Leave on for 20 minutes.

• Mix 2 tablespoons green clay with the juice of ½ lemon and enough mineral water to reach the desired consistency. Leave on for 20 minutes.

• Add ½ teaspoon honey *or* the juice of 1 small lemon to 1 egg white and beat until stiff. Leave on for 10 to 20 minutes.

• Make a smooth paste of oatmeal and water. Apply and leave on until it dries completely. Remove by rubbing off with your fingers. Rinse.

• Mix 1 tablespoon oatmeal flour, 1 tablespoon oil of your choice, and enough pure water to form a heavy dough. Leave on for 10 to 20 minutes.

• Mix ½ cup sesame seeds with ¼ cup water in a blender for 3 minutes. Strain. Leave on for as long as possible.

• Mix 1 tablespoon raw wheat germ with 2 tablespoons pure warm water, adding 1 egg yolk to form a heavy dough. Leave on for 10 to 15 minutes.

• Mix 1 tablespoon powdered yeast with 2 tablespoons pure warm water or 3 tablespoons yogurt. Add extra water or yogurt if needed. Leave on for 10 to 15 minutes.

• Mix 1 tablespoon honey, 1 teaspoon spring or mineral water, 1 teaspoon oil, and 1 capsule vitamin E (100–200IU). Leave on for 20 minutes.

• Mix 1½ teaspoons honey, juice of ½ lemon, and 1 small carton plain yogurt. Add 1 whipped egg white. Leave on for 15 minutes.

• Place 4 tablespoons oatmeal and 1 teaspoon dried mint leaves in a blender and mix well until finely ground. Add hot water to form a paste. Leave on for 15 minutes.

• Mash 1 tomato with 1 tablespoon each of honey, yogurt, and oatmeal. Leave on for 15 minutes.

See also Beauty Products.

FEATHERBEDS

See beds.

FEMININE HYGIENE SPRAYS

Aerosol propellants; ethanol; fragrance; glycerin; mineral oil; talc.

Most feminine hygiene sprays contain only a perfume and have no antibacterial ingredients to stop odor. Irritation is the most common problem, ranging from rashes and soreness to infection, open sores, and chemical burns.

SAFE ALTERNATIVES
Instead of using a feminine hygiene spray, rinse the vaginal area regularly while bathing with plain water. Using soap inside may cause irritation for you or your sexual partner.

See also Beauty Products and Douches.

FEMININE PROTECTION

Formaldehyde; fragrance; plastics (acrylonitrile, polyester).

Over 20 percent of the respondents in a *Consumer Reports* magazine survey had been warned by their doctors not to use deodorant tampons or pads. Even people who are not normally sensitive to perfume can, over time, develop irritations or allergic reactions to these deodorant scents.

All brands of tampons have, in addition, been associated with toxic shock syndrome, so approach the use of any tampon with caution.

SAFE ALTERNATIVES
Use unscented menstrual pads made from cotton. These come in two types, disposable and reusable. Reusable pads are less convenient since they have to be washed, and since they obligate you to carry soiled or damp pads with you when you are away from home.

Use small, soft, natural seasponges, which can be inserted like a tampon. The main disadvantage is that they tend to leak during a heavy flow if left in too long. They can be rinsed and reinserted and must be sterilized often.

Federal regulations prohibit the marketing of sponges "to insert into the body," so you will not find any sponges with instructions for use as a tampon. Before using a sponge for this purpose, first prepare the sponge by rinsing it several times in clean running water, and then sterilize the sponge by dropping it into a pot of boiling water, letting it boil for 30 seconds and allowing the sponge to sit in the water for a minute after turning off the heat.

Always wash your hands before removing or inserting the sponge. After removal, rinse the sponge well and squeeze it dry. It can then be reinserted. Store your sponge between periods in a clean, airy location. Do not put a damp sponge in a plastic or airtight container. If your sponge develops an odor, soak it overnight in a solution of white vinegar and water. Sponges should be resanitized before each period.

Frequent removal and rinsing of your sponge is recommended, as is alternating use with napkins. If the sponge is too big and fits too tightly, it can be cut to size. If it is too small, you may need two sponges. If you have trouble removing your sponge, tie a piece of silk thread or dental floss around the sponge to help pull it out.

Use a tampon made with natural fibers. In a study reported in the *American Journal of Obstetrics and Gynecology*, it was found that the presence of synthetic fibers dramatically increased the production of the bacterium that causes toxic shock syndrome and that the bacterium production *decreased* when it was grown on cotton fibers.

Brand Name/*Mail Order*

With the exception of tampons, which are readily available in supermarkets and drugstores, feminine protection products made from natural fibers may be hard to find. Ask your local natural-foods store to carry them or else order them by mail. Suitable small sponges may be available at bath shops and import stores.

Menstrual Pads

A Cycles Reusable Cloth Menstrual Pads (Cycles). Made from 100% cotton flannel covered with cotton calico print or unbleached muslin. Washable and reusable. Comes with a fabric-covered elastic belt. *Cycles.*

A *Red River Menstrual Pads.* Made with a white 100% cotton knit outer covering and a highly absorbant cotton inner lining. Washable, reusable, superabsorbant. "No chemicals . . . no synthetic materials, and no dyes." Handmade by two women living on the land in Arkansas.

Sponges

A *The Body Shop (England), Solviva.*

Tampons

Note: Manufacturers are not required by law to list tampon ingredients. The information listed here has appeared publicly in articles and advertisements. These are the only unscented brands that are made from natural fibers and claim to be chemically untreated.

A Tampax Original Regular Tampons (Tampax). 100% cotton.

B Kotex Security Tampons (Kimberly-Clark Corp.) Cotton and rayon in a plastic applicator. "No superabsorbent materials."

B O.B. (Johnson & Johnson). Cotton and rayon.

FIREPLACE CLEANERS

Ammonia; ethanol; kerosene; naphthalene.

SAFE ALTERNATIVES
Do-It-Yourself

• Clean the tiles around your fireplace with full-strength white vinegar or 1 cup washing soda dissolved in 2 gallons hot water. Rinse with clear water.

• Clean the flue by throwing a handful of salt into a blazing fire. The flame will turn yellow and the combination will help clean out excess soot.

See also Cleaning Products.

FISH & SEAFOOD

Benzyl alcohol/sodium benzoate; hydrogen peroxide; nitrates/nitrosamines.

Fish and seafood also contain water pollution contaminants (including DDT and other pesticides) that are present in the area from which they were taken. Fish can contain pollutants 2000 times more concentrated than the amounts present in the water where they were found. In less than one month fish can store up to 9 million times the PCB levels in surrounding waters.

SAFE ALTERNATIVES
Choose varieties of ocean fish, as there is a better chance that they will come from less polluted waters. Commonly available varieties include cod, halibut, pollack, and haddock.

Brand Name/*Mail Order*
Purchase fish and seafood fresh, wrapped in paper, from a fish market or butcher to avoid heat-sealed plastic containers. Check with your local dealer to see if any additives are applied to the fresh fish.

A *Bandon Sea-Pack.* "Chemically less contaminated" tuna and salmon packed in glass "with no additives, not even salt."

A *Briggs-Way Co.* "Fresh natural Alaska seafoods hand packed in glass."

A *Kennedy's Natural Foods.* Icelandic fish "from the most unpolluted waters. No antibiotics used in processing."

A *Shiloh Farms.* Fish from Iceland, "where the waters apparently are less contaminated than other ocean waters of the world."

See also Food and Water.

FLAVORING EXTRACTS

Benzyl alcohol/sodium benzoate; colors; flavors; glycerin.

SAFE ALTERNATIVES
Use herbs and spices for flavorings.

Brand Name/*Mail Order*
Flavoring extracts that use natural flavors can be purchased in natural-foods stores. Those that do not contain alcohol are preferred.

No Alcohol
B Bickford Flavors (Bickford Laboratories Co.).

B *Culpeper.* Natural flavor oils.

B Flavoroils (Solaray).

B Sorbee Natural Flavoring (Sorbee International). *Kennedy's Natural Foods.*

In Alcohol
BC *Walnut Acres.* Real vanilla beans and natural extracts in alcohol.

C Cook's Choice Pure Vanilla Extract (Cook Flavoring Co.).

C Nutriflavors (Cascade Continental Foods). *Erewhon Mail Order.*

C Schilling Pure Extracts (McCormick & Co.).

Do-It-Yourself

Instead of vanilla extract, make vanilla sugar or vanilla honey by keeping 1 or 2 vanilla beans in a tightly closed container with 2 cups of date sugar or honey. Then, simply replace part of the sweetener called for in the recipe with the vanilla sweetener.

See also Herbs & Spices.

FLOOR POLISH

See Furniture & Floor Polish.

FLOORING

Formaldehyde; plastics (acrylonitrile, latex, nylon, polyester, polyurethane, PVC/vinyl chloride).

SAFE ALTERNATIVES

Avoid synthetic wall-to-wall carpeting.

Use glazed ceramic tile, brick, stone, concrete, or hardwood floors.

If you need to install new hardwood floors, buy prefinished hardwood floor-tiles that have a baked-on finish, of which there are several types on the market. Choose those that come in six-inch squares and are held together with wire; avoid the twelve-inch squares that are glued together or have foam padding underneath. Remove the tiles from the box and air them outside in the sun for one day before installing. Lay the tiles on a particle-board or cement subfloor with white or yellow glue. Be sure to seal a particle-board subfloor first and allow it to dry thoroughly before applying glue, as it is yet unknown whether the dried glue and wood alone would form an adequate seal from the outgassing of formaldehyde from the particle board.

Less preferable would be to install a conventional hardwood strip floor. While it eventually would be nontoxic, during installation you would be exposed to toluene in the wood filler and fumes from the wood finish until it was thoroughly dry, which could take several weeks or months, depending on conditions and the type of finish used.

Some hard vinyl floor-tiles are also relatively inert. Avoid sheet linoleum and vinyl tiles that are soft and easily bendable, as they contain volatile plasticizers to keep them soft. Choose a hard vinyl tile that breaks when you bend it.

There are three basic types of hard tile: vinyl-asbestos with a "no-wax" surface; all-vinyl; and vinyl-asbestos with a plain surface. Vinyl-asbestos tiles are the best from an odor standpoint, and research done by *Consumer Reports* magazine concludes that the asbestos fibers are securely bonded into the vinyl and are not likely to be released unless the tiles are sanded. Vinyl-asbestos tiles with "no-wax" finishes are preferable to plain vinyl-asbestos tiles because the finish is baked on, eliminating the need for continuous application of toxic waxes.

Vinyl-asbestos tiles should be applied with one of the many water-based vinyl tile glues that can be found wherever tiles are sold. Self-adhesive tiles are sometimes recommended for people who are sensitive to petrochemicals, but the overwhelming smell of adhesive before it is laid on the floor makes it very difficult to prejudge how the finished floor will smell.

Before buying a roomful or houseful of any flooring, buy a small sample and lay it around on the floor to determine if you are willing to live with any possible odors.

Brand Name/*Mail Order*

Hardwood Floor Tiles (prefinished)
B   Color Tile (Color Tile Supermart).

B   Bruce Hardwood Floor Tiles (Bruce Hardwood Floors).

Vinyl-Asbestos Floor Tile
C   Kentile Reinforced Vinyl Tile—Beaux Arts Series (Kentile Floors). Many who are sensitive to plastics have used this tile with no ill effects.

See also Rugs & Carpets.

FLOUR

Chlorine; formaldehyde; pesticide residues.

SAFE ALTERNATIVES
Brand Name/*Mail Order*
Purchase unbleached whole flours, preferably made from organically grown foods, available in natural-foods stores.

A   Arrowhead Mills Flours (Arrowhead Mills).

A   *Culpeper.* From England, "100% wholewheat flour grown completely organically without chemical sprays or artificial fertilizers under the strict conditions of the Soil Association."

A   *Diamond K Enterprises.* Barley, brown rice, buckwheat, corn, millet, oat, pastry, rye, soy, triticale, and whole wheat flour.

A   *Jaffe Bros.* Rye flour.

A   *Leon R. Horsted.* Barley, buckwheat, corn, brown rice, soy, and wheat flour.

A   *Paul's Grains.* Stone-ground flour: whole wheat and whole wheat pastry, rye, soy, buckwheat, oat, barley, rice, and millet from grains grown on their own farm.

A   Shiloh Farms Flours (Shiloh Farms). *Shiloh Farms.*

A   *Special Foods.* White sweet potato, malanga, yam, and cassava flours. Recipes included for making bread, cookies, and other baked goods.

A   Westbrae Flours (Westbrae Natural Foods).

AB   *Butte Creek Mill.* Stone-ground barley, brown rice, buckwheat, corn, millet, oat, rye, soy, triticale, and wheat flour.

AB   *Deer Valley Farm.* Barley, buckwheat, corn, graham, oat, rice, rye, soy, garbanzo bean, whole wheat, and triticale flour.

AB   *Erewhon Mail Order.* Whole wheat, brown rice, corn, rye, soy, buckwheat, and sweet brown rice flour.

AB   *Kennedy's Natural Foods.* Barley, brown rice, buckwheat, and corn flour.

AB   Manna Milling Flours (Manna Milling Co.).

AB   *Walnut Acres.* Complete selection of "whole, freshly ground flours," including amaranth.

B   Elam's Flours (Elam's).

B   El Molino Unbleached Flours (El Molino Mills).

B Ener-G Flours (Ener-g Foods).

B *Lamb's Grist Mill.* Yellow and white cornmeal from "corn that does not have any of the chemicals and preservatives in it."

B Olde Mill Flours (Arrowhead Mills).

B *Old Mill of Guilford.* Stone-ground and water-ground whole-grain flours and meals.

B Stone-Buhr Flours (Stone-Buhr Milling Co.).

See also Food and Grains.

FOOD

Aerosol propellants; ammonia; benzyl alcohol/sodium benzoate; BHA/BHT; colors; chlorine; EDTA; flavors; formaldehyde; glycerin; hydrogen peroxide; lead; methylene chloride; mineral oil; nitrates/nitrosamines; saccharin; sulphur compounds; residues of hexane, paraffin, pesticides, phenol, and plastics (acrylonitrile, polyester, polyethylene, polyurethane, polystyrene, PVC/vinyl chloride, PVP).

Every food contains some type of food additive, derived either from plant, animal, or mineral sources, or else synthesized from petrochemicals. A food additive is defined by the Food Protection Committee of the Food and Nutrition Board as a "substance or mixture of substances other than a basic foodstuff, which is present in a food as a result of any aspect of production, processing, storage, or packaging."

Approximately 2800 substances are intentionally added to aid in processing or to improve the quality of food products; for example, nutrients, preservatives, antioxidants, colors, flavors, sweeteners, emulsifiers, stabilizers, and thickeners. Some 10,000 other incidental additives become part of foods during growing, processing, packaging, and storage: pesticides, hormones and stimulants, artificial colors in animal feed, chlorine from bleaching processes, fumigants, gas residues from roasting, solvent residue from extraction processes, polymers from plastic packaging, and many others.

One problem in testing food additives for safety is that they can have a synergistic effect and become more harmful as they combine with each other. This was clearly demonstrated in a study done by Dr. Benjamin Ershoff at the Institute for Nutritional Studies in California. Rats were given different combinations of three common food additives: sodium cyclamate, food dye Red No. 2, and polyoxyethelene sorbitan monostearate. At first the rats were fed only one of the three additives, and nothing happened. Then, the test animals were given sodium cyclamate and Red No. 2; they stopped growing, lost their hair, and developed diarrhea. When the rats were finally given all three additives, they lost weight rapidly and all died within two weeks.

SAFE ALTERNATIVES

Whenever possible, eat fresh, whole foods raised by "organic" methods: grown without synthetic fertilizers, pesticides, fumigants, artificial ripening processes, growth stimulants and regulators, or antibiotics and other drugs.

Since *organic* has been legally defined only in the states of California, Oregon, and Maine, find out, when buying foods represented as organic in other states, how the food is grown or raised and then use your own judgment as to whether or not it is truly organic. In California, the Organic Foods Act of 1979 requires that organic food be "produced, harvested, distributed, stored, processed, and packaged without application of synthetically compounded fertilizers, pesticides, or growth regulators . . . . Meat, poultry, or fish [must be] produced without the use of any chemical or drug to stimulate or regulate growth or tenderness, and without any drugs or antibiotics."

When food is sold as organic in the state of California, it must be prominently labeled, stating that it is ORGANICALLY GROWN IN ACCORDANCE WITH SECTION 26569.11 OF THE CALIFORNIA HEALTH AND SAFETY CODE. In addition, if the food is labeled "certified," the name of the person or organization providing the certification must appear. Information on specific growers of organic food must also be kept by the retailer and made accessible to the consumer.

Many states that do not have government regulations do have organizations that evaluate the growing methods of local farms and give a seal of approval according to their individual criteria. The California Certified Organic Farmers (CCOF), for example, inspect the land and the grower for one year, then give their seal of approval which can be displayed in natural-foods stores and on packaged goods, declaring that

1. Produce has not been sprayed with synthesized pesticides or insecticides.
2. No synthetically compounded fertilizer has been used except micro-nutrients, which may be applied as needed to maintain soil fertility.
3. A positive soil-building program is being employed to (a) develop, maintain or increase the humus content to 3% or more and (b) achieve a balanced soil fertility.

Even if a food is labeled "organic," recognize that between the farmer and the consumer a food passes through many stages where other forms of contamination may occur. For instance, one natural-foods store in California, now no longer in business, would spray organically grown produce in its refrigerator bin with a chemical "to keep flies away," but would still label it "organic."

Other possible sources of unintentional contamination include adjacent farms that use chemicals, a contaminated water supply, airborne pesticides from nearby crop dusting, chemical fertilizers or pesticides already in the soil, and unknown chemicals that may be in "organic" fertilizer. Remember, too, that sprayed crops grown in rotation with unsprayed crops are sometimes sold as organic.

There are, of course, occasions when nonorganic food is mislabeled or misrepresented by a natural-foods retailer and sold as organic, or when supermarkets buy seasonally low priced or surplus organic produce and sell it as nonorganic. In general, though, food not labeled as organic will contain pesticides and other additives, and organic foods will be significantly less chemically contaminated. Furthermore, organic foods are rarely gassed, waxed, colored, or otherwise additionally adulterated.

According to Michael Rozyne, an organic-foods buyer whose job is to investigate organic growers for the New England Food Cooperative Organization, "Ninety to ninety-five percent of growers and packers of organic food are legitimate. They are handling products that were grown to be more healthful that the average crop, and therefore exhibit unusual concern for high quality and care."

Currently, the majority of food in the United States is produced with chemicals. We are, however, moving in the direction of more organic farming. In 1980, the President's Council on Environmental Quality published *Integrated Pest Management*, which described a method that uses natural insect control as its base and chemicals only when necessary. In that same year, the United States Department of Agriculture issued *The USDA Report and Recommendations on Organic Farming*, which confirmed that organic farming could be the answer to the present economic, environmental, and health problems of the chemical-intensive agriculture industry. As of this writing, Friends of the Earth is working to pass the Agriculture Productivity Act, which would allot $10 million for research and expansion of organic farming in America. More information on this act can be obtained from Friends of the Earth (1045 Sansome St., San Francisco, CA 94111; 415/433-7373). Other organizations with programs that support organic

farming include the International Federation of Organic Agriculture Movements (B.P.S., F-84410 Bedoin, France), Friends of the Farm (Hopewell Farms, Rte. 1, Box 32, Dalton City, IL 61925); The Farallones Institute Rural Center (15290 Coleman Valley Rd., Occidental, CA 95465); and the New Jersey Coalition for Alternatives to Pesticides (PO Box 627, Boonton, NJ 07005).

Organic food can be purchased at most natural-foods stores. A listing of organic farmers in the United States, *The 1984 Directory: Wholesalers of Organic Produce/Products* can be ordered for $7.75 from the California Agrarian Action Project (433 Russell Blvd., Davis, CA 95616; 916/756-8518).

Eating fresh, unprocessed foods is the next-best thing to eating organic, and if you can't do that all the time, read labels carefully and choose natural-food products that do not contain petrochemical-derivative additives. Because the names of many additives do not identify their source as natural or synthetic, it is often impossible from reading a label to know if a food contains synthetic additives. In general, if the label says "artificial," or if you don't recognize an ingredient as a food, or if it doesn't say "natural" (as in "natural flavor" or "natural color"), you probably shouldn't buy it.

If a label says "100% natural," there should be *no* artificial colors, flavors, preservatives, or other synthetic additives added to the food product at all. Be careful, though, as some manufacturers use ingredients that already contain additives, such as ham or bacon or lard, and still call their products natural because they have not added any *other* artificial ingredients. Also beware of package labels that proclaim "No Preservatives!" or "No Artificial Flavors!"—the ingredients list may well reveal inclusion of other artificial additives.

Because consumers really do prefer natural foods, some manufacturers use deceptive advertising to capture a piece of this profitable market. Some of the tactics:

The Misleading Modifier. Brand X Natural Flavored Strawberry Ice Cream may contain many artificial ingredients, including artificial vanilla flavor, but has an accurate label because "natural" modifies "strawberry," not "ice cream."

Assumed Naturalness. Down-on-the-Farm Peanut Butter Granola Bars contain artificial flavors, BHA/BHT, hydrogenated oil, and sugar, but you think they are natural even if the label never refers to the granola bars as natural because of the picture of the farm on the package and descriptions of other farm-fresh natural foods.

"Printing Errors." Labels may claim "All Natural—No Preservatives," but when manufacturers are called on this, they'll explain that a preservative on the ingredients list is a "printing error."

Playing Up the Irrelevant. Labels loudly announce something the product doesn't contain (such as preservatives), hiding the fact that other artificial additives *are* contained (such as artificial flavors and colors). Be very careful with this one, because sometimes the additives are well hidden. For example, one label on a box of cookies reads, in part, ". . . Handmade foods free from artificial preservatives, flavorings, colors; an incentive for cottage industries." Sounds pure

and natural, but these cookies contain *margarine,* an ingredient *full* of additives that the law does not require to be listed on the label. A variation on this tactic is to announce that the product does not contain something that it wouldn't contain anyway, leading you to believe that other brands of the same product do contain this additive and are therefore inferior.

The Federal Trade Commission (FTC) has recommended new standards for food products labeled "natural," although these standards will not have the force of law until actually legislated:

> A food may be called natural only if it contains no artificial ingredients, and has no more processing than it would normally receive in a household kitchen . . . Minimal processing will include washing or peeling fruits or vegetables; homogenizing milk; freezing, canning, or bottling foods; grinding nuts; baking bread; and aging meats. Chemical bleaching would not be acceptable for food labeled "natural." The term could be used, however, if deviations from the standard are included in the advertisement and labeling, [such as], "Natural, but contains bleached flour."

According to the FTC, Congress has "temporarily tabled" this issue, and has not rescheduled it for additional review.

The Food and Drug Administration (FDA) does not give much help to consumers, either, in defining "health," "organic," or "natural" on food labels. According to the Consumer Federation of America, "The FDA has taken no position on their use in food labeling . . . because enforcement would be very difficult and costly."

In recent years, however, consumer pressure has resulted in the availability of many more packaged foods containing fewer additives than in the past. Most large corporate food manufacturers are removing artificial additives from selected products. Examination of ingredients in these products, available on any grocer's shelves, often reveals great similarity to the much more expensive "health food" brands.

The law requires most food products to have nearly all of their food additives listed on the label. For instance, any synthetic preservative must be specifically identified, while spices, colors, and flavoring need not be specifically identified, but simply mentioned as a group. Artificial colors and flavors, on the other hand, must be either specifically named or else described as artificial (except that artificial color need not be mentioned on butter, cheese, and ice cream labels, or on unprocessed fresh foods such as eggs and oranges). Natural colors and flavors may be indicated as such, or simply listed as "flavoring" or "color," or specifically identified.

Nevertheless, the presence of many other additives in food products may be legally concealed. Processed food may use ingredients already containing additives without being required to list these additives on the label. Ham included in processed foods, for instance, will contain nitrates and nitrites, and the shortening used may contain BHA and BHT, but only "ham" or "shortening" will appear on that product label.

Approximately 300 processed food products for which the FDA has set standards of identity need not list the ingredients they *must* contain to be identified by a specific generic term. Although the FDA encourages manufacturers to list *all* ingredients contained in these foods, often only the optional ingredients are listed. Products with standards of identity include some bakery products; cacao products; cereal flours and related products; canned fruit juices; fish and shellfish; food dressing and flavorings; frozen desserts; fruit butters, jellies, preserves, and related products; fruit pies; macaroni and noodle products; margarine; milk and cream; nonalcoholic beverages; and vegetable juice. For a complete list, see *United States Food Laws, Regulations and Standards* (John Wiley & Sons, New York, 1979). For complete regulations on each food product, see the *Code of Federal Regulations*, (Office of the Federal Register, General Services Administration, Washington, DC, 1981).

In addition to the above, those additives used in processing (such as detergents used to wash produce) which may leave a residue are not required to be listed on labels.

Whenever possible, avoid foods in lead-soldered cans, since the food absorbs lead from the solder. The FDA has estimated that approximately 20 percent of the lead found in the average person's diet comes from canned foods. Lead-soldered cans can increase the amount of lead in canned food by 200 to 300 percent. Furthermore, the contamination is significantly increased if the food is stored in the can after opening. Acidic foods such as orange and other fruit juices, tomatoes and tomato paste, and most fruits absorb the lead especially quickly and should be transferred to a nonmetal container before any continued storage.

Some foods are now canned in lead-free welded or one-piece aluminum cans. When you first start looking for lead-free cans, they all may look alike to you—probably because most of them will be lead-soldered. But once you come across a lead-free can, you will recognize it without a doubt. You will even be able to tell without removing the label, because enough of the seam will peek out for you to see.

A lead-soldered can has a top and bottom rim with an obvious, prominent side-seam, which may also reveal traces of solder on the outside. If you run your finger around the top or bottom of the can near the rim, you will feel the lumpy seam.

A lead-free welded can, on the other hand, has top and bottom rims with a very flat, narrow seam with a blue or black line running down the middle. (This sort of can is used by Progresso Italian soups and Health Valley products.) Its lead-free sibling, the lead-free aluminum can, has a rounded bottom, a rim only at the top, and no seam. Compare tuna cans to see this difference.

Even in a lead-free can, however, the can lining may still present problems. A gold-colored lining contains a phenol resin that may be absorbed by the food.

Alternately, look for foods packaged in glass, cellophane, or foil; even food packaged in plastic can absorb volatile components from the plastic.

For more information on additive-free foods, contact the Feingold Association (Box 6550, Alexandria, VA 22306), a volunteer national nonprofit organization dedicated to improving the health and behavior of hyperactive and learning-disabled children through dietary changes. This group engages in extensive research and verification of foods that do not contain artificial colors and flavors, BHA, BHT, TBHQ, and of restaurants that serve this food. The Feingold Association also publishes a monthly newsletter, *Pure Facts* ($12/year), and has local chapters all over the United States.

Adequate nutrition is mandatory in order for your body to maintain its ability to resist the harmful effects of toxic chemicals. Plan your menus to include fresh whole foods, and eat them raw or lightly cooked to preserve nutrients.

The human body particularly needs protein to produce an enzyme called P450. Recent research shows that this enzyme binds with fat-soluble chemicals and breaks them down by placing them next to oxygen molecules, and then expelling them from the body. Studies indicate that animals on low-protein diets had less than half the ability to break down toxic chemicals as did animals on diets with average amounts of protein. Compounds in fresh fruits and vegetables also increase production of enzyme P450.

Roughage from whole grains, vegetables, and fruits is necessary for intestinal regularity. Normal movement and elimination of food wastes is important because many chemicals in foods may be absorbed through the intestinal wall if the waste rests in the body for too long.

Intake of toxic chemicals can be minimized by your choice of foods. Analysis of foods by the FDA and the USDA shows that beef, chicken, turkey, veal, and high-fat dairy products such as cream, butter, high-fat cheese, and ice cream often are more heavily contaminated with pesticides than are other foods. This is due to the increased concentration of pesticides as you move up the food chain. Meat contains approximately fourteen times more pesticides than do plant foods, and dairy products five-and-a-half times more.

Based on these considerations, the ideal diet for avoiding toxic chemicals would be vegetarian, including

whole grains

legumes

fresh fruits and vegetables

eggs

nonfat milk and low-fat cheeses

ocean fish

honey, date sugar, barley malt powder/syrup, fig syrup, and rice syrup (in small quantities).

If you choose not to eat meat, take care to eat plant foods in proper combinations in order to get enough protein. Plant foods contain the same essential amino acids found in meat, but in different quantities. Equal amounts of each of the nine essential amino acids must be present for the others to be utilized. Usually, a plant will be missing a significant amount of one of the amino acids, making the others useless. When the missing amino acid is supplied by another food, it turns all the amino acids into "complete," high-quality protein. *Diet for a Small Planet* by Frances Moore Lappé and *Laurel's Kitchen* by Laurel Robertson (see Bibliography) are good reference books for food combining.

In general, vegetarians have a lower incidence of heart disease, high blood pressure, cancer, and obesity, but a strictly vegetarian diet is not optimum for everyone. Most people would thrive on a vegetarian diet, but approximately 30 percent of the population have metabolisms requiring some amount of meat in their diet, so check with your doctor before experimenting with any vegetarian regimen.

You might want to become what Fred Rohé calls in *The Complete Book of Natural Foods* an *omnivarian:* "a person who eats natural foods with an emphasis on plant foods, with complex carbohydrates as the principal foods, supplemented by all other types of foods, including or excluding meat and animal products according to individual discretion or circumstances."

Use pure water for all washing, soaking, and cooking of foods. Cook foods on electric appliances to avoid absorbing any combustion byproducts, and serve it on nonplastic dishware and glassware. Hot food especially can quickly absorb components of the plastic.

See also Alcoholic Beverages; Applesauce; Appliances; Baby Food; Baking Mixes; Baking Powder;

Barbecue Sauce; Bread; Butter; Cake; Candy; Cereal; Cheese; Chewing Gum; Chips; Chocolate; Coconut; Coffee; Cookies; Cookware; Crackers; Dried Fruits; Eggnog; Eggs; English Muffins; Fish & Seafood; Flavoring Extracts; Flour; Food Coloring; Food Processors; Food Storage; Fruitcake; Gelatin Desserts; Grains; Granola; Gravy; Herbs & Spices; Ice Cream; Ice Cream Cones; Jams, Jellies & Preserves; Juices & Fruit Drinks; Ketchup; Margarine; Mayonnaise; Meat & Poultry; Milk; Mustard; Nuts & Seeds; Oils; Olives; Pasta; Peanut Butter & Nut Butters; Pickles; Pies; Popsicles; Pretzels; Pudding; Salad Dressing; Salsa; Sauces; Sauerkraut; Seeds & Plants; Shortening; Sodas; Soy Sauce; Tea; Tortillas; Vinegar; Vitamins & Minerals; Water; and Yogurt & Kefir.

FOOD COLORING

Colors.

SAFE ALTERNATIVES
Brand Name/*Mail Order*
Natural-foods stores carry colors made from foods instead of petrochemicals.

B   Earth Grown Natural Food Coloring (Sorbee International). *Kennedy's Natural Foods.*

Do-It-Yourself
• Use fruit and vegetable juices for natural colorings:

beet juice for pink

carrot juice for orange

grape juice for lavender

chlorophyll for green

blueberry juice for blue

FOOD PROCESSORS

Plastic.
Food processors are very handy for preparing foods from scratch. All have plastic bowls, however. This does not seem to be much of a problem when processing cold foods for the extremely short period of time the food is in contact with the hard plastic, but hot foods processed for long periods (as when pureeing soup) may absorb some plastic.

SAFE ALTERNATIVES
Use a blender when possible, one that has a glass container. Or use a heavy-duty mixer with food-processing attachments.

Brand Name/*Mail Order*
Heavy-Duty Mixers
A   Kitchenaid Food Preparer K45SS or K5SS (Hobart Corp.). An all-metal mixer with a stainless-steel bowl modeled after commercial restaurant mixers with attachments for kneading, mixing, whipping, grinding, pureeing, slicing, shredding, and pasta making. *Sears, Whole Earth Access.*

A   Vitamix 3600 (Vita-Mix Corp.). Stainless-steel food processor that juices, mixes, chops, purees, shreds, makes peanut butter, kneads bread dough, chops ice, and even makes ice cream. *Vita-Mix Corp.*

FOOD STORAGE

Plastics (acrylonitrile, polyester, polyethylene, polystyrene, PVC/vinyl chloride).

SAFE ALTERNATIVES
Avoid plastic wraps or containers. If

you believe that plastic is stable and cannot contaminate food, try this: Close an empty plastic container for several days, then open it and sniff. If it has a plastic odor, the plastic polymers can be absorbed by the food. Since it really is impossible to know what type of plastic a food container may be comprised of, or which impurities might be present, or what the possible health effects may be, it's best to avoid them altogether.

Instead, use glass or ceramic containers, metal tins, or cellophane, a film produced from the cellulose in wood pulp (not to be confused with "plastic wrap").

Aluminum foil is also acceptable for almost everyone, except for those who are extremely sensitive to petrochemicals, since all aluminum foil manufacturers use mineral oil as a lubricating rolling oil in the milling process. The oil is burned off before packaging, but residues of both the oil and combustion by-products could still remain. If you do use foil, put the shiny side next to the food. *Webb Metals* carries a special, heavy-duty, reusable stainless-steel foil that does not have mineral oil residues.

Brand Name/*Mail Order*

Cellophane Bags
A *Erlander's Natural Products, Janice Corp., Kennedy's Natural Foods, Nu Vita Food Co.*

Cellophane Rolls
A *Erlander's Natural Products, H. D. Catty Corp.*

FOUNDATION MAKEUP

See Cosmetics.

FRAGRANCES

Aerosol propellants; benzyl alcohol; colors; ethanol; formaldehyde; fragrance (synthetic and natural); glycerin; phenol; trichloroethylene.

There has been very little scientific study on the health effects of synthetic fragrances beyond their ability to cause skin irritation. Nevertheless, even without scientific documentation, many people report a variety of ill effects.

SAFE ALTERNATIVES

The safest alternative is to avoid all fragrances and scented products.

If fragrance is important to you, use essential oils for a natural scent. But please use them *sparingly* for the benefit of those who are sensitive to all fragrances. There are three types of essential oils:

1. Natural—from a plant source; the fragrance is that of the plant (for example, a lemon yielding a lemon scent).

2. Synthetic—from a plant source; but the fragrance is different from that of the plant (for example, a geranium yielding a lemon scent).

3. Artificial (also called "perfume oil")—from petrochemicals.

When buying essential oils, make sure the oil has been obtained from a *natural* plant source. All natural essential oils are made from plants that are not sprayed with pesticides because the pesticides would become too concentrated in the oil.

Essential oils are removed by steam distillation. Those labeled "true," "absolute," or "concrete" are pure oils; "extracts" or "tinctures" have had grain alcohol added; and "extended oils" are extended with dipropylene glycol or diethyl phthalate (a plasticizer).

CAUTION: Use essential oils carefully, as they are extremely potent. Do not apply directly to skin without dilution, and do not apply to mucous membrane areas at all, even if perfume is made from the most natural essential oil.

Brand Name/*Mail Order*
Essential oils are available at most natural-foods stores.

A Attar Bazaar Essential Oils (Attar Bazaar). *Erewhon Mail Order.*

A Aura Cacia True Botanical Essenses (Aura Cacia). *Aura Cacia.*

A *Benson Enterprises.* Natural copies of famous fragrances.

A Colin Ingram Essential Oils (Colin Ingram). *The Herb Patch.*

A Crabtree & Evelyn Essential Oils (Crabtree & Evelyn). *Sunnybrook Farms.*

A Essential Oils. *Bear Meadow Farm, The Body Shop, The Body Shop (England), Caprilands Herb Farm, Clear Light Cedar Co., Culpeper, Denis Dumont, Hartenthaler's, Haussmann's Pharmacy, Hilltop Herb Farm, Homebody, Indiana Botanic Gardens, Lotions & Potions, Meadowbrook Herbs & Things, Merry Gardens, Misty Morning Farm, New Age Creations, Penn Herb Co., Ram Island Farm Herbs, Richter's, The Soap Opera, Sunnybrook Farms, Wide World of Herbs.*

A *Homebody.* Natural copies of famous fragrances.

A *Lotions & Potions.* Natural copies of famous fragrances.

A Star & Crescent Natural Essence Oils (Star & Crescent).

A Sunshine Scented Oils. (Sunshine Scented Oils). *Shiloh Farms.*

Do-It-Yourself
• To make perfume: Add a few drops of essential oil to one ounce of vegetable oil or vodka (100-proof if possible).

See also Beauty Products.

FREEZERS

See Appliances.

FRUIT BUTTER

See Jams, Jellies, & Preserves.

FRUITCAKE

Benzyl alcohol/sodium benzoate; BHA/BHT; colors; flavors; hydrogenated oil; pesticide residues; sucrose; sulphur compounds.

SAFE ALTERNATIVES
Brand Name/*Mail Order*
Fruitcakes made with dried fruits instead of candied fruits can be purchased at natural-foods stores.

A *Deer Valley Farm.* Whole wheat dried-fruit fruitcake.

A Shiloh Farms Honey Wheat Fruit Cake (Shiloh Farms). A whole wheat, dried-fruit fruit cake. *Shiloh Farms.*

B Festive Season "Honey Baked" Fruitcake (Golden Temple Bakery).

B Holland Honey Fruit Cake (Holland Honey Co.). Wheat free.

Contains "mixed fruit" with unspecified sweetener. *Kennedy's Natural Foods.*

B *Walnut Acres.* Whole wheat/honey/dried-fruit fruit cake. Also a honey-sweetened, whole wheat, vegetarian plum pudding.

C *Matthews 1812 House.* Dried-fruit (primarily apricot) and nut fruitcakes made with "no preservatives, rinds, peels, or candied fruit."

C Victoria's Dried Fruit Fruitcake (Curds & Whey).

See also Dried Fruit and Food.

FRUIT SPREADS

See Jams, Jellies, & Preserves.

FURNITURE

Formaldehyde; plastics (polyester; polystyrene; polyurethane; PVC/vinyl chloride).

One study showed that the addition of furniture to an otherwise empty house tripled formaldehyde levels.

SAFE ALTERNATIVES
Use wood or metal furniture.

Wood furniture should be checked carefully to make sure it is indeed solid wood. Often the front will be wood and the backs, sides, inside shelves, and drawer bottoms will be particle board or plywood. Particle board can be very convincingly veneered, but this wood veneer poses no barrier to the outgassing formaldehyde. Given the choice, plywood is preferable to particle board, and the older the plywood, the better.

Metal furniture is available in a number of styles: modern, high-tech functional, outdoor, and office. It can be more nontoxic than any other kind, if care is taken to avoid lubricating oils and synthetic seat-pads. If outdoor furniture is used, look for enamel or epoxy finishes and avoid PVC coatings. Check carefully to avoid particle board in metal furniture, particularly under plastic laminate desk-tops (such tops sometimes contain a metal backing with no particle board).

Consider buying used furniture, since new, solid-wood furniture and high-quality metal furniture are quite expensive. A great quantity and variety of both kinds is readily available and relatively inexpensive when bought used. Any problem materials have outgassed with time. For used furniture, look in the Yellow Pages under "Furniture Dealers—Used," and "Office Furniture & Equipment—Used."

One very useful piece of furniture is a set of wood or metal bookshelves with sliding or swinging glass or metal doors. This will allow storage of books and papers while providing protection from the outgassing of the ink.

Furniture should be upholstered with prewashed natural-fiber fabric and stuffed with cotton or wool batting or feathers.

Brand Name/*Mail Order*
A *A. Liss & Co.* Industrial-steel shelving, cabinets, and so on in bright decorator colors.

A *Able Steel Equipment Co.* Industrial-steel shelving, cabinets in "attractive colors that match any decor."

A   Cubics (Whittier Wood Products). Unfinished cube kits of kiln-dried western pine that can be mixed and matched to make custom storage systems.

A   Elfa (Elfa Ab). Modular steel baskets with baked-on epoxy finish to create all types of furniture and imaginative storage units. *Seabon Scandinavian Imports.*

A   *Equipto.* Large (127-page) catalog offers modular metal industrial-type shelving, drawers, cabinets in white and bright colors to create any type of storage or furniture you need.

A   *Outer Banks Pine Products.* Unfinished pine colonial corner china cabinets.

A   *Sears.* Metal shelving and drawer units in decorator colors; unfinished hardwood colonial furniture.

A   *Space Beds.* Solid hardwood beds with storage drawers, and other wood furniture finished with a natural oil.

A   *Zimmerman Chair Shop.* Unfinished solid-wood colonial chairs and tables.

AB   *Cornucopia.* Unfinished or finished hardwood tables and chairs.

AB   *Ikea.* Modern Swedish solid-wood furnishings, finished and unfinished, at low prices. Read descriptions carefully; many styles are of veneered particle board.

AB   *Shaker Workshops.* Solid-wood Shaker furniture.

AB   *Shaker Workshops West.* Wide selection of fine solid-wood Shaker furniture.

AB   *The Western Reserve Antique Furniture Kit.* Solid-wood Shaker furniture.

AB   *Yield House.* Solid-wood colonial furniture. Glassed-in shelving at good prices.

B   *Berea College Student Craft Industries.* Solid cherry tables and chairs.

B   *Charles Webb.* Pleasant and practical furniture, handmade from oak, cherry, or walnut.

B   *Fran's Basket House.* Large selection of rattan furniture and home accessories.

B   *Guild of Shaker Crafts.* Large variety of fine Shaker furniture, including items not found in other Shaker catalogs.

B   *L. L. Bean.* Wood-and-cotton-duck director's chairs and rockers.

B   *Laura Copenhaver Industries.* Limited selection of handmade hardwood bedroom furniture.

B   *Thos. Moser Cabinetmakers.* Fine solid-wood furniture in simple, original, timeless designs. Will do custom work.

B   *Walpole Woodworkers.* Cedar knock-down furniture for indoors and outdoors.

B   *Williams & Foltz.* Solid oak furniture with "natural oil finish" in clean, sleek styles.

Do-It-Yourself

Solid wood furniture can be obtained at significant savings by assembling

115

and finishing the furniture yourself from a kit. This also gives you complete control over the types of glue and finish used. Kits can be ordered from *The Bartley Collection, Cohasset Colonials, Design-Kit, Shaker Workshops, Shaker Workshops West, Southern Mobile Industries, The Western Reserve Antique Furniture Kit,* and *Yield House. Craft Pattern Studios* offers patterns for hundreds of furniture items to make yourself from wood.

Make a sofa bed out of a futon with a convertible wooden sofa frame available from *Arise Futon Mattress Co., Eugene Trading Co., The Futon Co., The Futon Shop,* and *Northwest Futon Co.* Additional cotton- or kapok-filled pillows can be ordered from *The Futon Co., The Futon Shop, Northwest Futon Co.,* and *Sleep & Dream.*

See also Futons, Wood, and Wood Finishes.

FURNITURE & FLOOR POLISH

Aerosol propellants; ammonia; detergents; fragrance (particularly lemon); glycols; nitrobenzene; paraffin; petroleum distillates; phenol; plastics (acrylic, polystyrene).

"DANGER: Harmful or fatal if swallowed. Keep out of reach of children."

SAFE ALTERNATIVES
Brand Name/*Mail Order*
C Old Craftsmen's Brand Lemon Oil with Beeswax Furniture Polish (Fox Run Craftsmen). Lemon oil and beeswax in a mineral oil base. Lemon scent.

C *Vermont Country Store.* Lemon oil in a "pure mineral oil base . . .

contains *no* silicones or petroleum distillates." Lemon scent.

Do-It-Yourself
Polishes Use a soft cloth to apply the following mixtures to furniture:
• Wipe with mayonnaise.
• Rub with cloth dipped in cool tea.
• Mix together 1 teaspoon olive oil, the juice of 1 lemon, 1 teaspoon brandy or whisky, and 1 teaspoon water. Make fresh each time.
• Mix 3 parts olive oil and 1 part white vinegar.
• Mix 1 part lemon juice and 2 parts olive oil or vegetable oil.
• Mix 1 cup white vinegar with 1 gallon warm water.
• For oak: Boil 1 quart beer with 1 tablespoon sugar and 2 tablespoons beeswax. When mixture is cool, wipe onto wood. When dry, polish with a dry chamois cloth.
• For mahogany: Mix equal parts white vinegar and warm water; wipe onto wood, then polish with a chamois cloth.

Special Problems
• For grease spots: Pour on salt immediately to absorb grease and prevent staining.
• For scratches: Mix equal amounts of lemon juice and salad oil. Rub this mixture into scratches with a soft cloth until they disappear.
• For water spots: Mix 10 drops lemon oil into 2 cups vodka. Dampen one corner of a soft cloth with this mixture and lightly rub the spots. Dry immediately with the dry end of the cloth.

See also Cleaning Products.

Futons

See Beds.

G

GELATIN DESSERTS

Colors; flavors; sucrose.

SAFE ALTERNATIVES
Brand Name/*Mail Order*
B   Hain Gel Dessert Mixes (Hain Pure Food Co.).

Do-It-Yourself
Add fruit and/or fruit juice (plus sweetener, if desired) to unflavored gelatin.

See also Food.

GLASS CLEANERS

Aerosol propellants; ammonia; colors; ethanol; fragrance; glycol; isopropyl alcohol; naphthalene; petroleum distillates.

Although many people find that old newspapers clean glass without streaking or leaving any lint behind, this is not recommended because of the fumes from the newsprint. Instead, a natural linen towel or other soft cloth, a clean damp chamois cloth, or a squeegee are best to use.

SAFE ALTERNATIVES
Do-It-Yourself
Never wash windows when the sun is shining directly on them; the cleaning solution will dry too fast and streak. When washing, use side-to-side strokes on one side and up-and-down strokes on the other so you can tell which side might need some extra polishing.

Cleaning Solutions
• Mix 2 tablespoons borax or washing soda in 3 cups water.
• Mix 2 tablespoons cornstarch and ½ cup white vinegar into 1 gallon warm water.
• Mix 1 tablespoon vinegar or lemon juice in 1 quart water. Spray on glass surface and wipe dry.
• Mix 1 cup vodka, 2 cups water, and 5 drops lactic acid. Spray on glass surface and wipe dry.
• Mix a little borax with water. Spray on glass surface and wipe dry.
• Use straight lemon juice or rub a fresh-cut lemon right onto the glass. Dry with a soft cloth.

For Foggy Windows
• Wash windows with plain soap rubbed directly onto a soft, damp cloth. Rinse and dry. The soap will leave a transparent film that will make the water molecules bead up instead of sticking to the glass as a mist.
• After cleaning and drying, wipe windows with a little glycerin on a clean, soft cloth.
• Clean glass with a solution of ½ cup vodka mixed with 1 quart water.

For Scratches
• Rub with toothpaste and a soft cloth.
• Rub with a paste of 1 part dry mustard and 1 part white vinegar.

To Clean Cut Glass
• Cover glass with wet potato peelings and leave for 24 hours. Rinse in cold water and dry.
• Apply a paste of calcium carbonate and water to glass. Let it dry slightly, then remove with a soft lintless cloth.
• Use a sprinkle of sodium hexa-

metaphosphate dissolved in water, adding enough so that the water feels slippery between your fingers.

• Sprinkle baking soda on a damp rag and clean glass. Rinse with clean water.

See also Cleaning Products, Soap, and Toothpaste.

GLUE & TAPE

Ammonia; ethanol; formaldehyde; glycols; hexane; naphthalene; phenol; plastics (acrylionitrile, epoxy resins, polyurethane, PVC/vinyl chloride, PVP).

SAFE ALTERNATIVES

Use staples or metal paper clips if possible. When glue is needed, use either a glue stick (a solid, very-low-odor white glue made from petrochemical derivatives); white glue (made from polyvinyl acetate plastic, has a slight odor when wet, but dries quickly); or yellow glue (made from aliphatic plastic resin, has a slight odor when wet, but dries quickly). When tape is needed, use aluminum or brown paper tape (avoid licking the adhesive back by moistening with a porcelain moistener, available at office-supply stores).

Brand Name/*Mail Order*

All brands listed below are odorless when dry. They can be purchased in office-supply, hardware, variety, and drugstores.

Glue Sticks

B Elmer's Glue Stick (Borden Co.).

B Glue Stic (Dennison Manufacturing Co.).

B Pritt Glue Stick (Ross Chemical Co./Henkel Corp.).

B Stix-A-Lot (The Carter's Ink Co.).

B Uhu Stic (Faber Castell). *Art Brown & Bro.*

White Glue

B Elmer's Glue-All (Borden Co.). *Art Brown & Bro.*

B Sanford Elephant Glue (Sanford Corp.).

Yellow Glue

B Elmer's Carpenter's Wood Glue (Borden Co.).

Aluminum Tape

B Sears Aluminum Foil Insulation Tape #42-88346 (Sears, Roebuck & Co.). *Sears.*

Do-It-Yourself

Paper, Glass, or Porcelain Glue

• Dissolve 6 tablespoons gum arabic in 1 cup water, add ½ cup plus 2 tablespoons natural glycerin, and mix well. Apply to both surfaces with a toothpick or tongue depressor. Hold together for 5 minutes. Make fresh each time.

Paper Glues

• Blend 4 tablespoons wheat flour and 6 tablespoons cold water to make a smooth paste. Boil 1½ cups water and stir in paste, cooking over very low heat for about 5 minutes. Use when cold.

• Blend 3 tablespoons cornstarch and 4 tablespoons cold water to make a smooth paste. Boil 2 cups water and stir in paste, continuing to stir until mixture becomes translucent. Use when cold.

• Completely dissolve 9 ounces white dextrin in 13 ounces water while heating to 140° F. In a separate bowl, dissolve ¼ fluid ounce alum, ½ ounce white sugar, and ½ fluid ounce glycerin in 2 fluid ounces water. Combine the two and heat to about 176° F until the solution becomes clear.

• Mix 2 ounces cornstarch and 1 ounce white dextrin in 4 fluid ounces water to make a smooth paste. Dissolve ½ ounce borax in 1 quart boiling water, then add 2 fluid ounces glycerin and the paste. Reheat to nearly boiling and stir for several minutes until smooth.

• Combine ¼ cup cornstarch, ¾ cup water, 2 tablespoons light corn syrup, and 1 teaspoon white vinegar in a medium saucepan. Cook over medium heat, stirring constantly, until mixture is thick. Remove from heat. In a separate bowl, stir together until smooth ¼ cup cornstarch and ¾ cup water. Add a little at a time to the heated mixture, stirring constantly. Will keep 2 months in a covered container.

GOLD CLEANER

See Metal Polishes.

GRAINS

Pesticide residues; talc.

SAFE ALTERNATIVES
Brand Name/*Mail Order*
Buy natural or organically grown whole grains at your natural-foods store; they are often sold in bulk.

A   Arrowhead Mills Grains (Arrowhead Mills).

A   *Diamond K Enterprises.* Barley, buckwheat, corn, millet, oats, popcorn, brown rice, rye, triticale, and wheat "grown in the midwest without chemical fertilizers, herbicides, or insecticides."

A   *Jaffe Bros.* Millet, oats, wheat, rye, buckwheat, popcorn, rice, and barley.

A   *Kennedy's Natural Foods.* Barley, buckwheat, corn, millet, popcorn, rice, wild rice, and wheat.

A   Lundburg Rices (Lundburg Farm). *Lundberg Farm.*

A   *Paul's Grains.* Corn, wheatberries, ryeberries, soybeans, buckwheat, oats, barley, popcorn, brown rice, millet, and flax grown on their own farm.

A   Shiloh Farms Grains (Shiloh Farms). *Shiloh Farms.*

A   Westbrae Grains (Westbrae Natural Foods).

AB   *Chico-San.* Brown rice, millet, buckwheat.

AB   *Deer Valley Farm.* Buckwheat, corn, barley, popcorn, brown rice, rye, wheat, and triticale.

AB   *Erewhon Mail Order.* Brown rice, wild rice, wheat, oats, corn, barley, millet, rye, buckwheat.

AB   *Walnut Acres.* Barley, buckwheat, millet, oats, popcorn, rice, rye, and wheat. Also 8 varieties of seasoned "gourmet grains."

B   *Butte Creek Mill.* Wheat, corn, rye, oats, brown rice, triticale, millet, barley, and popcorn.

B   Wolff's Buckwheat Kernels (The Birkett Mills).

See also Food.

GRANOLA & GRANOLA BARS

BHA/BHT; flavors; glycerin; hydrogenated oil; pesticide residues; sucrose.

SAFE ALTERNATIVES
Brand Name/*Mail Order*
Additive-free granolas and granola bars are sold in natural-foods stores and supermarkets.

Granola
B Branola (Aura Enterprises).

B Shiloh Farms Granolas (Shiloh Farms). *Shiloh Farms.*

B Sunburst Farms Granolas (Sunburst Farms Natural Foods).

C Arrowhead Mills Granolas (Arrowhead Mills).

C Back to Nature Vita Crunch Granola (Organic Milling Co.).

C Erewhon Granola (Erewhon).

C Granola 100% Natural Cereal (General Mills).

C Health Valley Real 100% Natural Granola (Health Valley Natural Foods).

C *Walnut Acres.*

Granola Bars
B Barbara's No Sugar & No Honey Granola Bars (Barbara's Bakery).

B Nature's Choice Fresh & Chewy Granola Bars. (Sunfield Foods).

See also Cereal, Food, and Grains.

GRAVY

BHA/BHT; colors; flavors; MSG; pesticide residues; sucrose.

SAFE ALTERNATIVES
Gravies made from meat drippings contain high levels of pesticides, which have concentrated in the fat. As an alternative, try one of the additive-free, nonfat vegetarian gravy mixes available at your natural-foods store.

Brand Name/*Mail Order*

Broths for Gravy (must be thickened):
A Organic Seasoning and Instant Gravy (Bernard Jensen Products).

B Dr. Bronner's "Balanced Protein-Seasoning" (All-One-God-Faith).

Gravy Mix
C Hain Brown Gravy Mix (Hain Pure Food Co.).

See also Food.

HAIRBRUSHES & COMBS

Plastics (nylon, PVC/vinyl chloride, and others).

SAFE ALTERNATIVES
Choose hairbrushes with wood handles and natural bristles, and use wood combs. Not only are they natural, but they will not produce the static electricity produced by plastic brushes and combs.

Brand Name/*Mail Order*
Buy natural hairbrushes and combs at drug, department, and natural-foods stores.

Natural-Bristle Hairbrushes

A *The Body Shop, Janice Corp., Kennedy's Natural Foods, Norm Thompson, The Soap Opera, Whole Earth Access.*

Wood Combs

A *Caswell-Massey, The Country Store & Farm, Erewhon Mail Order, Janice Corp., Kennedy's Natural Foods, Norm Thompson, Pure Planet Products, The Soap Opera, Vermont Country Store.*

HAIR COLOR

Ammonia; colors; detergents; EDTA; ethanol; fragrance; glycols; hydrogen peroxide; lead; mineral oil; sulphur compounds.

"WARNING: Contains an ingredient that can penetrate your skin and has been determined to cause cancer in laboratory animals." (Proposed FDA warning label that will not appear in hair dyes because of loopholes in regulations.)

The FDA has no power over hair dyes, which are mutagenic and suspected human carcinogens. Many hair dye chemicals, which can easily penetrate the scalp and enter the bloodstream, are not even tested for safety. One study suggests that women over the age of fifty who have used hair dyes for ten or more years have an increased risk of breast cancer.

Medical consultants for *Consumer Reports* magazine recommend that hair dyes be avoided entirely when pregnant or of childbearing age.

SAFE ALTERNATIVES

If you must use chemical dyes, *Consumer Reports* has some tips to help minimize the risk: don't use hair dyes more often than necessary; don't leave the dye on your head for any longer than necessary; flood your scalp thoroughly with water afterward; use a technique that involves minimal contact between the dye and your scalp; and put off using any hair dye to as late in life as possible.

Do-It-Yourself

Use henna. Many different shades of this natural coloring agent are available to darken or highlight. Henna gives hair a semipermanent protein coating, protecting it from sun damage and air pollution; it washes out gradually over a six-month period.

For best results, be sure to use 100-percent pure henna without metallic bases, "henna enhancers," or chemical dyes. On henna labels, "100% natural henna" doesn't necessarily mean "100% *pure* henna." There is some controversy about the different shades of henna. Several sources claim that any shade that is not orange-red may also contain chemical dyes. The FDA is currently investigating whether these "pure natural hennas" have been mislabeled.

You can also intensify the color by adding other ingredients:

red—paprika, beet juice, red zinger tea;

brown—ginger, nutmeg, hot coffee (instead of water);

gold—black or Ceylon tea, chamomile, onion juice.

To tone down the orange-red, add 1 part chamomile flowers to 2 parts henna.

Never use henna on eyebrows,

eyelashes, or facial hair, or if you already have a chemical dye on your hair or are about to get a permanent.

Take on temporary color with natural rinses made from plant materials. Because they are not as strong as chemical dyes, these rinses cannot effect drastic color changes, but they certainly can enrich your natural color and, when used repetitively, continue to be absorbed more and more into your hair. Because they are not permanent, they should be renewed occasionally or else the color will fade.

Pour liquid produced by the following formulas through hair 15 times, catching it in a basin below and rerinsing. Wring out excess and leave in hair for 15 minutes before finally rinsing with clear water.

Blonde *Note:* The effects of any blonde rinse will be heightened by drying your hair in the sun.
• Pour 3 cups hot water over 4 tablespoons chopped rhubarb root and simmer 15 minutes.
• Steep ½ cup chamomile flowers or any other yellow-blossomed flower or herb (calendula, mullein blooms and leaves, yellow broom flowers, saffron, turmeric, quassia chips) in 1 quart boiling water for ½ hour. Strain and let cool while you shampoo.
• Mix flower or herb tea for blonde rinse (see above) with an equal amount of lemon juice. Thicken by adding arrowroot to warm mixture and stirring over heat until it forms a gel. Apply to hair and sit out in the sun for an hour. Rinse with plain water.
• Mix 1 tablespoon lemon juice in 1 gallon pure, warm water. Use for final rinse.

Brown/Brunette
• Cook an unpeeled potato. Dip a cotton ball into the cooking water and saturate hair. Keep away from skin to prevent discoloration.
• Use strong black tea or black coffee for final rinse.

To Cover Gray
• Simmer ½ cup dried sage in 2 cups water for 30 minutes. Steep several hours. Pour strained liquid over clean hair 15 or more times, leave on hair until hair dries, then rinse and dry hair again. Apply weekly until desired shade is achieved, then monthly to maintain color.
• Crush walnut hulls in a mortar, cover with boiling water, add a pinch of salt, and soak for 3 days. Add 3 cups boiling water and simmer in a glass pot for 5 hours, replacing water as needed. Strain, then simmer liquid to one quarter of the original volume. Cool and add 1 teaspoon ground cloves or allspice and steep in the refrigerator for one week, shaking the mixture every day. Strain and use. *Caution:* This will stain everything you touch, so wear gloves and try to avoid skin contact.
• Mix 1 tablespoon apple cider vinegar in 1 gallon pure warm water. Use for final rinse.

Red
• Mix together 1 tablespoon each of henna, chamomile flowers, and vinegar, then steep in boiling water for 15 minutes. Cool and strain before using.
• Use a strong tea of rosehips or cloves.
• Use strong black coffee for final rinse.

See also Beauty Products.

HAIR CONDITIONERS

Aerosol propellants; ammonia; colors; fragrance; formaldehyde; glycols.

SAFE ALTERNATIVES
Brand Name/*Mail Order*

Unscented

A All Ways 100% Natural Indian Hemp Hair Conditioners (All Ways Natural Industries).

A Granny's Old-Fashioned Hair Conditioner (Granny's Old-Fashioned Products). *Granny's Old-Fashioned Products.*

A Infinity Hair Rinses (Infinity Herbal Products).

B *DP Laboratories.* DP Jo'ba Conditioner with jojoba oil.

C *The Body Shop.* Jojoba Oil Conditioner.

C *Common Scents.* Jojoba Oil Extra-Rich Conditioner.

C *Denis Dumont.* Several types of hair conditioners.

Natural Scent

A Aubrey Organics Hair Conditioners. (Aubrey Organics).

A *The Body Shop (England).* A variety of conditioners and rinses for all hair problems and types.

A Dr. Hauschka Neem Hair Lotion/Oil (Dr. R. Hauschka Cosmetics). *Meadowbrook Herbs & Things.*

A Jojoba Farms Jojoba Treatment Conditioner (Jojoba Farms).

A Nature de France French Clay Conditioners (Nature de France). *Erewhon Mail Order, Nature de France.*

A Nature's Naturals Hair Conditioner (Nature's Organics Plus).

A *New Age Creations.* Herbal Conditioning Vinegars and Herbal Hot Oil Treatment.

A Pure & Basic Conditioning Rinse (Head Shampoo).

A Weleda Rosemary Hair Conditioner/Lotion/Oil (Weleda). *Weleda, Wholesome Paks.*

B Carme Conditioner (Carme).

B Chenti Panthenol Bee Pollen Conditioners (Chenti Products).

B Country Roads Hair Conditioners (Golden California Co.).

B Desert Essence Jojoba Nutrient Conditioner (Desert Essence Cosmetics/Jojoba Products).

B Head Conditioner (Head Shampoo).

B Jason Hair Conditioners (Jason Natural Cosmetics). *Jason Natural Products.*

B Mill Creek Hair Conditioner (Mill Creek Natural Products).

B Nature's Gate Herbal Conditioner (Nature's Gate Herbal Cosmetics). *Common Scents, Deer Valley Farm, Erewhon Mail Order, Lotions & Potions, The Soap Opera.*

B Shikai Amla Conditioner for the Hair (Trans-India Products). *The Herb Patch.*

B Tom's Hair Conditioners (Tom's of Maine). *Erewhon Mail Order, Kennedy's Natural Foods, Walnut Acres.*

Do-It-Yourself

For Normal Hair

• Use neutral henna as directed on package.

• Saturate hair with olive, sesame, or corn oil. Make hot towels by running

• *hot* water over towels in washing machine and putting them through the spin cycle. Wrap head in aluminum foil and apply hot towels. Leave on for 20 minutes. Shampoo.

For Dry Hair
• Heat 1 cup olive oil and ¼ cup honey until warm. Pour into a bottle and shake well. Apply 1 or 2 tablespoons to scalp; massage. Cover head with a towel for several hours or wrap a hot damp towel around head for 10 minutes. Wash hair.
• Apply ½ cup mayonnaise to dry hair. Cover with a cellophane bag and wait 15 minutes. Rinse and shampoo.
• Puree 1 ripe avocado in blender or food processor. Massage into hair and wrap with a towel. Wait one hour before shampooing.

For Split Ends
• Massage scalp and hair ends with warm olive or avocado oil. Wrap head with a cotton towel, scarf, or diaper and leave on for 8 to 12 hours (all day or all night). Shampoo with regular shampoo to which 1 egg yolk has been added. Rinse with diluted lemon juice or vinegar.
• Massage 1 carton plain yogurt into hair and comb through. Rinse well.
• Mash 1 whole cucumber in a blender or food processor, adding a little water if necessary to make a paste. Apply to shampooed, towel-dryed hair and leave on for 10 minutes. Rinse well.

See also Beauty Products.

HAIR-REMOVAL PRODUCTS

Aerosol propellants; fragrance; mineral oil; paraffin.

SAFE ALTERNATIVES
Shave, tweeze, or have hair removed by electrolysis.

Brand Name/*Mail Order*
A *The Body Shop (England)*. Honey-based leg wax.
A Sessu Natural Hair Remover (Sessu-Haarentferner-Kosmetik). *Caswell-Massey*.

Do-It-Yourself
• Melt a small amount of beeswax in a small pan until very warm, but still cool enough to touch. After dusting skin with a body powder, apply warm wax to skin with a wooden spatula. Allow wax to dry for a few seconds, then remove quickly with a light tapping. The hairs will be removed with the wax. Soothe with a bit of cream or lotion.

See also Beauty Products and Shaving Creams.

HAIR-SETTING LOTION

Ammonia; colors; formaldehyde; fragrance; glycols; mineral oil; plastic (PVP).

SAFE ALTERNATIVES
Do-It-Yourself
• Dissolve 1 teaspoon sugar in 1 cup pure, warm water.
• Dissolve 1 teaspoon gelatin in 1 cup warm water. Use as a liquid or chill and use as a gel.
• Use stale beer.
• Towel-dry shampooed hair. Comb milk through hair to coat each strand. Set and dry.

See also Beauty Products.

HAIRSPRAY

Aerosol propellants; colors; ethanol; formaldehyde resins; fragrance; plastic (PVP).

Use of hairspray has long been associated with lung disease. In 1958, the lung disease thesaurosis was attributed to chronic inhalation of hairspray. Symptoms included shortness of breath, breathing difficulties, and reduced lung capacity. In most cases, the symptoms disappear after hairspray use is discontinued.

SAFE ALTERNATIVES
Consult with your hairdresser to find a style that doesn't need to be held in place with hairspray.

Brand Name/*Mail Order*

Unscented
A Aubrey Organics Natural Mist Hairspray (Aubrey Organics).

C Naturade Conditioning Hairspray with Jojoba. (Naturade Products).

Do-It-Yourself
• Chop 1 lemon (or 1 orange for dry hair). Place in a pot and cover with 2 cups pure, hot water. Boil until only half remains. Cool and strain. Add more water if needed. Refrigerate in a fine spray bottle. If desired, add 1 ounce vodka per cup of hairspray.

See also Beauty Products.

HAMMOCKS

See Beds.

HEATERS

See Appliances.

HEAT EXCHANGERS

See Air.

HERBS & SPICES

Artificial color; BHA/BHT; MSG; pesticide residues.

Herbs and spices may also be fumigated with ethylene oxide, a suspected mutagen.

SAFE ALTERNATIVES
Brand Name/*Mail Order*
Purchase whole dried herbs and spices at supermarkets, natural-foods stores, and gourmet shops and then grind them yourself at home. The flavor will be much fresher, and you'll know you won't be getting the fillers and anticaking ingredients sometimes found in ground seasonings. "Wild" herbs have been gathered from their natural habitat and then air dried. The only chemicals that might contaminate them are those from their natural setting. Organically grown herbs are also available.

A *Bear Meadow Farm.* Dried herbs and spices and salt-free culinary blends.

A *Culpeper.* Herbs, spices, and blends from England "naturally grown without artificial fertilizers or dangerous pesticides."

A *Deer Valley Farm.* Dried herbs, spices, and culinary blends.

A *Erewhon Mail Order.* Dried herbs and spices.

A Herbamare (Bioforce AG). *Deer Valley Farm, Erewhon Mail Order, Penn Herb Co.*

A Jory Farm Organically Grown Garlic Powder (Jory Farm).

A *Ram Island Farm Herbs.* Large selection of dried herbs "grown in our own gardens . . . or collected from our many acres of field, forest, and coast."

A *Richter's.* Dried herbs and spices. Books on uses of herbs.

A *S. & C. Huber, Accoutrements.* Freshly dried herbs from their own farm and other New England organic growers.

A *Walnut Acres.* Dried herbs and spices.

A *Weleda.* Biodynamically grown herbs and culinary herb mixtures.

AB *The Herb Patch.* "Superior quality" herbs & spices, "purchased organically grown when possible."

AB *Meadowbrook Herbs & Things.* Biodynamically grown herbs and herb mixtures, and spices from all over the world.

AB *Merry Gardens.* Rare and unusual dried herbs and culinary herb mixtures.

B Abundant Earth Seasonings (Abundant Earth Herb Co.).

B *Ahlswede's All Seasons.* Exclusive seasoning mixes made from the finest of pure ingredients without salt, sugar, MSG, sulphites, or fillers of any kind.

B *Bay Spice House.* Over 100 unusual herbs and spices. Also unusual ingredients for international cooking.

B Bell's All Natural Poultry Seasoning (William G. Bell Co.).

B *Capriland's Herb Farm.* Popular culinary herbs and salt-free herbal blends.

B *Earthsong Herb Shop.* Over 150 popular herbs and spices.

B Gaylord Hauser Seasonings (Modern Products).

B *Hartenthaler's.* Large selection of dried herbs and herbal syrups.

B *Haussmann's Pharmacy.* Dried herbs and spices.

B Helix Seasonings (Helix Corp). *Kennedy's Natural Foods, Pure Planet Products.*

B *Hilltop Herb Farm.* Salt-free culinary blends.

B *Indiana Botanic Gardens.* Over 300 varieties of dried herbs.

B *Misty Morning Farm.* Culinary herbs and salt-free seasoning blends.

B *Nature's Herb Co.* Large selection of dried herbs.

B *Nichols Garden Nursery.* Dried whole herbs and spices and salt-free herbal blends.

B Parsley Patch Seasonings (Parsley Patch Pure Spices).

B *Penn Herb Co.* Over 500 dried herbs.

B Seelect Seasonings (Seelect).

B Select Origins Seasonings (Select Origins).

B *Shaker Workshops.* Herb mixtures grown, dried, and packaged by the United Society of Shakers at Sabbathday Lake, Maine.

B Spice Islands Seasonings (Specialty Brands).

B *Sugar's Kitchen.* Sugar- and salt-free seasoning blends.

B Wagner's Herbs & Spices (John Wagner & Sons).

See also Seeds & Plants.

HONEY

See Sugar.

I

ICE CREAM

Colors; flavors.

Even though artificial colors and flavors are the only additives you will find regularly listed on ice cream labels, many other potentially harmful ingredients may be contained that do not have to be listed.

SAFE ALTERNATIVES
Ice cream is one of those foods with high pesticide concentrations because of large amounts of butterfat. To lower your exposure, eat sherbet, sorbet, or a low-fat frozen yogurt. Also, try ice cream made from soy milk.

Brand Name/*Mail Order*
Purchase an "all-natural" brand of ice cream at natural-foods stores and supermarkets. These brands can be reasonably relied upon to contain only those ingredients listed on their labels, and no artificial additives.

Made with Cow's Milk

B Alta-Dena Ice Creams (Alta-Dena).

B Natural Nectar Ice Creams (Natural Nectar Products Corp.).

B Shiloh Farms Ice Creams (Shiloh Farms). *Shiloh Farms.*

BC Double Rainbow Ice Creams (Double Rainbow).

BC Frusen Gladje Ice Creams/Sorbets (Frusen Gladje).

BC Haagen-Dazs Ice Creams/Sorbets (Haagen-Dazs).

BC Jacques La Creme Natural Ice Creams (Richmaid Ice Cream Co.).

C Dolly Madison All Natural Ice Creams (Seligco Food Corp.).

C Gelato Primo (Gelato Primo).

C Knudsen's Rich and Natural Ice Creams (Knudsen Corp.).

C Lucerne Our Natural Ice Creams (Safeway Stores).

C McConnell's Fine Ice Creams (McConnell's Fine Ice Creams of Santa Barbara).

C Tartufo Natural Italian Gourmet Ice Cream (Tartufo Italgelateria).

C Tres Chocolat (Tres Chocolat).

Made with Soy Milk

A Ice Dream (Garden of Eatin').

B Ice Bean (Farm Foods).

B Jollylicks (Living Lightly).

Frozen Yogurt

A Shiloh Farms All Natural Frozen Yogurt (Shiloh Farms). Made with milk from an organic dairy farm and sweetened with honey. *Shiloh Farms.*

See also Eggs, Food, Ice Cream Cones, Milk, and Sugar.

ICE CREAM CONES

Ammonia; colors; flavors; hydrogenated oil; sucrose.

SAFE ALTERNATIVES
Eat ice cream in a dish.

Brand Name/*Mail Order*
Purchase additive-free cones at natural-foods stores and supermarkets.

B The Natural Ice Cream Cone (Safe-T Pacific Co.).

C The Natural Gelato Cone (The Good Time Spice Couple Co.).

C Party Pride the Natural Ice Cream Cone (Safeway Stores).

See also Food and Ice Cream.

INSULATION

Dyes; formaldehyde; plastics (polyurethane, polystyrene).

Urea-formaldehyde foam insulation (UFFI) is the most dangerous of all insulations. After receiving numerous complaints that exposure to UFFI caused respiratory problems, dizziness, nausea, and eye and throat irritations, ranging from short-term discomfort to serious adverse health effects and hospitalization, and examining evidence that formaldehyde fumes cause cancer in laboratory rats, the Consumer Product Safety Commission (CPSC) banned the use of UFFI in residences and schools on 10 August 1982. One year later this ban was overturned by the Fifth Circuit Court of Appeals. The CPSC feels the court's decision was based on legal and factual errors and continues to warn consumers that available evidence indicates there are risks associated with the product.

UFFI is found in only about 500,000 American homes, most insulated in the 1970s. If you suspect you are having health problems because of UFFI, information on detection and proper removal can be obtained by calling the CPSC at 800/638-CPSC.

SAFE ALTERNATIVES
When installing new insulation, the two safest choices are fiber glass and blown-in cellulose. Blown-in cellulose insulation (made from old newspapers and sodium borate) is cheaper than fiber glass and gives greater insulating properties. It also may be least harmful; there is some speculation that inhalation of fiber glass fibers may cause adverse health effects similar to those from asbestos fibers.

If fiber glass is used, choose a foil-faced brand, rather than one that is asphalt impregnated, and place the foil side against the interior wall. Or, choose a brand without a vapor barrier and add your own. Fiber glass bats use a small amount of urea- and phenol-formaldehyde resin to keep them fluffy, so make sure there is an adequate barrier between the insulation and the living space.

Brand Name/*Mail Order*
B Insulsafe II (Certainteed). Undyed fiber glass blown-in insulation.

See also Vapor Barrier.

IRONING BOARD COVERS

Plastics (polyester, tetrafluoroethylene).

SAFE ALTERNATIVES
Brand Name/*Mail Order*

Buy all-cotton ironing board covers at hardware stores.

A *The Cotton Place.* Bleached muslin or barrier-cloth ironing board covers with cotton felt pad.

A *Janice Corp.* Prewashed cotton ironing board covers and pads. "Guaranteed to be free of all fabric finishes."

A *Limericks Linens.* Cotton ironing board covers and pads.

A Tug O' War 100% Cotton Ironing Board Covers and Pads (John Ritzenthaler Co.).

A *Vermont Country Store.* "Cotton ironing board cover and pad has a Press Cloth Fabric cover, the kind used by professional laundries . . . . Non-slip textured surface holds ironing in place."

See also Fabric and Textiles.

J

JAMS, JELLIES, & PRESERVES

Colors; pesticide residues; saccharin; sucrose.

SAFE ALTERNATIVES
Brand Name/*Mail Order*

Most brands of jams, jellies, marmalades, and preserves are additive free but do contain sugar. Choose one that is either unsweetened or else is sweetened with honey or rice syrup, available at your natural-foods store.

Fruit Butters

A Paul de Sousa's Apple Butter (Paul de Sousa's Co.). *Kennedy's Natural Foods, Pure Planet Products.*

A Shiloh Farms Apple Butter (Shiloh Farms). *Shiloh Farms.*

A Walnut Acres Apple Butter (Walnut Acres). *Walnut Acres.*

B Arrowhead Mills Fruit Butters (Arrowhead Mills). *Walnut Acres.*

B Gathering Winds Apple Butter (Gathering Winds Natural Foods). *Erewhon Mail Order.*

B Pure & Simple Fruit Butters (Pure Sales).

Fruit Spreads

AB Cascadian Farms Fruit Spreads (Cascadian Farms)

B The Cherry Tree Fruit Spreads (The Cherry Tree). *The Cherry Tree.*

B Gathering Winds Apple Spread (Gathering Winds Natural Foods). *Erewhon Mail Order.*

B L & A Pure Fruit Spreads (L & A Juice Co.).

B Paul de Sousa's Fruit Spreads (Paul de Sousa's Co.). *Pure Planet Products.*

B Westbrae Fruit Spreads (Westbrae Natural Foods). *Erewhon Mail Order.*

129

B   Whole Earth Fruit Spreads (Whole Earth).

Jams

A   *Special Foods.* Honey-sweetened and unsweetened jams made from such unusual fruits as papaya, guava, pomegranate, prickly pear, cherimoya, custard-apple, and star fruit.

A   Walnut Acres Jams (Walnut Acres). *Walnut Acres.*

B   Arrowhead Mills Jams (Arrowhead Mills).

B   Everything Natural Jams (Everything Natural).

B   Halgren's Jams (Halgren's).

B   Honey-Apricot (The Cherry Tree). Honey with bits of dried apricots. *The Cherry Tree.*

B   Kozlowski Farms No Sugar Jams (Kozlowski Farms).

Jellies

B   Everything Natural Jelly (Everything Natural).

B   Willis Wood's Cider Jelly (Willis Wood). "Our [apple] cider jelly is made without sugar or added sweeteners of any kind. Nothing is added to the fresh cider that we press and then evaporate into jelly here on our farm just as our family has for over 100 years." *Erewhon Mail Order, Wood's Cider Jelly.*

Preserves

A   Cascadian Farm Preserves (Cascadian Farm).

A   Paul de Sousa Preserves (Paul de Sousa's Co.). *Kennedy's Natural Foods, Pure Planet Products.*

A   Walnut Acres Preserves (Walnut Acres). *Walnut Acres.*

AB   Sorrell Ridge Conserves (Sorrell Ridge Farm). *Kennedy's Natural Foods.*

B   Hain Preserves (Hain Pure Food Co.).

B   L & A Preserves (L & A Juice Co.). *Kennedy's Natural Foods.*

B   Norganic Preserves (Norganic Foods).

B   Westbrae Preserves (Westbrae Natural Foods).

B   Whole Earth Preserves (Whole Earth).

B   William Escott's Preserves (William Escott's).

See also Food, Produce, and Sugar.

JUICES & FRUIT DRINKS

Colors; BHA/BHT; glycols; pesticide residues.

SAFE ALTERNATIVES
Brand Name/*Mail Order*

"Reconstituted" juices or those "made from concentrate" may contain polluted tap water. Pure juices can be purchased at natural-foods stores and supermarkets.

Juices

A   Biotta Vegetable Juices (Richter Bros.). *Deer Valley Farm, Penn Herb Co.*

A   *Culpeper.* English apple juice "made from organically grown apples that have not been sprayed."

A   *Four Chimneys.* "Certified organically grown" Concord grape juice.

A   Heinke's Organic Apple Juice (Heinke's).

A Jory Farm Zinfandel Grape Juice (Jory Farm).

A Marin Brand Gravenstein Select Apple Juice (Marin Food Specialties).

A Mendocino Juicers Organic Wine Grape Juice (Mendocino Juicers).

A R. W. Knudsen Family Organically Grown Juices (R. W. Knudsen & Sons).

A Shiloh Farms Fruit Juices (Shiloh Farms). *Shiloh Farms.*

A Walnut Acres Vegetable Juices (Walnut Acres). *Walnut Acres.*

A Westbrae Organically Grown Juices (Westbrae Natural Foods).

B *Alive Polarity Distributors.* Apple cider and "dealcoholized" sparkling and nonsparkling grape juices from France and Australia.

B Apple Time Apple Juice (Sebastopol Cooperative Cannery).

B Baron's Sparkling Natural Juice Drinks (Specialty Beverages).

B Bonnie Hubbard Apple Juices (United Grocers).

B C & W Frozen Valencia Orange Juice (California & Washington Co.).

B Chamay Silver Sparkling French Cider (Boyd Wilson International). Made in France. Has a champagnelike taste.

B The Cherry Tree Juices (The Cherry Tree). *The Cherry Tree.*

B Coastal Frozen Orange Juice (Ventura Coastal Corp.).

B Country Pure Coarse Filtered Apple Juice (Safeway Stores).

B Dare to Be a Juicer Juices (M. J. McDonald Juice Co.).

B Farmkist Fresh Prune Juice (Sugar Ripe Farms).

B Hain Juices (Hain Pure Food Co.). *Kennedy's Natural Foods.*

B Hansen's Natural Juices/Natural Cidre Sparkling Apple Juice (Hansen Foods).

B Health Mate Juices (Wagner Health Food Products).

B Heinke's Juices (Heinke's).

B Lakewood Fruit Juices/Sparkling Fruit Juices (Lakewood). *Deer Valley Farm, Walnut Acres.*

B Lehr's Juices (Richter & Co.).

B Martinelli's Apple Juice/Sparkling Apple Juice/Sparkling Cider (S. Martinelli & Co.).

B Minute Maid Frozen Juices (The Coca-Cola Co.).

B Mrs. Woods Farm Juices (John Woods Products).

B Mt. Madonna Fruit Juices (Mt. Madonna Natural Juices).

B Norganic Juices (Norganic Foods Co.).

B Pineyhill Vineyards Premium Wine Grape Juices (Pineyhill Vineyards). "No additives."

B Purely Delicious Frozen Juices (Ludford Fruit Products).

B R. W. Knudsen Family Juices/ Natural Fruit Fizzes (R. W. Knudsen & Sons). *Kennedy's Natural Foods.*

B Rock Island Natural Grape Juice (Rock Island Foods).

B S & W Unsweetened 100% Apple Juice (S & W Fine Foods).

B Seneca Frozen Apple Juice (Seneca Foods Corp.).

B Sunkist Frozen Orange Juice (Sunkist Growers).

B Town House 100% Pure Apple Cider/Juice (Safeway Stores).

B Tree Top Frozen Juices (Tree Top).

B Westbrae Juices (Westbrae Natural Foods).

Unsweetened Whole Fruit-Juice Concentrates

B Bernard Jensen (Bernard Jensen Products).

B Hain (Hain Pure Food Co.). *Deer Valley Farm.*

B Nu Life (Gides Nu Life).

See also Food, Produce, and Water.

K

KEFIR

See Yogurt & Kefir.

KEFIR CHEESE

See Yogurt & Kefir.

KETCHUP

Pesticide residues; sucrose.

SAFE ALTERNATIVES
Brand Name/*Mail Order*
Honey-sweetened ketchup is sold in natural-foods stores. It may be called "imitation ketchup" or be spelled a different way, because federal standards of identity require that ketchup contain a sucrose sweetener. (Despite this, some products not containing a sucrose sweetener still label themselves ketchups.)

A Walnut Acres Ketchup (Walnut Acres). *Kennedy's Natural Foods, Walnut Acres.*

B Bauman's Old-Fashioned Pennsylvania Dutch Ketchup (The Bauman Family). *The Great Valley Mills.*

B Gathering Winds All-Natural Ketchup/Table Sauce (Gathering Winds Natural Foods).

B Hain Naturals Imitation Catsup (Hain Pure Food Co.). *Kennedy's Natural Foods.*

B Health Valley 100% Natural Catch-Up Tomato Table Sauce (Health Valley Natural Foods).

B Johnson's Ketchup (Pure Sales).

B Sunburst Farms Un-Ketchup (Sunburst Farms Natural Foods).

B Westbrae Natural Hot & Spicy Catsup (Westbrae Natural Foods).

C Bonnie Hubbard Tomato Catsup (United Grocers).

C Del Monte Catsup (Del Monte Corp.).

C Heinz Tomato Ketchup (H. J. Heinz Co.).

C Hunt's Tomato Ketchup (Hunt-Wesson Foods).

C Town House Fancy Tomato Catsup (Safeway Stores).

See also Food.

L

LAUNDRY AGENTS

Ammonia; detergents; dyes (fluorescent brighteners); EDTA; ethanol; fragrance; isopropyl alcohol; naphthalene; phenol.

"CAUTION: May be harmful if swallowed."

"WARNING: Harmful if swallowed, irritating to eyes and skin. Keep out of reach of children."

(Some detergents with similar formulas have no warning on the label.)

SAFE ALTERNATIVES
Detergents were designed to clean synthetic fabrics. Natural fibers can be cleaned quite adequately with natural substances.

Cotton and Linen
Use borax, baking soda, washing soda, or a natural soap. Although most acids destroy the fiber, vinegar (acetic acid) can be used with no harmful effect. A drop or two of vinegar in the laundry water can help prevent colors from fading. Wash colors separately.

Mildew grows easily on cotton fibers, especially if they are stored under damp and dark conditions. The fungus stains the fiber and eventually causes it to rot. To prevent mildew, which starts its growth on soiled spots, keep clothing clean. Air clothes after wearing to allow any perspiration to dry, or wear clothes only once

before laundering. Using borax with the laundry soap will help retard the formation of mildew. Leaving a light on in the closet can provide warmth to keep clothes dry and will inhibit mold growth even in wet weather.

Silk
Hand wash in very cold water with a mild or castile soap, swishing the fabric around for a few minutes and allowing the water to soak into the fabric. Do not rub. Rinse with cold water and gently remove excess water by rolling the fabric in a towel. Do not wring. Dry away from direct sunlight until damp, then press on the wrong side with a dry iron. A few drops of vinegar will help keep colors from fading without harming the fabric. White vinegar used in the final rinse will also help keep white silks white. Wash colors separately.

Wool
Hand wash or delicately machine wash in lukewarm water (to prevent shrinkage) with mild soaps or diluted vinegar. Sweaters and knits should be reshaped to their original size while still damp. Do not use baking soda, as wool is quickly damaged by alkali. Dry cleaning of wool garments is not recommended because of the solvents used, and because mothproofing treatments may be applied.

Down and Feathers
Use a mild soap or baking soda. Dry in a tumble dryer at a cool temperature, as opposed to drying in the air. The machine dryer not only makes the items fluffier by putting more air between the feathers, but dries them more quickly, preventing possible

mold growth. Comforters and other large items should be dried in a commercial-size dryer to allow ample space for air circulation.

Brand Name/*Mail Order*

A *Culpeper.* Dried saporaria, a plant cleanser used since Roman times.

A *Erlander's Natural Products.* Washing Compound containing washing soda and baking soda.

B Country Safe Unscented Laundry Detergent (Marsdel).

B Green (Neo-Life Co. of America). *Walnut Acres* or your local Neo-Life distributor.

C Granny's Old-Fashioned Laundry Concentrate (Granny's Old-Fashioned Products). *The Allergy Store, Granny's Old-Fashioned Products.*

Do-It-Yourself

For Regular Fabrics

• Use soap. If you live in a hard-water area, you may need a water softener to help dissolve the soap properly. To find out if you need a water softener, put two cups of warm tap water into a quart jar, add a teaspoon of powdered soap-flakes or liquid soap, and shake hard. If you get lots of suds that last for several minutes, you don't need to add anything. If you don't get any suds, consult the Water Softeners entry in this book. When adding soap flakes to a wash of warm or cold water, dissolve the soap flakes in hot water first, and then add.

• Use baking soda.

• Use borax.

• Use washing soda.

• Use white vinegar.

• Use 1 tablespoon TSP per washer-load of clothes.

• Mix ¼ cup soap flakes or grated bar soap, 1 cup water, and ¼ cup borax in a saucepan and simmer until well blended.

For Delicate and Colored Fabrics

• Tie 1½ cups wheat bran in a piece of cotton cloth. Place in a pan containing 1 quart water and bring to a boil. Simmer for ½ hour, strain, and add 2 cups lukewarm water. Stir well. Use without soap.

See also Bleach, Cleaning Products, Soap, and Water Softeners.

LAUNDRY STARCH

Aerosol propellants; formaldehyde; fragrance; pentachlorophenol; phenol.

"CAUTION: Contents under pressure. Keep out of reach of children."

SAFE ALTERNATIVES

Choose a dry powdered starch, rather than one in an aerosol can.

Brand Name/*Mail Order*

Natural Scent

A Faultless Starch (Faultless Starch/Bon Ami Co.).

Do-It-Yourself

For Regular Fabrics

• Mix 1 to 3 tablespoons cornstarch with about 1½ tablespoons cold water to form a paste. Add paste to 1 pint boiling water and mix in ¼ teaspoon beeswax. Boil for 15 minutes, then strain through a double layer of cheesecloth. Dip items to be starched into the strained solution.

• Dissolve 1 tablespoon cornstarch in 1 pint cold water. Place in spray bottle. Shake before using.

For Delicate Fabrics
• Dissolve 1 package unflavored gelatin in 2 cups hot water. Dilute with at least one quart water and add clothes. Try a corner of the fabric first to make sure the solution does not end up sticky when dry. If it does, add more water and try again until you get it right.
• Dissolve 1 to 2 tablespoons granulated white sugar in 2 cups warm water. Dip in items to be starched.

See also Cleaning Products.

LIP GLOSS & LIPSTICKS

See Cosmetics.

LOOFAS

See Sponges.

LOTIONS, CREAMS & MOISTURIZERS

Ammonia; colors; EDTA; ethanol; fragrance; glycols; mineral oil; phenol.

SAFE ALTERNATIVES
Brand Name/*Mail Order*
Natural and unscented lotions, creams, and moisturizers can be purchased at drug and natural-foods stores.

Unscented
A   Earth Venus Moisturizer (Ida Grae/Nature's Colors). *The Allergy Store.*

A   Nature's Plus Vitamin E Cream (Nature's Plus).

B   *DP Laboratories.* DP Jo'ba Lotion with jojoba oil.

B   GK Outdoor Skin Protector (Pure Body Creations).

BC   *Homebody.* A variety of creams, lotions, and moisturizers.

BC   *Lotions & Potions.* A variety of creams, lotions, and moisturizers.

BC   *The Soap Opera.* A variety of lotions, creams, and moisturizers.

C   Basic Formula Pure Moisturizing Body Lotion/Pure Moisturizer (Dorothy Gray).

C   *Denis Dumont.* Lotions and moisture cremes.

C   Neutrogena Norwegian Formula Hand Cream (Neutrogena Corp.).

Natural Scent
A   Autumn-Harp Body Lotion (Autumn-Harp).

A   *The Body Shop (England).* Large selection of lotions and creams for all skin types.

A   Dr. Hauschka Lotions & Creams (Dr. R. Hauschka Cosmetics). *The Allergy Store, Meadowbrook Herbs & Things, Weleda.*

A   *Fluir Herbals.* Hand and body lotion, rose cream, and a lemon-scented heavy-duty hand cream.

A   *Heavenly Soap.* Lightly rose-scented Rose Night Cream.

A   Magic Lotion (Magic Lotion). *The Herb Patch.*

A   *New Age Creations.* Creams "made of the purest natural ingredients."

A   Sand-Oh-Sha Magic Musk Hand & Body Lotion (Sand-Oh-Sha)

A   Tom's Honeysuckle Body Lotion (Tom's of Maine).

A   Weleda Creams (Weleda). *Weleda, Wholesome Paks.*

B   Country Roads 87% Aloe Vera Moisturizing Lotion/Jojoba Moisturizing Cream (Golden California Co.).

B   Mill Creek Aloe Vera & Paba Moisturizing Lotion (Mill Creek Natural Products). *Kennedy's Natural Foods.*

B   Nature's Gate Moisture Lotion (Nature's Gate Herbal Cosmetics). *Erewhon Mail Order.*

B   Pure & Basic Aloe Vera Lotion (Head Shampoo).

B   Rachel Perry Aloe "E" All-Over Moisture Lotion (Rachel Perry).

B   Rocky Mountain Skin Trip (Rocky Mountain Ocean). *Erewhon Mail Order.*

B   Schiff Bee Pollen Remoisturizing Hand & Body Creme (Schiff Bio-Food Products).

Do-It-Yourself

• Combine 1 ounce natural glycerin or honey, 1 ounce avocado oil, 1 ounce sesame oil, 1 ounce olive oil, 2 ounces coconut oil, 2 ounces palm oil, ½ ounce spermaceti, and ½ ounce cocoa butter. Melt in a double boiler until completely dissolved. Beat the mixture with a wooden spoon until cold and put into jars. Keep refrigerated.

• Melt together 4 ounces almond butter (make by grinding almonds in a food processor or blender until butter is formed, or purchase at a natural-foods store), 4 ounces natural glycerin or honey, and 2 ounces coconut oil. In a separate pot, heat 16 ounces distilled water and dissolve 1 teaspoon borax into the water. Slowly add the water to the oil mixture. Beat well by hand or mix in blender or food processor. Place in bottles. Keep refrigerated.

• Simmer 1 cup rolled oats in 6 cups pure water for 30 minutes. Strain. Massage small amount of lotion into clean skin.

• Beat 2 eggs in a chilled bowl. While beating, slowly add 1 cup oil. When mixture begins to thicken, add 1 tablespoon fresh lemon juice or 1 tablespoon apple cider vinegar. Refrigerate in a covered glass container.

See also Beauty Products.

LUBRICATING OIL

Many aerosol or oil lubricants contain various strong-smelling solvents or scents.

SAFE ALTERNATIVES

Use plain castor or jojoba oil on hinges, doorknobs, and latches. Mineral oil also can be used, but avoid contact with skin, as irritation can result. For locks, use dry powdered graphite.

LUGGAGE

Plastics (nylon, polyester, PVC/vinyl chloride).

SAFE ALTERNATIVES

Buy luggage and purses made from cotton canvas.

Brand Name/*Mail Order*

A   The Original Stonemason Bag (Two Ducks). Expensive natural-color canvas luggage with leather trim.

AB *Patti Collins Canvas Products.* Cotton canvas luggage, purses, totes, backpacks at reasonable prices. Many styles and colors.

AB *Port Canvas Co.* Luggage in all shapes and sizes made from heavy-duty 100% cotton duck and webbing, with brass hardware. All seams double stitched; adjustable shoulder strap optional on all bags. Reasonably priced.

B *Coastside Creations.* Complete line of heavy-duty cotton canvas luggage, dufflebags, backpacks at reasonable prices. Handles custom orders.

B *Cotton Comfort.* Cotton canvas heavy-duty totebag with interior zippered pocket; also cotton backpacks.

B Ghurka Bags (Marley Hodgson). Expensive classic handmade luggage, originally designed for Her Majesty's troops in the provinces of the nineteenth century British Commonwealth. Made from specially woven 100% cotton twill and leather, both permanently treated to be resistent to soil and water by a process developed in England over 100 years ago. *Bullock & Jones, Cable Car Clothiers/Robert Kirk Ltd., Gokeys, Norm Thompson.*

B *Swaine Adeney Brigg.* Expensive canvas-and-leather luggage from England.

M

MAPLE SYRUP

See Sugar.

MARGARINE

Benzyl alcohol/sodium benzoate; colors; EDTA; flavors; glycols, hydrogenated oil.

All margarine is made from oil that has been hydrogenated, a process that totally changes the oil's chemical characteristics. Do not be misled by labels that state "made from 100% corn oil" or "made from 100% vegetable oil." By the time the oil has been hydgrogenated, bleached, filtered, and deodorized, it bears little resemblance to its original form.

SAFE ALTERNATIVES
Use natural vegetable oils or butter.

See also Butter, Food, and Oils.

MARKERS

See Pens & Markers.

MASCARA

See Cosmetics.

MATTRESS PADS

Plastic (polyester).

SAFE ALTERNATIVES
Brand Name/*Mail Order*
A *After the Stork.* Crib-size cotton flannel/rubber waterproof pads.

A *Big Sky Trading Co.* Sheepskin crib pads.

A *Cotton Brokers.* Best price on hospital-quality cotton felt pads. Also bassinet sizes.

A *The Cotton Place.* Hospital-quality cotton felt pads.

A *Cuddledown.* Cotton knit mattress pad filled with wool batting.

A *Erlander's Natural Products.* Cotton felt pads.

A *The Futon Shop.* "100% cotton laminated to a waterproof rubber sheet."

A *Garnet Hill.* Cotton-covered wool fleece pad and a pad made in Germany "of knit-backed Merino wool fleece on the sleeping side, wool batting in the center, and fine ultra-high thread-count cotton on the underside."

A *Golden Touch Lambskin Products.* Sheepskin crib pads.

A *Janice Corp.* "Unbleached, soft, fluffy cotton felt" seamless mattress pad.

A *New Zealand Lambskins.* Sheepskin crib pads.

A *Overland Sheepskin Co.* "Actual sheared sheepskin" mattress pads for "the plushest wool surface possible."

A *St. Patricks Down.* "Wool underlay," 2 inches thick, encased in cotton.

A *The Sheepskin Co.* Sheepskin crib pads.

A *Tender Touch.* Sheepskin pads for cribs and larger beds.

A *Vermont Country Store.* Cotton-covered wool fleece pad.

A Woolrest Sleepers (Woolrest USA). Fuzzy pad made of 100% wool in New Zealand. *JS&A, Norm Thompson, Overland Sheepskin Co., Woolrest USA.*

Do-It-Yourself

Sew together several layers of cotton flannel blankets. You can also add a thin layer of cotton or wool batting between the blankets (be sure to quilt the pad if you do, to keep the batting in place.)

For waterproof mattress pads use barrier cloth (several layers if necessary), or order flannel-covered rubber sheeting by the yard from *Vermont Country Store.*

See also Batting, Barrier Cloth, Blankets, and Textiles.

MATTRESSES & BOX SPRINGS

See Beds.

MAYONNAISE

EDTA; hydrogenated oil.

SAFE ALTERNATIVES
Brand Name/*Mail Order*
Natural-foods stores carry the brands listed below.

A *Special Foods.* Imitation mayonnaise made from recipes based on cooked white sweet potato, malanga, yam, or cassava.

A Walnut Acres Mayonnaise (Walnut Acres). *Walnut Acres.*

B Dr. Tima Soyannaise (Tima Brand).

B Eden Mayonnaise (Eden Foods).

B Featherweight Imitation Mayonnaise (Chicago Dietetic Supply). No eggs. *Chicago Dietetic Supply.*

B Hain Mayonnaises (Hain Pure Food Co.). *Deer Valley Farm, Kennedy's Natural Foods.*

B Hunza Natural Unsalted Mayonnaise (H & J Foods).

B Kraft Miracle Whip Salad Dressing (Kraft).

B Westbrae Mayonnaise (Westbrae Natural Foods).

See also Food.

MEAT & POULTRY

Artificial colors; nitrates/nitrosamines; pesticide residues; plastic residues (polyethylene, polystyrene).

Over 140 drugs (including antibiotics, stimulants, and tranquilizers) and pesticides have been identified by the federal General Accounting Office as being likely to leave residues in meat and poultry. Of these, 42 are suspected human carcinogens, 20 may be teratogens, and 6 may be mutagens. Approximately 14 percent of all meat and poultry sold may contain illegal amounts of these chemicals. This contaminated food is always passed along to the consumer because tests for contamination are not completed until after the meat and poultry has been purchased and consumed.

Several human carcinogens are commonly added to flesh foods. Arsenic is used in 90 percent of all chicken feed, and diethyl stilbesterol (DES) in 80 to 85 percent of all beef cattle and lamb feed; also, high levels of PCBs can be found in most fish-based feed, which further contaminates the mammals and birds.

SAFE ALTERNATIVES

Avoid eating liver, sweetbreads, and other organ meats, as toxins tend to accumulate there.

Eat fewer flesh foods and more fruits, vegetables, nuts, and whole grains. Flesh foods contain higher concentrations of pesticides than do foods lower down on the food chain.

Remove fat before cooking, as pesticides tend to accumulate there.

Avoid processed meats: bacon, sausage, salami, luncheon meats, frankfurters, and so on.

Remove the purple-inked USDA stamp from all meats before cooking.

Purchase meat and poultry fresh, cut to order, wrapped in paper from a butcher to avoid heat-sealed plastic containers.

Brand Name/*Mail Order*

Purchase meat and poultry from sources whose animals have been pasture grazed and raised without hormones or other chemicals to stimulate or regulate growth or tenderness, or without any drugs or antibiotics, or from animals that have been hunted in their natural habitat and contaminated only by those chemicals found in their environment. In some states, these flesh foods are referred to as "organic." They can be purchased at natural-foods stores or ordered by mail.

A *Country Pride Meats.* Buffalo meat.

A *Czimer Foods.* "Wild game meats and birds," including pheasant, duck, partridge, quail, wild turkey, Canadian geese, squab, venison, buffalo, elk, bear, wild boar, moose, reindeer, antelope, hippopotamus, lion, caribou, mountain sheep, wild goat, llama, kangaroo, zebra, giraffe, alligator, rattlesnake, beaver, and rabbit. Also some smoked meats and unusual fish and seafoods.

A *Deer Valley Farm.* Organically grown beef, pork, and poultry products and nitrate-free cured meats.

A Harmony Farms Meats (Harmony Farms).

A *Kennedy's Natural Foods.* "Uncontaminated" beef and lamb that have not been heat sealed in plastic. "Free of artificial hormones, antibiotics, injurious chemicals." Also additive-free bacon and hot dogs, chicken, turkey, and goat.

A Meadow-Raised Beef (Jimaino Ranches).

A Pel-Freez Rabbit (Pel-Freez Rabbit Meat). "No additives or preservatives, no added salt or water, and no added hormones."

A Shelton's Turkey Ranch Chicken (Shelton's Turkey Ranch).

A Shiloh Farms Meats/Poultry/Meat Products (Shiloh Farms). No nitrates or nitrites. Beef products from the range land of western Australia; poultry not fed antibiotics or hormones. *Shiloh Farms.*

A *Teel Mountain Farm.* Chickens. "No antibiotics, arsenic or other medications, no toxic pesticides, no preservatives or artificial coloring agents, no hormones or growth-stimulating chemicals; not raised in cages; free to run in their houses."

A *Walnut Acres.* Free range cattle and chickens fed "primarily on our homegrown grains and hay . . . . No hormones, growth-stimulants, and the like." Also products such as beans and franks and beef stew made from these meats.

A *Wish Poultry.* Turkeys and chickens raised "using no chemicals, no medicines, or preservatives."

A *Wolfe's Neck Farm.* Organic beef "raised without exposure to poisonous sprays, artificial growth stimulants, chemical fertilizers, or other harmful additives . . . since 1959. . . . All but 5% of the food is raised on this saltwater farm." Also sells organic lamb raised at other nearby farms.

Additive Free, but Not Organically Raised

B Country Sausage & Meat Sausages/Smoked Uncured Bacon/ Beef Frankfurters. (Country Sausage & Meat).

B Dick's Country Smoked Bacon (Dick's Country Smoked Meats).

B *Hans Mueller.* Natural all-meat sausages made by an American and European award winner. "Free from all preservatives like nitrites . . . no food colorings added . . . natural casings." Complete ingredients list with catalog.

B Health Valley Hot Dogs/Sliced Breakfast Pork/Sausage (Health Valley Natural Foods).

B Jones Dairy Farm Pork Sausages (Jones Dairy Farm).

See also Food.

METAL POLISHES

Ammonia; ethanol; fragrance; paraffin; petroleum distillates; sulphur compounds.

"DANGER: Harmful or fatal if swallowed. Irritating to eyes."

SAFE ALTERNATIVES
Brand Name/*Mail Order*

C E-Z-est Steeluster (E-Z-est Products Co.). This powdered cleanser has a slight peppermint scent, but none of the strong toxic fumes that other metal polishes have. Ingredients are unknown. Designed for use on copper, stainless steel, and aluminum.

Do-It-Yourself
Aluminum

• Use plain steel wool or steel wool and a nontoxic scouring powder. Rub in one direction only, since a circular scrubbing motion can damage the finish.

• Mix 2 tablespoons powdered alum and 1 cup TSP with enough water to form a thick paste. Rub this mixture on the aluminum with a soft cloth. Rinse with water.

• Soak in a solution of lemon juice or sliced lemons and boiling water. Or clean with a soft cloth dipped in straight lemon juice and rinse in warm water.

• Remove stains and discoloration from aluminum pots by boiling 3 tablespoons white vinegar and 2 cups water in the pot, or by rubbing the stain with a cut lemon. The boiling vinegar and water treatment is also good for removing lime scale from the bottom of an aluminum teapot, as is letting a mixture of vinegar and water sit in the teapot overnight.

• Boil in the pot a solution of 2 cups water and 2 teaspoons cream of tartar.

• Cook rhubarb, tomatoes, tart apples, sour milk, or buttermilk in the pot.

• Fill pot with water and add ½ to 1 teaspoon sodium hexametaphosphate. Bring water to a boil and simmer for 3 minutes.

Brass & Copper

• Use lemon juice or a paste of lemon juice and salt, or a slice of lemon sprinkled with baking soda. Rub with a soft cloth, rinse with water, and dry.

• Make a paste of lemon juice and cream of tartar. Apply, leave on for 5 minutes, then wash in warm water and dry with a soft cloth.

• Make a paste of salt, white vinegar, and flour. Apply the paste, let it set for a hour, then rub off, rinse, and polish with a soft cloth.

• Rub with hot white vinegar and salt.

• Rub with hot buttermilk or sour milk.

• Rub with tomato or rhubarb juice.

• Soak brass overnight in a solution of vinegar and salt, or boil in a pot of water with 1 tablespoon salt and 1 cup vinegar for several hours. Scrub with a brush, then wash with soap in hot water; rinse and dry.

• Polish with a soft cloth and Worcestershire sauce.

• Brass will look brighter and need less polishing if rubbed with olive oil after each polishing.

• If copper is tarnished, boil article in a pot of water with 1 tablespoon salt and 1 cup white vinegar for several hours. Wash with soap in hot water; rinse and dry.

• Boil 2 cups water in a medium-size pot and remove from heat. Add ½ cup soap flakes and stir until dissolved. Continue to stir while adding 3 tablespoons calcium carbonate and 2 tablespoons white vinegar. Beat until well blended and store in a jar with a tight lid.

Chrome

• Wipe with a soft cloth dipped in undiluted apple cider vinegar.
• Rub with a lemon peel, rinse, and polish with a soft cloth.
• Mix 3 cups washing soda, ¾ cup TSP, and 1¼ cups baking soda. Rub on with a damp cloth, rinse, and dry.
• Use a paste of calcium carbonate mixed with water.

Gold

• Wash in lukewarm soapy water. Dry with a cotton cloth, then polish with a chamois cloth.

Silver

• Apply a paste of baking soda mixed with water. Rub, rinse, and dry.
• Place silver in a pan, cover with sour milk or buttermilk, and let stand overnight. In the morning, rinse with cold water.
• Place items in a pan and cover with a mixture of 1 cup whole milk and either 2 teaspoons cream of tartar or 1 tablespoon white vinegar or lemon juice. Let stand overnight and rinse in the morning with cold water.
• Heat 1½ cups water and 2 tablespoons stearic acid in the top of a double boiler until the stearic acid melts. Remove from heat and add ½ teaspoon washing soda, ½ teaspoon TSP, and 1 cup diatomaceous earth. Stir into a paste. When cool, apply with a soft cloth, rub, and rinse with warm water.

• Dampen a cloth with some vodka and water, then sprinkle it with calcium carbonate. Apply, rub, and rinse with warm water.
• Put a sheet of aluminum foil in the bottom of a pan, add 2 or 3 inches of water, 1 teaspoon baking soda, 1 teaspoon salt, and bring to a boil. Add silver pieces, boil 2 to 3 minutes, making sure water covers silver. Remove silver, rinse, dry, and buff with a soft cloth.
• Fill a glass jar half full with thin strips of aluminum foil, then add 1 tablespoon rock salt and enough cold water to fill the jar. Keep covered. Dip silver items into the jar and leave for 2 minutes, then rinse well.
• For small items, rub the article with toothpaste and a soft cloth. Rinse with warm water and polish with a chamois cloth.
• Put items in an aluminum pan so that each piece touches the pan. Cover with 1 quart of almost boiling water into which 1 teaspoon TSP or 1 tablespoon baking soda has been dissolved. Let sit for several minutes, then remove silver and rinse dry.
• Apply a paste of calcium carbonate and olive oil and allow to dry. Rub off with a soft cloth and polish with chamois.

See also Cleaning Products and Scouring Powders.

MILK

BHA/BHT; formaldehyde; glycols; paraffin residues; pesticide residues; plastic residues.

Milk can also contain residues of antibiotics, hormones, and tranquilizers that have been fed to the cows, as well as residues of antiseptic solutions used to clean cow udders before milking. "Fortification" with vitamin A or D adds propylene glycol, alcohols, and BHT. All milk contains pesticide residues; no milk available in the United States today is free from them.

Most milk is pasteurized and homogenized before it reaches the consumer. Pasteurized milk has simply been heated to destroy bacteria. Homogenized milk has been mixed under pressure to reduce fat particles to a uniform size in order to improve taste, color, and a tendency to foam. Although pasteurization and homogenization do not in themselves add chemical contaminants, it is very rare to find pasteurized or homogenized milk that has not been fortified.

SAFE ALTERNATIVES
Drink "raw" milk, the unprocessed liquid direct from the cow or goat. It is graded according to levels of bacteria found in the milk. "Grade A" milk has the lowest bacteria count and in addition cannot, by law, contain detectable antibiotic residue. "Certified milk—raw" means that the milk conforms to the latest requirements of the American Association of Medical Milk Commissions. Since pesticides are stored in milk fat, it follows that low-fat or nonfat milk would contain lower levels of them.

If possible, buy milk in glass bottles. Some local dairies will deliver milk in glass bottles to your door. Milk in paper cartons would be a second choice.

Look for unfortified milk. Fortified milk will list vitamin A or vitamin D on the label. Raw milk, buttermilk, cream, and half-and-half are usually not fortified, and you may be able to get unfortified whole, low-fat, and nonfat milk from your local dairy.

Try soy milk, which can be made from organic soybeans.

Brand Name/*Mail Order*
Milk is sold regionally. Check with your natural-foods store for the brand of raw milk sold in your area, and for soy milk.

See also Food.

MOISTURIZERS

See Lotions, Creams, & Moisturizers.

MOLD AND MILDEW CLEANERS

Aerosol propellants; formaldehyde; fragrance; isopropyl alcohol; kerosene; pentachlorophenol; phenol.

"DANGER: Eye irritant. Keep out of reach of children. Use only in well-ventilated area."

SAFE ALTERNATIVES
Do-It-Yourself
• Keep areas dry and light. Never leave wet or damp fabric lying around.
• Allow room for air to circulate behind furniture that is right against the wall to help keep that area dry.
• Place a piece of charcoal in bookcases to help absorb dampness. If pages in a book have become damp, dry them by dusting the pages lightly with cornstarch, leaving it on until the moisture is absorbed, and then brushing off.
• Clean areas with a solution of borax and water.

• Clean areas with an aqueous solution of benzalkonium chloride 1:750 (brand name Zephirin, usually used for medical purposes).

See also Cleaning Products.

MOSQUITO NETTING

Plastics (polyester, nylon).

SAFE ALTERNATIVES
Brand Name/*Mail Order*
Order cotton mosquito netting by mail.

A *Heavenly Hammocks.* Cotton mosquito netting.

See also Textiles.

MOUTHWASH

Aerosol propellants; ammonia; colors; cresol; ethanol; flavors; formaldehyde; glycols; hydrogen peroxide; phenol.

SAFE ALTERNATIVES
Instead of using mouthwash, prevent bad breath with good dental hygiene, including regular brushing and flossing.

Brand Name/*Mail Order*
A Aubrey Organics Natural Mint Mouthwash (Aubrey Organics).

A Weleda Mouthwash Concentrate (Weleda). *Weleda, Wholesome Paks.*

B Tom's Natural Mouthwash (Tom's of Maine). *Kennedy's Natural Foods, Walnut Acres.*

Do-It-Yourself
• Use plain warm water to rinse food and loose debris from your mouth.
• Use 1 teaspoon baking soda in 1 glass pure water.

• Use sage, birch, or mint tea.
• Use warm salt water.
• Dissolve 7/8 teaspoon salt into 1 pint warm water.
• Use 1/2 teaspoon baking soda and 1/2 teaspoon salt in 1 pint warm water.
• Add 1/2 teaspoon essential oil of peppermint to 1 quart of water in a 2-quart bottle. Shake the bottle every other minute for 15 minutes. Let the mixture sit, covered, for 12 hours or longer, then filter through wet filter paper. Dissolve 1 teaspoon salt and 1/2 teaspoon baking soda into the peppermint water.

See also Beauty Products.

MUSTARD

Benzyl alcohol/sodium benzoate; EDTA; flavors.

SAFE ALTERNATIVES
Plain mustard is usually free of additives, but beware of flavored gourmet mustards, which often contain them.

Brand Name/*Mail Order*
B *Culpeper.* Several varieties made in England "without added color or preservatives."

B Eden Mustards (Eden Foods). *Erewhon Mail Order.*

B Featherweight Prepared Mustard (Chicago Dietetic Supply). *Chicago Dietetic Supply, Kennedy's Natural Foods.*

B French's Mustard (R. T. French Co.).

B Goldrush Mustard (Goldrush Enterprises).

B Grey Poupon Dijon Mustard (Heublein).

B Gulden's Spicy Brown Mustard (American Home Foods).

B Hain Naturals Stoneground Mustard (Hain Pure Food Co.). *Kennedy's Natural Foods.*

B Health Valley Stone Ground Mustard (Health Valley Natural Foods). *Kennedy's Natural Foods.*

B Morehouse Mustard (Morehouse Foods).

B Pure & Simple Mustard (Pure Sales).

B Westbrae Stoneground Mustard (Westbrae Natural Foods). *Walnut Acres.*

See also Food.

N

NAIL POLISH

Colors; ethanol; formaldehyde; glycols; hexane; phenol; plastics; toluene; xylene.

SAFE ALTERNATIVES
Brand Name/*Mail Order*
C P-Shine (P-Shine). A Japanese system that uses creams and powders to buff nails to a shine. Available at Neiman-Marcus and other fine department stores.

Do-It-Yourself
• Mix ¼ teaspoon powdered dried henna with enough water to produce a paste. Rub into the nails and allow to dry. Rinse, pat dry, and buff to desired shade.

See also Beauty Products.

NAPKINS

See Paper Napkins & Towels and Table Linens.

NUT BUTTERS

See Peanut Butter & Nut Butters.

NUTS & SEEDS

BHA/BHT; colors; glycerin; pesticide residues.

SAFE ALTERNATIVES
Avoid red pistachios and pecans, which are colored with coal-tar dyes.

Sometimes ethylene gas is used to loosen nuts to make them easier to shell; if the nuts seem to practically fall out of their shells, they probably have been so treated. To make untreated nuts easier to shell, warm them in the oven for a few minutes to dry them out.

Brand Name/*Mail Order*
Buy nuts and seeds (walnuts, peanuts, pumpkin seeds, sunflower seeds) in the shell, or buy unroasted and unsalted shelled nuts and seeds from your natural-foods store.

A *Gramma Gregg's Enterprises.* Chestnuts.

A *Jardine Ranch.* Almonds and walnuts.

A   Shiloh Farms Nuts & Seeds (Shiloh Farms). Peanuts and pecans; pumpkin, sesame, and sunflower seeds.

AB *Colvada Date Co.* Almonds, Brazil nuts, cashews, filberts, peanuts, pecans, pignolias, pistachios, pumpkin and sunflower seeds, and English walnuts.

AB *Deer Valley Farm.* Shelled and unshelled almonds, Brazil nuts, cashews, peanuts, pistachios, filberts, macadamia nuts, pecans, pine nuts, and walnuts. Also pumpkin, sesame, and sunflower seeds.

AB *Jaffe Bros.* Unfumigated shelled and unshelled almonds, peanuts, cashews, pecans, walnuts, and macadamias; also sunflower and sesame seeds.

AB *Kennedy's Natural Foods.* Raw and roasted almonds, Brazil nuts, cashews, filberts, peanuts, pistachios, pecans, pine nuts, and walnuts. Also alfalfa, chia, pumpkin, sesame, and sunflower seeds.

AB *Timber Crest Farms.* Almonds, Brazil nuts, and filberts.

B   *Erewhon Mail Order.* Raw shelled almonds, cashews, filberts, peanuts, pecans, pistachios, pine nuts, dried chestnuts, walnuts, and pumpkin and sesame seeds. Also tamari-roasted nuts and nut mixes.

B   *Walnut Acres.* Shelled and dry-roasted nuts.

See also Food and Peanut Butter & Nut Butters.

OILS

BHA/BHT; EDTA; hexane residues; pesticide residues; sulphur compounds.

Most common oils found in supermarkets have been solvent extracted—extracted with hexane, a petrochemical solvent. They have then been bleached, filtered, and deodorized into bland oil, each variety virtually indistinguishable from the others.

SAFE ALTERNATIVES

Purchase unrefined "pressed" or "expeller pressed" oils, squeezed from vegetables, nuts, and seeds by a mechanical process that does not use chemicals. These oils retain colors, flavors, and aromas from the original sources, so take care to use an oil compatible with whatever food it is being prepared with. Only seven types of these *unrefined* oils are available: corn, peanut, safflower, sesame, sunflower, soy, and olive.

Pressed olive oils are designated as "extra virgin" (from the very first pressing) or "virgin" (from the next pressing). "Pure" olive oil has been solvent extracted from either the pit or the remaining fruit pulp.

Beware of labels that say "cold-pressed." This has become meaningless health-food-store jargon with no legal definition. Often cold-pressed oils are solvent extracted, and should be avoided.

Brand Name/*Mail Order*

If you prefer a refined oil, choose one with "No Preservatives" on the label.

The brands listed below can be found in natural-foods stores and supermarkets. Only 3 brands of olive oil are recommended, since they are the only ones you are likely to come across that are organic. (In researching this book, as many as 26 kinds of nonorganic virgin and extra-virgin olive oil could be found in a single store.)

A *Jaffe Bros.* Cold-pressed olive and sesame oils.

A Sciabica Pure Virgin Olive Oil (Nick Sciabica & Sons). "Cold pressed and unrefined."

A Zorba Olive Oil (NEOPC).

B Arrowhead Mills Oils (Arrowhead Mills). "Unrefined." *Kennedy's Natural Foods, Shiloh Farms.*

B Belle Maison Grapeseed Oil (Belle Maison).

B Eden Oils (Eden Foods).

B Erewhon Oils (Erewhon). "Expeller-pressed, unfiltered, unrefined." *Erewhon Mail Order.*

B Hain Cold Pressed Oils (Hain Pure Food Co.). "Pure cold pressed." Expelled "by mechanical pressure, without using chemicals." *Deer Valley Farm, Kennedy's Natural Foods, Penn Herb Co.*

B Healthway Cold Pressed Oils (Healthway).

B Hollywood Cold Pressed Oils (Hollywood Health Foods).

B Walnut Acres Cold Pressed Oils (Walnut Acres). "All our oils are pressed only. No chemical solvents ever used." *Walnut Acres.*

B Westbrae Oils (Westbrae Natural Foods).

See also Food.

OLIVES

Pesticide residues.

SAFE ALTERNATIVES
Brand Name/*Mail Order*

Olives are generally free of additives, but most are packed in leaded cans. Choose a brand from your supermarket or natural-foods store packed in a glass jar or unleaded can.

A *Jaffe Bros.* Green ripe olives cured with only water and salt.

A *Leon R. Horsted.* Tree-ripened olives.

A Old Rancher's California Tree-Ripened Olives (Old Rancher's Co.). *Williams-Sonoma.*

B Adam's Olive Ranch Home-Cured Italian Style Spiced Olives (Adam's Olive Ranch).

B Bonnie Hubbard Spanish Olives (United Grocers).

B Co-op Ripe Black Olives (Universal Co-operatives). Unleaded can.

B "Homegrown" Ranch Style Olives (M. W. Armstrong-Lindsay).

B Marin Brand Marinated Inverno Olives (Marin Food Specialties).

B Old Monk Ripe Black Olives (Dolefam Corp.). Unleaded can. *Williams-Sonoma.*

B Star Spanish Olives (A. Giurlani & Bro.)

B Westbrae Natural Sicilian Style Olives (Westbrae Natural Foods).

See also Food and Produce.

OVEN CLEANERS

Aerosol propellants; detergents; fragrance (particularly lemon).

"DANGER: May cause burns to skin and eyes. Avoid inhaling vapors."

SAFE ALTERNATIVES

Prevent spills by cooking food in proper-sized containers. In addition, use aluminum oven liners or else line the bottom of the oven with aluminum foil to catch spills. Clean your oven as soon as food is spilled instead of waiting for accidents to bake on and become more difficult to remove.

Beware of brands advertising "no fumes." While it is true that these products have no *aerosol* fumes, they are still strong-smelling substances that require excellent ventilation if used at all.

Do-It-Yourself

• Use scouring powder and steel-wool pads.
• Use washing soda.
• Sprinkle a small amount of water in oven, then sprinkle on a large amount of baking soda. Use steel-wool pads and more water to loosen dirty areas. Wipe with a sponge.
• Mix 1 cup sodium perborate, ½ cup soda ash, ½ teaspoon TSP, and 2 tablespoons powdered soap. Apply with a damp sponge, let sit for an hour or 2, then rinse with clear water.

See also Cleaning Products.

P

PAINT

Aerosol propellants; ammonia; ethanol; formaldehyde; glycols; kerosene; lead; pentachlorophenol; phenol; plastics (acrylic, latex, phenol-formaldehyde resin, polyester, polyurethane, tetrafluoroethylene); trichloroethylene.

A Johns Hopkins University study found over 300 toxic chemicals and 150 carcinogens that may be present in paint.

SAFE ALTERNATIVES

Use old-fashioned, limestone-based whitewash (instructions on making it can be found in the Do-It-Yourself section below).

Use casein-based "milk paint," the most odorless commercial paint available. (Milk paint may tend to mold in damp locations such as kitchens or bathrooms.)

Use water-based latex paints, choosing a custom-mixed color to avoid the tetrafluoroethylene plastic in premixed shades. Odor can be reduced by adding one pound of baking soda, more or less, to each can of paint, stirring and adding until bubbling stops. Experiment for yourself—results can vary from excellent odor reduction to paint that will not stick on walls! Another way to help remove the smell of new paint is to put a bucket of warm water with a handful of hay in the room overnight.

If possible, have painting done professionally, or wear appropriate protection devices (available at paint and hardware stores) while doing it yourself. Ideally, do not occupy the newly painted area until paint is completely dry and odorless, a time period that will vary depending on the amount of ventilation and on weather conditions. Generally, water-based paints will be odor-free within two weeks. Paint during a warm, dry season, to encourage quick drying and so that windows can be left wide open to provide constant ventilation. As an alternative, close up a painted room and keep it well heated, airing occasionally.

Use oil-base paints with caution. Though ultimately they provide a harder, more durable, and more vapor-proof finish that will need repainting less often than will other types of paint, they are very toxic to apply and take months to become completely odorless. Once completely dry, however, oil-base paints are excellent. Do not use "low odor" varieties, as these are just as toxic, without the warning smell.

Brand Name/*Mail Order*
A Old-Fashioned Milk Paint (The Old-Fashioned Milk Paint Co.). *The Old-Fashioned Milk Paint Co., Shaker Workshops West.*

Do-It-Yourself

Whitewash
Apply in very thin coats to a damp surface so the wash will dry gradually. For best results, apply the wash so thin that you can see through it while it is wet.

• For wood, glass, or metal: Dissolve 15 pounds salt or 5 pounds dry calcium chloride in 5 gallons water. In a separate container, soak 50 pounds of hydrated lime in 6 gallons of water. Combine the two mixtures thoroughly and thin with plain water to the consistency of whole milk. Makes a little over 10 gallons.

• For masonry only (brickwork, concrete, cinder block, stone masonry, stucco): Mix 25 pounds white portland cement and 25 pounds hydrated lime in 8 gallons of water. Mix thoroughly, then add more water until the mixture is the consistency of heavy cream. Do not mix more than you can use in a few hours. Makes a little over 10 gallons.

• Colored interior whitewash: Stir 5 pounds hydrated lime into 1 gallon water and let sit overnight. Next morning, add powdered pigment to the lime water until you reach the desired shade. Remember that mixture will be further diluted and that paint will dry to a lighter color. Dissolve 1½ pounds salt in 2 quarts warm water and add to the lime mixture. Stir thoroughly and continue to stir every 10 minutes or so while applying the wash. Makes about 2½ gallons. Store leftovers in a tightly closed container.

• Colored exterior whitewash: Stir 5 pounds hydrated lime into 1 gallon water and let sit overnight. Next morning, add powdered pigment to the lime water until you reach the desired shade. Keep in mind further dilution of the mixture and that the paint will dry to a lighter color. Dissolve 1½ pounds salt and 1 pound alum in 3 quarts warm water, add to the lime mixture, and place on stove to heat. In a separate pot, melt 1 pound tallow. When both are hot, stir together and apply while still hot. Makes about 3 gallons.

Milk Paint
• Put 6 ounces hydrated lime into a bucket and add enough milk to make it the thickness of cream (you will need ½ gallon of milk in all). Stir in 4 ounces linseed oil, a little at a time, then add the rest of the milk. Sprinkle 3 pounds finely powdered calcium carbonate over the top and let it sink in before stirring it well into the mixture. Add powdered pigment for color, if desired.

• Pour just enough hot water to instant nonfat dry milk to reconstitute it into a smooth syrup. Add powdered pigment in small amounts until desired shade is reached. Apply to raw wood with a brush or rag while still warm. Will dry to a flat finish, much like latex wall paint.

PAINT REMOVERS

Benzene (now outlawed for this use, but may still be in older products); cresol; ethanol; methylene chloride; paraffin; phenol; toluene.

SAFE ALTERNATIVES
Use various small hand tools (there are over forty different ones to choose from) to scrape or sand the paint off. Local hardware stores offer a selection of hook scrapers, push scrapers, rasps, abrasive blocks, and sandpapers. For large jobs, such as removing old finish from a floor or old paint from a house, the appropriate equipment can be rented, or else professionals can be hired to do the sanding.

Take furniture to be stripped to a commercial paint stripper, listed in the Yellow Pages under "Furniture Stripping." Request that the item be sanded. If chemicals are used, air the item thoroughly before replacing it in the house. The greatest danger from a chemical paint remover is during use and cleanup; once dry, it should be relatively nontoxic.

Brand Name/*Mail Order*
Alkali Paint Removers Without Organic Solvents

B Brookstone Paint Stripper (Brookstone Co.). *Brookstone Co.*

B Peel Away (Macy-Havrda Co.). *Macy-Havrda.*

B Staples Dry Strip Paint Stripper (H. F. Staples & Co.). *Woodcraft.*

Do-It-Yourself
Wear rubber gloves when mixing and using these formulas.

General Removal
• Mix 1 pound TSP into 1 gallon hot water. Mop or brush it on, let it sit for about 30 minutes, then remove the softened paint with a scraper or putty knife.

For Walls
• Mix 1 part TSP with 2 parts calcium carbonate; then add enough water to make a thick paste. Apply a thickness of ⅜ inch to walls with a putty knife or trowel, leave on for about 30 minutes, then scrape off, taking the paint with it. Rinse with plain water.

For Old Brushes
• Mix 4 ounces TSP in 1 quart hot water. Press bristles of brush against the bottom of the can to work the

solution all the way into the brush, separating the bristles as the paint softens, and continuing until all the paint has been removed. Rinse thoroughly with plain water.

• Place brushes in an old saucepan and cover with white vinegar. Bring to a boil, then turn the heat down and simmer for a few minutes. Remove brushes and wash in soap and warm water.

PAINT THINNERS

Toluene; xylene.

SAFE ALTERNATIVES
Use water-base paint that can be thinned and cleaned up with water.

See also Paint.

PAPER NAPKINS & TOWELS

Dyes; formaldehyde.

SAFE ALTERNATIVES
Use cotton or linen towels and napkins.

See also Table Linens and Towels.

PASTA

Pesticide residues.

SAFE ALTERNATIVES
Brand Name/*Mail Order*
Although most have pesticide residues, pastas are generally additive free. Below are listed brands that are organic, whole grain, or for special diets.

Corn
B   Debole's Corn Pastas (DeBoles Nutrition Foods).

B   Westbrae Corn Pastas (Westbrae Natural Foods).

Wheat
A   Chico-San Udon Noodles (Chico-San). *Chico-San.*

A   Deboles Whole Wheat Pastas (DeBoles Nutrition Foods). *Deer Valley Farm.*

A   Eden Pastas (Eden Foods).

A   Erewhon Whole Wheat Pastas (Erewhon). *Erewhon Mail Order, Kennedy's Natural Foods.*

A   *Jaffe Bros.* Whole wheat pasta "made with very thin walls so it cooks more quickly."

A   Sunburst Farms Pastas (Sunburst Farms Natural Foods).

A   *Walnut Acres.*

AB Westbrae Pastas (Westbrae Natural Foods).

B   Johnson's Whole Wheat Pastas (Pure Sales).

B   Roman Meal Natural Foods Multi-Grain Spaghetti (Roman Meal Co.).

Miscellaneous
A   *Special Foods.* Pastas made from white sweet potato, malanga, yam, or cassava flours.

See also Flour and Food.

PEANUT BUTTER & NUT BUTTERS

Hydrogenated oil; pesticide residues; sucrose.

SAFE ALTERNATIVES
Brand Name/*Mail Order*
A   Deaf Smith Peanut Butter (Arrowhead Mills). *Kennedy's Natural Foods, Shiloh Farms.*

A   *Deer Valley Farm.* Peanut butter.

A *Jaffe Bros.* Organic Unsalted Peanut Butter.

A Marantha Almond Butter (Marantha Natural Foods).

A Westbrae Valencia Peanut Butter (Westbrae Natural Foods).

B Adams 100% Natural Peanut Butter (Adams Foods).

B Bread Spread Sesame Tahini (Pure Sales).

B Country Pure Peanut Butter (Safeway Stores).

B East Wind Peanut Butter (East Wind Community).

B Eden Peanut Butter/Sesame Butter (Eden Foods).

B Elam's Natural Peanut Butter With Defatted Wheat Germ (Elam's).

B Erewhon Nut Butters (Erewhon). *Erewhon Mail Order, Kennedy's Natural Foods.*

B Hain Nut Butters (Hain Pure Food Co.). *Kennedy's Natural Foods.*

B Health Valley 100% Natural Peanut Butter (Health Valley Natural Foods).

B Laura Scudder's Old-Fashioned Style Peanut Butter (Pet).

B Marantha Nut Butters (Marantha Natural Foods).

B Protein-Aid Sesame Butter/ Sesame Peanut Butter (International Protein Industries). *Shiloh Farms.*

B Smucker's Natural Peanut Butter (J. M. Smucker Co.).

B Spankey's Nut Butters (Marin Food Specialties).

B Sunburst Farms Peanut Butter (Sunburst Farms Natural Foods).

B *Walnut Acres.* Large variety of nut butters.

B Westbrae Nut Butters (Westbrae Natural Foods).

See also Food and Nuts & Seeds.

PENS & MARKERS

Acetone; ammonia; benzyl alcohol/ sodium benzoate; cresol; ethanol; glycols; naphtha; phenol; toluene; xylene.

SAFE ALTERNATIVES
Use a pencil.

Avoid solvent-base indelible inks in ball-point, fountain, and permanent felt-tipped pens and markers.

Brand Name/*Mail Order*
Art and office-supply stores carry pens and markers with odorless, water-base inks. Not all are alike, but the brands listed below seem to give off the least smell.

Pens

B Ceramicron (Pentel of America). Super-sharp refillable pen.

B Itoya Ceramique (Itoya). Metal ball point.

B Le Pen (Ushida of America Corp.). Fine-line plastic tip.

B Pentel Rolling Writer/Stylo (Pentel of America). Plastic ball tip. *Charette.*

B Pilot Precise Ball Liner/Fineliner/ Razor Point (Pilot Corp. of America). Plastic tip. *Art Brown & Bro., Charette.*

B Silvery Ink (Fisher Pen Co.). Ball point with silver aluminum ink.

B Stylist Fineline (Yasutomo & Co.). Plastic tip. *Charette.*

B Uniball/Micro (Mitsubishi Pencil Co.). Metal ball point. *Art Brown & Bro., Charette.*

Markers

B Illustrator Brush Tip Pens (Illustrator). Medium point.

B Insta-Brush Markers (Yasutomo & Co.). Medium brush tip.

B Marvy Markers (Ushida of America Corp.). Fine- and medium-point felt tips. *Charette.*

B Schwan Stabilayout 38/Stabilo-Pen 68 (Swan Pencil Co.). Wide- and medium-point felt tips. *Art Brown & Bro., Charette.*

PERFUME

See Fragrances.

PERMANENT WAVES

Ammonia; colors; fragrance; glycols; hydrogen peroxide; mineral oil.

SAFE ALTERNATIVES
Consult with your hairdresser to find a style appropriate for the natural wave in your hair or ask for an ammonia-free permanent.

See also Beauty Products.

PESTICIDES

Pesticides.

"CAUTION: Keep out of reach of children. Hazardous if swallowed or absorbed through skin. Do not get on skin, in eyes, or on clothing. Use only when area to be treated is vacated by humans and pets. Avoid breathing of mist. Avoid contact with eyes. Do not smoke while using. Should not be used in homes of the seriously ill or those on medication. Should not be used in homes of pollen-sensitive people or asthmatics."

Pesticides may also contain additives such as kerosene, xylene, nitrosamines, and dioxin as inactive ingredients or impurities.

Pesticides are used in or around 91 percent of all American households. These include insecticides (insect killers), acaricides (mite killers), nematocides (worm killers), herbicides (weed and brush killers), and rodenticides (rodent killers). They are specially formulated to resist natural decomposition processes. When used indoors, protected from sun and wind, they are even more long lasting. Pesticides can remain actively airborne for days or weeks, even up to twenty years.

Home-use pesticides pose a hazard to health from direct inhalation during application and from continued inhalation of residues. When combined, pesticides become even more toxic. Multiple exposures are encountered in homes, offices, public buildings, pets, water, air, and soil. Many pesticides can be stored in body fat and accumulate to toxic levels within the body.

The effects of long-term, low-level exposure to pesticides is not yet known. Infants, children, and adults with certain chronic illnesses are more susceptible to pesticide poisoning than are healthy adults. According to poison-control-center reports on pesticide exposures, 70 percent of the incidents involve children under five years of age. Over half of those who die from pesticide-related incidents are children.

Pesticides are regulated by the federal Insecticide, Fungicide, and Rodenticide Act, last amended by Congress in 1972. This act gives federal control to all pesticide applications and regulates both intrastate and interstate marketing of pesticides.

Since October 1977, the Environmental Protection Agency (EPA) has required extensive laboratory tests for safety at the manufacturer's expense before any new pesticide is allowed on the market. Included must be tests for acute exposure effects, the lethal dose in animals, and chronic exposure tests for carcinogenicity, mutagenicity, teratogenicity, and fertility.

Pesticides that were in use before 1977, however, have not undergone such testing and still continue to be used.

SAFE ALTERNATIVES

If you must use chemical pesticides, take these precautions recommended by the Center for Science in the Public Interest:

Read the label before buying or using pesticides. Use pesticides only for the purpose(s) listed and in the manner directed.

Do not apply more than the specified amount of pesticide. Overdoses can harm you and the environment.

Keep pesticides away from food and dishes.

Keep children and pets away from pesticides and sprayed areas.

Do not smoke while spraying.

Avoid inhalation of pesticides.

Do not spray outdoors on a windy day.

Pesticides that require special protective clothing or equipment should be used only by trained, experienced applicators.

Avoid splashing when mixing pesticides.

Avoid spills and breakage of pesticide containers.

If a pesticide is spilled on skin or clothing, wash with soap and water and change clothing immediately.

Store pesticides under lock in the original containers with proper labels. Never transfer a pesticide to a container, such as a soft drink bottle, that would attract children.

Dispose of empty container safely. Wrap single containers of home-use products in several layers of newspaper, tie securely, and place in a covered trash can. Never burn boxes or sacks. In case of farm or ranch use, single containers may be buried where water supplies will not be contaminated. Dispose of large quantities in special incinerators or special landfills.

Wash with soap and water after using pesticides, and launder clothes before wearing again.

If a pesticide is swallowed, check the label for first-aid treatment. Call or go to the doctor or hospital immediately, keeping the pesticide label with you.

Check out fumigators to make sure they are dependable.

Don't use the house when fumigated. The need to keep the house closed means that the inhabitants will not have enough fresh air. Airing out will simply reduce the effectiveness of the operation.

Try to discourage general use of fogging devices by neighbors or municipal authorities, and if this can't be helped, protect the home by closing doors and intake fans.

Brand Name/*Mail Order*

Safe retail products include herbal repellents (which work well for moths and some other bugs), adhesive pest traps, and ultrasonic pest repellers.

Herbal Repellents

A *Bear Meadow Farm.* Herbal moth and flea repellents.

A *Cedar-Al.* Cedar oil steam distilled from Western Red Cedar Chips.

A *Clear Light Cedar Co.* Cedar needles or cedar and lavender in a bag.

A *The Country Store and Farm.* "Proven herbal" Moth Out.

A *Erlander's Natural Products.* Aromatic cedar shavings.

A *Fluir Herbals.* Mothaway Sachet filled with rosemary, lavender, patacholy leaves, cedar, vetiver, bay leaves, and chamomile.

A *Misty Morning Farm.* Cedar chips.

A Moth-Away Herbal Moth Repellant (Sun-Ray Industries). "An organic compound of natural herbs, spices, and oils. Contains absolutely no poisonous chemicals." *Cuddledown, Garnet Hill, Vermont Country Store.*

A Moth-B-Gone (Heritage House of California). Made from aromatic red cedar. No chemicals added.

A *New Age Creations.* Herbal Moth & Bug Repellant.

A *Overland Sheepskin Co.* Bag filled with hand-gathered, sun-dried cedar needles.

A *Ram Island Farm Herbs.* Sachet bags filled with moth-repelling sweet and bitter herbs.

B Cedarstows (Jokari/US). Made of cedar boards and military-duck canvas with brass fittings. Closet or under-bed models. *Agatha's Cozy Corner, The Sharper Image, Vermont Country Store.*

Adhesive Pest-Traps

B Aeroxon Fly-Catcher (Fr. Kaiser GmbH).

B Black Flag Roach Motel Roach Traps (Boyle-Midway).

B d-Con Roach Traps (d-Con Co./ Sterling Drug). *Walnut Acres.*

B Fly Stik Fly Trap (Farnam Companies).

B Fly Trap Fly Catcher Strip (Willert Home Products).

B Roatel (Fumakilla). *Nigra Enterprises.*

B Stick-A-Roach Roach Glue Traps (J. T. Eaton Co.).

B Stick-Em Rat & Mouse Glue Traps (J. T. Eaton Co.).

Ultrasonic Pest Repellers

B Deci-Mate Ultrasonic Pest Repellers (El Mar Corp.) *The Sharper Image.*

B *J S & A.* Ultrasonic Bug Zapper.

PESTICIDES

Do-It-Yourself

Maintain your home or workspace so it is not attractive to pests. Keep living areas clean, and especially eliminate food crumbs that attract pests indoors. Empty garbage cans frequently. Remove indoor water sources by repairing leaky faucets, pipes, and clogged drains. Remove clutter (papers, boxes, and the like) that provide shelter. Examine your building structure and fill holes and cracks that provide entry points for pests.

Ants

- Keep things clean; don't leave any crumbs or garbage around.
- Wipe up a line of ants with a wet sponge so that other ants will not follow. Wipe up any stray ants that may be out looking for food for others.
- Sprinkle powdered red chili pepper, paprika, dried peppermint, or borax where ants are coming in.
- Plant mint around the outside of the house to discourage ants from entering.

Beetles

- Put a bay leaf in each container of cereal, crackers, cookies, flour, and other grain products.
- Kill them manually when you see them.
- Store flour and grains in a cool cabinet, or preferably in the refrigerator. This will also help keep whole grains and whole-grain flour fresh.

Cockroaches

- Mix equal parts powdered oatmeal or flour with plaster of paris. Spread on the floor of infested area.

- Mix equal parts baking soda and powdered sugar. Spread around infested area.
- Mix by stirring and sifting 1 ounce TSP, 6 ounces borax, 4 ounces granulated sugar, and 8 ounces flour. Spread on the floor of infested area. Repeat after 4 days and again after 2 weeks to kill newly hatched roaches.
- Mix 2 tablespoons flour, 1 tablespoon cocoa powder, and 4 tablespoons borax. Spread around infested area.
- Use cucumber rinds in infested area.
- Use bay leaves in infested area.
- Trap them: Set an uncapped 1-quart Mason jar upright, with grease on the inside of the neck and a piece of banana inside for bait. Place a tongue depressor against the side of the jar so they can walk up the "plank" and fall, trapped, into the jar.

Fleas

- Feed your pet brewer's yeast by mixing the powdered form with his food or giving him tablets.

Flies

- Hang clusters of cloves in a room.
- Make flypaper by boiling sugar, corn syrup, and water together and placing mixture onto brown paper.
- Use a fly swatter.
- Put screens on windows and doors.
- Scratch the skin of an orange and leave it out; the citrus oil released will repel flies.

Mosquitoes

- Put screens on windows and doors.
- When you see them sitting on walls at night, suction them up with the long attachment on the vacuum cleaner.

Moths

• Don't worry about moths if you can see them. The moths that cause damage are a specific variety of clothes moth that are too small to notice. It is the larvae of these moths that eat fabric.

• Kill moth eggs before they hatch by placing items in the sun or by running the dry item through a warm clothes dryer. This should be done when the item is first purchased and at periodic intervals while being stored.

• Protect uninfested items by storing them in airtight containers, such as a paper packages or cardboard boxes, with all edges carefully sealed with paper tape.

• Store items in a clean condition; moth larvae especially love areas soiled with food stains.

• Washing destroys all forms of the moth.

• Make sachets of dried lavender or equal parts of dried rosemary and mint with cotton, linen, or silk, and place into drawers and closets.

• Put dried tobacco in closet or chest.

• Use whole peppercorns.

• Use cedar oil or chips.

Rats & Mice

• Use mousetraps.

• Get a cat.

• Starve them by making sure no food is left in open places (including food in unopened cardboard containers). Keep garbage in tightly covered metal containers.

• Remove their shelter by keeping storage spaces orderly, and keeping stored items off the floor. Seal holes around the bottom of walls.

• Keep them out of the house by closing any holes in exterior walls and keeping doors closed.

• Make a mixture of 1 part plaster of paris and 1 part flour with a little sugar and cocoa powder added and sprinkle where rats and mice will find it.

Silverfish

• Make a trap out of an empty cold-cream jar without a lid. Put ½ teaspoon flour inside for bait and run a piece of adhesive tape (sticky side down) at an angle up the side so they can climb up and fall, trapped, inside.

Spider Mites

• Put fresh banana peels in infested areas. Keep adding fresh peels to the old ones to repel all the mites.

• Mix 4 cups wheat flour and ½ cup buttermilk into 5 gallons water. Spray on plants to get rid of mites.

Termites

• Use heat. Apply 140° F for 10 minutes with a heat lamp.

• Use copper chromate or cryolite or other nonvolatile insecticide.

• Keep area very dry.

Further information on alternatives to chemical pesticides for both indoor and outdoor pest management can be obtained from the Bio-Integral Resource Center (1307 Acton St., Berkeley, CA 94706, phone 415/524-2567). They have many publications, for both professionals and lay people, covering alternatives for all types of pest problems.

PETROLEUM JELLY

Petroleum jelly is generally considered to be harmless; nevertheless, it is a petrochemical derivative and should be approached with caution by anyone who is sensitive.

SAFE ALTERNATIVES
Brand Name/*Mail Order*
Buy petroleum-free "petroleum jelly" at natural-foods stores.
A Unpetroleum Jelly (Pure Body Creations).

See also Beauty Products.

PICKLES

Benzyl alcohol/sodium benzoate; colors; EDTA; sulphur compounds; sucrose.

SAFE ALTERNATIVES
Brand Name/*Mail Order*
Natural-foods stores and supermarkets carry additive-free pickles.

A Bolinas Foods Dill Pickles (Bolinas Foods).

A Chico-San Yamaki Daikon Radish Pickles (Chico-San). *Chico-San.*

A Mrs. Woods' Pickles (John Woods Products). *Kennedy's Natural Foods.*

A Walnut Acres Dilled Zucchini Spears. (Walnut Acres). *Walnut Acres.*

B Dessaux Cornichons (Dessaux Fils).

B Erewhon Pickles (Erewhon).

B Star Imported Pickled Onions (A. Giurlani & Bro.).

B Westbrae Honey-Sweetened Pickle Relish/Home-Style Dill Pickles (Westbrae Natural Foods).

C Del Monte Pickles (Del Monte Corp.).

See also Food.

PIES

Benzyl alcohol/sodium benzoate; colors; flavors; hydrogenated oil; sucrose.

SAFE ALTERNATIVES
Brand Name/*Mail Order*
A *Deer Valley Farm.* Honey-sweetened, whole-grain fruit pies.

B Natural Nectar Frozen Pies (Natural Nectar Products Corp.).

PILLOWS

Plastics (polyester, polyurethane).

SAFE ALTERNATIVES
Brand Name/*Mail Order*
Purchase ready-made pillows covered with 100-percent cotton ticking and filled with cotton batting, down or feathers, kapok, or buckwheat hulls from department or furniture stores, or by mail. Pillows filled with down and feathers are available in varying proportions: all down, all feather, or mixtures of the two. The larger the percentage of feathers in a pillow, the firmer it will be.

A *Agatha's Cozy Corner.* Goose down or two down/feather mixtures.

A *Cuddledown.* Goose down and down/feather. They also have a unique design with a firm feather core surrounded by soft down.

A *Dona Shrier.* Organic cotton batting covered with bleached white cotton muslin prewashed in baking soda.

A   *Erlander's Natural Products.* Kapok. Cotton cover "prewashed with pure soda ash plus baking soda." Also kits for making cotton-filled pillows and cotton pillow ticks.

A   *Essential Alternatives.* Buckwheat hulls, down/feather.

A   *Eugene Trading Co.* Kapok or buckwheat hull pillows.

A   *The Futon Shop.* Goose-down/feather and buckwheat hull.

A   *Garnet Hill.* Goose down.

A   *Great Lakes Futons.* Buckwheat hulls.

A   *Janice Corp.* Cotton cover prewashed in baking soda and vinegar. Filled with 100% cotton batting "garnetted without oil or pesticides."

A   *KB Cotton Pillow Co.* Pillows in 100% cotton; cotton ticking prewashed in baking soda.

A   *Limericks Linens.* Duck and goose down or feathers. Also white cotton pillow ticks.

A   *Northwest Futon Co.* Buckwheat hull pillows.

A   *Peach Blossom Futon.* "Pure, white, odorless, long staple fibre cotton . . . free of all linters, seeds, dust, and allergy-producing oils."

A   *Vermont Country Store.* White goose down, feather, or wool. Also cotton damask pillow covers from Belgium.

A   *Xhaxhi.* Kapok, cotton, buckwheat hulls.

AB *New Moon.* Buckwheat hull, lambswool, or down pillows.

B   *Dreamy Down Fashions.* Goose down or 90% feathers/10% down.

B   *Euroquilt.* Medium-fill white goose-down pillows.

B   *Feathered Friends.* All-down and several firmnesses of down/feather blends.

B   *J. Schachter.* Goose down, down/feather.

B   *Quiltessence.* Goose down or 50/50 down and feathers.

B   *Warm Things.* Goose down, duck down, or a 50/50 combination.

Do-It-Yourself
Make your own pillows by stuffing prewashed cotton pillow ticks with prewashed cotton towels, diapers, thermal blankets, or cotton or wool batting. To stuff with batting, simply unroll batting, fold into pillow shape, and stitch around the edges to hold batting in shape.

See also Batting and Textiles.

PLACEMATS

See Table Linens.

POPSICLES

Colors; flavors; sucrose.

SAFE ALTERNATIVES
Brand Name/*Mail Order*
Additive-free popsicles are sold at natural-foods stores and supermarkets.

B C & W Natural Fruit Pops (California & Washington). *Shiloh Farms.*

B Garden of Eatin' Frozen Joy (Garden of Eatin').

B Knudsen Real Fruit Bars (Knudsen Corp.).

B Natural Nectar Freeze Bars (Natural Nectar Products Corp.).

C Minute Maid Orange Juice Bars (The Coca-Cola Co.).

C Popsicle Natural Popsicles (Popsicle Industries).

C Shamitoff's Natural Fruit Bars (Shamitoff Foods).

C Welch's Grape Juice Bars (Tomorrow Products).

Do-It-Yourself
Freeze fruit juice in paper cups. When juice becomes slushy, insert a wooden stick. Freeze solid, peel paper off, and eat.

See also Food and Juices & Fruit Drinks.

POTHOLDERS

Dyes; plastic (polyester).

Old potholders lying around your house may contain asbestos; new ones do not.

SAFE ALTERNATIVES
Brand Name/*Mail Order*
Buy cotton potholders at hardware, cookware and variety stores.

A *Janice Corp.* Potholders made from prewashed, undyed cotton fabric, stuffed with pure cotton batting.

B Ritz Potholders (John Ritzenthaler Co.). Thick cotton terrycloth potholders.

Do-It-Yourself
Sew together several thicknesses of cotton terrycloth towels.

See also Textiles and Towels.

POULTRY

See Meat & Poultry.

PRESERVES

See Jams, Jellies, & Preserves.

PRINTER'S INK

Ammonia; benzyl alcohol; cresol; ethanol; formaldehyde; glycerin; naphtha; phenol; plastic (acrylonitrile); toluene; xylene.

Commercial inks continuously give off fumes as they dry on the printed page. Daily newspapers are notorious for this problem since they are printed with a particularly odiferous ink and are delivered within hours of printing. Inexpensive paperback books are printed with a similar type of ink. When completely dry, inks become relatively inert; but some inks dry instantly, while others take years.

SAFE ALTERNATIVES
Accelerate the drying process by airing printed material or placing it in the sun for a few hours, if possible.

To minimize inhalation of vapors, read next to an open window or outdoors, or else sitting next to an air filter, which can be aimed either toward your face or between your nose and the reading matter.

Use the public library system. It's free, conserves resources, and offers lots of aired-out books, magazines, and newspapers to read.

To avoid printer's ink altogether, listen to books on cassette tapes. Look for tape books at your local bookstore or rent tape cassettes (over 700 titles) from *Books on Tape*. State libraries sometimes offer taped books as well, but often these can be used only with a note from your doctor. (Although tapes contain plastic, this is less toxic than printer's ink.)

To block fumes, place the glass from a picture-frame over the book while reading, or place the entire book in a reading box, a specially designed airtight box with a glass top. A variety of different devices can be used to turn pages within the box, such as cotton gloves attached through the sides, or sticks inserted through the slots.

Brand Name/*Mail Order*

Reading Boxes
A *Safe Haven.* Reading boxes with special vacuum attachments in various sizes: portable lap-size; giant newspaper-size; and a desktop size large enough to be used by hyperactive children (hyperactivity may be caused by fumes from the print). Made of lightweight aluminum with a white, baked enamel finish, welded seams, tempered glass, and cotton or natural chamois cuffs.

A *Webb Metals.* Galvanized-steel reading boxes, each with a charcoal-filtered vent. Comes with cotton cuffs or gloves. Will also make boxes in custom sizes to accommodate such things as electric typewriters.

Do-It-Yourself

Reading Boxes
• Buy a picture-frame of wood or metal (with a glass insert) in the desired size. Build a box of cardboard that is open at the top, and cut a small hinging door on one side. If necessary, fasten edges with glue or foil tape. Wrap the entire box with aluminum foil or other nontoxic covering, if you like. Place book inside, cover the open top with picture frame, and read through the glass. Turn pages through the side door. Alternately, purchase a picture frame to cover an existing box.
• Turn a large aquarium on its side and cover the open end with a cotton towel. Read through the glass and turn pages by reaching under the towel.
• To read a paperback book while lying down, or if you need a more mobile solution when you can't bring your reading box along, put the book in a cellophane bag and read through the cellophane.

See also Air and Copy Machines.

PRODUCE

Colors; detergent residues; mineral oil; paraffin; pesticide residues; phenol; plastic residues; sulfur compounds.

SAFE ALTERNATIVES
Buy certified organically grown produce, that is certain to have been grown by true organic methods. The produce offered at natural-foods stores may be labeled with a variety of descriptive terms, some of which may be misleading.

"Certified Organically Grown"

Grown by organic methods and certified by an association of organic growers (such as California Certified Organic Farmers) who verify that member farms meet particular criteria. The name of the certifying organization should accompany this label. Some organizations have logos that are easy to recognize from store to store.

"Organically Grown" or "Organic"

Generally meaningless, unless the store has its own definition posted near the produce bin. Sometimes this term is used by stores that have signed statements from the grower, describing the precise growing practices. In these cases, the store must take the grower's word as truth, for there is neither time nor money to send knowledgable people to inspect the farms, run pesticide tests, or perform all the other necessaries to certify the produce.

"Represented" or "Claimed Organic"

Generally used when the farmer has told the store that the produce is organic, but nobody has checked on it. Usually no signed statement of growing practices has been submitted.

"Ecologic"

Grown on a farm that may be in the process of converting to organic methods, or on one using Integrated Pest Management (whereby a small amount of pesticides may be used if necessary, but only as a last resort).

"Unsprayed"

Not sprayed with pesticides. Also usually not colored, gassed, or waxed, but probably not from a farm with a soil-building program, nor especially carefully harvested and packaged.

Your natural-foods store should provide some explanation of what its terms mean, since only three states (California, Oregon, and Maine) have actual legal definitions. If you don't see adequate labeling, ask! Find out how insects, weeds, and diseases are controlled and what fertilizers are used. Become acquainted with the produce buyer and encourage informative labeling and responsible buying practices.

Organic produce is often recognizable by how it looks. Fruits and vegetables are often smaller than their chemicalized siblings, slightly misshapen, and not of uniform color. That tiny, slightly squashed looking orange that's a little green around the edges will probably be the sweetest, juiciest you have ever eaten.

Try to avoid imported foods; they may have been sprayed with pesticides long since banned in the United States as too dangerous, and have certainly been fumigated before being allowed into the country (even fruits from Hawaii are fumigated before allowed to enter the mainland). Coffee, cocoa, papayas, mangos, guavas, pineapples, bananas, and other tropical fruits fall into this category.

Avoid produce that has been artificially dyed: some oranges (all Florida citrus sold before January); some red "new" potatoes (regular potatoes dyed to resemble the more expensive variety); some red "yams" (really altered sweet potatoes). How to tell if they're dyed? It is often not possible, but one is more likely to get dyed produce from a supermarket than from a natural-foods store.

Avoid potatoes and onions that have been treated with maleic hydrazide, a potential human carcinogen. Treated potatoes and onions tend to sprout on the inside instead of the outside, so if you slice one open and see it sprouting or beginning to brown, you know it has been treated. Test a potato and an onion from the store you regularly buy from by keeping it several weeks and then slicing it open when you see no exterior signs of sprouting. You can assume that store's potatoes and onions to be consistent—one way or another—since grocers repeatedly buy from the same source.

Buy tomatoes, bananas, oranges, lemons, cantaloupes, persimmons, and pears in season only, as out of season they are likely to be ripened artificially with ethylene gas.

Remove peels from produce that may be coated with paraffin: carrots, oranges, lemons, limes, apples, pears, plums, peaches, melons, parsnips, eggplants, summer squash, potatoes, tomatoes, green peppers, rutabagas, turnips, cucumbers, grapefruits, and tangerines. This will help to some degree, but paraffin cannot be completely removed since the wax sticks to cut surfaces. In addition to its carcinogenic impurities, paraffin food-coatings entrap pesticide, dye, and gas residues.

Eat foods that are less likely to be contaminated by pesticide sprays: carrots, white potatoes, beets, turnips, celery root, radishes, onions, parsnips, mushrooms, sweet potatoes, and yams.

Remove pesticide residues as much as possible. (Manufacturers of the following methods *claim* them to be effective.)

• Soak produce for 5 minutes in 1 gallon pure water mixed with 1 tablespoon sodium hexametaphosphate.

• Use Clean Green Veggie Bath (Sydnor Research Associates), an old Swedish formula made from water, citric acid, and an "organic cleansing agent" that claims to remove solubilizing pesticide residues, dirt, grime, germs, bacteria and viruses, and odor absorbed from other foods in storage; it also acts as an antibrowning agent. Mill Creek Old-Fashioned Pure Castile Soap (Mill Creek Natural Products) also claims in ads to "wash veggies of spray so no chemicals stay."

Note: These methods might remove the pesticide *residues* on the *outside* of the fruit or vegetable. Produce, however, is sprayed repeatedly and nothing can remove the pesticides inside.

Encourage your local markets to furnish paper instead of plastic bags to hold your selected produce in.

Brand Name/*Mail Order*

All mail-order sources listed have produce available only *seasonally*, and may require ordering in advance.

A *Ahlers Organic Date & Grapefruit Garden.* White marsh seedless grapefruit.

A Barbara's Organic Mashed Potatoes (Barbara's Bakery). *Kennedy's Natural Foods.*

A Cascadian Farm Frozen Strawberries (Cascadian Farm).

A *Effie May Organic Fruits & Vegetables.* Good variety of fruits and vegetables from an organic farm that "began more than 10 years ago, on soil that had not been cultivated for almost 50 years."

A *George W. Park Seed Co.* Mushroom farm to grow 5 weeks worth of mushrooms indoors in your own home.

A *Kennedy's Natural Foods.* Large selection of seasonally available produce. Also some frozen produce.

A *Lee's Fruit Co.* Oranges and grapefruits with a "substantially higher food content in minerals and vitamins" due to use of sea solids to replace minerals in the soil.

A *Quiet Meadow Farm.* Cherries, peaches, apricots, plums, and grapes.

A *Rebecca Lang.* Blueberries.

A Shiloh Farms Frozen Fruits & Vegetables (Shiloh Farms). *Shiloh Farms.*

A *Starr Organic Produce.* Bananas, avocado, papaya, oranges, tangelos, and grapefruit.

A *Valley Cove Ranch.* All varieties of citrus, pomegranates, and avocados. Organically grown using "pure mountain water. Our fruit is not dyed or gassed, and no chemical processing is used in our packing operation, nor are the cartons chemically treated."

A *W. Atlee Burpee Co.* Mushroom farm to grow about 3 months worth of mushrooms indoors in your own home.

A *Walnut Acres.* Potatoes, beets, carrots, and onions. Also other vegetables, beans, and fruits packed in lead-free cans.

A Yahtae Farm Frozen Blackberries (Yahtae Farm).

Do-It-Yourself

Grow your own produce without synthetic fertilizers or pesticides.

A highly nutritious organic food you can easily grow yourself is sprouts. Simply soak seeds overnight, then drain and place in a wide-mouth jar with cheesecloth fixed over the top with rubber bands (or you can buy sprouting kits at your natural-foods store). Rinse and drain several times a day and watch your sprouts grow.

Many different types of seeds can be used. Try alfalfa, cabbage, clover, radish, or sunflower seeds; beans such as black-eyed peas, garbanzos, mung beans, soy beans, or lentils; or even whole corn and wheat berries. Each has its own distinct flavor. Choose nonchemically treated seeds from your natural-foods store or order them by mail from *Deer Valley Farm, Diamond K Enterprises, Earthsong Herb Shop, Erewhon Mail Order, Jaffe Bros., Nichols Garden Nursery, Pure Planet Products, Walnut Acres,* or *West Wind Farm.*

See also Food.

PUDDING

Colors; flavors; pesticide residues; sucrose.

SAFE ALTERNATIVES
Brand Name/*Mail Order*

B Hain Pudding Dessert Mixes (Hain Pure Food Co.).

B *Walnut Acres.* Cornstarch-free Malty Carob Pudding Mix.

See also Food.

Q

QUILTS

See Comforters & Quilts.

R

RANGES

See Appliances.

READING BOXES

See Printer's Ink.

REFRIGERATORS

See Appliances.

RICE SYRUP

See Sugar.

ROOFING

The most harmful of all roofing materials is tar. Not only is it especially noxious during installation, it continues to release fumes for long periods, especially in warm weather.

SAFE ALTERNATIVES
Any other type of roofing is accept-

able that is compatible with your building structure. If you already have a tar roof and it needs to be re-tarred, try one of the new asphalt-free "rubber" roofs, made of sheets of synthetic rubber or plastic that can be heat-welded, nailed, or glued into place. Installation costs two to three times more than a tar roof, but these rubber roofs are extremely durable and could last up to five times longer than tar.

Brand Name/*Mail Order*
There are many brands of rubber roofs. Ask your local roofing contractor, or call the manufacturer of the brand listed below for a dealer near you.

Rubber Roofs
C Whaleskin (Kelley Energy Systems).

RUG, CARPET, & UPHOLSTERY SHAMPOO

Aerosol propellants; ammonia; colors; detergents; dyes (fluorescent brighteners); ethanol; fragrance; isopropyl alcohol; naphthalene; perchlorethylene; pine oil (contains naturally occurring phenolic compounds).

"Keep Out of Reach of Children."

SAFE ALTERNATIVES
Brand Name/*Mail Order*
A Granny's Old-Fashioned Carpet Shampoo (Granny's Old-Fashioned Products). *Granny's Old-Fashioned Products.*

Do-It-Yourself
Clean spills on your rugs and carpets immediately, before they become

stains; keep carpets fresh with regular vacuuming.

Keeping Carpets Clean

• Deodorize: Sprinkle baking soda liberally over entire carpet, making sure carpet is dry. Use several pounds for a 9' × 12' area. Wait 15 minutes or longer, then vacuum. For persistent odors, wait overnight before vacuuming. Repeat procedure if necessary.

• Brighten colors: Vacuum first to remove dust. Mix together 1 quart white vinegar and 3 quarts boiling water. Apply to rug with a wet rag, taking care not to saturate the backing. Dry thoroughly and air until dry. Then rub the surface with warm breadcrumbs and vacuum.

Stains

• Blood: Gently sponge the stain with cold water and dry with a towel. Repeat until stain is gone.

• Grease: Cover with baking soda, rubbing lightly into the rug. Leave on for 1 hour, then brush off. Repeat as needed.

• Oil and grease: Cover spots with cornstarch. Wait 1 hour, then vacuum.

• Ink: Put cream of tartar on the stain and squeeze a few drops of lemon juice on top. Rub into the stain for a minute, brush off the powder with a clean brush, and sponge immediately with warm water. Repeat if needed. If the ink is still wet, cover with a paste of Fuller's earth and water and let dry. Brush off and repeat if necessary. Or pour a mound of table salt immediately on the wet spot. Let sit for a few moments, then brush up and continue to reapply and remove until all moisture is absorbed and stain is bleached out.

• Soot: Cover thickly with salt, then sweep it up carefully.

• Urine: Rinse with warm water, then apply a solution of 3 tablespoons white vinegar and 1 teaspoon liquid soap. Leave on for 15 minutes, then rinse and rub dry.

See also Cleaning Products.

RUGS & CARPETS

Formaldehyde; pesticides (mothproofing); plastics (acrylonitrile, latex, nylon, polyester, polyurethane, PVC/vinyl chloride).

SAFE ALTERNATIVES

Avoid synthetic wall-to-wall carpeting. If your floor is laid with it, seriously consider removing it and the padding beneath and installing some type of nontoxic flooring. These carpets not only release minute particles of synthetic materials in the air as they wear, but they and the polyurethane foam padding underneath often outgas vapors of toxic chemicals such as formaldehyde and pentachlorophenol (from the backing), and are treated with mothproofing, soil repellents, moisture repellents, and other finishes. If the subfloor is particle board, remove it or thoroughly seal it from any living space above and below, because it heavily outgasses formaldehyde.

Use area rugs made of cotton, cotton/wool blend, sheepskin, or unmothproofed wool without jute or latex backing. Oriental rugs are often acceptable if they have not been mothproofed. Cotton, cotton/wool blend, or unmothproofed wool wall-to-wall carpets can also be used over a nontoxic subfloor.

Brand Name/*Mail Order*

Import stores, department stores, and interior decorators have access to natural-fiber rugs and carpets.

A *Icemart.* Long-hair Icelandic fleece area rugs.

A *Janice Corp.* Off-white rag rugs handwoven in the Blue Ridge Mountains of North Carolina.

A *Monarch Trading Co.* Lambskin area rugs from New Zealand.

A *Tibetan Refugee Self-Help Centre.* Custom rugs of any size, design, or color made of wool imported from Nepal or Tibet and dyed with vegetable dyes.

AB *Collins Designers.* "Broadloom carpeting, entirely cotton, to 18-foot widths or irregular shapes; loomed to order in almost any color dyed to order."

AB *Dellinger.* Cotton carpet (style 3333 Linwood) available without dyes or latex backing, custom dyed.

AB *Holster's Ruddy Duck Rugs.* Handwoven cotton or wool rag rugs. Will custom make with specified fabric and color.

AB *Homespun Crafts.* Cotton rag rugs.

AB *Peerless Imported Rugs.* Largest selection of natural-fiber area rugs, in all price ranges; imported from all over the world.

B *Charles W. Jacobsen.* Fine wool oriental area rugs.

B *Country Rag Rugs.* Crocheted and woven cotton rag rugs, stair treads, and hall runners. Ready made, kits, and rags by the pound for making your own.

B *Erlander's Natural Products.* Wool and cotton area rugs with oriental designs.

B *Guild of Shaker Crafts.* Handwoven cotton or wool 2' × 4' area rugs in traditional Shaker patterns.

B *Ikea.* Swedish cotton or wool area rugs.

B *Import Specialists.* Cotton or wool area rugs handloomed in India.

B *Laura Ashley.* Wool area rugs and "cotton rugs" made from canvas printed with tapestry designs.

B *Shaker Workshops.* Wool area rugs handwoven in New England.

B *Shaker Workshops West.* Handwoven cotton or wool area rugs in traditional Shaker patterns. Will make custom sizes and attempt custom color combinations.

See also Flooring, Textiles, and Wood Finishes.

S

SALAD DRESSING

Benzyl alcohol/sodium benzoate; BHA/BHT; colors; EDTA; flavors; glycols; hydrogenated oil; pesticide residues; sucrose; sulfur compounds.

Brand Name/*Mail Order*

Additive-free salad dressings are sold in supermarkets and natural-foods stores.

A Walnut Acres Salad Dressings (Walnut Acres). *Walnut Acres.*

B Bernstein's 100% Natural Salad Dressings (Nalley's Fine Foods).

B Cardini's Dressings (Caesar Cardini Foods).

B Hain Salad Dressings/Salad Dressing Mixes (Hain Pure Food Co.). *Deer Valley Farm, Kennedy's Natural Foods.*

B Hollywood All Natural Salad Dressings (Hollywood Health Foods).

B Lifespice Salad Dressings (SanSel).

B Marie's Salad Dressing (Marie's Quality Dressings).

B Newman's Own Olive Oil and Vinegar Dressing (Salad King).

B Paul de Sousa's Herbal Salad Dressing (Paul de Sousa's Co.). *Pure Planet Products.*

B Postilion's Salad Dressings (The Postilion).

B Rondele Salad Dressing (InoFood Corp.).

B The Source Herb French Dressing (Caesar Cardini Foods).

B Sunburst Farms Salad Dressings (Sunburst Farms Natural Foods).

BC Peggy Jane's Honey Salad Dressings (Peggy Jane's Special Products).

C Casablanca Salad Dressings (Casablanca Food Products).

C El Molino Herbal Secrets Salad Dressings (El Molino Mills).

C Papaya Seed Dressing (Hawaiian Plantations).

See also Food.

SALSA

Benzyl alcohol/sodium benzoate; pesticide residues.

SAFE ALTERNATIVES
Brand Name/*Mail Order*

Additive-free salsas can be found in natural-foods stores and supermarkets.

A Walnut Acres Chili Sauce (Walnut Acres). *Walnut Acres.*

B Bauman's Old Fashioned Pennsylvania Dutch Chili Sauce (The Bauman Family). *The Great Valley Mills.*

B Desert Rose Salsa (Desert Rose Salsa Co.).

B Embasa Home Style Mexican Sauces (Albino Garcia Y Fco.).

B Hot Cha Cha Garden Fresh Texas Salsa (Hot Cha Cha).

B Ortega Green Chili Salsas (Ortega Mexican Foods).

B Pace Picante Sauce (Pace Foods).

B Pure & Simple Salsa (Pure Sales).

B Sunburst Farms Salsa Picante (Sunburst Farms Natural Foods).

B Wizard Baldour's Hot Stuff (Linden's Elf Works). *Shiloh Farms.*

C Homade Chili Sauce (Sona Food Products Co.).

See also Food.

SANITARY NAPKINS

See Feminine Protection

SAUCES

Pesticide residues; sucrose.

SAFE ALTERNATIVES
Brand Name/*Mail Order*
Purchase additive-free sauces at natural foods stores and supermarkets but watch out for sucrose.

A Walnut Acres Sauces (Walnut Acres). *Walnut Acres.*

B Eden Spaghetti Sauce (Eden Foods).

B Enrico's All Natural Spaghetti Sauce (Ventre Packing Co.).

B Gathering Winds Cooking Sauces (Gathering Winds Natural Foods).

B Hain Naturals Italian Spaghetti & Cooking Sauces (Hain Pure Food Co.).

B Health Valley Bellissimo True Italian Natural Pasta Sauce (Health Valley Natural Foods).

B Johnson's Spaghetti Sauces (Pure Sales). *Erewhon Mail Order, Kennedy's Natural Foods.*

B Judyth's Mountain Pasta Sauces (Judyth's Mountain).

B L & A Spaghetti Sauce (L & A Juice Co.). *Kennedy's Natural Foods.*

B Mark's Natural Spaghetti Sauces (Erewhon). *Erewhon Mail Order.*

B Mrs. Gooch's Pasta Sauce (Mrs. Gooch's Ranch Markets).

B Nature's Cuisine Spaghetti Sauce (Nature's Best).

B Newman's Own Industrial Strength All-Natural Venetian Spaghetti Sauces (Newman's Own).

B Progresso Spaghetti Sauces (Progresso Quality Foods/Ogden Food Products).

B Ragu Italian Cooking Sauces (Ragu Foods).

B Westbrae Sauces for Pasta (Westbrae Natural Foods).

C Golden Grain Spaghetti Sauce (Golden Grain Macaroni Co.).

C Prego Italian Sauce (Campbell Soup Co.).

See also FOOD.

SAUERKRAUT

Pesticide residues; sulfur compounds.

SAFE ALTERNATIVES
Brand Name/*Mail Order*
Purchase additive-free sauerkraut at natural foods stores.

A Mrs. Woods' Sauerkraut (John Woods Products).

B Gathering Winds Natural Style Sauerkraut (Gathering Winds Natural Foods). *Erewhon Mail Order.*

B Kozmic Kraut (NEOPC).

B Pure & Simple Sauerkraut (Pure Sales).

See also Food.

SCOURING PADS

Colors; fragrance; plastic.

SAFE ALTERNATIVES
Use scouring pads made of plain steel

wool, plain copper, or stainless-steel coils and balls.

For items that might scratch easily, use one-inch slices of loofa sponges.

For added cleaning power, use scouring pads with recommended scouring powders.

Brand Name/*Mail Order*

A Brillo Copper Knit Cleaning Pads/ Brass Cleaning Pads (Purex Corp.).

A Chore Boy Copper Scouring Puff (Airwick Industries).

A Kurly Kate Multipurpose Brass Cleaning Pads (Purex Corp.).

A Supreme Steel Wool Balls (Purex Corp.).

See also Scouring Powder and Sponges.

SCOURING POWDERS

Colors; chlorine; detergents; talc.

SAFE ALTERNATIVES
Brand Name/*Mail Order*
Choose a scouring powder that does not contain chlorine, available at supermarkets and hardware stores.

A Bon Ami Cleaning Powder (Faultless Starch/Bon Ami Corp.). *Erlander's Natural Products.*

B Bon Ami Polishing Cleanser (Faultless Starch/Bon Ami Corp.).
Do-It-Yourself
• Sprinkle baking soda, borax, or dry table salt on surface or on a sponge, then scour and rinse.
• Apply liquid soap to surface and sprinkle with dolomite powder. Scour with scouring pad.
• Mix 9 parts calcium carbonate with 1 part soap flakes or TSP.

• Mix 12 parts washing soda, 7 parts powdered soap, and 81 parts pumice.
• Mix 20 parts powdered soap, 5 parts borax, 5 parts washing soda, and 35 parts pumice.
• Dissolve ¼ cup soap flakes and 2 teaspoons borax into 1½ cups boiling water. Cool to room temperature and add ¼ cup calcium carbonate.
• For bleaching action, add a small amount of sodium perborate to any of the above formulas.

See also Cleaning Products.

SEAFOOD

See Fish & Seafood.

SEASONINGS

See Herbs & Spices.

SEEDS

See Produce, Nuts & Seeds, and Seeds & Plants.

SEEDS & PLANTS

Pesticides

Some seeds are fumigated with lindane or other toxic chemicals, but it is questionable how much of that would end up in an otherwise organically grown food. The main reason to buy unfumigated seeds is that they would probably grow a healthier plant.

Brand Name/*Mail Order*

A *Abundant Life Seed Foundation.* "Untreated and open-pollinated" seeds for herbs and vegetables.

A *Bear Meadow Farm.* Herb plants.

A *Borchelt Herb Gardens.* Herb seeds.

A *Butterbrooke Farm.* Pure, open-pollinated, chemically untreated vegetable seeds from a co-op of organic growers and seed savers.

A *Exotica Seed & Rare Fruit Nursery.* Unusual varieties of seeds and plants.

A *Johnny's Selected Seeds.* Vegetable and herb seeds. "We do not chemically treat our seeds . . . We depend on composting, cover crops, and other classic organic techniques, and we avoid the use of chemical pesticides wherever possible. . . . While we strive to supply seed grown with minimal chemicals, it should be made clear that top quality, high germination, vigor, and trueness-to-type is our primary emphasis . . . and as far as we know we are the largest seed company in the States with this commitment." Will send a leaflet describing sources of seeds on request.

A *Meadowbrook Herbs & Things.* Herb seeds from a farm that has had "strict adherence to organic/biodynamic growing practices over the past 16 years."

A *Merry Gardens.* Herb seeds.

A *Misty Morning Farm.* "Plants and seeds . . . grown with care, organic soil amendments and bio-dynamic compost."

A *Peace Seeds.* Over 3,000 varieties, many unusual.

A *Richter's.* Seeds for herbs and spices.

A *Taylor's Herb Gardens.* Over 100 varieties of live herb plants and seeds. Catalog contains a guide to companion planting for poison-free gardening.

A *Vita Green Farms.* Herb and vegetable seeds.

B *Bay Spice House.* Seeds for growing herbs.

B *Caprilands Herb Farm.* Small selection of herb plants and seeds.

B *Gurney's Seed & Nursery Co.* Wide selection of standard and unusual fruit and vegetable trees and small plants.

B *Henry Field Seed & Nursery Co.* Large catalog of seeds and plants of all types of fruits and vegetables.

B *Hickory Hollow.* Herb seeds.

B *Horticultural Enterprises.* Chiles and peppers (31 varieties), plus other Mexican vegetables. Ahameim hot chile, Hungarian hot wax peppers, Romanian sweet peppers, and Santa Fe grande hot peppers are treated with a fungicide; others are not.

B *Kitazawa Seed Co.* Small catalog of seeds for oriental vegetables.

B *Le Jardin du Gourmet.* Good prices on about 250 varieties of common plant seeds and specialty seeds from France, Holland, Germany, Africa, Russia, and Romania. Also inexpensive sets for shallots, garlic, and leeks. Offers 20-cent sample packets because, "When you buy a packet of seeds—let's say basil—you might get from it hundreds of plants and, frankly, who needs that many basil plants."

B *Merry Gardens.* Live rare and unusual herb plants and seeds.

B *Nichols Garden Nursery.* Herb seeds and plants; seeds for common and unusual vegetables.

B *Redwood City Seed Co.* Small catalog of unusual seeds for all types of plants.

B *The Sandy Mush Herb Nursery.* Large selection of live herb plants and seeds grown in a high mountain farm in North Carolina.

B *Stokes Seeds.* Large variety of standard and unusual vegetable seeds.

B *Sunnybrook Farms.* Large selection of herb seeds and plants.

B *Vermont Bean Seed Co.* Large catalog of unusual varieties of common vegetables.

B *W. Atlee Burpee Co.* Seeds and plants for common vegetables, fruits, and herbs.

B *Well-Sweep Herb Farm.* Over 500 varieties of live herb plants.

SHAMPOO

Ammonia; colors; cresol; detergent; EDTA; ethanol; formaldehyde; fragrance; glycols, nitrates/nitrosamines; plastic (PVP); sulfur compounds.

In addition to the above, antidandruff shampoos contain coal-tar solutions or other toxic ingredients. Selenium sulfide, for example, can cause degenerative lesions to the liver, kidney, heart, spleen, stomach, bowels, and lungs if swallowed. Another toxic chemical used in antidandruff shampoos, recorcinol, is very easily absorbed through the skin.

SAFE ALTERNATIVES
Brand Name/*Mail Order*
These recommended shampoos, available at natural-foods stores, drugstores, and by mail, remove grime, dirt, and excess oils from the hair, but let the natural oils remain. Thus, your hair will not feel "squeaky clean," as it does with detergent-based shampoos that completely strip the hair.

Unscented

A All Ways Natural Indian Hemp Shampoo (All Ways Natural Industries).

A Golden Lotus Shampoos (Golden Lotus).

A Granny's Old-Fashioned Shampoo (Granny's Old-Fashioned Products). *Granny's Old-Fashioned Products.*

A Infinity Shampoos (Infinity Herbal Products).

A *New Age Creations.* Olive oil castile Shampoo Soap.

A Vega Shampoo (Marie Vega & Associates).

B *Common Scents.* Pure Shampoo.

B DP Laboratories. DP Jo'ba Shampoo with jojoba oil.

B *Homebody.* Pure Shampoo.

B *Lotions & Potions.* Pure Shampoo.

B Olive Oil Shampoo (Heritage Products).

B Real Aloe Vera Shampoo (The Real Aloe Co.). Yellow label is unscented, green label is scented.

BC *The Body Shop.* Jojoba Oil Shampoo and pH Shampoo.

BC *Denis Dumont.* Several shampoos that can be customized to your hair type with the addition of protein, wheat-germ oil, jojoba oil, natural glycerine, almond oil, coconut oil, or apricot oil.

C Simple Shampoo (Simple Soap). *Common Scents, Janice Corp.*

C *The Soap Opera.* Jojoba Shampoo.

Natural Scent

A *The Body Shop (England).* Large variety of shampoos for all hair types.

A *Community Soap Factory.* Nettle-rose Herbal Conditioning Shampoo.

A Dr. Hauschka Neem Shampoo (Dr. R. Hauschka Cosmetics). *The Allergy Store, Meadowbrook Herbs & Things.*

A Granny's Old-Fashioned Shampoo (Granny's Old-Fashioned Products).

A Jeanne Rose's Specialty Shampoo (New Age Creations).

A Jojoba Farms Shampoo (Jojoba Farms).

A Natural's Shampoo (Nature's Organics Plus).

A Nature de France French Clay Shampoos (Nature de France). *Erewhon Mail Order, Nature de France.*

A *New Age Creations.* "Pure organic shampoos, made with herbs for a particular hair type in an olive oil castile base."

A O'Naturel Saisons Shampoos (O'Naturel).

A Pré de Provence Shampoos (Justin Mathew).

A Pure & Basic Shampoos (Head Shampoo).

A Tom's Shampoos (Tom's of Maine). *Deer Valley Farm, Erewhon Mail Order, Kennedy's Natural Foods, Walnut Acres.*

A Weleda Shampoos (Weleda). *Meadowbrook Herbs & Things, Weleda, Wholesome Paks.*

B Carme Shampoos (Carme).

B Chenti Panthenol Bee Pollen Shampoo (Chenti Products).

B Country Roads Natural Keratin Shampoo (Golden California Co.).

B Desert Essence Jojoba Spirulina Shampoo (Desert Essence Cosmetics/Jojoba Products).

B Hain Avocado Shampoo (Hain Pure Food Co.).

B Head Shampoo (Head Shampoo).

B Jason Shampoos (Jason Natural Cosmetics). *Jason Natural Products.*

B Mill Creek Shampoos (Mill Creek Natural Products).

B Naturade Shampoos (Naturade Products).

B Nature's Gate Herbal Shampoos (Nature's Gate Herbal Cosmetics). *Deer Valley Farm, Erewhon Mail Order, Lotions & Potions, The Soap Opera.*

B Shikai Shampoo (Shikai Products). Shampoo made from the fruit of the acacia tree. *The Herb Patch.*

Do-It-Yourself

• Blend 1 cup liquid castile soap (can be made from castile bar soap by grating bar and mixing with pure water in a blender or food processor) with ¼ cup olive, avocado, or almond oil.

Add ½ cup distilled water. Place in bottles. Use sparingly.

• Mix 1 egg with 1 cup liquid castile soap in a blender until well beaten. Store in refrigerator. For added protein, as you blend pour in 1 package unflavored gelatin, a small amount at a time, until mixed. Store in refrigerator no longer than 2 weeks.

• Beat 2 eggs with 2 tablespoons vodka. Apply to dry hair and massage well. Wrap a hot towel around your head; after 10 minutes rinse hair well with warm water.

• Use baking soda. Simply rub a handful of dry baking soda into wet hair and rinse. For the first several weeks of use, hair will be drier than normal, but then the natural oils will begin to make your hair very soft. Great for dandruff.

• Use liquid soap.

• To remove dulling soap film: Add 1 teaspoon sodium hexametaphosphate to 1 gallon warm water. Wet hair thoroughly with solution, then wash hair with soap or shampoo. Rinse with what's left of the solution, then with plain water.

See also Beauty Products and Soap.

SHAVING CREAMS

Aerosol propellants; ammonia; BHA/ BHT; colors; ethanol; fragrance; glycerin; mineral oil; phenol; talc.

SAFE ALTERNATIVES

Instead of using an electric razor, which requires an alcohol-based preshave, use a safety razor and soap applied with a natural-bristle shaving brush or a natural shaving cream, available at your natural-foods store.

Brand Name/*Mail Order*

Unscented

A   Oregon Dairy Goats Unscented Shaving Soap (Oregon Dairy Goats).

AB *The Body Shop.* Shaving Gel and Shaving Soap.

BC *Denis Dumont.* Aloe-Jojoba Shaving Gelee and a shaving cream.

Natural Scent

A   *The Body Shop (England).* Foaming Sandalwood Shaving Cream.

A   Tom's Shaving Creams (Tom's of Maine). Scented with peppermint or orange oil. *Erewhon Mail Order, Kennedy's Natural Foods, The Soap Opera.*

See also Beauty Products and Soap.

SHOE POLISH

Aerosol propellants; ethanol; methylene chloride; nitrobenzene; perchloroethylene; trichloroethane; trichloroethylene; xylene.

Never use shoe polish while drinking alcoholic beverages or immediately afterward, as the toxic effects of nitrobenzene are compounded by the presence of alcohol in the system.

SAFE ALTERNATIVES

Wear suede or canvas shoes that do not require polishing.

If you must use a commercial shoe care product, apply sparingly in a well-ventilated area, preferably outdoors, away from an open window that will draw fumes back into the house. Allow shoes to dry thoroughly outdoors before wearing.

Do-It-Yourself
• Use walnut oil or other nut oil, or else olive oil, and buff with a chamois cloth to a shine.

See also Shoes.

SHOES

Dyes; formaldehyde; plastics (acrylic, polyurethane, PVC/vinyl chloride).

SAFE ALTERNATIVES
Wear shoes made entirely of leather or else wear cotton espadrilles. To avoid formaldehyde, look for leather shoes that are stitched instead of glued. Most leather shoes are made from dyed leather, but according to leading dermatologists, the dye is so firmly fixed to the leather that reactions to it would be extremely rare.

Brand Name/*Mail Order*
Brand name shoes are not listed here because so many fine brands are available. Look for them in better department, clothing, and shoe stores. Unnatural materials will bear a "man made" legend on the shoe or the box. Ask the salesperson.

Abbreviations used: (M)—men's; (W)—women's; (C)—children's and infants'.

A *Berg.* (MW) Inexpensive Dutch wooden shoes made from lightweight poplar wood, "not heavier than a pair of tennis shoes."

A *Gohn Bros.* (MW) Sheepskin sole liners.

B *A Child's Garden.* (C) Leather Pedibares.

B *After the Stork.* (C) Leather Pedibares and suede moccasins.

B *Beckwith Enterprises.* (C) "Top grain leather" moccasins.

B *Biarritz.* (W) Good prices on cotton canvas and leather espadrilles in a variety of unusual styles.

B *Caput Magnum Designs.* (W) Colorful leather sandals handmade in England.

B *The Cordwainer Shop.* (MW) Custom handcrafted leather footwear.

B *Cotton Dreams.* (MWC) Chinese cotton shoes with vinyl soles, and cotton canvas shoes with natural rubber soles.

B *The Cotton Place.* (MWC) Leather moccasins.

B *French Creek Sheep & Wool Co.* (MW) Gray 100%-pure wool "chalet shoes," handmade in Austria.

B *Good Things Collective.* (MWC) Good selection of Chinese cotton shoes with vinyl or cotton soles.

B *Kow Hoo Shoe Co.* (MW) Custom shoes made from American calfskin, suede, cordovan leather, lizard skin, sea turtle skin, baby alligator skin, or silk. "Send us pictures or drawings chosen from a magazine [and] your foot measurements."

B *Lee Kee.* (MW) Hong Kong shoe and boot maker will custom make from your choice of leathers. "Order any design by sending us a picture from an advertisement, or a photograph, or even a clearly drawn sketch."

B *Life Tools Co-op.* (W) Chinese cotton shoes with vinyl soles.

B *Moonflower Birthing Supply.* (C) Leather "Storkenbirks."

B *Natural Child.* (C) Chinese shoes, "100% cotton right down to the triple-layered soles."

B *Nature's Little Shoes.* (C) Natural leather shoes.

B *Northern Lights.* (MW) High-quality traditional Swedish clogs anatomically designed by medical doctors; made from wood and "natural untreated leather."

SHORTENING

BHA/BHT; flavors; hydrogenated oil; pesticide residues.

All shortening is made from oil that has been hydrogenated, a process that totally changes the oil's chemical characteristics. Do not be misled by labels that say "100% vegetable shortening." While it is true that shortening may have started out as vegetable oil, after hydrogenation, bleaching, filtering, and deodorizing, it bears little resemblance to its original form.

SAFE ALTERNATIVES
Use natural vegetable oils or butter.

See also Butter and Oils.

SHOWER CAPS

Plastic.

SAFE ALTERNATIVES
Brand Name/*Mail Order*
A *Janice Corp.* Cotton barrier-cloth shower caps with covered elastic.

Do-It-Yourself
Sew a cotton shower cap from barrier cloth.

See also Barrier Cloth and Textiles.

SHOWER CURTAINS

Plastics (polyester, PVC/vinyl chloride).

SAFE ALTERNATIVES
Enclose your shower stall with glass doors.

Brand Name/*Mail Order*
Purchase cotton shower curtains by mail.

A *The Cotton Place.* White.

A *Good Things Collective.* White.

A *Janice Corp.* White.

A *Ras Distributors.* White.

A *Vermont Country Store.* White.

AB *Erlander's Natural Products.* White, solid colors, and a windowpane check.

See also Textiles.

SILVER POLISH

See Metal Polishes.

SKIN CLEANSERS (NONSOAP)

Colors; ethanol; fragrance; mineral oil.

SAFE ALTERNATIVES
Brand Name/*Mail Order*
Unscented
A Granny's Old-Fashioned Hand, Face & Body Soap (Granny's Old-Fashioned Products). *Granny's Old-Fashioned Products.*

B *The Body Shop.* Clarifying Cleanser.

Natural Scent
A Dr. Hauschka Cleansing Cream (Dr. R. Hauschka Cosmetics). *The Allergy Store.*

A Weleda Cleansing Lotion With Iris (Weleda). *Weleda.*

B *Denis Dumont.* Minty Body & Face Gelées.

B Rachel Perry Aloe Vera All-Over Body Wash (Rachel Perry). *Common Scents.*

Do-It-Yourself

Cleansing Cream

• Whip plain sweet (unsalted) butter. Can be stored at room temperature, but keep away from heat since butter melts easily.

Cold Creams

• Combine 10 ounces apricot kernel oil, 2 ounces cocoa butter, and 2 ounces beeswax. Melt in a double boiler until completely dissolved. Beat the mixture with a wooden spoon until cold, and put into jars. Keep refrigerated.

• Melt 4 ounces beeswax and add 2 cups almond oil. In a separate pan, warm 5 ounces water and dissolve in it 1½ teaspoons borax. Mix borax solution with beeswax/oil mixture, stirring constantly until cool. Store in cool place.

• Beat together 2 tablespoons aloe vera gel and 3 ounces almond oil in the top of a double boiler. Add 1 ounce lanolin and melt together. Remove from heat and add 2 ounces plain water or rose water. Beat continuously until mixture has cooled and spoon into jar.

Other Cleansers

• Combine ½ cup water and 1 teaspoon cornstarch in a double boiler and stir until thickened. Add 2 to 3 tablespoons cocoa butter, ½ teaspoon freshly grated lemon peel, and 1½ tablespoons freshly squeezed and strained lemon juice. Stir well and store in cool, dry place.

• Apply fresh milk to skin with a cotton ball. Allow a few minutes for milk to dry before rinsing. Or blend 1 teaspoon powdered milk with ¼ cup warm water and apply.

• Mix ⅛ teaspoon oil, 1 tablespoon whole milk and ⅛ teaspoon honey. Apply to skin and remove by blotting with a cotton cloth. Rinse with warm water.

• Rub fresh yogurt or yogurt mixed with fresh crushed garlic into the skin and allow it to sit for a few minutes before rinsing.

• Splash face with warm water and then rub with 1 to 2 tablespoons oatmeal flour.

• Rub a slice of raw potato or tomato over skin. Rinse.

• Place thin slices of white potato or cucumber on skin and leave on for 5 minutes. Rub skin with fresh potato slices, then rinse.

• Mix a few drops lemon juice into 3 tablespoons cream or half-and-half. Smooth onto skin with a cotton ball. Leave on for a few minutes and rinse.

• Apply mayonnaise for a few minutes. Rinse with warm water.

• Apply a mashed, overripe banana. Rinse with warm water.

See also Beauty Products.

SLEEPING BAGS

Plastics (nylon, polyester).

SAFE ALTERNATIVES
Buy a natural-fiber sleeping bag or put natural-fiber sleeping bag liners inside your synthetic sleeping bag to

prevent skin contact with the synthetic material.

Brand Name/*Mail Order*

Sleeping Bags

A *Erlander's Natural Products.* Sleeping bags filled with cotton or wool batting, covered with cotton fabric prewashed with soda ash. Also cotton flannel liners.

Sleeping Bag Liners

A *Clothcrafters.* White 100% cotton sleeping bag liners.

A *Life Tools Co-op.* White 100% cotton sleeping bag liners.

A *Limericks Linens.* White 100% cotton sleeping bag liners.

B *The White Pine Co.* Silk knit sleeping bag liners.

See also Textiles.

SLEEPWEAR

See Clothing.

SLIPPERS

Plastics (acrylic, nylon, PVC/vinyl chloride).

SAFE ALTERNATIVES
Brand Name/*Mail Order*

Purchase slippers made from natural sheepskin.

Sheepskin Slippers

AB *Cable Car Clothiers/Robert Kirk, The Country Store and Farm, French Creek Sheep & Wool Co., Golden Touch Lambskin Products, Janice Corp., L. L. Bean, Land's End, Monarch Trading Co., Norm Thompson, Orvis, Ramus International, Reekie's of Grasmere, Sick-*

afus Sheepskins, Vermont Country Store.

See also Textiles.

SOAP

Ammonia; BHA/BHT; color; EDTA; formaldehyde; fragrance; glycols; phenol.

Soap is not considered to be a cosmetic and therefore is not affected by the cosmetic labeling laws which require ingredients to be listed. Although a few companies voluntarily disclose their ingredients, most do not. Basically, soap is made from a combination of an animal or vegetable fat with sodium hydroxide. Natural glycerin, a by-product of this combination, is also used as a base for soap. Herbs, scents, colors, and other ingredients can be added to either type of soap.

The most popular and most heavily advertised soaps are the antimicrobial "deodorant" soaps. An FDA advisory review panel has questioned the safety of using these potent germ-killers on a regular day-to-day, year-after-year basis. There is concern about the possible dangerous consequences when these substances are absorbed through the skin and accumulate in the liver and other organs. As a result, the panel has declared "not safe" or "not proved safe" those deodorant soaps containing chloroxylenol (PCMX), cloflucarban, dibromsalan (DBS)*, fluorosalan*, hexachlorophene*, phenol, tetrachlorosalicylanilide (TSCA)*, tribromsalan (TBS)*,

---

*No longer marketed over the counter in the United States, but may be present in prescription soaps.

triclocarban, or triclosan. In addition, the panel could find no evidence to prove that these potentially hazardous substances actually helped stop body odor any more effectively than did plain soap. It also warned that deodorant soaps should not be used on infants under six months of age.

In nondeodorant soaps, the most common and troublesome ingredient is synthetic fragrance. The fragrances in deodorant and luxury toilet soaps are clearly recognizable, but some of the other soaps commonly regarded as "pure" also end up containing added synthetic fragrances as well. Moreover, some soaps represented as "natural" contain synthetic fragrance (of, say, coconut or oatmeal) to enhance the scent of the natural ingredient. Not only are fragrances totally unnecessary to the effectiveness of soap, they are often irritating and can cause dry skin, redness, and rashes. Scented soaps usually also contain fixatives to keep you smelling "springtime fresh" all day. From an aesthetic point of view, these scents might clash with any natural fragrance you may choose to apply separately.

SAFE ALTERNATIVES
Buy pure, plain, unscented, uncolored soap. Body odor is best prevented by regular bathing with pure soap and hot water.

Some advertisers claim that soap is "drying to the skin." This is true for some soaps, especially those made primarily from coconut oil, so if dry skin is a problem, choose a glycerin soap or one made from olive oil.

Brand Name/*Mail Order*
Brands listed below can be purchased at natural foods stores, bath shops, drugstores, hardware stores, cookware stores, or by mail.

Bar Soap: Unscented

A *The Body Shop.* Vegetable glycerin soap.

A Bon Ami Cleaning Cake (Faultless Starch/Bon Ami Corp.). Heavy-duty soap with feldspar added as an abrasive. *Erlander's Natural Products, The Country Store & Farm, Vermont Country Store, Williams-Sonoma.*

A Caswell-Massey Pure Castile Soap (Caswell-Massey Co.). *Caswell-Massey.*

A The Chef's Soap (Beh Housewares Corp.). *Janice Corp., Buffalo Shirt Co.*

A Colonial Garden Castile Soap (Colonial Gardens Kitchens).

A *Common Scents.* Vegetable glycerin soap.

A Conti Castile Soap with Olive Oil (J. B. Williams Co.).

A Druide Natural Coconut Oil Soap (Druide).

A *Erlander's Natural Products.* Olive oil and wine olive oil Jubilee Soaps.

A *Heavenly Soap.* Homemade basic soap.

A Kirk's Original Coco Hardwater Castile Soap (Procter & Gamble).

A Kiss My Face Pure Olive Oil Soap (Kiss My Face). "Made without artificial color, fragrance, foamers, preservatives, or animal ingredients." *The Herb Patch, Kennedy's Natural Foods, Kiss My Face.*

A La Taste Forcalquier Soaps (La Taste Forcalquier). *The Allergy Store.*

A Les Enfants (Beh Housewares Corp.).

A Le Sportif (Beh Housewares Corp.).

A *Lotions & Potions.* Vegetable glycerin soap.

A Neutrogena Original Formula (Unscented) (Neutrogena Corp.).

A Olde Tyme Soap (Bentley Springs Farm).

A Oregon Dairy Goats Unscented Goat Milk Soap (Oregon Dairy Goats). *Common Scents, The Soap Opera.*

A Pears Transparent Soap (A. & F. Pears/DEP Corp.). *Common Scents, The Soap Opera.*

A Physician & Surgeons Cocoa Butter Soap (Sigma Pharmaceutical Corp.) *Common Scents.*

A Pré de Provence Olive Oil Soap (Pré de Provence). *Common Scents, The Country Store & Farm.*

A Provender Kitchen Soap (Provender Kitchen Soap).

A Rokeach Kosher Kitchen Soap (I. Rokeach & Sons).

A Simple Soap (Simple Soap). *Common Scents, Janice Corp.*

A Sirena Soap (Tropical Soap Co.). *Common Scents, Deer Valley Farm, The Herb Patch, Janice Corp., Kennedy's Natural Foods, The Soap Opera.*

A *The Soap Opera.* Vegetable glycerin soap and a Greek olive oil soap.

A Soapure (Winthrop Laboratories/ Sterling Drug). "Unscented, free of harsh chemicals and detergents."

A *Williams-Sonoma.* Natural Glycerine Hand Soap.

Bar Soap: Natural Scent

A *The Body Shop (England).* Variety of unusual soaps.

A *Cal Ben Soap Co.* Pure bar soap without "artificial additives, coloring dyes, irritating allergy-prone disinfectants, sticky deodorants, lanolins, useless creams, and harmful polluting detergents." Very slight almond scent.

A *Dr. Bronner's Magic Soap* (All-One-God-Faith). *Pure Planet Products, The Soap Opera.*

A Loanda Natural Herbal Soaps (Loanda Products). Formerly called Beyond Soap. No added fragrance, but smells faintly of the herbs used. *Erewhon Mail Order, Erlander's Natural Products, The Herb Patch, Lotions & Potions, The Soap Opera.*

A Nature de France French Clay Soaps (Nature de France). *Erewhon Mail Order, Nature de France, The Soap Opera.*

A *Richter's.* Scented herbal soaps.

A *The Soap Opera.* A large selection of natural imported soaps.

A Tom's Soaps (Tom's of Maine). *Erewhon Mail Order, Kennedy's Natural Foods.*

A *Walnut Acres.* "Old-fashioned formulas free of additives."

A Weleda Soap (Weleda). *The Allergy Store, Meadowbrook Herbs & Things, Moonflower Birthing Supply, The Soap Opera, Weleda, Wholesome Paks.*

Liquid Soap: Unscented
A *Erlander's Natural Products.* Olive oil and wine olive oil Jubilee Soaps.

A Granny's Old-Fashioned Liquid Hand Cleanser (Granny's Old-Fashioned Products) *Granny's Old-Fashioned Products.*

Liquid Soap: Natural Scent
A *The Body Shop.* Liquid Castile Soap with lemon oil.

A *Cal Ben Soap Co.* Pure liquid soap without "artificial additives, coloring dyes, irritating allergy-prone disinfectants, sticky deodorants, lanolins, useless creams, and harmful polluting detergents." Very slight almond scent.

A *Community Soap Factory.* Liquid soap "all natural and 100% pure, and free of animal products . . . no artificial ingredients of any kind." Almond or peppermint scent.

A Dr. Bronner's Pure Castile Soap (All-One-God-Faith). *Erewhon Mail Order, Kennedy's Natural Foods, Lotions & Potions, Pure Planet Products, The Soap Opera.*

A Mill Creek Pure Castile Soap (Mill Creek Natural Products).

Soap Flakes: Unscented
A Boraxo Powdered Hand Soap (United States Borax & Chemical Corp.).

A White King Natural Soap (White King).

Do-It-Yourself
• Make liquid soap from any bar soap or soap flakes by mixing 2 cups grated bar soap or soap flakes with 1 gallon water in a pot, and heating the mixture to boiling over low heat, stirring until the soap dissolves. Lower heat and simmer for 10 minutes. Allow to cool.

See also Beauty Products.

SOCKS & STOCKINGS

See Clothing.

SODAS

Aspartame; BHA/BHT; colors; glycols; saccharin; sucrose.

SAFE ALTERNATIVES
Drink sparkling mineral waters that have added natural flavors without adding sweeteners: lemon, lime, mint, and orange, or a soda sweetened with honey or juice.

Brand Name/*Mail Order*
Additive-free sodas are sold at natural-foods stores and supermarkets.

Note: Natural sodas sweetened with fructose may also contain sucrose, the same sweetener found in white sugar. Sodas listing "high-fructose corn syrup" among the ingredients may end up being sweetened with 55% sucrose, even though the label says "no sucrose." These, along with sugar-sweetened sodas, are rated "C."

B Dr. Tima Sodas (Tima Brand).

B Honey Pure Sodas (Honey Pure Corp.). *Deer Valley Farm, Shiloh Farms, Walnut Acres.*

B Hopping's Honey Sodas (Hopping Bottling Co.).

B Napa Naturals Sodas (Adams Natural Beverage Co.). Sweetened with fruit juices.

B Original New York Seltzer (Original New York Seltzer). Sweetened with "fructose syrup."

C Chico Natural Sodas (Chico Soda Works).

C Corr's Rush Sodas (Corr's Beverage Co.).

C Hansen's Natural Sodas (Hansen Foods).

C Health Valley Sodas (Health Valley Natural Foods).

C Naturàle 90 Sodas (Great Lakes Beverages Corp.).

C Orelia Sodas (Orelia West).

C Paradise Gold Sodas (Hawaiian Pacific Wholesale).

C Seven-Up (Seven-Up Co.).

C Spree All Natural Sodas (Shasta Beverages).

Do-It-Yourself
Mix your favorite fruit juice or fruit concentrate with sparkling mineral water.

See also Juices & Fruit Drinks and Water.

SOUP MIXES

BHA/BHT; colors; hydrogenated shortening; MSG; pesticide residues.

SAFE ALTERNATIVES
Brand Name/*Mail Order*
A Walnut Acres Soups (Walnut Acres). Organic ingredients and untreated deep-well water in

lead-free cans. *Kennedy's Natural Foods, Walnut Acres.*

B Fearn Soup Mixes (Fearn Soya Foods).

B Hain Dry Soup Mixes/Hearty Home Style Soups. (Hain Pure Food Co.). Lead-free cans. *Kennedy's Natural Foods.*

B Health Valley Soups (Health Valley Natural Foods). **Lead-free** cans. *Kennedy's Natural Foods.*

B Magic Gardens Natural Soups (Magic Gardens). *Shiloh Farms.*

B Natural & Kosher Frozen Soups (Natural & Kosher Foods).

See also Food.

SOY SAUCE

Benzyl alcohol/sodium benzoate; pesticide residues; sucrose.

SAFE ALTERNATIVES
Brand Name/*Mail Order*
Additive-free soy sauce is sold at supermarkets and natural-foods stores.

A Chico-San Lima Organic Soy Sauce (Chico-San). *Chico-San.*

A Westbrae Organic Shoyu (Westbrae Natural Foods).

B Arrowhead Mills Tamari Soy Sauce (Arrowhead Mills).

B Eden Tamari/Shoyu (Eden Foods).

B Erewhon Tamari (Erewhon) *Erewhon Mail Order, Kennedy's Natural Foods.*

B Kikkoman Milder Soy Sauce (Kikkoman Corp.). Other Kikkoman varieties contain sodium benzoate.

B Pure & Simple Tamari Shoyu (Pure Sales).

B San-J Tamari Natural Soy Sauce (Pure Sales).

B Soken Natural Soy Sauces (Soken Trading Co.).

B Westbrae Tamari (Westbrae Natural Foods). *Kennedy's Natural Foods.*

C Chung King Soy Sauce (RJR Foods).

See also Food.

SPICES

See Herbs & Spices.

SPONGES

Dyes; plastics (polyurethane foam).

SAFE ALTERNATIVES
Use natural sponges: Loofas are long, stiff sponges made from gourds (very good if you need to scrub something). Sea sponges—large, soft corals gathered from the ocean—are soft and "spongy," and come in many sizes. If neither loofas nor sea sponges are available, use natural beige-colored sponges made from processed cellulose.

Brand Name/*Mail Order*
Natural sponges can be purchased at drug, hardware, art supply, and natural-foods stores.

Loofas
A *The Body Shop, The Body Shop (England), Common Scents, Deer Valley Farm, Erewhon Mail Order, Janice Corp., The Herb Patch, Kennedy's Natural Foods, Lotions & Potions, Pure Planet Products, The Soap Opera, U. S. Health Club.*

Sea Sponges
A *The Body Shop, The Body Shop (England), Caswell-Massey, Common Scents, Erewhon Mail Order, Erlander's Natural Products, Hearthsong, Homebody, Janice Corp., Kennedy's Natural Foods, Lotions & Potions, Pure Planet Products, The Soap Opera.*

Do-It-Yourself
Nichols Garden Nursery sells loofa seeds and instructions for curing them into sponges.

SPOT REMOVERS

Aerosol propellants; ammonia; benzene; chlorine; EDTA; fragrance; isopropyl alcohol; naphthalene; perchloroethylene; toluene; trichloroethylene.

"CAUTION: Eye irritant. Vapor harmful. Keep out of reach of children."

SAFE ALTERNATIVES
Brand Name/*Mail Order*
C Granny's Old-Fashioned Stain Remover (Granny's Old-Fashioned Products). *Granny's Old-Fashioned Products.*

Do-It-Yourself
Remove spots just as soon as they happen.
• Blood: Soak fabric in cold water, then wash with soap and cold water. If necessary, bleach white fabrics in a solution of 1/4 cup borax and 2 cups water, then wash as usual.
• Cocoa, chocolate, and coffee: Sponge stain with cold water, then with a solution of 2 tablespoons borax in 2 cups water. Wash as usual.

• Fruit and fruit juice: Stretch the fabric over a basin and pour boiling water over the stain. Wash as usual.

• Grass: Rub with glycerin and let set for 1 hour. Wash as usual.

• Ink: Soak fabric in cold water, then wash as usual. If stain has set on a white fabric, wet fabric with cold water, then apply a paste of cream of tartar and lemon juice and let sit for 1 hour. Wash as usual.

• Mildew: Wash in hot, soapy water. Rinse and dry in the sun.

• Milk: Soak fabric in equal parts glycerin and warm water, rubbing gently. Then wash in slightly cooler soapy water, rinse, and dry.

• Mud: Brush off excess dried mud with a soft brush, then rub the stain with water from boiling potatoes, or a solution of 2 tablespoons borax in 2 cups water. Rinse well and wash as usual.

• Perspiration: Sponge stains with a weak solution of white vinegar or lemon juice and water, or soak the fabric in water in which 2 aspirins have been dissolved.

• Tea: Stretch the fabric over a basin and pour boiling water over the stain. Wash as usual.

• Urine: Sponge the stain with a solution of baking soda and water, then rinse in warm water and wash as usual.

• Water: Hold fabric in hot steam until damp, shaking frequently, then press with a warm iron.

See also Cleaning Products, and Rug, Carpet & Upholstery Shampoo.

SPROUTS

See Produce.

SUGAR

BHA/BHT; pesticide residues; sucrose.

Sugar has many names: Barbados molasses/sugar, blackstrap molasses, brown sugar, cane sugar/syrup, corn syrup, dextrose, invert sugar, invert sugar/syrup, kleenraw sugar, maple sugar/syrup, muscavado sugar, raw sugar, ribbon cane syrup, sorghum syrup, and turbinado sugar. They may come from different sources, look different, and taste different, but they are all the same thing—sucrose.

More diseases have been linked to eating sucrose than to any other aspect of nutrition. One of the most important characteristics of sucrose to be concerned about is that as a simple carbohydrate it cannot be digested, assimilated, or utilized by the body without the help of other nutrients that must be provided from somewhere else. So in order to accommodate sucrose, the missing nutrients are taken from nutritious food in your diet, from nutrients in your blood, and even from nutrient reserves stored in your bones.

Sucrose also inhibits the ability of the white blood cells in your immune system to curb bacteria. This effect lasts for about four hours, so if you eat sucrose for breakfast, lunch, and dinner, this is likely to leave your body vulnerable to bacteria most of the time.

While there is still controversy as to whether sugar will actually bring on illness, evidence is mounting against sugar, and there is no question that it will weaken your system. Among the ailments sucrose consumption is likely to aggravate, if not cause, are tooth decay, diabetes, hypoglycemia, coronary disease, obesity, ulcers, high blood pressure, vaginal yeast infections, osteoporosis, and malnutrition.

Fructose is often used as a substitute for sucrose in health-food products. Even though its name suggests it might be healthier, the fructose used in commercial products bears about as much resemblance to the natural sugar found in fruits as refined white sugar does to sugar cane. Generally manufactured from corn syrup, it too is a simple carbohydrate. Although it is easier to metabolize than sucrose and you need to use less (the sweetening power is almost twice that of sucrose), fructose cannot be relied upon as a substitute sweetener because usually it is a high-fructose corn syrup that contains 55 percent sucrose.

Refined white sugar is the most heavily contaminated of the sucrose sweeteners, having been sprayed with multiple pesticides, processed over a natural gas flame, and chemically bleached. Beet sugar, additionally, is processed with BHA or BHT, and both beet and cane sugar contain residues of sulfur compounds.

SAFE ALTERNATIVES

Eat naturally sweet foods. Add fruit juices or fresh or dried fruits to dishes that need to be sweetened.

Use one of the following sweeteners that do not rely on sucrose as their sweetening agent:

Barley Malt

This natural sweetener composed mainly of maltose is made by soaking and sprouting the barley to make malt, then combining it with more barley and cooking it until the starch is converted to sugar. The mash is then strained and cooked down to syrup, or dried into powder.

Barley malt syrup is only about 40 percent as sweet as sucrose, so use 2 cups syrup for each cup of sugar. Since it is a liquid sweetener, decrease the liquid in the recipe by ¼ cup for each ¾ cups syrup used.

Barley malt powder, on the other hand, is *2000 percent* sweeter than sucrose. Be very careful when measuring; it is easy to get too much. Use only 2 to 2½ teaspoons of barley malt powder per cup of sugar.

Date Sugar

This sweetener is made by dehydrating dates to 2 percent moisture and grinding them very finely into a granulated-type sugar. This natural fructose sweetener is equal to sugar in its sweetening power and so can be substituted for white sugar cup for cup. It is especially good in recipes that call for brown sugar.

Fig Syrup

Syrup made simply from figs and water and works very well as a substitute for molasses when substituted cup for cup.

Honey

Composed of glucose and fructose, honey generally is the least chemically contaminated sweetener because bees exposed to pesticides usually don't make it back to the hive.

Legally, for a bottle to be labeled "honey" it must contain "the nectar and floral exudations of plants gathered and stored in the comb by honeybees." Honey is always honey—"raw," "natural," "organic," regardless of how it is labeled. Filtering to remove bee parts and pollens is the only processing sometimes used. "U. S. Grade A" or "Fancy" honey refers to the level of filtration and does not give any indication of quality or freedom from chemical contamination.

There are many different types of honey. The lighter-colored honeys usually have a more delicate flavor, while darker-colored honeys have a very strong, distinct flavor. For sweetness without too much flavor, try clover, star thistle, mountain wildflower, or orange blossom honey. Iron-bark tree honey tastes like butterscotch. Tupelo is best for baking. Other types of honey include alfalfa, black-eyed bean, buckwheat, cabbage, conifer, grapefruit, Hawaiian wild lava plum, hawthorne, heather, lemon blossom, lime, manzanita, mesquite, rosemary, safflower, and thyme.

Honey is 140 percent as sweet as sugar, so replace each cup of sugar with ½ to ¾ cup honey and reduce liquid in recipe by ¼ cup for each ¾ cup honey used.

One problem with honey is that the flavor may come through in the finished product even when a light honey is used. By using less honey than is called for in the recipe, you will get the sweetness without the honey taste.

Maple Syrup/Sugar
Along with honey, has been a mainstay natural-food sweetener for years, as it is simply boiled-down maple tree sap. Unfortunately, its sweetener is sucrose, but because its method of processing does not add the contaminants found in cane and beet sugars, it is the best sucrose sweetener to use. You might want to limit your consumption, however, and save it for Sunday pancakes while using some other alternative for your all-purpose sweetener.

Maple trees are grown without fertilizers or pesticide sprays, but in America the law permits injection of the trees with formaldehyde pellets to increase the flow of sap, and does not require this to be stated on the label. The Canadian Food and Drug Directorate, on the other hand, does not allow this practice.

Government regulations stipulate that all maple syrup be maple-sap syrup, be free from foreign material, and weigh not less than eleven pounds per gallon. The syrup is then graded by color according to the U.S. color standards; the lighter the syrup, the higher the quality and the more delicate the flavor. Grade Fancy—Light Amber is the highest quality, the first syrup made each season. Grade A—Medium Amber is produced in greatest quantity, with a medium maple flavor. Grade B—Dark Amber has the strongest maple flavor that really comes through in recipes.

Rice Syrup
A natural sweetener composed mainly of maltose. It is made by combining barley malt with rice and cooking it until all the starch is converted to sugar. The mash is then strained and cooked down to syrup.

Rice syrup is best used just as it comes from the jar, on pancakes, waffles, toast, and rice cakes, or in cooking, when only a touch of sweetness is needed. Because it is only 20 percent as sweet as sugar, it is impractical as a sugar substitute in recipes.

The following cookbooks all contain recipes using non-sucrose sweeteners:

Barkie, Karen E. *Sweet and Sugar-free*, New York: St. Martin's Press, 1982.

California Honey Advisory Board. *Honey . . . Anytime.* (PO Box 32, Whittier, CA 90608.)

Chico-San. *Yinnie's Rice Syrup Cookbook.* (Free; PO Box 810, Chico, CA 95927.)

Farmilant, Eunice. *The Natural Foods Sweet-Tooth Cookbook.* New York: Jove Publications, 1973.

Geiskopf, Susan. *Putting It Up with Honey.* Ashland, OR: Quicksilver Productions, 1979.

Kohrman, Katherine. *The Common Ground Dessert Cookbook.* Berkeley, CA: Ten Speed Press, 1983.

Martin, Faye. *Rodale's Naturally Delicious Desserts and Snacks.* Emmaus, PA: Rodale Press, 1978.

Mayo, Patricia Terris. *The Sugarless Baking Book.* Boulder, CO: Shambhala, 1983.

Opton, Gene, and Hughes, Nancy. *Honey Feast—A Sampler of Honey Recipes.* Berkeley, CA: Ten Speed Press, 1975.

Parkhill, Joe M. *Honey! A Sugarless Cookbook.* Berryville, AZ: Country Bazaar Publishing, 1982.

Warrington, Janet. *Sweet and Natural.* Trumansburg, NY: The Crossing Press, 1982.

Brand Name/*Mail Order*
Natural sweeteners are sold in natural-foods stores.

Barley Malt Powder
B Barley Malt Powder. *Walnut Acres.*

B Dr. Bronner's Barleymalt Sweetener (All-One-God-Faith).

B Dr. Bronner's Calcium-Food Malt (All-One-God-Faith). Barley malt powder supplemented with high-nutrient food powders.

Barley Malt Syrup
B Eden Barley Malt Syrup (Eden Foods).

B Pure Malt Extract (Jake's Products). *Kennedy's Natural Foods.*

Date Sugar
A *Colvada Date Co.* Raw date sugar made from dates grown on the company's own farm.

Fig Syrup
B Miss Figgy Pure Fig Syrup (R. W. Knudsen & Sons).

Honey
Brand names are not listed here because hundreds are available, many only regionally. Since some makes of honey are diluted with corn syrup, choose a brand with "undiluted" on the label.

A *Culpeper.* "Reasonably priced honey from places and districts likely to be free from pollution": Spain, Tasmania, Guatemala, the Andes Mountains, Honduras, and New Zealand.

A *Glorybee Honey.* Offers 100% natural, raw, unfiltered honey and comb honey in bulk at very low prices. Also a full line of beekeeping supplies and several honey cookbooks.

A *Kennedy's Natural Foods.* Many brands of pure honey.

A *Smoot Honey Co.* A family-owned and operated honeybee business on the eastern slopes of the northern Rocky Mountains, with a production area covering "over 20,000 square miles of some of the most pollution free country remaining in the U.S." Honey is a "100% natural product of honeybees." Also a honey cookbook.

A *Thousand Island Apiaries.* Honey "produced without chemicals; our bees are not fed sugar or drugs during the honey-producing season."

A Walnut Acres Honey (Walnut Acres). "Produced without the use of chemicals . . . bees are not fed sugar, sulfa drugs, or antibiotics . . . . Not "cooked," not adulterated with corn syrup, sugar, or anything else." *Walnut Acres.*

Maple Syrup
Because of its sucrose content, all brands are rated "C."

C *Brookside Farm.* Vermont maple syrup "as organic as we know how to make it. . . . No sprays in the groves, no pellets in the tapholes, no artificial defoamers in the evaporator, no preservatives in the syrup."

C Bucket Boy Maple Syrup (Mille Lacs Maple Co.).

C Camp Maple Syrup (Camp). Canadian. *Kennedy's Natural Foods.*

C Cary's Pure Maple Syrup. (Doxsee Food Corp.). "100% maple . . . produced solely from the sap of the maple tree, containing absolutely nothing else."

C Citadelle Pure Maple Syrup (The Maple Sugar Producers of Quebec). Canadian.

C *Clark Hill Sugary.* Old-fashioned maple syrup. "We lift the sap from our own New Hampshire maple trees in the same gentle way. . . . We don't add anything extra."

C *Dan Johnson's Sugar House.* New Hampshire "pure maple syrup. . . . No additives. . . . A natural food."

C Jones Dairy Farm Pure Maple Syrup (Jones Dairy Farm).

C Macdonald's Pure Maple Syrup (Ault Foods). Canadian.

C New Hampshire Pure Maple Syrup (Kings Inn Farm).

C Norganic Maple Syrup (Norganic Foods Co.).

C Old Colony Pure Maple Syrup (American Maple Products Corp.). *Mrs. Appleyard's Kitchen.*

C Pure, Unfiltered, Organic Maple Syrup (Jake's Products).

C Shady Maple Farms Maple Syrup (Shady Maple Farms).

C Spring Tree Pure Maple Syrup (Spring Tree Corp.). Canadian.

C *Sugarbush Farms.* Vermont maple syrup "made right here on our farm . . . collected the old-fashioned way with a team of horses, and boiled down in our sugar house with a wood fire."

C *Walnut Acres.* "Produced in Pennsylvania and Canada. . . . No taphole pellets, no formaldehyde, no defoamers, no corn syrup or other adulterant."

C Westbrae Maple Syrup (Westbrae Natural Foods).

Maple Sugar

C *Kennedy's Natural Foods.*

C Old Colony Pure Maple Sugar (American Maple Products Corp.). *Mrs. Appleyard's Kitchen.*

C Pure Maple Syrup Granules (Vermont Country Maple).

C *Sugarbush Farms.*

C *Walnut Acres.*

Rice Syrup

B Traditional Rice Malt (Mitoku Co.).

B Yinnie's Rice Syrup (Chico-San). *Chico-San, Erewhon Mail Order, Kennedy's Natural Foods.*

SUNTAN LOTION

Ethanol; fragrance; glycols; mineral oil.

SAFE ALTERNATIVES
Brand Name/*Mail Order*
Natural suntan lotions are sold at natural-foods stores.

Unscented

A Aubrey Organics Nature Tan (Aubrey Organics).

A *The Body Shop (England).* Lotions with cocoa butter and Paba.

A *Heavenly Soap.* Moisturizing/Tanning Lotion.

B *Denis Dumont.* Paba lotion, tanning oil, and Hawaiian coconut oil with vitamin E.

B *Homebody.* Aloe vera and cocoa butter tanning lotions.

B Nature's Gate Herbal Suntan Lotion (Nature's Gate Herbal Cosmetics). *Deer Valley Farm, Erewhon Mail Order.*

B Nature's Life Suntanning & Body Lotion (M.K. Health Food Distributors).

Natural Scent

A *Heavenly Soap.* Moisturizing/Tanning Lotion.

A Rachel Perry Aloe-Paba Tanning Formula (Rachel Perry).

B Country Roads Natural Sea & Slope Tanning Lotion (Golden California Co.).

B Mill Creek Old-Fashioned Dark Tanning Oil (Mill Creek Natural Products).

Do-It-Yourself
• Use plain sesame oil, which screens about 30% of the sun's ultraviolet rays in addition to softening the skin with natural vitamin E.

• Use cocoa butter.

• Use a mixture of olive oil and cider vinegar.

• Boil ¾ cup pure water and brew strong tea with 3 black tea bags. Put ¼ cup tea into a blender with ¼ cup lanolin and ¼ sesame oil. Blend at low speed. Add remaining tea steadily.

• Warm together ¼ cup mink oil, ¼ cup sesame oil, 1 tablespoon liquid lecithin, and 2 tablespoons lanolin. Use as is, or add ⅓ cup strong black tea and ¼ teaspoon borax by first mixing the borax with the tea and then combining the two mixtures slowly with an electric beater (the tea will slightly stain your skin to "deepen" the tan). Make sure they are both the same temperature so they will mix well.

See also Beauty Products.

T

TABLECLOTHS

See Table Linens.

TABLE LINENS

Dyes; formaldehyde; plastics (polyester, PVC/vinyl chloride).

SAFE ALTERNATIVES
Brand Name/*Mail Order*

A   *Homespun Crafts.* Tablecloths, napkins, and placemats in a cotton colonial homespun fabric, embroidered or with lace.

A   *Homespun Fabrics & Draperies.* Fringed tablecloth/napkin sets made of "raw" or bleached cotton.

A   *Janice Corp.* White 100% cotton placemats handwoven in the Blue Ridge Mountains of North Carolina.

A   *Testfabrics.* Untreated cotton tablecloths, napkins, and placemats.

AB   *E. Braun & Co.* Pure Belgian linen monogrammed placemats, napkins, and tablecloths.

AB   *Vermont Country Store.* Cotton placemats, tablecloths, and napkins in several styles. Also cotton "silence cloth" to place under tablecloth to prevent dishes from rattling.

B   *Berea College Student Craft Industries.* Cotton placemats in a variety of colors.

B   *Blowing Rock Crafts.* Handwoven cotton tablecloths in colonial patterns.

B   *Clothcrafters.* White 100% cotton tablecloths with stitched colored borders, blue stripe 100% cotton denim placemats, and inexpensive white cotton napkins with stitched colored borders by the dozen. "A daily substitute for paper napkins."

B   *The Cotton Co.* Homespun placemats and napkins.

B   *The Country Store & Farm.* Cotton damask tablecloths and napkins in red- or blue-and-white checks.

B   *Gurian's.* Handloomed cotton tablecloths embroidered with dyed wool.

B   *Homespun Weavers.* Custom-made cotton tablecloths, napkins, and placemats in colonial homespun patterns.

B   *Import Specialist.* Multicolored cotton rag placemats handloomed in India.

B   *Limericks Linens.* Cotton and linen tablecloths and napkins.

B   *Mather's.* Cotton homespun-weave tablecloths.

See also Fabric and Textiles.

TAMPONS

See Feminine Protection.

TAPE

See Glue & Tape.

TEA

Pesticide residues.

Some tea bags contain heat-sealant adhesives.

SAFE ALTERNATIVES
Drink herb teas; black teas contain caffeine.

Brand Name/*Mail Order*
Buy loose tea and brew with metal tea-balls or cotton tea bags, or choose brands whose tea bags are folded and stapled.

Herb Teas & Tea Blends
A Abundant Earth Herb Teas (Abundant Earth Herb Country).

A Chico San Lima Ohsawa Organic Twig Tea (Chico-San). *Chico-San.*

A Erewhon Organic Kukicha Stem Tea (Erewhon). *Erewhon Mail Order.*

A Herb Teas. *Bear Meadow Farm, Deer Valley Farm, The Herb Patch, Meadowbrook Herbs & Things, Merry Gardens, Misty Morning Farm, Ram Island Farm Herbs, Richter's, Weleda.*

A Walnut Acres (Walnut Acres). *Walnut Acres.*

A Westbrae Organic Green Tea (Westbrae Natural Foods).

B Alive Polaritea (Alive Polarity Distributors). *Alive Polarity Distributors.*

B Alvita Teas (Alvita Products Co.). *Deer Valley Farm.*

B Celestial Seasonings Herb Teas (Celestial Seasonings). *Deer Valley Farm, Hartenthaler's, Walnut Acres.*

B Fixminze Pompadour (Pompadour). *Le Jardin du Gourmet.*

B Herb Teas. *Bay Spice House, Earthsong Herb Shop, Haussmann's, Merry Gardens, Nichols Garden Nursery, Penn Herb Co., Shaker Workshops, Wide World of Herbs.*

B Magic Mountain Herb Teas (Magic Mountain Herb Tea Co.).

B San Francisco Herb Tea (San Francisco Herb & Natural Food Co./Nature's Way Products).

B Satori Teas (Satori Products). Unusually sweet natural herbal tea blends.

B Traditional's Herb Tea Blends (Traditional Medicinals). Natural hemp and wood bags. *The Herb Patch.*

Cotton Tea Bags
A Cotton Tea Bags. *The Country Store & Farm, Penn Herb Co.*

See also **Herbs & Spices.**

TELEPHONES

Plastic.

SAFE ALTERNATIVES
Use a speaker phone from several feet away.

Use an old telephone. Most have metal or wood bases with receivers made of old outgassed Bakelite (phenol-formaldehyde resin) or hard natural rubber. If you can find a local dealer who specializes in old telephones, he may be able to make a metal receiver.

Purchase a new phone made entirely of wood and metal with cloth cords.

Use a small headset.

Note: If you must use special telephone equipment because "hearing, speech, visual, or motion impairment interferes with the use of the telephone," you can apply to your local telephone company for a reduction in certain charges and exemption from some other charges. Pacific Telesis calls its form "Application for Reduction in and Exemption from Charges for Telephone Services." Ask your local telephone company representative if similar rates are available.

Brand Name/*Mail Order*

Phones made of natural materials can be purchased at phone-center stores, telephone shops, or by mail.

B *Billard's Old Telephones.* Large selection of old telephones and parts. Will also put modern phone works into old phones.

B Butcher Block Phones (AT&T).

B Country Junction Phones (AT&T). Desktop model only. Others have plastic parts. *Sears.*

C Telephone Headsets (ACS Communications). Though made mainly of plastic, they are so small that one's exposure to the plastic is proportionally much less than with regular phones. *JS & A, The Sharper Image.*

TEXTILES

Dyes; formaldehyde; phenol; plastics (acrylonitrile, nylon, polyester, polyethylene, polyurethane, polyvinyl chloride/vinyl chloride).

Since World War II, hundreds of synthetic "miracle" fibers have been developed and are now in popular use. Although little scientific evidence exists to conclusively prove that these fibers themselves are harmful, chemicals such as toxic phenol, carcinogenic vinyl chloride, and other harmful plastics that are used to make them may be absorbed by the skin.

In addition to their potentially toxic effects, plastic fibers are not very comfortable. As a group, none absorb moisture very well, making you uncomfortably hot, sticky, and clammy in warm weather, providing an ideal environment for bacteria growth. They are also poor choices for winter wear, as they are not good conductors of heat.

Plastic fibers are also difficult to clean because they tend to absorb oil from the skin and hold oily stains that can be effectively removed only with specially developed synthetic detergents (which also pollute and cause health problems).

"Static cling" is another problem unique to synthetic fibers, caused by an electric charge created by the friction of the synthetic fiber against the body. To solve this problem, even more synthetic chemicals are used in fabric softeners and antistatic agents.

Many textile products are treated with formaldehyde. Even if not stated on the label, all polyester/cotton blend fabrics have formaldehyde finishes. Polyester/cotton bedsheets have a particularly heavy finish because of their continuous use and frequent laundering. Formaldehyde is also used on nylon fabrics to make them flameproof. Some pure cotton fabrics have been treated with formaldehyde finishes for easy care. Even though it is not required by law, clothing labels will usually reveal a finish that makes them "crease resistant," "permanent pressed," "durable pressed," "no-iron," "shrink proof," "stretch proof," "water repellent," "waterproof," or "permanently pleated," since these are qualities considered desirable to the consumer. These finishes combine formaldehyde resin directly with the fiber, making the formaldehyde irremovable. At the end of processing, new textile products often contain free formaldehyde levels of 800 ppm to 1000 ppm (parts-per-million). Simple washing can lower these levels to 100 ppm, but formaldehyde continues to be released as the resin breaks down during washing, ironing, and wear.

Flame retardants are another problem, especially since most polyester fibers are treated with them. Even though the carcinogenic TRIS, a leading flame retardant, was banned by the Consumer Product Safety Commission (CPSC) in children's sleepwear, it is still legally used in adult sleepwear, hospital gowns, industrial uniforms, wigs, and other textile products we use daily.

SAFE ALTERNATIVES
Use natural fibers and stuffing/insulation materials—cotton, linen, silk, all the various types of wool, down, feathers, kapok (a fiber taken from the seed pod of the tropical kapok, or silk-cotton tree), and natural-fiber blends: cotton/silk, linen/cotton, and wool/cotton (commonly known as Viyella). With the exception of the use of pesticides during growing periods, very few chemicals are used in the processing of natural fibers. Unlike synthetic fibers, where the only

way to get rid of all the petrochemicals is to destroy the fiber itself, the finishes and dyes used in the processing of natural fibers can either be avoided or effectively removed.

Cotton
Cotton is a natural cellulosic fiber, taken from hairs that develop around the seed pod of the cotton plant. After it is picked, the pod is placed into the cotton gin, which separates the seed, the lint, and the linters. The lint is then spun into yarn and the shorter linters used for cotton batting, in making rayon, and in the production of paper.

Cotton quality is determined by the length of the fiber in the seed pod. Long-staple varieties, such as Sea Island, Egyptian, and Pima are the highest quality.

Two terms that you will frequently find on labels of cotton items are "sanforized" and "mercerized." Sanforized fabrics have been precompressed to the size to which they would shrink after washing by way of a mechanical process that controls shrinkage, involving no chemicals and considered harmless. Mercerized fibers have undergone a nontoxic process by which they have been immersed under tension in a strong solution of sodium hydroxide (derived from salt), which is then washed off. This permanently improves the strength, absorbancy, and appearance of the fabric as well as providing excellent colorfastness.

Cotton is soft, nonirritating, absorbs body moisture, allows the skin to breathe, and is cool in summer and warm in winter. Nevertheless, it is the most contaminated of all the natural fibers because of heavy pesticide spray. In Guatemala, where there are huge cotton plantations, the cotton can be sprayed up to fifty times in a single three-month growing cycle. A woman who has a small mail-order business selling cotton products writes:

I have my own personal conflict with cotton. Cotton in itself is a natural fiber created by our great Creator for our own use and enjoyment. But modern agriculture and big business have made a monster out of this gentle giant. I would say that about 30 percent of the people who live in this farming community valley suffer from the intensive cotton spraying. Cotton is sprayed in the early spring with a fungicide, then in the fall with a defoliant to rid the plants of their leaves so that the farmer will get more money for his crop. (Leaf matter in the cotton pickings lowers the grade and hence the quality and price received for the fiber.) I hear all too often that local people have colds, allergies, etc. when I know that they are suffering from the cotton spraying. And the hospital nurses record that more babies are born with defects nine months after the spraying. I love cotton and still consider it one of our best fiber friends. I do question its growing practices.

After processing, however, whatever pesticide residues remain in the final fabric seem to be harmless, except for those people extremely sensitive to pesticides.

Linen

Linen is made from fibers from the inner bark of the flax plant. The bark is first removed from the plants and left in the field so that natural bacterial action can loosen the fibers. The stems are then crushed mechanically and the fibers removed. At the mill, the fibers are combed to separate the different lengths and align them in preparation for spinning.

Linen is often used in its natural beige shade, or bleached to make a lighter color, rather than being dyed.

Silk

A protein fiber, silk is taken from the cocoon of the "silkworm" caterpillar. Each cocoon is spun of one continuous silk filament extruded from the body of the silkworm inside. Most silk is produced by cultivated silkworms. The cultivation process begins with the laying of the eggs by silk moths. After incubation, the young silkworms are fed mulberry leaves until ready to begin spinning the cocoon. The cocoons are made of the silk filaments and a gummy substance that holds them together. The gum is first softened with warm water, allowing the filaments to be separated and formed into strands of yarn, and then removed entirely with a soap solution.

Wool

A natural miracle fiber, wool is naturally fire resistant. It is warm in winter and cool in summer; it breathes, and it also resists soil so is easy to care for. Wool is a sign of quality and looks good for many years.

The term *wool* is a general one, referring to protein fibers spun from fleece of the sheep or lamb or from the hair of the angora or cashmere goat, the camel, the alpaca, the llama, or the vicuña.

After shearing, the wool fleece is washed a number of times in a soapy alkaline solution. This "scouring" removes the lanolin, a natural oil that keeps the fleece soft and waterproof. "Unscoured" wool retains the natural water repellency of the lanolin.

If significant amounts of dirt, burrs, sticks, and other vegetable matter remain after scouring, the fleece is carbonized with sulfuric acid to remove the extraneous matter. The wool is then carded and combed, the fibers separated with fine wire teeth in preparation for spinning.

Wool fleece of various qualities is taken from over 200 different breeds of sheep and several exotic animals.

Sheep's Wool—comprises the largest percentage of wool manufactured. Higher-quality sheep's wool is sheared from live sheep; poorer-quality wool is removed from slaughtered animals with chemicals or natural bacterial action and is generally blended with other types of wool.

Merino Wool—from Merino sheep, is considered to be the highest-quality sheep's wool.

Lamb's Wool—fleece from sheep eight months old or younger.

Icelandic Wool—from sheep with coats that are naturally longer, silkier, and more water repellent than those of other sheep, producing a bulky yet lightweight yarn. Most Icelandic wools are sold undyed in their natural shades of brown, charcoal, gray, and white. The yarn is unscoured and untreated, retaining the lanolin that makes it naturally water and soil resistant.

Alpaca—from one of the domesticated breeds of camel-like South African animals related to the wild vicuña. The alpaca live in Peru at an elevation of 14,000 to 16,000 feet. Alpaca hair is long, uncommonly soft, and has insulating qualities sufficient to keep the animals warm in the freezing temperatures of the Andes Mountains.

Vicuña—from a wild South American mammal resembling a llama. It has soft, delicate wool, much like its domesticated relative, the alpaca.

Angora—made from the hair of the angora rabbit. It is often blended with sheep's wool.

Yak—from the long-haired ox that lives on the high plateaus of Tibet and central Asia.

Cashmere—fiber obtained from the fleece of the Kashmir goat, an animal native to the Himalaya Mountains of India, China, and Tibet. Only the fine under-hair of the fleece is used, gathered by combing the animals during the shedding season.

Camel's Hair—from the hair of the two-humped Bactrian camel of central Asia. In the spring, the camels begin to shed their hair, and the caravans they travel in are followed from place to place by a trailer collecting the hair as it drops. The soft, downy hair is used to make camel's hair cloth, usually a natural light brown or tan, but sometimes dyed to darker colors.

Sheepskin—soft sueded leather with woolen fleece on one side. It is used for coats, rugs, bedspreads, slippers, seat covers, and other products.

Shearling is sheepskin from a young lamb that has never been sheared.

Because wool is highly susceptible to attack by moths, many companies treat their woolens with one of two types of mothproofing. The first involves chemically changing the disulfide cross-linkages in the fiber to create larger and stronger linkages. Moths cannot digest this chemically altered fiber, and starve. The other type is simply an insecticide (sodium fluorosilicate, DDT, or dieldrin) that is poisonous to the moth larvae, applied during manufacture or dry cleaning. Some insecticide treatments are durable through laundering and dry cleaning, while some are removable and must be renewed with each cleaning. Because it is difficult or impossible for the consumer to distinguish chemically altered mothproofing from durable or removable insecticide treatments, it is much safer to buy an entirely unmothproofed product.

Most wool imported from the British Isles, South America, Iceland, and Greece is unmothproofed unless specified. Domestic stores and distributors often treat woolens on the premises to prevent problems with moths. Check with the retailer before purchase to see if mothproofing has been used. Often, by advance request, they will hold for you an unmothproofed garment from a future shipment.

Wool can also be treated to be "washable," either with chlorine gas or liquid chlorine compounds or with petrochemical resins. Finishes of this sort will be noted on the label, and should be avoided.

If you are "allergic to wool," try a softer variety of a natural unbleached wool; your allergy may be to the bleaches and dyes.

Down and Feathers

All are taken from the bodies of ducks and geese; goose down is the highest quality and most expensive. They are processed only by washing and sanitizing, as chemicals would break down the proteins in the feathers and destroy them.

You can buy down and feathers by the pound from *Feathered Friends* and *Limericks Linens*.

Natural-fiber products are easy to identify because the Textile Fiber Products Identification Act, passed in 1960, requires that each textile product be labeled with the generic names of the fibers from which it is made. The generic names are established by the Federal Trade Commission (FTC) and include twenty-one man-made fiber groups, plus the natural fibers. This law applies to all yarns, fabrics, household textile articles, and wearing apparel. Imported goods must also adhere to this law, and moreover the label must reveal the country of origin. Exempt from this regulation are upholstery stuffing; outer coverings of furniture, mattresses, and box springs; linings, interlinings, stiffenings, or paddings incorporated for structural purposes and not for warmth; sewing and handicraft threads; and bandages and surgical dressings. This labeling appears along with the name of the manufacturer, the size of the garment, and cleaning instructions, and it is usually attached to the seam of a garment near the waist or hemline.

Fibers must be listed in descending order, according to the percentage by weight of the fiber that is present in the product (for example, "80% polyester, 20% cotton"). Trademark names are permitted in addition, but must be capitalized if listed: "100% Fortrel polyester." If a fiber present comprises less than 5% of the total weight, it must be listed as "other fiber" unless it has a specific purpose, as in "4% spandex added for elasticity." Fibers of unknown origin (miscellaneous scraps, rags, odd lots, textile by-products, second-hand materials, or waste materials) are listed as "undetermined fiber." Fibers comprising less than .5% of the total weight need not be revealed. Technically, this would allow a manufacturer to make a fiber labeled "100% cotton" that actually is 99.5% cotton and .5% polyester, but the National Cotton Council feels that no manufacturer would go to the trouble to make a fabric containing .5% polyester because an amount that small of synthetic fiber would not affect the performance of the fabric; textile products labeled as being made from 100% natural fibers most probably are.

Label information seems to apply only to the fibers used in the body of the garment or item. Sometimes labels will read "100% natural fiber, exclusive of decoration," without revealing the fabric of the decoration. Sweaters labeled "100% cotton" often have nylon threads running through the bottom edge and sleeve cuffs to help retain the shape. Cotton chamois shirts sometimes have nylon interfacings behind the buttons. Polyester thread may be used in natural-fiber garments as well as synthetic zippers, elastic, trims, linings, and interfacings, and plastic buttons and hooks. Many less-expensive cotton undergarments especially will have synthetic elastic and trim.

In addition to government regulations, independent organizations sell logos to manufacturers, giving information about the fiber content or performance of the textile products that bear them. The use of these logos is regulated, and products are tested to make sure they live up to their claims.

The *Seal of Cotton* is a trademark of Cotton, Incorporated, and can only be used with its permission. Created in 1973, this brown-and-white logo indicates that the item is made from 100 percent domestic cotton. It is used on fabrics, garments, bed linens, and towels.

The *Natural Blend* seal, in use since 1974, is also a trademark of Cotton, Incorporated, and can be used only on fabrics that contain 60 percent or more cotton.

The *Woolmark* is a registered certification owned by the Wool Bureau, Incorporated, a division of the International Wool Secretariat. Labels are purchased by manufacturers for apparel, knitwear, floor covering, upholstery materials, blankets, and bedspreads. Since 1964, over 14,000 companies in over fifty countries have been licensed to use it. Items bearing this logo must be of pure wool and be labeled "100% pure wool," "100% virgin wool," "All pure wool," or "All virgin wool."

The *Woolblend Mark* was introduced in 1972 by the Wool Bureau, Incorporated. Products displaying this logo must contain at least 60 percent wool, and identify all nonwool components by their generic names.

Superwash is a registered certification mark used in conjunction with the Woolmark and the Woolblend Mark. This logo indicates that the wool product has been "chemically treated" to make it felt resistant.

Look for products with the Seal of Cotton and the Woolmark to ensure that the item is made from 100 percent natural fiber. The other logos will help you identify which items contain synthetic fibers or chemical finishes that you may want to avoid.

As a second choice, wear rayon, a man-made fiber that, unlike other synthetic fibers, is comprised of cellulose, a substance found in all plants. Cellulose used in making rayon is taken from cotton linters, old cotton rags, paper, and wood pulp. The cellulose is broken down with petrochemicals and then reformed into threads resembling cotton or silk.

Launder all textiles before use to remove any finishes that may be present (this includes fabric for beds or upholstery). If simple laundering is not sufficient, try several launderings or soaking the fabric in hot water with baking soda or vinegar for several hours or overnight. Sometimes several soakings are needed.

Avoid textile products with formaldehyde finishes. These are sometimes difficult to detect because label information about fabric finishes is not required by law. Types of finishes are sometimes voluntarily included on the label, but only when the addition of the finish is a favorable selling point to the consumer. What the finish is made from is never revealed.

Avoid textile products with fire-retardant finishes. To fireproof fabrics, dip the fabric in a solution of ¼ cup alum dissolved in 1 gallon water. Or use naturally flame-resistant wool.

Avoid fabrics with dyes that bleed; if the dye comes out in water, it can be released by perspiration and absorbed by the skin. Because no laws require the dye type to be listed on the label, it is impossible to tell if the dye used on any particular fiber might be carcinogenic or simply cause an allergic reaction.

Choose natural- and light-colored fibers, and fabrics such as mercerized cotton that are colorfast. Wash fabrics well before wearing to remove any excess dyes. Ideal—however impractical for most people—would be to buy untreated, undyed fabric and yarn, and color them yourself using natural dyes.

See also Afghans, Barrier Cloth, Batting, Beds, Bedspreads, Blankets, Bumper Pads, Clothing, Comforters & Quilts, Diapers, Dyes, Elastic, Fabric, Feminine Protection, Ironing Board Covers, Luggage, Mattress Pads, Mosquito Netting, Pillows, Potholders, Rugs & Carpets, Shoes, Shower Caps, Shower Curtains, Sleeping Bags, Table Linens, Thread, Towels, Toys, Umbrellas, Window Coverings, and Yarn.

THREAD

Plastics (nylon, polyester).

SAFE ALTERNATIVES
Brand Name/*Mail Order*
Buy cotton or silk thread at your local fabric store.

AB *Cerulean Blue*. Silk sewing thread.

AB *The Cotton Place*. Cotton sewing, quilting, and button thread; silk sewing thread.

AB *Erlander's Natural Products*. Cotton quilting, sewing thread, and linen thread.

AB *Gohn Bros*. Cotton quilting thread.

B *Norton Candle and Handiwork House*. Colored 100% cotton quilting thread.

B *The Oriental Rug Company*. Cotton thread, black and white only.

B *S. & C. Huber, Accoutrements*. Silk embroidery floss.

B *Sureway Trading Enterprises*. Silk sewing and embroidery thread.

B *Utex Trading Enterprises*. Silk sewing and embroidery thread.

See also Textiles.

TISSUES

Colors; formaldehyde; fragrance.

SAFE ALTERNATIVES
Use plain white cotton handkerchiefs. Even plain white tissues still may contain formaldehyde.

TOFU

Tofu is "curd" or "cheese" made from soybeans and natural minerals. It can be fried like meat, stir-fried with vegetables, mashed and blended with dips and salad dressings, and used as a cheese replacement.

Brand Name/*Mail Order*
Natural-foods stores and supermarkets all carry tofu. All brands are additive free; those listed below are made from soybeans.

A Erewhon Tofu (Erewhon).

A Health Valley Tofu-Ya (Health Valley Natural Foods).

A Living Lightly Tofu (Living Lightly).

A Sunburst Farms Organic Tofu (Sunburst Farms Natural Foods).

See also Food.

TOILET PAPER

Colors; formaldehyde; fragrance.

While not scientifically proven, it has been observed by many that toilet paper containing dyes and scents can cause all types of genital irritation, sometimes even misdiagnosed as herpes.

SAFE ALTERNATIVES
Brand Name/*Mail Order*
Buy unscented, white toilet paper. It still may contain formaldehyde, but I have no do-it-yourself toilet paper to propose!

B Chiffon Unscented Tissue (Crown Zellerbach Corp.).

B Co-op Toilet Paper (Universal Co-operatives).

B Generic Toilet Paper (Orchid Paper Products).

B Marina Toilet Paper (Crown Zellerbach Corp.).

B MD Unscented Twin Quilted Tissue (Georgia Pacific Corp.).

B   Scotch Buy Toilet Paper (Safeway Stores).

B   Scottissues (Scott Paper).

B   Truly Fine Bathroom Tissue (Safeway Stores).

TOOTHBRUSHES

Plastics (nylon, PVC/vinyl chloride).

SAFE ALTERNATIVES
Brand Name/*Mail Order*
Choose a natural-bristle toothbrush, preferably with a handle of a natural material, from your natural-foods store.

A   *Cambridge Chemists.* Bone-handle, and natural-bristle toothbrushes, made in the same manner since 1805.

A   *Janice Corp.* "Handmade in England of bone and the finest natural white bristle."

A   Ohdee Natural Toothbrush (Dalco). A wooden stick that you can form into a natural-bristle toothbrush. Still in use after thousands of years in Africa, Asia, and the Middle East.

A   *Pure Planet Products.* Bone-handle toothbrush from China.

B   Fuchs Toothbrushes (Fuchs). Plastic handle. *Pure Planet Products, Whole Earth Access.*

B   Tom's Toothbrushes (Tom's of Maine). Plastic handle. *Erewhon Mail Order, Erlander's Natural Products, Kennedy's Natural Foods.*

See also Toothpaste.

TOOTHPASTE

Ammonia; benzyl alcohol/sodium benzoate; colors; ethanol; flavors; fluoride; formaldehyde; glycols; mineral oil; plastic (PVP); saccharin.

SAFE ALTERNATIVES
Brush regularly with plain water, and floss to remove food particles.

Brand Name/*Mail Order*
Most of the brands listed below can be purchased at your natural-foods store.

A   Amway Natural Ingredient Toothpaste (Amway Corp.). From Amway distributors.

A   Chico-San Toothpaste/Dentie Tooth Powder (Chico-San). *Chico-San.*

A   Dr. Bronner's Calcium Carrot Powder (All-One-God-Faith). *Deer Valley Farm, Pure Planet Products.*

A   Erewhon Dentie Toothpowder (Erewhon). Charred eggplant and sea salt. *Erewhon Mail Order.*

A   Paul de Sousa's Chlorophyll Tooth Powder (Paul de Sousa's Co.). *Pure Planet Products.*

A   Peelu Tooth Powder (Ahmad's Peelu). A powder made from the branches of the peelu tree. Claims to whiten teeth better than any commercial toothpaste, remove plaque, and prevent cavities.

A   Sabertooth Natural Tooth Powder (Sabertooth).

A   Weleda Toothpastes (Weleda). *Meadowbrook Herbs & Things, Weleda, Wholesome Paks.*

B   Barth's Toothpastes (Barth Vitamin Corp.). *Barth's of Long Island, Pure Planet Products, The Soap Opera.*

B Care Natural Chlorophyll Dentifrice (Sunstar).

B Holistic Propolis Toothpaste (Holistic Products Corp.).

B Nature's Gate Herbal Toothpastes (Nature's Gate Herbal Cosmetics). *Erewhon Mail Order, The Herb Patch, The Soap Opera.*

B Nature de France Toothpastes (Nature de France). *Erewhon Mail Order, Nature de France, The Soap Opera.*

B Neem Herbal Toothpaste (Nandi Imports).

B Peelu Toothpaste (Uni-Pac Labs).

B Phytomer Mint Toothpaste (Sea-N-Earth Distributor).

B Tom's Natural Toothpastes (Tom's of Maine). *Erewhon Mail Order, Erlander's Natural Products, Kennedy's Natural Foods, The Soap Opera, Walnut Acres.*

B Tom's Natural Toothpaste with Fluoride (Tom's of Maine). Contains naturally occurring calcium fluoride.

B Xylitol All-Natural Toothpaste (Finnfoods). *Pure Planet Products, The Soap Opera.*

Do-It-Yourself
• Use plain baking soda, or mix baking soda with a few drops peppermint extract or oil, or other extract or oil of your choice.
• Use plain salt or mix 1 part salt with 2 parts baking soda.
• Mix ½ cup powdered pumice with ¼ cup honey or glycerin to form a paste.
• Mashed strawberries. Freeze them in cubes when in season and use during the winter months.

• Use calcium ascorbate (the salt of vitamin C, not ascorbic acid).
• Soak 1 teaspoon dried Irish moss in 1 cup water for 15 minutes in a small enamel pot. Bring to slow boil and simmer. Strain the gel through cheesecloth into a small glass container and add 1 teaspoon salt and 1 teaspoon baking soda. Mix completely, then add a few drops chlorophyll and 2 drops essential oil of licorice, fennel, or anise.
• Use plain calcium carbonate or mix with a little essential oil of wintergreen, spearmint, or peppermint.
• Run dried lemon peel in a blender to make ½ cup of powder and mix with ¼ cup baking soda.

See also Beauty Products and Toothbrushes.

TOWELS

Plastic (polyester).

SAFE ALTERNATIVES
Brand Name/*Mail Order*
Buy natural-fiber kitchen and bath towels wherever towels are sold.

A *Cotton Brokers.* "The most absorbant towel you can get . . . not available in retail stores," and at the best price.

A *The Cotton Co.* "The softest, thickest towels ever!" Cotton, of course.

A *Janice Corp.* Heavy white cotton terry towels.

AB Cannon Fulfillment/Magnificence/Royal Classic/Royal Touch (Cannon). *Erlander's Natural Products, J. Schachter, Ras Distributors.*

AB Fieldcrest Royal Velvet (Fieldcrest Mills). *E. Braun & Co., Homespun Crafts.*

AB J. P. Stevens Echelon/Indulgence (J. P. Stevens).

AB *Laura Ashley.* Cotton terry towels in unusual colors.

AB *Limericks Linens.* British cotton bath towels.

AB Martex Gentle Touch/Invitation/Luxor Pima/Patrician Pima/Splendor (Westpoint Pepperell). *E. Braun & Co.*

AB Pratesi (Pratesi). *Pratesi.*

AB *Vermont Country Store.* Commercial-grade cotton hotel towels.

100% Cotton Kitchen Towels

A *Cotton Brokers, Janice Corp.*

AB *The Chef's Catalog, Erlander's Natural Products, Vermont Country Store, Williams-Sonoma.*

B *Clothcrafter's, Homespun Weavers, Limericks Linens.*

See also Textiles.

TOYS

Plastics (polyester, polyethylene, polystyrene, PVC/vinyl chloride).

SAFE ALTERNATIVES
Choose toys made from wood, metal, or natural fibers.

Brand Name/*Mail Order*
Most of the brand-name toys listed below can be purchased at any large toy-store.

A *After the Stork.* "Happy toys of select hardwoods, carefully sanded and rounded. Nontoxic, non-splintering, and safe for teething."

A *Alafoss Icewool.* Sheep and polar bears made of Icelandic wool shearling.

A *Carjeanne Enterprises.* Handcrafted stuffed animal toys. "Fabrics are washed in baking soda, stuffing is organically grown cotton, all threads and trims are 100% cotton. . . . No toys are made in the presence of tobacco smoke or animals."

A *Castlemoor.* Cuddly animals made from "pure British wool fleece."

A Discovery World (Small World Toys). Wooden dinosaur and insect model kits.

A *Frontier Toys.* Handmade trains, cars, airplanes, and pull toys made from unpainted Oregon-grown pine.

A *Golden Touch Lambskin Products.* A stuffed sheepskin lamb.

A *Mountain Toy Makers.* Wooden cars, trains, animals, and so on, of original design and handmade to be sturdy and safe. "We have always resisted the temptation to finish our toys as a matter of principle. Since toys spend upwards of 50% of playtime in a small child's mouth, we feel that the risk to the child, even from so-called nontoxic paint, is too great to warrant a finish."

A *Overland Sheepskin Co.* Furry sheepskin animals.

A *Ramshead.* Furry sheepskin animals.

A *Reekie's of Grasmere.* Furry sheepskin animals.

A Woodkrafter Kits (Woodcrafter Kits). Hardwood kits for small airplanes, boats and "earth movers."

AB *Hearthsong.* Imaginative playthings and handmade stuffed dolls made with natural materials. Also beeswax crayons, "modeling beeswax," and books on toy making.

AB *Ramus International.* Stuffed sheepskin animals.

AB *Wide World Games.* Table-top games, board games, puzzles, building blocks, checkerboards, push and pull toys, and other games from around the world made from birch, oak, maple, walnut, and cherry. Read descriptions carefully, as many items are made from plywood.

B *Berea College Student Craft Industries.* Solid-wood board games: skittles, checkers, Chinese checkers, and so on.

B *Bill Muller, Toymaker.* Imaginative wooden toys that rock or roll or puzzle, each "individually handcrafted and carefully sanded.... We never use plastic, and there are no artificial finishes—no paint or varnish."

B BRIO (Brio). All types of wooden toys including fantastic elaborate pieces to build a train system with a whole city around it. *Hanna Andersson.*

B *Childcraft.* Wooden blocks, train sets, and the like in a catalog that has mostly plastic toys.

B *Easy Pieces.* A variety of wooden puzzles "backed with hard-board . . . natural wood stain (nontoxic)."

B *Erlander's Natural Products.* Stuffed toy kits that include untreated cotton batting for filling. Also kapok-filled "monkey sock" toys.

B Fast 111's Cars (Kenner Products).

B *Finger Prints.* Hand-cut hardwood toys made in Holland, "painted and varnished with nontoxic materials."

B Hot Wheels Cars (Mattel).

B Klein & Trumbly Hardwood Kindergarten Blocks (Klein & Trumbly). Oak and alder blocks with a natural finish.

B Lock-Ups Cars (Kidco).

B Matchbox Cars (Lesney Product Corp.).

B *Mountain Craft Shop.* Over 202 kinds of authentic American folk toys, reproductions of those once made at home and handed down through the generations. Includes toys such as "skyhook" (a gravity-defying device), "flying machine," several varieties of tops, many noisemakers, puzzles, and puppets, as well as clothespin, corncob, rope, and spool dolls.

B Playskool Blocks (Playskool/Milton Bradley).

B Pocket Cars (Tomy Corp.).

B *The Puzzle People.* Wood block puzzles.

B *Tryon Toymakers.* Handmade wooden toys, hand painted with "nontoxic enamel paint."

Puzzles, swings, and toy designs derived from original mountain toys.

B *Tully Toys.* A zoofull of adorable rocking animals made from "the finest of Southern hardwoods."

B Uncle Goose Alphabet Blocks (Uncle Goose Alphabet Blocks). "Child-safe nontoxic colors" on wood blocks.

See also Textiles.

TYPEWRITER CORRECTION FLUID

Cresol; ethanol; glycerin; naphthalene; plastic.

SAFE ALTERNATIVES
Use a word processor or a self-correcting typewriter.

Brand Name/*Mail Order*
Buy adhesive correction tapes or "white-out" tapes that strike a white powder over the error. They are sold at stationery and office-supply stores.

Adhesive
B Avery Self Adhesive Correction Tape (Avery Label).

B Pres-A-Ply 1-Line Correction Tape (Dennison Manufacturing Co.).

B Scotch Brand Post-It Cover-Up Tape (3M).

White-Out
B Carter's X-Pert Correction Tabs (Dennison Manufacturing Co.).

B Dixon Taperaser (Joseph Dixon Crucible Co.).

B Ko-Rec-Type (Eaton-Allen Corp.).

B Touch & Go Typing Correction Tape (Eberhard Faber).

See also Computers.

U

UMBRELLAS

Plastics (nylon, polyester, PVC/vinyl chloride).

SAFE ALTERNATIVES
Brand Name/*Mail Order*
Umbrellas made of 100% cotton and silk do exist, although some of the cotton ones are not very effective at keeping you dry once the water-repellent finish begins to wear off. Choose a nylon umbrella rather than a vinyl umbrella as the least toxic, most inexpensive, most effective way to stay dry in the rain. Or have an umbrella custom covered with a very tightly woven (250 threads per inch or more) cotton cloth.

B *Janice Corp.* Water repellent wood-handled umbrella covered with natural-color cotton.

B *Swaine Adeney Brigg.* Expensive silk umbrellas with wood handles.

B *Uncle Sam Umbrella Shop.* "No repair has ever stumped Sam. Let him solve your umbrella problem." Fine handmade umbrellas. Carries waterproofed cotton umbrellas. Can custom make, offering a choice of over 2000 handles; will cover in cotton, silk, or your own fabric.

B *Vermont Country Store.* Water-repellent cotton poplin umbrellas.

See also Textiles.

UNDERGARMENTS

See Clothing.

UPHOLSTERY SHAMPOO

See Rug, Carpet, & Upholstery Shampoo.

VAPOR BARRIER

Most vapor barriers are impregnated with asphalt.

Vapor barrier (also called building paper or roofing felt) is a necessary part of wall construction. When constructing new walls, the vapor barrier is fitted to minimize the amount of pollutants that could leak inside from the building materials. Walls generally contain an interior wall surface, insulation, vapor barrier, sheathing, and an exterior wall surface.

SAFE ALTERNATIVES
Use an unperforated foil-backed paper and install with staples or foil tape. If the vapor barrier is placed against the inside of the *exterior* wall, fumes from treated woods, insulation, caulking, and electrical wires are pulled into the room. Instead, place the vapor barrier against the inside of the *interior* wall, next to the insulation, to block fumes from building materials and force them outdoors.

Foil vapor barrier is also excellent for many other uses when it is necessary to block fumes. It is available either with foil on one side and brown paper on the other, or with foil on both sides, and it can be used to line particle-board cabinets, to cover plastic items, and is even durable enough to be used as a temporary floor covering.

Brand Name/*Mail Order*
If your local building-supply store doesn't carry foil vapor barrier, ask to order it.

B Denny Foil Vapor Barrier (Denny Co.).

VINEGAR

Pesticide residues.

SAFE ALTERNATIVES
Brand Name/*Mail Order*
Because of their acidic nature, vinegars do not need preservatives, and so are as safe as any other nonorganic, additive-free food. Flavored vinegars contain natural herbs, spices, and fruits. So enjoy yourself, and let the many different varieties add a lift to your menus. The following vinegars are organic, and for that reason, particularly recommended.

A Chico-San Seitai Temple Rice Malt Vinegar (Chico-San). *Chico-San.*

A De Sousa's Apple Cider Vinegar (Paul de Sousa's Co.). *Kennedy's Natural Foods.*

See also Food.

VITAMINS & MINERALS

Benzyl alcohol/sodium benzoate; BHA/BHT; colors; flavors; formaldehyde; glycerin; mineral oil; plastic (PVP); sucrose; sulfur compounds; talc.

Certain nutrient deficiencies can make us more susceptible to the negative health effects of specific chemical substances.

Deficiency	Susceptibility
Vitamin A	DDT, hydrocarbon carcinogens, PCBs
Vitamin C	arsenic, cadmium, carbon monoxide, chromium, DDT, dieldrin, lead, mercury, nitrates, ozone
Vitamin E	Lead, ozone
Calcium	Lead
Iron	Hydrocarbon carcinogens, lead, manganese
Magnesium	Fluoride
Phosphorus	Lead
Protein	DDT and other insecticides
Riboflavin	Hydrocarbon carcinogens, lead, ozone
Selenium	Cadmium, mercury, ozone
Zinc	Cadmium

The proper supplements, however, can help our bodies fight back against unavoidable pollutants. Especially important are the antioxidants: vitamin A, vitamin C, vitamin E, beta-carotene, glutathione, and cysteine. Be careful, though, about taking too much of some supplements; not more than 25,000 units of vitamin A or 500 mcg of selenium should be taken per day.

SAFE ALTERNATIVES

Vitamins come from two sources: food (natural) and petrochemicals (synthetic). There is a real controversy over which is better.

Despite the fact that synthetic and natural vitamins have identical chemical structures, they have subtle biological differences and different levels of biological activity, which affect how much of the vitamin can actually be used by the body. Many reports show that natural vitamins with their higher levels of biological activity are better utilized than are synthetic forms.

Impurities do exist in both natural and synthetic vitamins. Dr. Theron G. Randolph, a pioneer in the treatment of chemical sensitivities, has observed that "synthetically derived substances may cause a reaction in a chemically susceptible person, while the same material of natural origin may be tolerated—even though the two substances have identical chemical structures."

Taking into consideration the present state of the vitamin industry, the most reasonable way to take vitamins for most people is to combine natural with synthetic.

The only truly natural vitamins are those that come directly from a food source, being either a highly nutritious food itself (bee pollen, for example), a powdered concentrate of the food with the moisture and fiber removed (as in barley leaf juice powder), or the isolated component of a food (as in wheat germ oil). One indicator that the supplement is from a food source is a label that lacks a vitamin potency listing, since being a natural substance, the potency will change with each batch. Natural vitamins generally are low potency, will list their food source on the label, and come in liquid form or large-size tablets, or require that you take multiple doses several times per day. For many people, the added nutrients found in the following supplemental foods are adequate for their needs.

Alfalfa
Chlorophyll, vitamins A, D, E, K, and U, and many minerals and trace elements.

Barley Leaf Juice Powder
Vitamins B and C, calcium, iron, magnesium, and over 100 enzymes. Studies in Japan have shown that barley leaf juice powder can neutralize the harmful effects of PVC, cadmium, nicotine, strontium, and mercury by changing them into insoluble salts, and can deactivate the mutagenicity of nitrogen compounds in automobile exhaust.

Bee Pollen
Complete protein, all vitamins, minerals, trace elements, hormones and enzymes. Buy pure granules, as tablets may contain unneccessary additives.

Bone Meal
Calcium.

Brewer's Yeast
Complete protein and B complex vitamins. Look for brands whose labels state "not blended or fortified." If potencies for vitamins B_1, B_2, and B_6 are identical, the product has added vitamins.

Chlorophyll
Trace minerals.

Cod Liver Oil
Vitamins A and D.

Desiccated Liver
Complete protein, B complex vitamins, and iron.

Kelp
Minerals and trace elements.

Spirulina
Complete protein, minerals, B vitamins, and vitamin E.

Wheat Germ Oil
Vitamin E.

Synthetic vitamins are high-potency vitamins in little pills. Most of the so-called natural vitamins on the market today are either fortified (low-potency natural vitamins mixed with high-potency synthetic vitamins) or synthetic in a natural base (the label will say something like "in a natural base containing . . ."). Heavily advertised, brightly colored high-potency vitamins with clever names are always synthetic and frequently contain many additives.

If you really need to take high doses of vitamins, then fortified vitamins or synthetic vitamins in a natural base are acceptable. Completely natural vitamins would be too cumbersome and prohibitively expensive. High-quality, additive-free synthetic vitamins have a minimum of impurities and the benefits of taking them far outweigh the harmful effects of whatever contaminants may be left in them. Be careful, however, of taking high doses of supplements for long periods of time without medical supervision.

Brand Name/*Mail Order*
Natural-foods stores are your best source for natural and additive-free dietary supplements.

Natural Supplements

A Bio-Strath (Naturally Vitamin Supplements). "Chemical-free concentrated yeast and herb liquid."

A Floradix (Salus of America). Mixed extracts of vegetables and herbs.

A Green Magma (Green Foods Corp.). *Erewhon Mail Order, Kennedy's Natural Foods.*

A *The Herb Patch.* "Completely natural" low-potency supplements "from pure food and herbal concentrates without sythetics added." Includes vitamin A from vegetable carotene, vitamin C "100% compounded from acerola cherries without any laboratory-synthesized ascorbic acid," vitamin E from vegetable oils, and calcium from carrots.

A *Jay Parker.* Pure selenium Se.

A Malabar (Malabar Formulas). Made from dried organ meats.

A Schoenberger Vegetable Crystals (Bio-Nutritional Products).

Additive-Free Synthetic Supplements

B Allergy Research Group (Nutricology). *Nutricology.*

B Carlson (Carlson).

B Kal (Kal).

B Mega VM (Scientific Consulting).

B Naturally (Naturally Vitamin Supplements).

B N F Factors (NF Factors).

B Plus (Plus Products).

B Schiff (Schiff Bio Food Products).

B Solgar (Solgar Co.).

B Thompson (W. M. Thompson Co.).

B Twin Lab (Twin Lab).

The following mail-order sources carry a large variety of natural and additive-free supplements: *Barth's of Long Island, Boudry Distributors, Bronson Pharmaceuticals, Deer Valley Farm, Eden Ranch, Elm Enterprises, Erewhon Mail Order, Great Earth Vitamins, Haussmann's Pharmacy, Kennedy's Natural Foods, Klaire Laboratories, Nature Food Centres, RVP the Health Savings Center, Shiloh Farms, Sivad Bioresearch, Sunburst Biorganics, Swanson Health Products, U.S. Health Club, Vitaline Formulas, Vitamin Specialties Co., Walnut Acres, Western Natural Products.*

Pathway makes individual formulas by prescription only from pure powdered natural or synthetic vitamins and minerals, according to your needs.

See also Food.

WALL CLEANERS

Ammonia; kerosene.

SAFE ALTERNATIVES
Do-It-Yourself
• Make a paste of water and cornstarch or Fuller's earth. Cover stain with paste and let set for 1 hour. Brush off the powder and repeat if necessary.

See also Cleaning Products.

WALLPAPER CLEANERS

Ammonia; naphthalene.

SAFE ALTERNATIVES
Do-It-Yourself
• Rub spots on wallpaper with an artist's gum eraser; the inside of a stale loaf of rye bread or a slice of rye bread; wheat bran sewn in an old sock; or borax.
• Make a paste of borax and water. Apply to spot and let set for a few minutes. Brush off with a soft cloth and repeat if necessary.
• Sprinkle baking soda on a damp cloth and rub onto spot, then rub lightly with fine steel wool.

See also Cleaning Products.

WATER

Asbestos; benzene; chlorine; fluoride; lead; methylene chloride; nitrates/nitrosamines; pesticides; plastic (vinyl chloride); toluene; trichloroethane; trichloroethylene; xylene.

Water can also contain BCEE, carbon tetrachloride, selenium, arsenic, cyanide, PCBs, dioxin, and dichloroethylene. Chlorine frequently combines with natural organic matter in the water (dead leaves and humus in soil, silt, and mud) to form trihalomethanes (THMs), the most common being the carcinogen chloroform. According to the Environmental Protection Agency (EPA), THMs are found in virtually every chlorinated drinking water supply in the United States.

In all, the EPA has identified more than 700 pollutants that occur regularly in drinking water. At least 22 are known carcinogens; others have not been tested. It has been estimated that the 700 identified pollutants may represent as little as 10 percent of the actual number of pollutants that exist in drinking water supplies, because adequate tests have not yet been invented to detect all the hazardous substances that may be present.

In addition, three different types of pipe also contribute pollutants. Metal pipes can leach cadmium, copper, iron, lead, or zinc. Asbestos cement pipes can release asbestos fibers. And even though the plastics industry insists that PVC pipe is safe, a 1980 study sponsored by the California Health Services Department showed that a wide variety of toxic and carcinogenic substances leach from the pipes into the water, including methyl ethyl ketone (MEK), dimethylformamide (DMF), cyclohexanone (CH), tetrahydrofuran (THF), trihalomethanes (THMs), carbontetrachloride, tetrachloroethene, trichloroethane, di-(2-ethylhexyl) phthalate (DEHP), dibutyl phthalate, and butylated hydroxy-toluene (BHT). These substances have not yet been examined by government agencies for safety, although the solvents used for installation have been tentatively associated with toxic effects on the liver and central nervous system. Water standing in the pipes for any length of time will additionally become contaminated with vinyl chloride.

The EPA has complete authority over drinking water from public water supplies, including all chemical additives—both those added for a specific purpose and those that find their way into the water supply accidentally. At present, the quality of our public water supply is controlled by National Interim Primary Drinking Water Regulations (Code of Federal Regulations Title 40, Part 141), developed by the EPA in accordance with the Safe Drinking Water Act of 1974, an amendment to the Public Health Service Act. Effective since 24 June 1977, these maximum contaminant levels were set "at a level at which, in the administrator's judgment based on such report, no known or anticipated adverse effects on the health of persons occur and which allows an adequate margin of safety."

Unfortunately, maximum contaminant levels exist for only eight inorganic chemicals (arsenic, barium, cadmium, lead, mercury, nitrate, selenium, and silver) and ten organic chemicals (endrin; lindane; methoxychlor; toxaphene; 2,4-D; 2,4,5-TP; and the trihalomethanes: bromodichloromethane, dibromochlor-omethane, bromoform, and chloroform). No regulations exist to protect us from an estimated 30,000 other hazardous substances found in tap water.

In some areas, even the inadequate federal drinking water standards may not be in effect, as the EPA expects each state to enforce the federal laws itself. While some states have refused to comply with the standards, even among the law-abiding states are some water districts that do not submit samples for examination.

According to the Safe Drinking Water Act, even if a maximum contaminant level has been set, the public water supply does not have to meet those standards: "A required treatment technique for a contaminant for which a recommended maximum contaminant level has been established . . . *shall reduce such contaminant to a level which is as close to the recommended maximum contaminant level for such contaminant as is feasible* . . . with the use of the best technology, treatment techniques, and other means, *which the administrator finds are generally available (taking cost into consideration)* [italics mine]."

Since most municipal water treatment facilities were built in the early 1900s for the purpose of disinfecting water rather than purifying it, these water treatment facilities are not designed to deal with the new pollutants found in our water today. The federal government projects that it would take billions of dollars and ten to fifteen years to upgrade these systems. Small communities are often financially unable to upgrade their water treatment facilities to improve water quality.

SAFE ALTERNATIVES

Use a water purification system to decontaminate water for drinking, food preparation, brushing teeth, and bathing. To avoid breathing chlorine fumes and to reduce skin contact with other contaminants while washing dishes or bathing, an entire house filtration system can be rented or purchased, or else filters can be attached to individual faucets.

Water purification systems use one or more of three basic types of water purification: activated carbon, distillation, and reverse osmosis. Each method works in a different way and each removes different pollutants. Examine each system's method and compare laboratory tests on water samples to determine which system best suits your personal needs.

A comparison of pollutants removed by the different methods shows that the purest water would be obtained from a system using a distiller or reverse-osmosis unit in conjunction with a carbon prefilter.

Activated Carbon Filtration

Also known as charcoal filtration, this is the most inexpensive and readily available water filtration method. It removes chlorine, pesticide residues, and other organic chemicals by adsorption, a process by which the pollutants are attracted by and stick to the carbon. It will *not* remove fluoride, salts, minerals, or nitrates, although carbon block will remove bacteria and heavy metals.

Activated carbon comes in filters of many different styles and capacities, from a carbon-filled straw you can suck water through to systems that filter water for the whole house. The least expensive brands are made from hard plastic. Though this does not seem to affect the water quality if water contacts the plastic only briefly while being filtered, water sitting in plastic over long periods of time will absorb polymers from the plastic. If you are extremely sensitive to plastics, you may not be able to tolerate even the slight exposure the water has while passing through the tube, and you will need an all-stainless-steel unit.

COMPARISON of POLLUTANTS REMOVED by WATER PURIFICATION METHODS

	Activated carbon granular	Activated carbon block	Distillation	Reverse osmosis
Asbestos	Some	Yes	Yes	Yes
Bacteria & viruses	Some	Yes	Yes	Some
Chlorine	Yes	Yes	No	No
Fluoride	No	Some	Yes	Yes
Heavy metals	No	Yes	Yes	Yes
Minerals	No	No	Yes	Yes
Nitrates	No	No	Yes	Yes
Organic chemicals	Yes	Yes	Some	Some
Salts	No	No	Yes	Yes

"Bacteriostatic" devices contain granulated carbon with silver added to kill bacteria; these are not recommended. Independent laboratory tests have shown that residual silver from these devices can find its way into the finished water product. While excess intake of silver has not yet been proven to be harmful to health, silver is nevertheless a heavy metal and frequent ingestion should be approached with caution. Furthermore, EPA studies indicate that silver does not actually reduce the bacteria count. Many manufacturers state that bacteriostatic devices should be used only on "municipally treated water" (which has already killed bacteria with the chlorination process).

Bacteria is a major problem in carbon units. Most bacteria that grow in the units are harmless, but a Canadian government health agency has identified almost a dozen potentially dangerous species of bacteria that can grow on the carbon. Conditions within the unit can encourage any bacteria that gets inside to multiply many times over, so units should be used only with water that is microbiologically safe. Bacteria counts increase when units are left unused for a period as short as five days. *Consumer Reports* magazine found that bacterial counts in the water could be greatly reduced if the first ten to thirty seconds of water that emerges from the unit is discarded. A carbon system made from a solid block of activated carbon acts as a strainer, trapping the bacteria between the highly compressed carbon granules where there is no room for them to multiply.

The small activated-carbon units that attach to faucet heads and are found in most department, drug, and discount stores are inexpensive and convenient, but do not contain a sufficient filter medium to effectively remove chemicals from the volume of water that passes through. Larger and more expensive units are available, however, that do an adequate job of removing chlorine and organic chemicals, provided that the carbon is changed regularly. You may want a carbon filtration system for your whole house to filter water for drinking, cooking, and bathing. If you live in an apartment or condominium with a central water source for the whole building, use smaller filters on separate faucets or shower heads.

One of the most important criteria for choosing a carbon unit is the relationship between the quantity of water going through the filter and the amount of carbon in the filter. Unfortunately, there is no formula for optimum performance. Use common sense and choose a filter large enough to do the job.

There are basically two types of units. Over-the-counter units sit on top of the counter and work either by your pouring the water through it manually, or by having a diverter to the tap, which can then either dispense the filtered water from the filter or back through the tap. Undersink models are mounted to the pipes beneath the sink and dispense the water either through the regular tap or through an additional tap installed for that purpose. These contain more carbon and are free flowing, purifying all the water that comes through.

The effective life of the activated carbon within a unit varies, depending on the amount of carbon present in relation to the amount of water used. At some point, the carbon will become saturated with pollutants and begin releasing them into the finished water product. This may happen at 50, 100 or 500 gallons. *Consumer Reports* found this to occur more often in those units using powdered carbon in a pad, and so recommends a unit with a granulated carbon cartridge.

Need for a carbon change can be signalled by a change in taste, a chlorine smell, or a reduced rate of water flow (a clogged filter will not allow as much water through). Don't rely on these indicators, however, to ensure pure water. Granulated carbon should be changed at least every six months; carbon block, once a year.

As mentioned before, how often you change the carbon really depends on the amount of carbon used and the amount of water flow. Try to figure out how much water you use on a daily basis and compare that with the estimated life of the carbon. Mark the date on your calendar and change the carbon when that time has passed, even if you think it is unnecessary. It doesn't hurt to change the carbon too often, and besides, you can't really tell exactly when it must be done without having a water sample analyzed. Frequent filter changes will also help to keep the bacteria count low. This applies if you are using your carbon filter by itself or in conjunction with a distiller or reverse osmosis unit.

Activated carbon units are recommended for use with cold water only. Labels specifically warn that the carbon will not remove contaminants effectively from hot water. The units will, however, significantly reduce the level of chlorine fumes when used on hot water taps in showers and on kitchen sinks, even though the filtered hot water itself may not be suitable for drinking.

Reverse Osmosis (R/O)

These systems can be used to further enhance the abilities of carbon filtration. R/O purifies water by causing it to pass through a plastic or cellulose membrane that lets in water molecules but not pollutants. A similar method can be found in plant life, where water passes through cellulose, which purifies nutrients and disposes of waste fluids. R/O will remove asbestos, bacteria and viruses, fluoride, heavy metals, minerals, salts, and nitrates not removed by the carbon.

Because of the amount of plastic involved in an R/O unit, the water it produces should not be used for drinking without additional carbon filtration. If you do get an R/O system, be sure to clean or change the membrane every two years.

Distillation

This method comes closest to duplicating nature's own system for water purification—the hydrologic cycle. Within the cycle, evaporating water rises from the earth's surface, leaving the impurities behind, then condenses and returns to earth in its pure form as precipitation.

Water distillers work by boiling water to turn it into steam and then condensing it into "pure" water. Boiling the water destroys bacteria and other living materials that the distilling process leaves behind in the boiling tank, along with inorganic chemicals, heavy metals, trace minerals, and other inert impurities that are too heavy to rise with the water vapor. Early versions of water distillers concentrated only on the removal of organic solid materials such as salts, calcium, silt, dirt, iron, and nitrates.

Some of the newer water distillers attempt to remove volatile organic chemicals with a "volatile gas vent." This vents the steam from these chemicals when they pass their vaporization point. Often many of them do not escape but are instead condensed into the final distilled water product. An alternative method for removing organic chemicals would be to leave the cover off an air-cooled system for one to two minutes after the water has come to a boil, and then to cover it for the distillation process. If you are considering purchasing a distiller, make sure you choose a complete distillation system that includes an adequate activated carbon prefilter.

A number of different types of home-use distillers are available on today's market, differing primarily in materials they are made from and the methods used in heating the water and in condensing the steam back into liquid form.

Distillers are made from glass or stainless steel. Glass is best, because the stainless steel tends to erode over time. Water is heated most often by electricity, either by immersing a heating element directly into the water or by positioning the element under the boiling chamber. Other distillers can operate over camp stoves, or wood- or gas-fired heaters.

Condensation can be achieved by cooling the steam with either air or water. In some air-cooled systems, the steam passes through stainless-steel condensation coils that are cooled by an electric fan located near the coils. Other systems use "ambient" or "natural" cooling, where large cooling surfaces are exposed directly to the room-temperature air. Water-cooled distillers either circulate an independant flow of cooling water around the condensation coils, or use water incidentally for cooling as it is being preheated before entering the boiling chamber. The preheating process (known as fractional distillation or multi-stage flash distillation) also is more efficient in removing volatile organic chemicals.

Once the water is distilled, make sure it is not recontaminated by being passed through the wrong type of output water line. Gray polybutylene tubing should not be used, since DEHP (known to be carcinogenic to animals) has been found in samples of polybutylene pipe.

Distillation has several disadvantages. One is that the boiling chamber must be cleaned frequently to remove the contaminants that have been left behind. It also requires time and produces a limited amount of water.

Another alternative is to drink bottled water. Purchase a brand bottled in glass directly from the natural source. Water in plastic bottles should not be used, as the water absorbs plastic polymers from the containers.

The purity of bottled water is regulated by the FDA and, as a food, is controlled under the federal Food, Drug, and Cosmetic Act. "Bottled water" is defined by the FDA as "water that is sealed in bottles or other containers and intended for human consumption." Mineral and soda waters are specifically exempt from this definition.

Legally acceptable sources for bottled water are wells, springs, and public water right from the tap. No requirements specify that the source of the water or any treatment it has undergone be listed on the label; but if any information is given at all, it must be truthful and not misleading. An excellent selling point for manufacturers is to tell the consumer if the water has come from a well or a spring, so if the source of the water is not revealed, chances are it is only treated tap water.

Bottled waters are divided into two types: "still" water (without bubbles) and "sparkling" water (with bubbles). Even though there are no state or federal regulations for the labeling of bottled water containers, the labels do use certain generalized descriptive terms:

Drinking Water—tap or well water processed in some way before bottling.

Spring Water—water that emerges from the earth's surface under its own pressure, sometimes through a pipe. Water in bottles labeled "spring water" must come from a spring; "natural spring water," unlike plain spring water, may not be processed in any way before it goes into the bottle. Beware of companies with the word "spring" in the company name, rather than in the name of the product, or companies referring to the product as "spring-fresh," "springlike," or

"spring-pure." Do not mistakenly assume that this water is from a spring.

Mineral Water—water containing a legally specified level of minerals. "Natural mineral water" is sparkling or still water, usually from a spring, which contains only the naturally occurring minerals. Regular "mineral water" may have had minerals added or removed. Mineral waters are specifically exempt from federal regulations for bottled waters.

Sparkling Water—water that contains bubbles made by carbon dioxide gas. "Naturally sparkling" water contains the bubbles when it is underground; when the water is drawn from the spring, the natural carbon dioxide is removed separately and reinjected during bottling. Some still waters are artificially carbonated, either with natural or manufactured carbon dioxide.

Many consumers believe that bottled waters are of higher quality than tap water, although legally this need not be true. Federal regulations require that bottled waters whose marketing involves interstate commerce meet the federal standards for public drinking water (established in 1962) which, according to the FDA, "does not represent an optimum level or even an average level of quality, but only the minimum acceptable level of quality for bottled water.* Those bottled waters sold only within individual states need only meet the

*FDA quality standards for bottled drinking water can be found in the *Code of Federal Regulations*, Title 21, Section 103.35, Office of the Federal Register, General Services Administration, Washington DC, 1982.

state requirements, which can be either lower or more stringent than the federal standards.

Club sodas and seltzer waters are marketed in competition with bottled waters, although neither are controlled by federal regulations. Both are merely filtered and carbonated tap water; club soda also contains added mineral salts. The quality of these waters will differ greatly, depending on the quality of the local water and the method of filtration used. Many bulk waters that are home delivered in five-gallon bottles are also simply processed tap water.

When choosing a bottled water, the FDA suggests you select one that is controlled by federal regulations and preferably one that indicates its source. Most companies have a water analysis report available for inspection. Request a copy of the report before settling on a bottled water to be your regular source of drinking water.

Bottled water can be reasonably relied upon to be free of chlorine. *Consumer Reports* magazine, in September 1980, did not test their thirty-eight different bottled waters for chlorine specifically, but found that the levels of chloroform (formed by the reaction of chlorine with organic matter), other trihalomethanes, and pesticides in all thirty-eight brands tested were lower than their instruments could detect. Levels of chloride, nitrate, cadmium, iron, and lead were all within the federal standards, and none contained harmful quantities of bacteria. The mineral waters had levels of purity similar to those waters regulated by the government. The magazine did find, however, a number of brands that had excessively high levels of both sodium and fluoride.

Bottled waters differ greatly in their taste, depending on their mineral content and the presence of other contaminants. Many waters, such as those from famous spas and resorts, are bottled because of the reputed health benefits of their minerals. Although certain amounts of trace minerals are necessary to health, excesses may be harmful or cause adverse reactions.

If tap water is all that is available to you, some pollutants can be removed using the following methods:
• Bring water to a boil in a glass pot, boil it for 10 minutes, and allow it to cool until steaming stops. This will kill bacteria and remove chlorine, chlorine by-products (five minutes of boiling removes over 99 percent of THMs), and pesticides, but it will not remove inorganic chemicals, heavy metals, and trace minerals.
• Add a pinch of vitamin C crystals or a bit of a vitamin C tablet to a glass of water. The acid in the vitamin C combines with the chlorine to neutralize its harmful effects, but will not do anything to any of the other pollutants.
• Add 1/2 grain (several crystals or 1/960 of an ounce) sodium thiosulfate to one to six gallons of water, depending on the amount of chlorine. This will change the dangerous chlorine to harmless chloride, but will not affect the other pollutants.

Brand Name/*Mail Order*
Most water filters available at your local stores are probably ineffective. If you are committed to clean water, make the investment and order a filter by mail.

For home delivery of spring water in five-gallon glass bottles, call local water companies. Some natural-foods stores sell local spring or well water in bulk that you can fill into your own glass containers. Supermarkets sometimes have pure-water vending machines that dispense filtered municipal water. The brands listed below can be found in supermarkets, liquor stores, and natural-foods stores.

Mineral Water (carbonated)

A Apollinaris (Apollinaris Brunnen, A. G.).

A A Sante (A Sante). Bottled in Calistoga.

A Badoit Naturally Sparkling Mineral Water (S. A. des Eaux Minerales d'Evian). Bottled in France.

A Calistoga Sparkling Mineral Water (Calistoga Mineral Water Co.).

A Contrexeville (Société Genérale de Grandes Sources d'Eaux). Bottled in France.

A Crystal Geyser Sparkling Mineral Water (Crystal Geyser Water Co.). Drawn from the pure, deep recesses of the fabled Napa Valley geyser country.

A Ferrarelle Naturally Sparkling Mineral Water (Sangemini International). Bottled in Riardo, Italy, from a volcanic spring.

A Fiuggi (Ente Fiuggi S.p.A.). Bottled in Italy.

A Gerolsteiner Sprudel Natural Mineral Water (Gerolsteiner Sprudel/GMBH & Co.). Bottled in West Germany.

A Levissima Natural Mineral Water (Bertolli America). Bottled in Italy.

A Manitou Naturally Sparkling Pure Rocky Mountain Mineral Water (Manitou Corp.). Water taken from an aquifer one mile below the base of Pike's Peak, protected from all contamination. Bottled at the source.

A Mendocino Naturally Sparkling Mineral Water (Mendocino Mineral Water).

A Perrier Natural Sparkling Mineral Water (Great Waters of France).

A Peters Val Mineral Water (Peterstaler Mineralquellen/Huber GMBH & Co.). Bottled in the mountains of the Black Forest in West Germany.

A Ramlösa Sparkling Mineral Water (A. B. Ramlösa Hälsobrunn). Bottled at the Ramlösa spa in Sweden.

A Royal Hawaiian Sparkling Artesian Water (Royal Hawaiian Beverage & Water). Water filtered and aged 25 years through porous volcanic rock. Bottled in Hawaii.

A S. Pellegrino Pure Mineral Table Water (San Pellegrino S.p.A.). Bottled in the Alps at Bergamo, Italy.

A San Benedetto Natural Sparkling Mineral Water (G. Raden & Sons). Bottled in Italy.

A Sonoma Mission Inn Sparkling Water (Sonoma Mission Inn). Bottled at the Sonoma Mission Inn.

A Stiles Natural Mineral Water (Parastar). Watsatch Rocky Mountain Artesian Well Water.

A Vichy Springs Sparkling Mineral Water (Vichy Springs Mineral Water Corp.). Bottled in California.

A Vittelloise (Societé Genérale des Eaux Minerales de Vittel). Natural spring water fortified with carbonation. Bottled in France.

Spring Water (noncarbonated)
A Applegate Spring Water (Applegate Spring Water Co.). Bottled in California.

A Evian Natural Spring Water (S. A. des Eaux Minerales d'Evian). Bottled in the Alps near Mont Blanc.

A Heavenly Hawaiian Waters (Koolau Distributors). Bottled in Hawaii.

A Mountain Valley Water (Mountain Valley Water). From Hot Springs, Arkansas, 100% pure spring water bottled in glass only, since 1871. Nationwide home delivery available.

Ceramic water crocks for storing and dispensing water from 5-gallon bottles are available by mail from *Bill Pruzan, Spring Well Dispensers, and Whole Earth Access.*

Activated Carbon (granulated)
A AMF Cuno Aqua-Pure AP600 (AMF/Cuno). Whole house filter. *Nigra Enterprises.*

A EPS Filter (Environmental Purification Systems). *Environmental Purification Systems, Nigra Enterprises.*

A *P.E.R. Corp.* Whole house filter. PSSAC-20 Activated Carbon Filter.

B Shower/Tub Filters. *Environmental Purification Systems, Nigra Enterprises.*

Carbon Block
AB Multi-Pure (Multi-Pure Drinking Water Systems). Over-the-counter plastic or stainless-steel units. *E. L. Foust Co., Environmental Purification Systems, Nigra Enterprises.*

B Water Dome (Neo-Life Co. of America). Local Neo-Life distributors.

B Water-Safe TOC-200 (Coast Filtration). Under-the-sink 10-inch carbon block plus a 5-micron prefilter. *Coast Filtration, Nigra Enterprises.*

Reverse Osmosis
B Water-Safe WS/R05 (Coast Filtration). On-the-counter and under-sink carbon units with reverse osmosis. *Coast Filtration, Nigra Enterprises.*

Distillers
A Durastill (Durastill). Made from stainless steel. *Durastill, Nigra Enterprises.*

A *New World Distiller Corp.* Stainless-steel distillers.

A Pure Water Distillers (Pure Water). Six different styles and sizes of stainless-steel distillers. *The Allergy Store, Pure Water.*

A Scientific Glass Distillers (Scientific Glass Co.). Made from Pyrex glass. *Nigra Enterprises, Scientific Glass Co.*

WATER FILTERS

See Water.

WATER HEATERS

See Appliances.

WATER SOFTENERS

Fragrance.

"CAUTION: May be harmful if swallowed. Eye irritant."

SAFE ALTERNATIVES

Use sodium carbonate, sodium hexametaphosphate, washing soda, or borax.

Do-It-Yourself

Add your own water softener to warm or hot water 1 minute before adding soap.

To find out how much water softener to use, dissolve ½ teaspoon of softener in 1 gallon of 140° water. Half-fill a quart jar with softened water, add ½ teaspoon soap, cap the jar, and shake for 10 seconds. If good suds form and hold for 5 minutes, that is the right amount of softener. Try again, using less softener, to find out if a smaller amount will still make good suds. If the original amount of softener doesn't make good suds, repeat the test, adding more softener until good suds form. Multiply this amount by the number of gallons your washer holds and add that amount with each washer load.

See also Cleaning Products.

WINDOW COVERINGS

Plastic (polyester).

Sun shining on polyester curtains heats them up and causes additional outgassing of plastic fumes.

SAFE ALTERNATIVES

Hang natural-fiber curtains or drapes. Use ready-made cotton curtains or make your own from other natural-fiber fabric.

Hang wooden shutters; leave them unfinished, or else coat them with a nontoxic wood finish.

Hang metal blinds.

Hang rice-paper shades.

Hang cloth shades. Vinyl shades are not recommended, nor are ready-made cloth shades, which contain the original sizing as well as additional stiffeners and adhesives with unknown components. Make your own cloth shades with kits that use wooden rollers and prewashed materials of your choice, stiffened with a nontoxic starch.

Brand Name/*Mail Order*

A *Essential Alternatives.* Rice-paper shades.

A *Eugene Trading Co.* Rice-paper shades.

A *Homespun Fabrics & Draperies.* "Raw" or bleached cotton custom draperies.

A *Ikea.* Rice-paper shades.

A *Laura Copenhaver Industries.* Cotton muslin curtains with handmade cotton fringes and lace.

A *Mather's.* Early American unbleached cotton curtains and pleated draw drapes.

A *New Moon.* Rice-paper shades.

A *Northwest Futon Co.* Rice-paper shades.

A *S. & C. Huber, Accoutrements.* Custom-made natural-fiber curtains.

A *Vermont Country Store.* Curtains, 100% cotton in colonial designs.

A *Xhaxhi.* Rice-paper shades.

AB *Homespun Crafts.* Curtains, 100% cotton in colonial designs.

See also Fabric and Wood Finishes.

WINE

See Alcoholic Beverages.

WOOD

Formaldehyde; plastics (phenol-formaldehyde resin, urea-formaldehyde resin); pentachlorophenol, phenol.

"WARNING: This product is manufactured with a urea-formaldehyde resin and will release small quantities of formaldehyde. Formaldehyde levels in the indoor air can cause temporary eye and respiratory irritation and may aggravate respiratory conditions or allergies. Ventilation will reduce indoor formaldehyde levels."

Most wood products today are made of particle board or plywood instead of solid wood. Particle board, made from small wood shavings saturated with urea-formaldehyde resin and pressed into a woodlike form, is easily recognizable because you can see the pressed-together shavings on all sides. Plywood is harder to recognize because it has a wood grain on the outside. A cross-section, however, reveals several sheets of wood sandwiched together with phenol-formaldehyde resin.

SAFE ALTERNATIVES
Solid wood that has not been treated is safest.

All new plywood is made with phenol-formaldehyde resin, instead of the urea-formaldehyde resin used in particle board. The phenol-formaldehyde resin, though also produced from formaldehyde, has much less of a tendency to decompose, and is therefore safer. Nevertheless, some outgassing may still occur (estimates vary from 5 percent to 10 percent as much), and some residual unreacted formaldehyde from the manufacturing process may also outgas from the plywood resin for a time. If you find you must use plywood in new construction, at least minimize its use inside your home or else seal it in the same manner as particle board, with one of the products recommended below. Aging before use will also help.

Before the last ten years or so, all plywood used in interior construction as well as cabinets, wood-grained paneling, and furniture was made with urea-formaldehyde resin. This did not seem to cause as much of a problem as with particle board, because there was more wood and much less of the resin in the plywood. Plywood already installed in your house, whether built-in or part of your cabinets or furniture, will tend to be aged and probably will not be a problem. If you are concerned and cannot remove it, consider sealing it with a finish, or else increase ventilation.

Get rid of your particle board if possible, or try to completely seal it off. Even old particle board will continue to outgas at some level. Pace Industries, manufacturer of the formaldehyde sealant "Right On" Crystal Aire I, has performed tests showing that applying four coats of this product reduces formaldehyde levels by 95 percent. Hyde-Check (Mortell Co.), a water-based latex sealer, reduces formaldehyde emissions from 15 ppm to .02 ppm (over 99 percent). Other wood finishes or paint may confine formaldehyde fumes if an object is totally and thoroughly coated, but there is no research to confirm this. Foil will definitely seal formaldehyde in, if airtight in application. Instead of flimsy aluminum foil, use foil vapor barrier and aluminum foil tape.

Brand Name/*Mail Order*
A Wolmanized Lumber (Koppers Co./Forest Products). Wood that is resistant to water, rot, and termites, preserved with odorless inorganic salts of copper chromium arsenic.

B Masonite (Masonite Corp.). Composition hardboard made from wood chips compressed with steam at high pressure, then waterproofed with a paraffin-based emulsion.

See also **Vapor Barrier** and **Wood Finishes.**

WOOD FINISHES

Aerosol propellants; benzene; ethanol; formaldehyde; lead; plastic (acrylonitrile).

The biggest problem with wood finishes is that they have a very strong chemical odor when applied, and may pollute the air for the weeks or months it may take for them to dry sufficiently to cease emitting noticeable vapors.

SAFE ALTERNATIVES
The most natural wood finish is shellac, made from a natural resin secreted by the insect *Laccifer lacca* mixed with alcohol, available at any hardware or paint store. The alcohol may continue to evaporate for up to six months before becoming completely dry and odor free, but most people will not notice it after several days. Disadvantages are a long drying period and clean-up with alcohol.

Brand Name/*Mail Order*
B "Right On" Crystal Aire I (Pace Industries). This water-based, casein-derived product is by far the fastest-drying wood finish on the market. Volatile alcohol drying agents are released when the finish is applied, but "these agents are 50% dispersed within the first few minutes of application and 90% within 30 to 60 minutes. After 24 hours, surface emission is virtually unmeasurable." It can be used for any purpose, from furniture (only pure lemon oil is needed for maintenance) to highly trafficked floors. It can also be used to block chemical fumes of all types; tests have shown that 4 coats applied with a 30-minute drying period between each coat will reduce formaldehyde emissions from particle board by 95%. Other products offered by the same company include Crystal Aire II, which acts as a binder to prevent release of asbestos fibers, and Pace-Creme, a fast-drying water-based wood stain, available in 10 shades. *Nigra Enterprises, Pace Industries, Peter Philhower.*

WOOD STOVES

See Appliances.

WORCESTERSHIRE SAUCE

Sucrose; pesticide residues.

SAFE ALTERNATIVES
Brand Name/*Mail Order*
B Robbie's "All Natural" Worcester-shire Sauce (Robbie's).

B St. James Worcestershire Sauce (The Clipper Tea & Produce Co., England).

See also Food.

Y

YARN

Dyes; pesticides (mothproofing); plastics (acrylic, polyester, nylon).

SAFE ALTERNATIVES
Brand Name/*Mail Order*
Purchase undyed, unmothproofed natural-fiber yarns at a yarn store or by mail.

A *Brown Sheep Co.* Natural gray or white wool fiber for spinning, and natural wool yarns.

A *Cheryl Kolander.* Silk yarn, 36 types, in either natural cream-to-beige shades or hand-dyed in 45 colors using natural dyes.

A *Hearthsong.* Plant-dyed wool yarns imported from Switzer-land.

A *The Manning Handweaving School & Supply Center.* White rug wool for dyeing; fibers for spinning (alpaca, silk, camel, flax, cotton, goat, llama, wool, mohair and yak); and natural unscoured yarns made of cotton, cotton/linen, wool, silk, and alpaca.

A *Old Mill Yarn.* Wool yarn in natural grays, whites, and browns. Specify "untreated" when requesting information.

A *The Oriental Rug Co.* Natural-color cotton yarn.

A *Paula Simmons.* Yarn in many natural light, dark, and variegated shades. "We raise our own sheep, do not use chemicals, use no dye or bleach on the fleeces or the yarn."

A *Rammagerdin of Reykjavik.* Wool yarn from Icelandic sheep in the natural colors of the sheep—10 shades of whites, grays, and browns.

A *S. & C. Huber, Accoutrements.* Fibers for spinning: wool fleece, flax, cotton, raw and cocoon silk, cashmere, camel, and fleece from their own llamas. Wool yarns in natural colors or dyed with vegetable dyes; cotton yarns in two natural shades or dyed with natural indigo; and linen yarn in either natural or bleached white.

A *Straw into Gold.* Fibers for spinning: silk, wool, alpaca, mohair, camel's hair, yak, cotton, linen, and cashmere. Undyed natural yarns of cotton, linen, or wool.

A *Sureway Trading Enterprises.* Silk yarn and fiber for spinning.

A *Woodsedge Wools.* Undyed and vegetable-dyed wool fiber for spinning; undyed wool and silk yarns.

AB *Art Needlework Industries.* Cotton, alpaca, wool/silk blends, and many kinds of British wools including the wool used to weave Harris Tweed.

AB *Babouri's Handicrafts.* Handspun wool yarns from Greece in natural and dyed colors.

AB *Bartlett Yarns.* Undyed wool yarns and fibers for spinning in natural sheep colors. Also dyed yarns.

AB *Briggs & Little Woolen Mills.* Untreated and dyed wool yarns.

AB *Cambridge Wools.* Natural-color and dyed wool yarns.

AB *Contessa Yarns.* Natural-color wool, silk, and mercerized and unmercerized cotton. Also some dyed natural-fiber yarns.

AB *Cotton Clouds.* Untreated and dyed cotton yarns.

AB *The Cotton Place.* Several types of cotton yarn.

AB *Craftsman's Mark.* Wool, cotton, and linen yarns, mostly undyed, from England.

AB *Elizabeth Zimmerman/Meg Swansen.* Unbleached, natural sheep's wool; unspun, undyed Icelandic wool; and dyed wool imported from Scotland and Canada.

AB *Les Filatures de Paris.* Unique cotton, silk, and wool yarns from France. Price list in French.

AB *The Pendleton Shop.* Wool, yak, camel, cotton, silk, goat, angora, and mohair fibers for spinning. Navajo-type wool yarn for rug making.

AB *Romni Wools & Fibres.* Undyed fibers for spinning: wool, mohair, alpaca, angora, camel, cotton, flax, goat, silk, yak, and cashmere. Undyed and dyed yarns made from cotton, linen, wool, angora, mohair, and silk. Also wood knitting needles and crochet hooks.

AB *R. S. Duncan & Co.* Cotton and wool yarns made in the United Kingdom.

AB *Stavros Kouyomoutzakis.* Natural-color and dyed wool yarns from Greece.

AB *Utex Trading Enterprises.* Silk knitting/weaving yarns.

B *Daft Dames Handcrafts.* Several types of cotton yarn.

B *Harrisville Designs.* Dyed wool yarns.

B *Wondercraft.* Dyed cotton and wool yarns.

YOGURT & KEFIR

Colors; flavors.

SAFE ALTERNATIVES
All brands of plain yogurt are free from artificial additives, but harmful ingredients are often found in fla-

vored yogurts. Buy plain yogurt and add your own sweeteners and toppings, or buy an additive-free brand.

Kefir is similar to yogurt, but is a liquid and made from a different culture. Kefir cheese has had some of the liquid removed and tastes like sour cream mixed with cream cheese. It is not available flavored.

Brand Name/*Mail Order*

The following ratings are for *flavored* yogurt. No products have been rated "A" because all the milk used contains pesticide residues.

Yogurt

B Brown Cow Farm Natural Yogurt (Brown Cow Farm).

B Honey Hill Farms Nonfat Yogurt (Honey Hill Farms Cultured Specialties).

B Mountain High Natural Yogurt (Mountain High).

B Mystic Lake Dairy Goat Milk Yogurt (Mystic Lake Dairy).

B Nancy's Honey Yogurt (Springfield Creamery).

B Natural & Kosher Yogurt (Natural & Kosher Foods).

C Alta-Dena Raw Yogurt (Alta-Dena).

C Dannon Yogurt (Dannon Co.).

C Knudsen Yogurt (Knudsen Corp.).

C Yoplait Yogurt (Yoplait USA).

Kefir

B Alta-Dena Kefir (Alta-Dena).

B American Kefir Low Fat Kefir (American Kefir Corporation).

B Nancy's Kefir (Springfield Creamery).

Kefir Cheese

B Alta-Dena Kefir Cheese (Alta-Dena).

B Vasa Continental Kefir Cheese (Continental Culture Specialists).

Do-It-Yourself

Make your own yogurt and kefir with cultures from your natural-foods store or from *Daisyfresh Dairy Cultures, Deer Valley Farm, International Yogurt Co., Nichols Garden Nursery,* or *Walnut Acres.*

See also Milk.

THE NO-SMOKING SECTION:
How to Avoid Secondhand Cigarette Smoke

"WARNING: The surgeon general has determined that cigarette smoking is dangerous to your health."

New warnings that will go on cigarette packages in 1985:

SURGEON GENERAL'S WARNING: Smoking causes lung cancer, heart disease, emphysema, and may complicate pregnancy.

SURGEON GENERAL'S WARNING: Quitting smoking now greatly reduces serious risks to your health.

SURGEON GENERAL'S WARNING: Smoking by pregnant women may result in fetal injury, premature birth, and low birth weight.

SURGEON GENERAL'S WARNING: Cigarette smoke contains carbon monoxide.

Smoking must be included in this book because cigarettes are probably the most toxic of consumer products, yet we often feel helpless to control our exposure to their devastating effects.

Only 4 percent of the total smoke produced by a cigarette is inhaled by the smoker. The other 96 percent becomes sidestream waste, containing more than twice the concentration of pollutants the smoker inhaled. Possible symptoms for the *nonsmoker* who inhales this smoke include burning eyes, nasal congestion and drainage, sore throat, cough, headache, and nausea. It is a significant health hazard for infants, children, pregnant women and their yet-to-be-born children, for people with cardiovascular disease, for asthmatics, and for others with impaired respiratory function, or with heart disease, lung disease, or allergies. Children of smoking parents have an increased incidence of upper respiratory infections, bronchitis, asthma, pneumonia, and a significant decrease in respiratory function. Prolonged exposure to sidestream smoke can increase the risk of disease in healthy people who do not smoke, including higher risk of lung cancer, respiratory infection, angina, decreased blood oxygen levels, decreased exercise tolerance, decreased respiratory function, broncho-constriction, and broncho-spasm. In *The Health Consequences of Smoking: Chronic Obstructive Lung Disease*, the surgeon general of the United States reports that there is very solid evidence that nonsmokers suffer lung disease from exposure to the smoke of those who do use cigarettes.

Smokers will smoke, so it is up to you to protect yourself from this hazardous practice. Organizations that can provide information and assistance (and which need your support) include:

Action on Smoking and Health (ASH), 2013 H St. NW, Washington, DC 20006; 202/659–4310.

American Lung Association, 1740 Broadway, New York, NY 10019; 212/245–8000.

Californians for Nonsmokers' Rights, 2054 University Ave., Suite 500, Berkeley, CA 94704; 415/841–3032.

Group Against Smokers' Pollution (GASP), PO Box 632, College Park, MD 20740; 301/474–0967.

The workplace is the area of most concern to nonsmokers, because in many cases health is impaired and work suffers, yet a living must be made. If you have a private office space, either request that people not smoke within or display a NO SMOKING sign. If you work in a common area, ask your fellow workers not to smoke while working. If they refuse, talk to your employer. The law requires employers to provide a safe and healthful working environment and it prohibits people from engaging in any activity that causes physical injury to others. More information on this law and how it applies to your office situation can be obtained from ASH. A 1982 California State Court of Appeals ruling upholds the right of employees to protest a smoke-filled environment as presenting a hazardous working condition without the fear of being fired. Any employee subsequently fired can then go to court and sue the company for damages.

It is to your employer's benefit to honor your request for no smoking. A Dow Chemical Company study showed that smokers used 80 percent more sick leave than did nonsmokers, that 50 percent of the nonsmokers had difficulty working near a smoker, and that 7 percent used sick leave because of illness due to tobacco smoke exposure at work. In addition, smokers cost employers more money than nonsmokers do in increased absenteeism and medical care, property damage and maintenance, time lost on the job, and early mortality. One study estimates that employers can save up to $4,700 per employee each year, reduce cleaning costs and sick leave, and increase productivity when smoking is discontinued.

The providing of no-smoking work areas is definitely on the rise. At least fifty companies in America have now either partially or fully banned smoking during working hours and many cities have passed local ordinances placing the nonsmoker's right for clean air above the smoker's right to smoke. The 6 January 1984 edition of *Insurance Week* warns that "grave economic consequences may face employers who do not put in force a smoking policy for their employees." In a number of cases nonsmokers have won disability benefits and other compensation from their employers for ailments caused by involuntary smoking.

To keep the air clean in your workplace, provide an area for smokers (preferably in a room separate from nonsmokers) and then purify the smoke-filled air with an activated carbon air filter to remove toxic gasses along with a negative-ion generator to remove particulates. Smoke levels can also be reduced by having smokers use ashtrays such as the Pollenex Nosmoke Ashtray (Associated Mills), which draws smoke into the inside of the plastic receptacle with a small fan and absorbs it with activated carbon, or the Smoke Zapper Ashtray (order by mail from *J S & A*), which works on the same principle but also has a negative-ion generator.

For more information on how to establish a no-smoking policy in your workplace, contact the **American Lung Association** (1740 Broadway, New York, NY 10019); the **Health at Work Program** (Group Health Cooperative of Puget Sound, Center for Health Promotion, 200 15th Ave. East, CX-2, Seattle, WA 98112), or the **Clean Indoor Air Educational Foundation** (25 Deaconess Rd., HH421, Boston, MA 02215).

Express your views on no smoking to businesses you patronize. Always ask for a no-smoking section in restaurants, airlines, and other public places even if it is obvious that none exists. Ask people who may be smoking next to you not to smoke.

The only way businesses know you want no smoking is for you to ask. Public pressure really works. Praise and patronize those businesses that do have smoking regulations so they know you appreciate it. ASH and Californians for Nonsmokers' Rights both sell stickers requesting a no-smoking section, which can be affixed to the bills you receive. Or you can be creative and have your own message printed on inexpensive labels from *Walter Drake*. Having some stickers thanking businesses for their nonsmoking policies would be a good idea, too.

The following businesses are committed to helping consumers avoid secondhand cigarette smoke.

AIRLINES

Most airlines have no-smoking sections unless they fly very small planes. If you are flying first class, ask for a seat in the very first row. When requesting a no-smoking seat in coach, ask for a seat in the *center* of the no-smoking section. If you ask for a seat as far from the smoking section as possible, you are likely to be given one right next to the first class smoking section. If you don't specify, you might be seated in the last row of the no-smoking section right next to the coach's smoking section. Check each time you fly to find out the particular pattern used, and choose a seat as far away as possible.

Airlines that have banned smoking altogether include:

Air North (Massachusetts, Vermont, Washington, DC)

Atlantic Express (New York, Massachusetts, Washington, DC)

Civil Aviation Administration of China (China; smoking banned on flights within China only)

Golden West Airlines(California)

Muse Air (Texas)

Pacific Coast Airlines (California)

Rocky Mountain Airways (Colorado, Wyoming, Nebraska).

HEALTH SPAS

Alive Polarity Inn, PO Box 90, Emigrant Gap, CA 95715; 916/389–8237.

Alive Polarity Inn & Vegetarian Health Resort, 1880 Lincoln Ave., Calistoga, CA 94515; 707/942–4636.

The Ashram, Box 8, Calabasas, CA 91302; 213/888–0232.

The Fountain of Youth Spa, Star Rte. 1, PO Box 12, Niland, CA 92257; 714/348–1340.

Meadowlark, 26126 Fairview Ave., Hemet, CA 92343; 714/927–1343.

Rancho La Puerta, Tecate, CA 92080; 714/478–5341.

Sky Valley Park, 74–565 Dillon Rd., Desert Hot Springs, CA 92240; 714/329–7415.

Vita Dell Spa, 13495 Palm Dr., Desert Hot Springs, CA 92240; 714/329–6200.

Wilbur Hot Springs, Wilbur Springs, CA 95987; 916/473–2306.

LODGING

Cambridge Inn, 10135 100th St., Oklahoma City, OK; 403/426–3636.

Continental Inn, 9735 I.H. North, San Antonio, TX 78233; 512/655–3510.

The Directory Hotel, 7900 South Lewis, Tulsa, OK 74136; 918/492–5000.

Drury Inns, 800/325–8300. Hotels in Texas, Oklahoma, Kansas, Missouri, Illinois, Indiana, and Tennessee.

Excelsior Hotel, 101 West 100 North, Provo, UT 84601; 800/223–5672 or 801/377–4700. Ninety of 250 rooms have been designated for no smoking since the hotel first opened, and there are no-smoking sections in the hotel's restaurants.

Excelsior Hotel, 616 West 7th, Tulsa, OK 74136; 918/587–8000.

Executel at the Airport, 100 Airport Plaza Dr., Midland, TX 79701; 915/561–8000.

Four Seasons Hotel, Houston Center, 1300 Lamar St., Houston, TX 77010; 713/650–1300.

Hilton Hotels in Manila, Taipai, Dusseldorf, and Strasbourg.

Hyatt on Sunset, 8401 Sunset Blvd., Hollywood, CA 90069; 213/656–4101.

Hyatt Regency, 711 South Hope St., Los Angeles, CA 90017; 213/683–1234.

Inn on the Park, Four Riverway, Houston, TX 77056; 713/871–8181.

La Maida House, 11159 La Maida St., North Hollywood, CA 91601; 213/769–3857.

La Quinta Motor Inns, PO Box 32064, San Antonio, TX 78216; 512/366–6000. No-smoking rooms in 122 inns in 25 states across the country.

The Lincoln, 5410 LBJ Freeway, Dallas, TX 75240; 214/934–8400.

Los Cuartos Inn, 7800 C.A. Henderson Blvd., Oklahoma City, OK 73139; 405/632–6666, and 1100 Highway 34, Elk City, OK 73648; 405/225–9210.

Non-Smokers' Inn, 9229 Carpenter Freeway, Dallas, TX 75247; 214/631–6633. Entire inn is for nonsmokers.

Oak Tree Inn, Vinegar Hill, Highway 110, Heber Springs, AR 72543; 501/362–6111.

Ramada Inn—Metrocenter, 12707 North 28th Drive, Phoenix, AZ 85029; 602/866–7000.

Westin Hotel, 10135 100th St., Edmonton, Alberta, Canada.

For information on other hotels with no-smoking rooms, contact your local Thrifty Rent-A-Car.

RENTAL CARS

Thrifty Rent-A-Car. Reservations for smoke-free rental cars can be made in over 400 locations across the country by calling 800/331–4200.

RESTAURANTS

Nationwide restaurants that have established policies of providing no-smoking sections include **Coco's Famous Hamburgers, Denny's, Furr's Cafeteria, The Magic Pan Crêperie, Morrison's Cafeteria, The Plank-house, Red Lobster Inn, Reuben's, Victoria Station,** and **Wyatt Cafeteria.**

Guide to Smoke-Free Dining, a nationwide, city-by-city directory of restaurants that prohibit smoking or have no-smoking sections can be ordered for $6.75 from Environmental Press, 1201 Dusky Thrush Trail, Austin, TX 78746.

In the future, perhaps the Yellow Pages of the telephone directory will list restaurants with no-smoking sections. Write to them and suggest it.

SINGLES

Non-Smoking Singles, 4397 West 146 St., Cleveland, OH 44135.

TRAVEL

Cebu Cruises, 1017–168th Ave. SE, Room 2, Bellevue, WA 98008; 206/746–3414. No-smoking cruises, eight to eleven days, along the coast of the Pacific Northwest from May through September.

Christian Fellowship Tours, PO Box 633, Niagra Falls, Ontario, Canada. Tours to the Holy Land and China.

Noseworthy Travel, 1315 E. Katella, Orange, CA 92667.

Rocky Mountain River Tours, PO Box 126, Hailey, ID 83333; 208/756–4808. Smoke-free summer raft trips on the Salmon River in Idaho.

Smoke-Free Float Trips, PO Box 126, Hailey, ID 83333; 208/788–9300.

The Nonsmokers' Travel Club of GASP, 8928 Bradmoor Dr., Bethesda, MD 20817. Plans foreign and domestic trips for groups of nonsmokers. Past trips: Mexico, Europe, Canada, Barbados, Scandinavia, Hawaii, and many domestic locations. Also a newsletter that reports on the latest information relating to leisure activities for nonsmokers. Subscription $4/year.

Tours for Non-Smokers, 1815 West Glenoaks Blvd., Glendale, CA 91201; 213/500–8914.

ADDITIONAL RESOURCES

Magazines in which nontoxic and natural products are frequently advertised include *Bestways, Co-Evolution Quarterly, East West Journal, Let's Live, The Mother Earth News, Mothering, Mother Jones, New Age Journal, The New Farm, New Shelter, Organic Gardening, Prevention, Vegetarian Times,* and *Whole Life Times.*

Although there is no one organization as yet that focuses solely on nontoxic and natural products, several groups in related fields also address this consumer issue and problems surrounding it:

Ecological Illness Law Report, PO Box 1739, Evanston, IL 60204–1739. A bimonthly independent publication founded in 1983 "dedicated to providing news and analysis on the legal aspects of ecological illness," including illness caused by toxic consumer products. The *Report* is an excellent clearinghouse for information on legal cases relating to all types of toxins, from smoking to formaldehyde and pesticides, and can provide invaluable resources for attorneys working on related cases. The people who publish it will also refer you to an attorney in your area who will understand your case. Memberships range from $15/year for members of related nonprofit groups to $30/year for attorneys with active practices.

Friends of the Earth (FOE), 1045 Sansome St., San Francisco, CA 94111. "A dynamic, aggressive, politically astute group promoting nonviolent and democratic environmentalism for a sustainable future and a livable world." In addition to saving endangered species, their activities include strengthening federal laws for clean air and water and controlling toxic waste, as well as acquisition of federal funds to support organic farming. Their highly acclaimed monthly newsletter, *Not Man Apart,* reports on all environmental matters (including new nontoxic and natural products). Memberships begin at $25/year; subscription only, $15.

Human Ecology Action League (HEAL), PO Box 1369, Evanston, IL 60204. A national nonprofit organization formed in 1976 "to focus the energies, activities, and attention of all people vitally interested in good 'Human Ecology' and its reverse 'Ecological Illness.' " It is concerned with the effects of all substances on human health, and methods of living to avoid harmful substances. Its quarterly newsletter, *The Human Ecologist,* is a clearinghouse of information on environmental illness and wellness. The league can also refer you to over fifty local groups and to newsletters that would have information on how to find nontoxic and natural products in your area; it also offers a list of books for sale relating to environmental illness. Memberships start at $15/year.

Save Us from Formaldehyde Repercussions (SUFFER), Waconia, MN 55387–9583; 612/448–5441. A grass-roots national nonprofit organization of families exposed to formaldehyde, joined together with the goal of educating the public on the hazards of formaldehyde and where it is found in consumer products. Their quarterly newsletter, *The Environmental Guardian*, reports on all matters relating to formaldehyde exposure including political, legal, and medical issues. Membership is $20/year; $50/year for professionals.

Society for Clinical Ecology (SCE), 109 West Olive St., Fort Collings, CO 80524. A nonprofit international association of physicians and associated professionals who study the clinical aspects of environmentally induced illnesses. The organization can refer you to a physician in your area who understands illness caused by toxic chemicals (for referrals, write to SCE at 2005 Franklin St., Suite 490, Denver, CO 80205). Their quarterly medical journal, *Clinical Ecology*, includes studies, case histories, and abstracts of papers in related fields. Yearly conferences are open to everyone. Membership is $24/year.

Appendix One

HARMFUL EFFECTS OF COMMON SUBSTANCES

Included here is a representative list of harmful substances most commonly found in consumer products, along with their potential health effects. This is not to suggest that everyone will experience the following symptoms upon any amount or type of exposure to these chemicals; this is simply to condense the toxicological data available on these substances.

Everyone reacts differently, individually, to all things. Some people can tolerate exposure to large amounts of chemicals with no ill effect, while others develop complex symptoms to even small exposures—very much as some people can "eat like a horse" and remain slender, while others gain weight consuming less food.

The harmful substances listed here fall into one of two categories: The first covers those ingredients found in consumer products that are classified and known to be hazardous. Fourteen of these—asbestos, benzene, lead, naphthalene, nitrates/nitrosamines, nitrobenzene, pentachlorophenol, aldrin/dieldrin, chlordane, heptachlor, acrylonitrile, vinyl chloride, toluene, trichloroethylene—are so dangerous that they are included on the Environmental Protection Agency (EPA) list of sixty-five "priority pollutants" recognized as being hazardous to human health. The second category includes substances that may appear to be safe for many people but pose a problem for those who are sensitive to petrochemical derivatives or have specific other reactions (such as allergy to perfume or hyperactivity related to food additives). Read the descriptions of the possible health effects to decide for yourself which of these substances you choose to avoid.

If you have health problems, avoiding any of these chemicals may make a difference.

AEROSOL PROPELLANTS

Heart problems, birth defects, lung cancer, headaches, nausea, dizziness, shortness of breath, eye and throat irritation, skin rashes, burns, lung inflammation, and liver damage. If misdirected, aerosol sprays can cause chemical burns and eye injury.

The most commonly used aerosol spray is Freon, a lung irritant and central-nervous-system depressant. In high concentrations, Freon can cause coma or even death.

Aerosol gases can also turn into other more toxic gases, including fluorine, chlorine, hydrogen fluoride, chloride, and phosgene (military poison gas).

Many aerosol products also contain other toxic ingredients that can more easily get into eyes and lungs than if dispensed by some method other than aerosol cans or pump spray bottles. These can lead to high particle retention in the lungs and cause respiratory problems.

AMMONIA (including AMMONIUM CHLORIDE, AMMONIUM HYDROXIDE, BENZALKONIUM CHLORIDE, and QUATERNARY AMMONIUM COMPOUNDS)

Irritation of eyes and respiratory tract, conjunctivitis, laryngitis, tracheitis, pulmonary edema, pneumonitis, skin burn, and vestication.

ASBESTOS

Autopsy reports show 100 percent of urban dwellers to have asbestos in lung tissue. Asbestos exposure can affect almost every organ of the body. Illnesses: asbestosis, a chronic lung disease, and mesothelioma (an often fatal form of cancer). Asbestos diseases can result from very brief exposures and even exposure to other people who have been exposed (who may have asbestos fibers in their hair or clothing), and may take up to forty years to appear. The EPA announced in 1972 that there is no safe level of asbestos exposure, as *any* exposure to the fibers involves some health risk.

ASPARTAME (NUTRASWEET)

According to a letter from Dr. Richard J. Wurman to the *New England Journal of Medicine,* NutraSweet, an FDA-approved natural sweetener made from amino acids, can change levels of chemicals in the brain that affect behavior, especially affecting people with underlying brain disorders such as Parkinson's disease and insomnia. Aspartame also might cause brain damage in children suffering from phenylketonuria. Because it has not been widely used, the long-term effects are unknown.

Nevertheless, scientific tests performed on aspartame to establish its safety prior to FDA approval resulted in brain tumors and grand mal seizures in rat studies, and depression, menstrual irregularities, constipation, headaches, tiredness, and general swelling in human test groups. Furthermore, during human evaluations, two of the subjects underwent cancer operations (aspartame has not been tested for carcinogenicity).

When exposed to heat, aspartame breaks down into toxic methyl alcohol. This may occur even at temperatures reached by diet sodas during regular storage.

BENZENE

Carcinogenic. Can also cause drunken behavior, lightheadedness, disorientation, fatigue, and loss of appetite.

BENZYL ALCOHOL/SODIUM BENZOATE

Intestinal upsets and allergic reactions. Although these substances are usually considered relatively safe, clinical observation by medical doctors has shown them to cause adverse reactions in people who are sensitive to petrochemical derivatives.

BHA (BUTYLATED HYDROXYANISOLE)/BHT (BUTYLATED HYDROXYTOLUENE)

BHT is a suspected human carcinogen. Studies show not only that BHT is carcinogenic to mice, but indicate also that it promotes existing tumors. Moreover, animal studies reveal BHA and BHT to cause metabolic stress, depression of growth rate, loss of weight, damage to the liver, baldness, and fetal abnormalities.

Clinical observation by medical doctors has shown that BHA and BHT can cause adverse reactions in those who are sensitive to petrochemical derivatives. The late Dr. Benjamin Feingold, of Kaiser-Permanente Medical Center has widely publicized BHA and BHT to be a cause of hyperactivity and behavioral disturbances in children. Although it has been very difficult to substantiate this with scientific studies, the observations of parents and doctors for over fifteen years confirm that avoidance of BHA and BHT has significantly improved their children's condition.

CHLORINE (including CHLORINE DIOXIDE and SODIUM HYPOCHLORITE)

Pain and inflammation in the mouth, throat, and stomach and erosion of mucous membranes, vomiting, circulatory collapse, confusion, delirium, coma, swelling of the throat, severe respiratory tract irritation, pulmonary edema, and skin eruptions. Exposure has been linked to high blood pressure, anemia, diabetes, heart disease, and causes a 44-percent greater risk of gastrointestinal or urinary tract cancer.

Clinical observation by medical doctors has shown that reactions to chlorine can also occur from chlorine fumes rising from hot or cold running tap water, including such symptoms as red eyes, sneezing, skin rashes, and fainting or dizziness while taking a shower or washing dishes.

COLORS

F D & C colors, also called U.S. certified colors and artificial colors, are colors made from coal-tar that can be used in foods, drugs, and cosmetics (hence the initials F D & C). There is a great deal of controversy about their use because almost all have been shown to be carcinogenic in animal studies.

The FDA determines the safety of coal-tar colors by testing for acute oral toxicity, primary irritation, sensitization, subacute skin toxicity, and carcinogenicity by skin application. There are six coal-tar colors permanently listed as being "safe" (even though most are animal carcinogens), and others in current use that are on a FDA provisional list awaiting further proof of safety or toxicity. Technical materials on F D & C colors warn, "CAUTION: Consult the latest government regulations before using this dye in foods, drugs, and cosmetics."

Food colors have been widely publicized by Dr. Benjamin Feingold of Kaiser-Permanente Medical Center and the Feingold Association as a cause of hyperactivity and behavioral disturbance in children. While it has been very difficult to substantiate this with scientific studies, the observations of parents and doctors for over fifteen years confirm that avoidance of artificial colors has significantly improved their children's condition.

F D & C Yellow #5 causes allergic reactions in those sensitive to aspirin. The World Health Organization estimates that half the aspirin-sensitive people plus nearly 100,000 others are sensitive to this color, which can cause many different symptoms including life-threatening asthma attacks. Because of this, all foods produced after 1 July 1982 must list this color on the label separately from any other artificial colors.

D & C colors are coal-tar colors that can be used only in drugs and cosmetics. "Ext. D & C" on a label before a color listing means that it is approved for exterior use only in drugs and cosmetics and may not be used on the lips or mucous membranes. "Lakes of D & C" before a color indicates that a form of aluminum, calcium, barium, potassium, strontium, or zirconium has been added to the coal-tar dye.

There are several different types of D & C colors. Azo dyes are made from phenol and are easily absorbed through the skin. Anthraquinone dyes, which are currently being studied for carcinogenicity, are made from benzene. Aniline dyes cause intoxication, lack of oxygen in the blood, dizziness, headaches, and mental confusion.

HC colors are aniline, azo, or peroxide dyes, approved only for hair coloring. Symptoms from peroxide dyes include skin rash, eczema, bronchial asthma, gastritis—and occasionally, from complications arising from the above, death.

Colors in cleaning products are regulated by the Consumer Product Safety Commission (CPSC), which oversees the makeup of all cleaning products. All the commission requires is that products display warning labels if they contain "hazardous" ingredients; it is not necessary to list what the hazardous ingredient(s) is. According to the CPSC, no laws exist regulating the type of dye that may be used to color cleaning products.

CRESOL

Affects the central nervous system, liver, kidneys, lungs, pancreas, and spleen and can be fatal. Can be absorbed through the skin and mucous membranes. Symptoms: dermatitis, digestive disturbances, faintness, vertigo, mental changes, sweating, pallor, weakness, headache, dizziness, ringing in the ears, shock, delirium, and skin numbness and discoloration.

DETERGENTS

Detergents are responsible for more household poisonings than any other substance. Dermatitis, flulike and asthmatic conditions, severe eye damage; severe upper-digestive-tract damage if ingested.

DYES

Direct dyes (the do-it-yourself-at-home type) contain highly carcinogenic dichlorobenzidene, which is very easily absorbed through the skin. Can also cause anemia, jaundice, damage to the central nervous system, kidneys, and liver, as well as death. Azoic, basic, disperse, fiber-reactive, and vat dyes all can cause allergic reactions, as can fluorescent whitening agents.

EDTA (ETHYLENEDIAMINE TETRAACETIC ACID)

Numbness and tingling in fingers, lightheadedness, dizziness, vertigo, sneezing, nasal congestion, abdominal cramps, diarrhea, fever followed by chills, myalgia, headache, anorexia, nausea, urinary frequency and urgency, skin irritation, asthma attacks. EDTA is on the FDA list of food additives to be studied for toxicity.

ETHANOL

Central nervous system depression, anesthesia, feelings of exhilaration and talkativeness, impaired motor coordination, diplopia, vertigo, flushed face, nausea and vomiting, drowsiness, stupor, coma, dilated pupils, shock, hypothermia, and possibly death.

FLAME RETARDANTS

TRIS, a leading flame retardant, has been proved to be both mutagenic and carcinogenic to animals. Studies have shown that TRIS can be absorbed through the skin from garments washed more than fifty times. Materials treated with tetrakis hydroxyl-methyl phosphonium chloride (THPC), another retardant, release formaldehyde when the fabric is wet. Additional flame retardants include tetrakis hydroxyl-methyl phosphonium (THP), phenol, polybrominated biphenyls (PBBS), and polychlorinated biphenyls (PCBs).

FLAVORS

More than 1500 different petrochemical-derivative flavoring agents are currently in use. Usually they are listed as a group as "artificial" or "imitation" flavors, although occasionally a particular flavoring, such as vanillin, will be listed separately.

Most artificial flavorings are considered to be safe, but clinical observation by medical doctors has shown that artificial flavors can cause adverse reactions in those who are sensitive to petrochemical derivatives.

Dr. Feingold has widely publicized artificial flavors as a cause of hyperactivity and behavioral disturbances in children. While it has been very difficult to substantiate this with scientific studies, the observations of parents and doctors for over fifteen years confirm that avoidance of artificial flavors has significantly improved their children's condition.

FLUORIDE

Carcinogenic. Over 10,000 cancer deaths per year are linked to fluoridated water. Can also cause tiredness and weakness, mottling of the teeth, wrinkled skin, a prickly sensation in your muscles, kidney and bladder disorders, constipation, vomiting, itching after bathing, excessive thirst, headaches, arthritis, gum diseases, nervousness, diarrhea, hair loss, skin disorders, stomach disorders, numbness, brittle nails, sinus problems, mouth ulcers, vision problems, eczema, bronchitis, and asthma. Excessive fluoride can also reduce blood vitamin C levels, weaken the immune system, and cause birth defects and genetic damage. The use of fluoride has been banned in ten European countries.

FORMALDEHYDE

Suspected human carcinogen. Has been related to teratogenic and mutagenic changes in bacteriological studies. The National Academy of Sciences estimates that 10 to 20 percent of the general population may be susceptible to the irritant properties of formaldehyde at extremely low concentrations. Symptoms from inhalation of vapors: cough, swelling of the throat, watery eyes, respiratory problems, throat irritation, headaches, rashes, tiredness, excessive thirst, nausea, nosebleeds, insomnia, disorientation, bronchoconstriction, and asthma attacks. Symptoms from ingestion: nausea, vomiting, clammy skin and other symptoms of shock, severe abdominal pain, internal bleeding, loss of ability to urinate, vertigo, and coma, possibly leading to death. Symptoms from skin contact: skin eruptions. Long-term exposure can cause allergic sensitization. A preliminary scientific study speculates that formaldehyde may be a contributing factor in sudden infant death syndrome (SIDS).

FRAGRANCE

"Fragrance" on a label can indicate the presence of up to 4000 separate ingredients that are not listed at all. Most or all of them are synthetic. Complaints to the FDA have included headaches, dizziness, rashes, skin discoloration, violent coughing and vomiting, and allergic skin irritation. Clinical observation by medical doctors has shown that fragrances can cause all types of central nervous system symptoms including depression, hyperactivity, irritability, inability to cope, and other behavioral changes.

GLYCOLS

Glycols can be derived from petrochemicals or obtained from natural materials as a by-product of soap manufacture. On labels glycol appears as one of the following: natural (natural glycerin, vegetable glycerin); unspecified (glycerol, glycerin); and petrochemical (glycol, glyceryl, ethylene glycol, PEG or polyethylene glycol, and propylene glycol). Most forms of both natural and synthetic glycols are considered safe, although an FDA study showed polyethylene glycol to be highly allergenic. Ethylene glycol has been known to cause central nervous system depression, nausea and vomiting, abdominal pain, dehydration, weakness, muscle tenderness, coma, and death. Clinical observation by medical doctors has shown that any type of synthetic glycols can cause symptoms in those who are sensitive to petrochemical derivatives.

HEXANE

Cough, depression, heart problems, nausea, vomiting, abdominal swelling, and headache.

HYDROGEN PEROXIDE

Will burn skin and eyes on contact; inhalation can cause breathing difficulties.

HYDROGENATED OIL

Hydrogenation of oil into hard fat (margarine, vegetable shortening) destroys or deforms the essential fatty acids in the oil. Lack of essential fatty acids can contribute to neurological disease, heart disease, arteriosclerosis, skin diseases, cataracts, arthritis, high blood-cholesterol levels, and cancer.

KEROSENE

Intoxication, burning sensation in chest, headaches, ringing in the ears, nausea, weakness, uncoordination, restlessness, confusion and disorientation, convulsions, coma, burning in mouth, throat, and stomach, vomiting and diarrhea, drowsiness, rapid breathing, tachycardia, low-grade fever, and death.

LEAD

Early symptoms of lead poisoning: abdominal pains, loss of appetite, constipation, muscle pains, irritability, metallic taste in the mouth, excessive thirst, nausea and vomiting, shock, muscular weakness, pain and cramps, headache, insomnia, depression, and lethargy. Chronic low-level exposure has been found to produce permanent neuropsychological defects and behavior disorders in children, including low IQs, short attention spans, hyperactive behavior, and motor difficulties. In high doses, lead can cause brain damage, nervous system disorders, and death. Can also affect the kidney, liver, gastrointestinal system, heart, immune system, nervous system, and blood-forming system, and cause malformations in male sperm and low sperm counts. There is no demonstrably safe level for lead.

Because of the overuse of lead products in the past, virtually all air, water, food, and living beings are contaminated. Lead exposure can be lessened, but not completely avoided.

METHYLENE CHLORIDE

Suspected human carcinogen. Mutagenic.

MINERAL OIL

Suspected human carcinogen. Interferes with vitamin absorption in the body. Forbidden as a food coating in Germany. Is less dangerous if inhaled than if ingested or rubbed on skin.

MSG (MONOSODIUM GLUTAMATE)

Symptoms: Chinese Restaurant Syndrome—numbness, weakness, heart palpitations, cold sweat, and headache. Animal studies show MSG can cause brain damage, stunted skeletal development, obesity, and female sterility. It is also on the FDA list of additives that need further study for mutagenic, subacute, and reproductive effects. Pregnant women and people on sodium-restricted diets should not use MSG.

NAPHTHALENE

Suspected human carcinogen. Skin irritation, headache, confusion, nausea and vomiting, excessive sweating, urinary irritation; in sufficient quantity can lead to death.

NITRATES/NITROSAMINES

Relatively harmless, naturally occurring nitrates are changed within the body to nitrites, which cause fall in blood pressure, headache, vertigo, palpitations, visual disturbances, flushed skin, nausea, vomiting, diarrhea methemoglobinemia in infants, coma, and death. They can also turn into nitrosamines, which are carcinogenic.

NITROBENZENE

Symptoms: bluish skin, shallow breathing, vomiting, and death.

PARAFFIN

Impurities in paraffin are carcinogenic. In addition, clinical observation by medical doctors has shown that paraffin can cause adverse reactions in those who are sensitive to petrochemical derivatives.

PENTACHLOROPHENOL

Coughing, breathing difficulty, convulsions, nausea, loss of appetite, anesthesia, sweating, coma, and death.

PERCHLOROETHYLENE

Carcinogenic. Can also cause central nervous system depression, lightheadedness, dizziness, sleepiness, nausea, tremor, loss of appetite, disorientation, and liver damage.

PESTICIDES, HERBICIDES, FUNGICIDES

Over 1500 pesticides, herbicides, and fungicides are used in consumer products, combined with approximately 2000 other possibly toxic substances to make nearly 35,000 pesticide products. Over 100 of these in common use are thought to be carcinogenic, mutagenic, or teratogenic.

Some pesticides are extremely long lasting in the environment. An EPA study detected residues of chlordane inside homes twenty years after application. These pesticides also tend to be stored in the fatty tissue, and can accumulate over time to high levels in the body.

Health effects of some commonly encountered pesticides include paralysis, neuritis, sterility, convulsions, dizziness, weakness, tiny pupils, blurred vision, muscle twitching, slowed heartbeat, aplastic anemia, nausea, cough, diarrhea, tremors, damage to liver, kidney, and lungs, headaches, respiratory difficulty, coronary edema, coma, suppression of immune function, depression, irritation to ear, nose, and throat, hyperirritability, brain hemorrhages, central nervous system effects, decreased fertility and sexual function, and altered menstrual periods.

PHENOL

Suspected human carcinogen. Can also cause skin eruptions and peeling, swelling, pimples, hives, burning, gangrene, numbness, vomiting, circulatory collapse, paralysis, convulsions, cold sweats, coma, and death.

PLASTICS

All plastics present a problem with their "outgassing," a constant release of sometimes undetectable fumes, especially when heated. A good example of this outgassing effect occurs in new cars. That "new car smell" is caused by the outgassing of the plastic materials used in the interior of the car. You can see it as well as smell it, in the scum that forms on the inside of the windshield. In a study done by the National Aeronautics and Space Administration (NASA), polyester was found to be the synthetic material that released the most fumes.

Acrylonitrile ("Lucite"/"Plexiglas") is a suspected human carcinogen. Can also cause breathing difficulties, vomiting, diarrhea, nausea, weakness, headache, fatigue, and increased incidence of cancer in humans.

Epoxy Resins are a suspected human carcinogen.

Latex is one of the least toxic plastics. Usually considered relatively safe, clinical observation by medical doctors has shown that latex can cause adverse reactions in those who are sensitive to petrochemical derivatives.

Nylon is usually considered to be relatively safe, but clinical observation by medical doctors has shown that nylon can cause adverse reactions in those who are sensitive to petrochemicals. Both benzene and phenol are used to make nylon, and minute amounts of these substances that might still be present in the finished product may account for these adverse reactions.

Phenol-Formaldehyde Resin ("Bakelite") releases minute amounts of formaldehyde when new.

Polyester can cause eye and respiratory-tract irritation and acute dermatitis.

Polyethylene is a suspected human carcinogen.

Polyurethane can cause bronchitis, coughing, skin and eye problems. It also releases toluene diisocyanate, which can produce severe pulmonary effects and sensitization.

Polyvinyl Chloride (PVC) releases *Vinyl Chloride,* especially when the product is new. Vinyl chloride is carcinogenic, mutagenic, and teratogenic, and can cause mucous membrane dryness, numbness to the fingers, stomach pains, hepatitis, indigestion, chronic bronchitis, ulcers, Raynaud's syndrome, and allergic skin reactions.

Polyvinylpyrrolidone (PVP) is carcinogenic and can also cause thesaurosis, a lung disease affecting some users of hairspray, causing enlarged lymph nodes, lung masses, and changes in blood cells. Disease is reversible if hairspray is avoided.

Tetrafluoroethylene ("Teflon") can be irritating to eyes, nose, and throat, and can cause breathing difficulty. Tetrafluoroethylene produces poisonous gases when burned and may also produce these gases to a lesser degree when heated.

SACCHARIN

Label warning: "Use of this product may be hazardous to your health. . . . Contains saccharin, which has been determined to cause cancer in laboratory animals."

SUCROSE (sugar, corn sugar/syrup, dextrose, glucose syrup, invert sugar/syrup, maple sugar/syrup).

Symptoms: nutritional deficiencies, lowered resistance to disease, tooth decay, diabetes, hypoglycemia, coronary disease, obesity, ulcers, high blood pressure, vaginal yeast infections, and osteoporosis.

SULFUR COMPOUNDS (including potassium and sodium bisulfate and metabisulfite, sulfur dioxide, and sulfuric acid)

Can cause fatal allergic anaphylactic shock, asthma attacks, destroys vitamin B_1 (thiamin), has mutagenic effects on viruses, bacteria, and yeast, can act synergistically with carcinogens to make them more potent.

TALC

May be contaminated with carcinogenic asbestos.

TOLUENE

Nervous system and mental changes, irritability, disorientation, depression, and damage to liver and kidneys.

TRICHLOROETHYLENE

Suspected human carcinogen. Mutagenic. Symptoms: gastrointestinal upsets, central nervous system depression, narcosis, heart and liver malfunctions, paralysis, nausea, dizziness, fatigue, psychotic behavior.

XYLENE

Nausea, vomiting, salivation, cough, hoarseness, feelings of euphoria, headaches, giddiness, vertigo, ringing in the ears, confusion, coma, and death.

REFERENCE BOOKS

Bommersbach, Jane. "The Case Against NutraSweet." *Westword,* 25 January 1983.

Brobeck, Stephen, and Averyt, Anne C. *The Product Safety Book: The Ultimate Consumer Guide to Product Hazards.* New York: E. P. Dutton, 1983.

California State Department of Consumer Affairs. *Clean Your Room! A Compendium Describing a Wide Variety of Indoor Pollutants and Their Health Effects, and Containing Sage Advice to Both Householders and Statespersons in the Matter of Cleaning Up.* Sacramento: California State Department of Consumer Affairs, February 1982.

Freydberg, Nicholas, Ph.D., and Gortner, Willis A., Ph.D. *The Food Additives Book.* New York: Bantam Books, 1982.

Fritsch, Albert J., ed. *The Household Pollutants Guide.* Garden City, NY: Anchor Press/Doubleday, 1978.

Gosselin, R. E., et al. *Clinical Toxicology of Commercial Products.* 4th ed. Baltimore: The Williams & Wilkins Co., 1976.

Hunter, Beatrice Trum. *Beatrice Trum Hunter's Additive Book.* New Canaan, CT: Keats Publishing, 1980.

Hunter, Beatrice Trum. *Consumer Beware! Your Food and What's Been Done to It.* New York: Simon & Schuster, 1971.

Lipske, Michael. *Chemical Additives in Booze.* Washington, DC: Center for Science in the Public Interest, 1982.

Makower, Joel. *Office Hazards.* Washington, DC: Tilden Press, 1981.

Regenstein, Lewis. *America the Poisoned.* Washington, DC: Acropolis Books, 1982.

Samuels, Mike, M.D., and Bennett, Hal Zina. *Well Body, Well Earth: The Sierra Club Environmental Health Sourcebook.* San Francisco: Sierra Club Books, 1983.

Weiss, G., ed. *Hazardous Chemicals Data Book.* Park Ridge, NJ: Noyes Data Corporation, 1980.

Winter, R. *A Consumer Dictionary of Cosmetic Ingredients.* New York: Crown Publishers, 1978.

Winter, R. *A Consumer Dictionary of Food Additives.* New York: Crown Publishers, 1978.

Appendix Two

DESCRIPTION AND SOURCES FOR SUBSTANCES USED IN THE DO-IT-YOURSELF FORMULAS

Note: Because people can have allergic reactions to things they least expect, it is wise to do a "patch test" before using substances to make your own formulas, especially cosmetics that are used on the skin. Simply wet a patch of skin about the size of a quarter with the substance and cover loosely with a bandage for twenty-four hours. Any sign of redness, tenderness, or itching indicates sensitivity.

Alum powder. A mineral. For external use only; keep out of reach of children. Available at drugstores. *Romni Wools & Fibres; S. & C. Huber, Accoutrements; Straw into Gold.*

Baking soda (bicarbonate of soda, sodium bicarbonate). A mineral. Available in bulk at natural-foods stores and supermarkets. Arm & Hammer Baking Soda (Church & Dwight Co.).

Beeswax. Wax from the honeycomb of virgin bees. Available at hardware, hobby, and natural-foods stores. *Cerulean Blue; Glorybee Honey; Haussmann's Pharmacy; Kennedy's Natural Foods; New Age Creations; Penn Herb Co.; S. & C. Huber, Accoutrements; Wide World of Herbs.*

Borax (sodium borate). A mineral. Irritating to eyes and skin. Harmful if swallowed; keep out of reach of children. Available at supermarkets. Twenty Mule Team Borax (United States Borax & Chemical Corp.).

Calcium ascorbate. Vitamin C. Natural-foods stores.

Calcium carbonate (chalk, whiting). A mineral. Art-supply, drug, paint, and chemical-supply stores.

Calcium chloride. A mineral. Drug and chemical-supply stores.

Chlorophyll. The component of plants that makes them green. Pharmacies and health-food stores. *New Age Creations.*

Clay. A fine powder consisting of a variety of natural minerals. The particular color and composition are determined by the region where the clay was mined, although other minerals may be added to create desired hues. Natural-foods stores.
Abracadabra Clay (Abracadabra). Pure clay. May contain iron oxides. Comes in several different colors for different skin types. *The Body Bar, The Herb Patch.*
Facial Kleening Clay. (Green Valley Marketing).
Lewis Marketing. Natural desert clay.
Nature de France Clays (Nature de France). Mined in Tremblay-les-Gonesse, 100% French clay powders. *Erewhon Mail Order, Nature de France, The Soap Opera.*
Nevalite Products. Mined in Nevada, 100% clay from a bed that was once an inland sea.
New Age Creations. An assortment of clays for different skin types.
Pascalite. Pure, cream-colored clay containing natural antibiotics.
Wide World of Herbs. White clay.

Cocoa butter. A solid fat from cocoa beans. Known to cause allergic skin reactions. Natural-foods stores. *The Body Shop, Indiana Botanic Gardens, New Age Creations, Wide World of Herbs.*
Aura Cacia Pure Cocoa Butter (Aura Cacia). *Aura Cacia.*
Jason's Generic & Natural 100% Pure Cocoa Butter (Jason's Beauty Products). *Jason Natural Products.*
Woltra Cocoa Butter (Woltra Co.). *The Soap Opera.*

Diatomaceous earth. A pure silica formed from the fossils of one-celled algae with shells. Swimming pool supplies.

Dolomite. A mineral. Natural-foods stores.

Fuller's earth. A clay. Building materials and ceramic supply stores.

Glycerin. Natural glycerin is obtained as a by-product when natural fats, oils, and minerals are combined in soap manufacture. Natural-foods and drugstores. *New Age Creations, Penn Herb Co.*

Gum arabic. From acacia trees. Can cause reactions such as hay fever, asthma, and dermatitis to those who are allergic. Drugstores.

Henna. The dried, powdered leaves of a small tree native to southwest Asia and north Africa. Available only as a heavily fumigated import, it occurs naturally in three basic colors: red, black, and neutral; other shades are

obtained by carefully mixing these. Natural-foods stores. *The Body Shop (England), Cerulean Blue, Pure Planet Products, The Soap Opera, Wide World of Herbs.*
Born Again Hair (Le Vision Care Products). Purest Egyptian henna.
Helix Henna (Helix Corp.). Pure henna.
Rainbow Henna (Rainbow Henna Corp.). Pure henna.

Hydrated lime. From limestone. Skin irritant; take precautions to avoid excessive inhalation of dry particles. Building supplies.

Irish moss. From red algae. Natural-foods stores.

Lactic acid. Made from milk. Caustic in concentrated form. Hardware and paint stores.

Lanolin (wool fat, wool wax). Secretions from the oil glands of sheep. Common skin sensitizer. Drugstores and chemical-supply houses. *Indiana Botanic Gardens, New Age Creations, Penn Herb Co.*
Lanolin (Joy of Health).
Liquid Lanolin (Heritage Products).

Lecithin. Derived from eggs or soybeans. Natural-foods stores.

Lemon oil. Extracted from lemon peels. Known to cause allergic skin reactions. Drug and hardware stores.

Linseed oil. From the seeds of the flax plant. Use only unboiled, as boiled contains toxic drying agents. Art-supply and natural-foods stores.

Magnesium carbonate. A mineral. Drugstores.

Mason sand. A mineral. Building-materials stores.

Mink oil. From mink fur. Drugstores.

Oils. Cosmetic oils are more highly refined than are the oils sold for eating. They are filtered, cleaned, and purified to be as neutral and pure as possible. Cosmetic-grade oils have a better hypoallergenicity than do edible-grade refined or unrefined oils, since most allergic reactions are caused by small particles of the seed or nut that remain and act as irritants. Allergenicity is further reduced by a lower bacteria count than is found in edible-grade oils. On the other hand, most cosmetic-grade oils are taken from the seed or nut by solvent extraction, using the petrochemical hexane, whereas edible-grade oils are available that have been "cold-pressed" without chemicals. Cosmetic-grade oils are found in natural-foods stores and body-care shops. *The Body Shop, The Body Shop (England), Caswell-Massey, Common Scents, Denis Dumont.*

Plaster of paris (calcium sulfate, gypsum). A mineral. Hardware and building-supply stores.
Dowman's Plaster of Paris (Dowman Products).

Potassium bicarbonate. A mineral. Drugstores.

Pumice. A volcanic rock. Hardware and paint stores.

Sodium hexametaphosphate. Made from minerals. Calgon is pure sodium hexametaphosphate, but is scented. Chemical-supply houses.

Sodium perborate. Made from borax and soda ash. For external use only; keep out of reach of children. Drugstores and chemical-supply houses.

Spermaceti. A wax from the head of the sperm whale. Drugstores and chemical-supply houses. *Haussmann's Pharmacy.*

Stearic acid. Made from tallow. Known to cause allergic skin reactions. Hobby shops.

TSP (trisodium phosphate). A mineral, TsP (Santa Monica Chemical Corp.) is a scented mixture of sodium carbonate and sodium sesquicarbonate and does not contain any trisodium phosphate. For external use only; skin irritant; keep out of reach of children. Hardware stores, variety stores, janitor supplies, and paint stores.
Dowman's TSP (Dowman Products).
Oakite Trisodium Phosphate (Oakite).

Washing soda (sal soda, sodium carbonate decahydrate). A mineral. For external use only; keep out of reach of children. Arm & Hammer Washing Soda is scented and reportedly contains other chemical additives. Drug and chemical-supply stores. *Cerulean Blue, Erlander's Natural Products, Straw into Gold.*

White dextrin. Made from starch. Chemical supplies.

White Portland cement. A combination of various minerals. Building supplies.

Zinc oxide. From zinc. Drugstores and ceramic shops.

Directory One

MAIL-ORDER SOURCES

When dealing with mail-order companies, be very specific about what you are interested in. A letter requesting information about nitrate-free sausages might get an immediate response, while a simple catalog request will be answered whenever catalogs are next printed (sometimes six months later). Moreover, some of the companies listed have several catalogs and may discard your request rather than take either the time to find out which catalog you are interested in or the expense of sending all of them. *Always* write your full name and address on the request letter itself; by the time it is read, the envelope on which you wrote your return address will have long parted company with its enclosure. While most of the catalogs are free, some mail-order companies charge a fee, often refundable with your first order. Overseas companies have requested that you make an exception to the no-cash-in-the-mail rule and send your catalog fee in *cash* because of the processing fees involved with out-of-the-country checks. Other companies ask that you enclose a SASE—a self-addressed, stamped (#10 letter-sized) envelope—with your catalog request to ensure a prompt reply.

You will notice that each address is followed by the code "Dept. NN." Mail-order companies use these codes to keep track of where their customers found out about them. *Please use this code so that these businesses can know you read about them in this book.*

A. Liss & Co.
35–03 Bradley Ave., Dept. NN
Long Island City, NY 11101
800/221–0938
212/392–8484
Free catalog

Able Steel Equipment Co.
50–02 23rd St., Dept. NN
Long Island City, NY 11101
212/361–9240
Free catalog

Abundant Life Seed Foundation
PO Box 772, Dept. NN
Port Townsend, WA 98368
206/385–5660
$3 catalog

A Child's Garden
320 Penwood Rd., Dept. NN
Silver Spring, MD 20901
301/593–0712
Free catalog

ACS Hoval
935 N. Lively Blvd., Dept. NN
Wood Dale, IL 60191
312/860–6860
Free catalog

Adams Mattress Co.
PO Box 7025, Dept. NN
Fort Worth, TX 76111
817/838–2395
No catalog

After the Stork
PO Box 1832, Dept. NN
Bisbee, AZ 85603
602/432–3683
Free catalog

Agatha's Cozy Corner
Woodbury Plaza, Dept. NN
Portsmouth, NH 03801
800/258–0857
Free catalog

Ahlers Organic Date & Grapefruit Garden
PO Box 726, Dept. NN
Mecca, CA 92254
714/396–2337
Free catalog

Ahlswede's All Seasons
PO Box N164, Dept. NN
Northfield, IL 60093
312/441–8441
Free catalog

Aireox Research Corp.
PO Box 8523, Dept. NN
Riverside, CA 92515
714/689–2781
Free catalog

Alafodd Acewool
c/o Daphne Imports
7 Norden Lane, Dept. NN
Huntington Station, NY 11746
800/228–5000
Free catalog

Alice in Wonderland Creations
Rte. 1, PO Box 405, Dept. NN
Millstone, WV 25261
$1 catalog

Alive Polarity Distributors
28779 Via Las Flores, Dept. NN
Murrieta, CA 92362
714/677–7451
Free catalog

The Allergy Store
7345 Healdsburg Ave., Suite 511, Dept. NN
Sebastopol, CA 95472
800/824–7163
Free catalog

Allermed Corp.
4324 Sunbelt Dr., Dept. NN
Dallas, TX 75248
214/248–0782
Free catalog

Andean Products
PO Box 472, Dept. NN
Cuena, ECUADOR
Free catalog

Ann Taylor
PO Box 805, Dept. NN
New Haven, CT 06503
800/228–5600
800/642–8777
Free catalog

Annie Cole
73 Princes Way, Dept. NN
Wimbledon
London SW19 6HY, ENGLAND
Free catalog

Arise Futon Mattress Company
37 Wooster St., Dept. NN
New York, NY 10013
212/925–0310
212/925–0369
Free catalog

Art Brown & Bro.
2 West 46th St., Dept. NN
New York, NY 10036
212/575–5555
Free catalog

Art Needlework Industries
7 St. Michael's Mansions, Dept. NN
Ship St.
Oxford OX1 3DG, ENGLAND
Free catalog

Ascot Chang
41 Man Yue St., Dept. NN
2/F Block D
Hunghom, Kowloon
HONG KONG
Free catalog

Aura Cacia
PO Box 391, Dept. NN
Weaverville, CA 96093
916/623–4999
Free catalog

Avoca Handweavers Ltd.
Ballinacor House, Dept. NN
Church Rd.
County Dublin, IRELAND
$3 catalog

Babouris Handicrafts
56 Adrianou St., Dept. NN
Athens 116, GREECE
No catalog

Baldwin Hill Bakery
Baldwin Hill Rd., Dept. NN
Phillipston, MA 01331
617/249–4691
Free catalog

Banana Republic
PO Box 77133, Dept. NN
San Francisco, CA 94107
415/777–5200
Free catalog

Bandon Sea-Pack
PO Box 5488, Dept. NN
Charleston, OR 97420–0614
503/347–3914
503/888–4600
Free catalog

Barth's of Long Island
270 W. Merrick Rd., Dept. NN
Valley Stream, NY 11582
800/645–2328
516/561–2233
Free catalog

Bartlett Yarns
Dept. NN
Harmony, ME 04942
207/683–2251
Free catalog

The Bartley Collection
747 Oakwood Ave., Dept. NN
Lake Forest, IL 60045
312/295–2535
Free catalog

Bay Spice House
2343 Birch St., Dept. NN
Palo Alto, CA 94306
415/326–8811
Free catalog

Bear Meadow Farm
RFD 2, Moore's Rd., Dept. NN
Florida, MA 01247
413/664–6453
413/663–9241
$1 catalog

Beckwith Enterprises
PO Box 2204, Dept. NN
Bloomington, IN 47402
Free catalog

Benson Enterprises
PO Box 5736, Dept. NN
Hacienda Hts., CA 91745
213/794–6527
Free catalog

Berea College Student Craft Industries
Dept. NN
Berea, KY 40404
606/986–9341
Free catalog

Berg
3707 Robinson, Dept. NN
Austin, TX 78722
Free catalog

Berner International Corp.
216 New Boston St., Dept. NN
Woburn, MA 01801
617/933–2180
Free catalog

Better Gooses & Garments
1232 Sawyers Bar Rd., Dept. NN
Etna, CA 96027
$.20 catalog

Bettywear
97 Nichols Ave., Dept. NN
Shelton, CT 06484
No catalog

Biarritz
PO Box 590, Dept. NN
Auburn, ME 04210
Free catalog

Big Sky Trading Co.
PO Box 1, Dept. NN
Arlee, MT 59821
406/726–3214
Free catalog

Billard's Old Telephones
21710 Regnart Rd., Dept. NN
Cupertino, CA 95014
408/252–2104
Free catalog

Bill Muller, Toymaker
PO Box 40, Dept. NN
Oak Hall, VA 23416
804/824–4373
Free catalog

Bill Pruzan
50 Berry St., Dept. NN
San Francisco, CA 94107
415/441–5444
No catalog

Bill Tosetti's
17632 Chatsworth, Dept. NN
Granada Hills, CA 91644
213/363–2192
Free catalog

Biobottoms
57 Grant Ave., Dept. NN
Petaluma, CA 94952
707/778–7945
Free catalog

Blowing Rock Crafts
PO Box 16, Dept. NN
Blowing Rock, NC 28605
704/295–3577
Free catalog

Blue Heron Futons
764 Elm, Dept. NN
Lawrence, KS 66044
913/841–9443
Free catalog

The Blue Ribbon Bedding Co.
PO Box 780, Dept. NN
New York, NY 10013
212/966–2625
$1 catalog

The Body Shop
1621 Fifth St. Dept. NN,
Berkeley, CA 94710
415/524-0216
Free catalog

The Body Shop (England)
1 Crane St., Dept. NN
Chichester
West Sussex, PO19 1LH, ENGLAND
Free catalog

Books on Tape
PO Box 7900, Dept. NN
Newport Beach, CA 92658–0900
800/626–3333
Free catalog

Borchelt Herb Gardens
474 Carriage Shop Rd., Dept. NN
E. Falmouth, MA 02536
Free catalog

Boudry Distributors
31220 La Baya Dr., Suite 110, Dept. NN
Westlake Village, CA 91362
805/497–3565
Free catalog

Briar Shepherd
Keeper's Cottage, Moor Lane, Dept. NN
N. Yorkshire, Skipton, ENGLAND
Free catalog

Briggs & Little Woolen Mills
York Mills, Dept. NN
Harvey Station NB EOH 1HO, CANADA
Free catalog

Briggs-Way Co.
Dept. NN
Ugashik, AK 99683
Free catalog

Bright Future Futon Co.
2424 Garfield SE, Dept. NN
Albuquerque, NM 87106
505/268–9738
Free catalog

Britches of Georgetowne
PO Box 428, Dept. NN
Alexandria, VA 23313–0428
703/548–0200
Free catalog

Britex-by-Mail
146 Geary, Dept. NN
San Francisco, CA 94108
415/392–2910
$2 catalog

British Isles Collection
Mt. Washington Valley, Rte. 16, Main
St., Dept. NN
North Conway, NH 03860
603/356–9311
Free catalog

Bronson Pharmaceuticals
4526 Rinetti Lane, Dept. NN
La Cañada, CA 91011
213/790–2646
Free catalog

Brooks Brothers
350 Campus Plaza, Dept. NN
Edison, NJ 08817
800/247–1000
201/225–4860
Free catalog

Brookside Farm
Dept. NN
Tunbridge, VT 05077
Free catalog

Brookstone Co.
127 Rose Farm Rd., Dept. NN
Peterborough, NH 03458
Free catalog

Brown Sheep Co.
Rte. 1, Dept. NN
Mitchell, NE 69357
308/635–2198
Free catalog

Buffalo Shirt Co.
345 Main St., Dept. NN
Half Moon Bay, CA 94019
415/726–3194
Free catalog

Bullock & Jones
340 Post St., Dept. NN
San Francisco, CA 94108
415/392–4243
800/227–3050
Free catalog

Butte Creek Mill
PO Box 561, Dept. NN
Eagle Point, OR 97524
503/826–3531
Free catalog

Butterbrooke Farm
78 Barry Rd., Dept. NN
Oxford, CT 06483
203/888–2000
Free catalog

The Butterfield Co.
Rte. 4, Box 234, Dept. NN
Fairfield, IA 52556
515/472–8691
Free catalog

C. D. Fitzhardinge-Bailey
St. Aubyn, 15 Dutton St., Dept. NN
Bankstoun, New South Wales 2200
AUSTRALIA
Free catalog

Cable Car Clothiers/Robert Kirk Ltd.
150 Post St., Dept. NN
San Francisco, CA 94108
415/397–7733
Free catalog

Cal Ben Soap Co.
9828 Pearmain St., Dept. NN
Oakland, CA 94603
415/638–7091
Free catalog

Calef's Country Store
Dept. NN
Barrington, NH 03825
603/664–2231
Free catalog

Cambrian
Llanwrtyd Wells, Dept. NN
Powys, LD5 4SD, ENGLAND
Free catalog

Cambridge Chemists
702 Madison Ave., Dept. NN
New York, NY 10021
212/838–1885
212/838–1884
No catalog

Cambridge Wools Ltd.
PO Box 2572, Dept. NN
Auckland 1, NEW ZEALAND
Free catalog

Camp Beverly Hills
9615 Brighton Way, Suite 210, Dept. NN
Beverly Hills, CA 90210
213/202–0069
$1 catalog

Capriland's Herb Farm
Silver St., Dept. NN
Coventry, CT 06238
203/742–7244
Free catalog

Caput Magnum Designs
Station St., Dept. NN
Holbeach, Spalding
Lincolnshire, PE12 7LF, ENGLAND
Free catalog

Carjeanne Enterprises
PO Box 21874, Station 16, Dept. NN
Lakewood, CO 80228
303/986–9604
Free catalog

Carol Brown
Dept. NN
Putney, VT 05346
802/387–5875
Free catalog

Castlemoor
Castle St., Dept. NN,
Bampton
Devon EX16 9NS ENGLAND
$2 catalog

Caswell-Massey Co.
111 Eighth Ave., Dept. NN
New York, NY 10011
212/620–0900
Free catalog

Cedar-Al Products
Dept. NN
Clallam Bay, WA 98326
206/457–8638
Free catalog

Cerulean Blue
PO Box 21168, Dept. NN
Seattle, WA 98111
206/625–9647
$3.25 catalog

Charette
31 Olympia Ave., Dept. NN
Woburn, MA 01888
617/935–6000
Free catalog

Charing Cross Kits
PO Box 798, Dept. NN
Meredith, NH 03253
603/279–8449
Free catalog

Charles W. Jacobsen
401 S. Salina St., Dept. NN
Syracuse, NY 13201
315/422–7832
315/471–6522
Free catalog

Charles Webb
28 Church St., Dept. NN
Cambridge, MA 02138
617/491–2389
Free catalog

Cheese Junction
1 W. Ridgewood Ave., Dept. NN
Ridgewood, NJ 07450
800/631–0353
Free catalog

The Chef's Catalogue
725 County Line Rd., Dept. NN
Deerfield, IL 60015
312/480–9400
$1 catalog

The Cherry Tree
PO Box 361, Dept. NN
Sonoma, CA 95476
707/938–3480
Free catalog

Cheryl Kolander
440 Blair, Dept. NN
Eugene, OR 97402
503/863–6330
503/683–2359
Free catalog

Chicago Dietetic Supply
405 E. Shawmit Ave., Dept. NN
LaGrange, IL 60525
312/352–6900
Free catalog

Chico-San
PO Box 810, Dept. NN
Chico, CA 95927
916/891–6271
Free catalog

Childcraft
PO Box 500, Dept. NN
Edison, NJ 08818
800/631–5657
201/572–6100
Free catalog

Cindy-Kit
31 Nagle Ave., Dept. NN
New York, NY 10040
Free catalog

Clark Hill Sugary
Dept. NN
Canaan, NH 03741
603/523–7752
Free catalog

Clear Light Cedar Co.
PO Box 551–M, Dept. NN
Placitas, NM 87043
505/867–2925
Free catalog

Cleo
18 Kildare St., Dept. NN
Dublin 2, IRELAND
$2 catalog

Clothcrafters
Dept. NN
Elkhart Lake, WI 53020
414/876–2112
Free catalog

Coast Filtration
142 Viking Ave., Dept. NN
Brea, CA 92621
714/990–4602
Free catalog

Coastside Creations
PO Box 101, Dept. NN
Half Moon Bay, CA 94019
415/756–3194
Free catalog

Cohasset Colonials
Dept. NN
Cohasset, MA 02025
617/383–0110
$1 catalog

Collette Modes
66 S. Great George St., Dept. NN
Dublin 2, IRELAND
Free catalog

Collins Designers
317 Presidential Way, Box 536,
Dept. NN
Guilderland, NY 12084
518/456–6845
No catalog

Colonial Garden Kitchens
270 W. Merrick Rd., Dept. NN
Valley Stream, NY 11582
800/228–5656
800/642–8777
Free catalog

Colvada Date Co.
PO Box 908, Dept. NN
Coachella, CA 92236
619/398–3441
Free catalog

Common Scents
3920A 24th St., Dept. NN
San Francisco, CA 94114
415/826–1019
Free catalog

Community Soap Factory
PO Box 32057, Dept. NN
Washington, DC 20007
202/347–0186
Free catalog

Contessa Yarns
PO Box 37, Dept. NN
Lebanon, CT 06249
203/423–3479
Free catalog

Cording of Piccadilly
19 Piccadilly, Dept. NN
London W1V OPE, ENGLAND
Free catalog

The Cordwainer Shop
Wild Orchard Farms, Dept. NN
Deerfield, NH 03037
603/463–7742
$3 catalog

Cornelius Furs
Box 3775 G P O, Dept. NN
Sydney 2001, AUSTRALIA
Free catalog

Cornucopia
PO Box 44, Westcott Rd., Dept. NN
Harvard, MA 01451–0044
617/456–3201
Free catalog

Cotton Brokers
PO Box 148, Dept. NN
Richfield, MN 55423
Free catalog

Cotton Clouds
PO Box 604, Dept. NN
Safford, AZ 85546
602/428–7000
Free catalog

The Cotton Co.
PO Box 631, Dept. NN
Chattanooga, TN 37401
800/421–4548
Free catalog

Cotton Comfort
5000 Belt Line Rd., Suite 590, Dept. NN
Dallas, TX 75075
800/527–4384
214/458–7375
Free catalog

Cotton Cookie Clothing Co.
PO Box 569, Dept. NN
Woodacre, CA 94973
415/488–0705
Free catalog

Cotton Dreams
PO Box 1261, Dept. NN
Sebastian, FL 32958
305/589–0172
Free catalog

The Cotton Loom
398 W. Camino Gardens Blvd. #106,
    Dept. NN
Boca Raton, FL 33432
$1 catalog

The Cotton Place
PO Box 59721, Dept. NN
Dallas, TX 75229
214/243–4149
$3 catalog

Cotton Togs North
PO Box 2180, Dept. NN
Dixmont, ME 04932
Free catalog

Cottontails
1325 43rd St., Dept. NN
Los Alamos, NM 87544
505/662–4558
$1 catalog

Country Pride Meats
PO Box 6, Dept. NN
Ipswich, SD 57451
605/426–6343
605/426–6288
Free catalog

Country Rag Rugs
465 North St., Dept. NN
Dalton, MA 01226
Free catalog

The Country Store & Farm
Rte. 2, Box 304, Dept. NN
Vashon, WA 98070
206/463–3655
$1 catalog

Craft Pattern Studios
2200 Dean St., Dept. NN
St. Charles, IL 60174
$2 catalog

Craftsman's Mark
Tone Dale Mill, Dept. NN, Wellington,
Somerset TA21 OAW, ENGLAND
Free catalog

Cresset Farm Cheese
RD 1, Rte. 34B, Dept. NN
Aurora, NY 13026
315/364–7286
Free catalog

Crowley Cheese
Dept. NN
Healdsville, VT 05758
802/259–2340
Free catalog

Cuddledown
106 Main St., Dept. NN
Yarmouth, ME 04096
207/846–9781
Free catalog

Culpeper
Hadstock Rd., Linton, Dept. NN
Cambridge CB1 6NJ, ENGLAND
$2 catalog

The Custom Shop
157th Ave., Dept. NN
Franklin, NJ 07416
800/221–9982
800/522–5229
Free catalog

Cycles
PO Box 23123, Dept. NN
San Jose, CA 95153
Free catalog

Czimer Foods
Rte. 7, PO Box 285, Dept. NN
Lockport, IL 60441
312/460–2210
312/460–3503
SASE catalog

Daisyfresh Dairy Cultures
PO Box 36–Y, Dept. NN
Santa Cruz, CA 95063
Free catalog

Dan Johnson's Sugar House
Rte. 1, PO Box 265, Dept. NN
Jaffrey, NH 03452
603/532–7379
Free catalog

David Morgan
PO Box 70190, Dept. NN
Seattle, WA 98107
206/282–3300
Free catalog

Daybreak
PO Box 177, Dept. NN
Monterey, MA 01245
Free catalog

Deer Valley Farm
RD 1, Dept. NN
Guilford, NY 13780
607/764–8556
Free catalog

Deerlick Springs
PO Box 56, Dept. NN
Douglas City, CA 96024
916/623–2957
Free catalog

Deerskin Trading Post
119 Foster St., Dept. NN
Peabody, MA 01960
617/532–2810
Free catalog

Dellinger
PO Drawer 273, Dept. NN
Rome, GA 30161
404/291–7402
No catalog

Denis Dumont
1433 Polk St., Dept. NN
San Francisco, CA 94109
415/441–0341
Free catalog

Denny Andrews
Clock House Workshop, Dept. NN
Colehill, Near Swindon
Wiltshire, ENGLAND
Free catalog

Des Champs Laboratories
PO Box 440, Dept. NN
E. Hanover, NJ 07936
201/884–1460
Free catalog

Design-Kit
Drawer D, Dept. NN
Bloomingburg, NY 12921
914/733–1991
$1 catalog

Deva
PO Box F83, Dept. NN
Burkittsville, MD 21718
301/473–4900
Free catalog

Diamond K Enterprises
R.R. 1, Box 30, Dept. NN
St. Charles, MN 55972
507/932–4308
Free catalog

Dona Shrier
825 Northlake Dr., Dept. NN
Richardson, TX 75080
214/235–0485
Free catalog

Down Home Comforters
PO Box 440, Dept. NN
Willits, CA 95490
707/459–4241
Free catalog

Down Lite Products
7818 Palace Dr., Dept. NN
Cincinnati, OH 45242
513/772–2233
Free catalog

DP Laboratories
2724 Third Ave., Dept. NN
San Diego, CA 92103
619/233–7213
Free catalog

Dreamy Down Fashions
287 W. Butterfield Rd., Dept. NN
Elmhurst, IL 60126
312/941–3840
$1 catalog

Dublin Woolen Co.
Metal Bridge Corner, Dept. NN
Dublin 1, IRELAND
Free catalog

Dunham's of Maine
PO Box 707, Dept. NN
Waterville, ME 04901
800/341–0471
Free catalog

Durastill
4200 Birmingham Rd., Dept. NN
Kansas City, MO
800/821–6000
No catalog

E. Braun & Co.
717 Madison Ave., Dept. NN
New York, NY 10021
212/838–0650
Free catalog

E. L. Foust Company
PO Box 105, Dept. NN
Elmhurst, IL 60126
312/834–4952
Free catalog

Earthen Joys
1412 Eleventh St., Dept. NN
Astoria, OR 97103
503/325–0426
Free catalog

Earthsong Herb Shop
330 N. First #4, Dept. NN
Sandpoint, ID 83864
208/263–8312
SASE catalog

East Wind
Box 152 Cohasset Stage Rte., Dept. NN
Chico, CA 95926
916/342–9178
Free catalog

Easy Pieces
PO Box 194, Dept. NN
Harbor Springs, MI 49740
616/526–5471
Free catalog

Eden Ranch
PO Box 370, Dept. NN
Topanga, CA 90290
213/455–1336
Free catalog

Effie May Organic Fruits and Vegetables
19550 Hidden Glen Rd., Dept. NN
Alpine, CA 92001
619/445–9918
Free catalog

Eichten's Hidden Acres Cheese Farm
Country Rd. 82, Dept. NN
Center City, MN 55012
612/257–4752
Free catalog

Eileen's Handknits
Dept. NN
Ardara, Donegal, IRELAND
Free catalog

Eiler's Cheese Market
Rte. 2, Dept. NN
DePere, WI 54115
414/336–8292
Free catalog

NONTOXIC & NATURAL

Elisabeth the Chef
St. Mary's Road, Sydenham Farm,
Dept. NN
Leamington Spa CV31 1QE, ENGLAND
Free catalog

Elizabeth Forbes
44 Monterey Blvd., Dept. NN
San Francisco, CA 94131
415/585–1121
Free catalog

Elizabeth James
PO Box 357, Dept. NN
Beverly, MA 01915
617/927–6171
Free catalog

Elizabeth Zimmerman/Meg Swansen
6899 Cary Bluff, Dept. NN
Pittsville, WI 54466
Free catalog

Elm Enterprises
PO Box 2325, Dept. NN
Corrales, NM 87048
Free catalog

Environmental Purification Systems
PO Box 344, Dept. NN
Danville, CA 94526
415/838–2457
Free catalog

Equipto
Dept. NN
Aurora, IL 60507
312/859–1000
Free catalog

Erewhon Mail Order
236 Washington St., Dept. NN
Brookline, MA 02146
617/738–4516
Free catalog

Erlander's Natural Products
PO Box 106, Dept. NN
Altadena, CA 91001
213/797–7004
Free catalog

Especially Maine
US Rte. 1, Dept. NN
Kennebunkport, ME 04046
207/985–3749
Free catalog

Esprit
950 Tennessee St., Dept. NN
San Francisco, CA 94107
800/4-ESPRIT
Free catalog

Essential Alternatives
38 Center St., Dept. NN
Rutland, VT 05701
802/773–8834
Free catalog

Eugene Trading Company
651 E. 13th, Dept. NN
Eugene, OR 97401
503/344–7006
Free catalog

Euroquilt
461 Rte. 46 West, Dept. NN
Fairfield, NJ 07006
800/631–1092
201/227–4586
Free catalog

Exactitude
91 Stillman St., Dept. NN
San Francisco, CA 94107
415/543–5190
Free catalog

Exotica Seed and Rare Fruit Nursery
1742 Laurel Canyon Rd., Dept. NN
Los Angeles, CA 90046
213/851–0990
$2 catalog

Exotic Silks!
252 State St., Dept. NN
Los Altos, CA 94022
415/948–8611
Free catalog

FBS
659 Main St., Dept. NN
New Rochelle, NY 10801
800/228–5200
914/636–8600
Free catalog

Feathered Friends
155 Western Ave. W, Dept. NN
Seattle, WA 98119
800/426–2724
206/622–0974
Free catalog

Finger Prints
1848 Clay St., Dept. NN
Port Townsend, WA 98368
206/385–3101
Free catalog

Fluir Herbals
PO Box 49, Dept. NN
Stroudsburg, PA 18360
Free catalog

Four Chimneys
Hall Road, Dept. NN
Himrod-on-Seneca, NY 14842
607/243–7502
Free catalog

Fran's Basket House
Rte. 10, Dept. NN
Succasunna, NJ 07876
201/584–2230
Free catalog

French Creek Sheep & Wool Co.
Dept. NN
Elverson, PA 19520
800/345–4091
215/286–5700
Free catalog

Frette
787 Madison Ave., Dept. NN
New York, NY 10021
212/988–5221
Free catalog

Funn Stockings
PO Box 102, Dept. NN
Steyning
W. Sussex, ENGLAND
Free catalog

The Futon Co.
412 W. Franklin, Dept. NN
Chapel Hill, NC 27514
919/933–2222
Free catalog

The Futon Shop
178 W. Houston St., Dept. NN
New York, NY 10014
212/620–9015
Free catalog

Garnet Hill
PO Box 262, Dept. NN
Franconia, NH 03580
603/823–5545
Free catalog

General Wax & Candle
PO Box 9398, Dept. NN
N. Hollywood, CA 91609
818/765–6357
No catalog

George W. Park Seed Co.
PO Box 31, Dept. NN
Greenwood, SC 29646
800/845–3369
Free catalog

Gill Imports
PO Box 73, Dept. NN
Ridgefield, CT 06870
203/438–7409
$1 catalog

Glenn's Optiques
10611 Garland Rd., Suite 216,
Dept. NN
Dallas, TX 75218
214/321–6753
No catalog

Glorybee Honey
1006 Arrowsmith St., Dept. NN
Eugene, OR 97402
503/485–1649
Free catalog

Godiva Chocolatier
701 Fifth Ave., Dept. NN
New York, NY 10022
800/223–6005
212/593–2845
Free catalog

Gohn Bros.
PO Box 111, Dept. NN
Middlebury, IN 46540–0111
219/825–2400
Free catalog

Gokey's
84 S. Wabash St., Dept. NN
St. Paul, MN 55107
800/328–9374
612/224–4432
Free catalog

Golden Touch Lambskin Products
PO Box 41, Dept. NN
Oregon, WI 53575
608/835–9026
608/833–9323
Free catalog

Good Things Collective
1 Cottage St., Dept. NN
Northampton, MA 01027
413/527–6403
413/527–6400
$1 catalog

Gramma Gregg's Enterprises
PO Box 793, Dept. NN
Yureka, CA 96097
916/475–3521
No catalog

Granny's Old-Fashioned Products
3581 E. Milton, Dept. NN
Pasadena, CA 91107
213/577–1825
No catalog

Great Earth Discount Vitamins
2020 Cotner Ave., Dept. NN
W. Los Angeles, CA 90025
Free catalog

Great Lakes Futons
1428 N. Farwell Ave., Dept. NN
Milwaukee, WI 53202
414/272–3324
414/272–3319
Free catalog

The Great Valley Mills
101 SW End Blvd., Dept. NN
Quakertown, PA 18951
215/536–3990
Free catalog

Guernsey Knitwear
6 The Bridge, St. Sampson's, Dept. NN
Channel Islands, ENGLAND
Free catalog

Guild of Shaker Crafts
401 W. Savidge St., Dept. NN
Spring Lake, MI 49456
616/846–2870
Free catalog

Gurian Fabrics
276 Fifth Ave., Dept. NN
New York, NY 10001
212/689–9696
Free catalog

Gurney's Seed & Nursery Co.
Dept. NN
Yankton, SD 57079
Free catalog

H.D. Catty Corp.
Church & Mill Sts., Dept. NN
Huntly, IL 60142
Free catalog

Haf-a-Jama
14 Mica Lane, Dept. NN
Wellesley, MA 02181
617/235–5340
Free catalog

Hanna Andersson
5565 SW Hewett Blvd., Dept. NN
Portland, OR 97221
503/292–8664
Free catalog

Hans Mueller
2459 Southwell, Dept. NN
Dallas, TX 75229
214/241–2793
Free catalog

Happy Baby Bunz
PO Box 745, Dept. NN
Carmichael, CA 95608
916/486–0882
SASE catalog

Harrisville Designs
Dept. NN
Harrisville, NH 03450
Free catalog

Hartenthaler's
Delcroft Shopping Ctr., Dept. NN
Folcroft, PA 19032
215/583–1644
Free catalog

Hartman's
4237 Bettina, Dept. NN
San Mateo, CA 94403
415/343–1131
No catalog

Harvie & Hudson
77 Jermyn St., Dept. NN, St. James's
London SW1, ENGLAND
Free catalog

Haussmann's Pharmacy
534–536 W. Girard Ave., Dept. NN
Philadelphia, PA 19123
215/627–2143
Free catalog

Hawthorne Valley Farm
RD 2, Harlemville, Dept. NN
Ghent, NY 12075
518/672–4882
Free catalog

Hayashi Kimono
Intl Arcade, 4–2, Yiraku-Cho, Dept. NN
Tokyo, JAPAN
Free catalog

Hearthsong
2211 Blucher Valley Rd., Dept. NN
Sebastopol, CA 95472
707/829–0900
Free catalog

Hearty Mix Co.
1231 Madison Hill Rd., Dept. NN
Rahway, NJ 07065
201/382–2432
Free catalog

Heavenly Hammocks
PO Box 25, Dept. NN
Santa Cruz, CA 95063
408/335–3160
Free catalog

Heavenly Soap
5948 E. 30th St., Dept. NN
Tucson, AZ 85711
602/790–9938
Free catalog

The Herb Patch
PO Box 583, Dept. NN
Boulder City, NV 89005
702/456–1547
Free catalog

Helen McGroarty
7 Grafton Arcade, Dept. NN
Dublin 2, IRELAND
Free catalog

Henry Field Seed & Nursery Co.
Dept. NN
Shenandoah, IA 51602
Free catalog

Hickory Hollow
Rte. 1, Box 52, Dept. NN
Peterstown, WV 24963
SASE catalog

Hilltop Herb Farm
PO Box 1734, Dept. NN
Cleveland TX 77327
Free catalog

Holster's Ruddy Duck Rugs
Misery Bay Route, Dept. NN
Toivola, MI 49965
Free catalog

Homebody
8521 Melrose Ave., Dept. NN
Los Angeles, CA 90069
213/659–2917
Free catalog

Homespun Crafts
PO Box 1776, Dept. NN
Blackburg, SC 29702
800/458–3491
800/438–7939
Free catalog

Homespun Fabrics & Draperies
10836 Washington Blvd., Dept. NN
Culver City, CA 90230
213/839–6984
Free catalog

Homespun Weavers
530 State Ave., Dept. NN
Emmaus, PA 18049
215/967–4550
SASE catalog

Hortocultural Enterprises
PO Box 810082, Dept. NN
Dallas, TX 75381
Free catalog

House of Hammocks
PO Box 211, Dept. NN
Newton Highlands, MA 02161
617/244–1545
Free catalog

Huntington Clothiers
2258 E. Main St., Dept. NN
Columbus, OH 43209
800/848–6203
614/237–5695
Free catalog

Icemart
Keflavik International Airport, Dept. NN
ICELAND
$1 catalog

Ikea
1224 Dundas St. East, Dept. NN
Mississauga ON L4Y 2C1, CANADA
Free catalog

Import Specialists
82 Wall St., Dept. NN
New York, NY 10005
212/248–1633
800/334–4044
Free catalog

Indiana Botanic Gardens
PO Box 5, Dept. NN
Hammond, IN 46325
219/931–2480
800/348–6434
Free catalog

International Yogurt Co.
628 N. Doheny Dr., Dept. NN
Los Angeles, CA 90069
213/274–9917
Free catalog

Irish Cottage Industries
44 Dawson St., Dept. NN
Dublin 2, IRELAND
$1 catalog

J. Crew Outfitters
22 Lincoln Pl., Dept. NN
Garfield, NJ 07026
800/562–0258
201/471–7084
Free catalog

J. Jill Ltd.
Stockbridge Rd., Dept. NN
Great Barrington, MA 01230
413/528–1500
Free catalog

J. Schachter Corp.
115 Allen St., Dept. NN
New York, NY 10002
212/533–1150
Free catalog

Jaffe Bros.
PO Box 636, Dept. NN
Valley Center, CA 92082
619/749–1133
Free catalog

Janice Corp.
12 Eton Dr., Dept. NN
N. Caldwell, NJ 07006
201/226–7753
Free catalog

Janice Jacobsen
2142 Prosser Ave., Dept. NN
Los Angeles, CA 90025
No catalog

Jankits
Dept. NN
Ingomar, MT 59039
406/354–6621
$1 catalog

Jantz Design & Manufacturing
502 Bonnardel, Dept. NN
Sebastopol, CA 95472
No catalog

Jardine Ranch
Rte. 1, Box 195, Dept. NN
Paso Robles, CA 93446
805/238–2365
Free catalog

Jason Natural Products
707–711 S. Hampton Dr., Dept. NN
Venice, CA 90291
213/396–3171
Free catalog

Jay Parker
216 Juanita Way, Dept. NN
San Francisco, CA 94127
$2 catalog

Johnny's Selected Seeds
Dept. NN
Albion, ME 04910
207/437–9294
Free catalog

Jos. A. Bank Clothiers
109 Market Pl., Dept. NN
Baltimore, MD 21201
301/837–8838
Free catalog

J S & A
1 J S & A Plaza, Dept. NN
Northbrook, IL 60062
800/323–6400
312/564–7000
$2.50 catalog

Kangaroo Kits
PO Box 106, Dept. NN
Epsom, NH 03234
Free catalog

Karess
PO Box 642, Dept. NN
Cayucos, CA 93430
805/995–1505
Free catalog

KB Cotton Pillow Co.
PO Box 5578, Dept. NN
Clearwater, FL 33518
813/796–4389
Free catalog

Kennedy's Natural Foods
1051 W. Broad St., Dept. NN
Falls Church, VA 22046
703/533–8484
$2 catalog

Kennedy's of Ardara
Ardara County, Dept. NN
Donegal, IRELAND
Free catalog

Kid Cottons
197 Main St., Dept. NN
Northfield, MA 01360
413/498–4423
Free catalog

The Kids Warehouse/White Creek Co.
Brownell Hollow Rd., Dept. NN
Eagle Bridge, NY 12057
518/677–8214
Free catalog

Kinloch Anderson
John Knox House, 45 High St.,
Dept. NN
Edinburgh EH1 1SR, SCOTLAND
Free catalog

Kiss My Face
PO Box 804, Dept. NN
New Paltz, NY 12561
Free catalog

Kitazawa Seed Co.
356 W. Taylor St., Dept. NN
San Jose, CA 95110
408/292–4420
Free catalog

Klaire Laboratories
PO Box 618, Dept. NN
Carlsbad, CA 92008
619/438–1083
SASE catalog

Kow Hoo Shoe Company
23 Hennessy Rd., Dept. NN
Wanchai, HONG KONG
Free catalog

Kron Chocolatier
506 Madison Ave., Dept. NN
New York, NY 10022
212/486–0265
212/486–0266
Free catalog

L. L. Bean
Dept. NN
Freeport, ME 04033
207/865–3111
Free catalog

Lamb's Grist Mill
Rte. 1, Box 66, Dept. NN
Hillsboro, TX 76645
817/582–2405
No catalog

Lands' End
Land's End Lane, Dept. NN
Dodgeville, WI 53595
800/356–4444
Free catalog

Landau
PO Box 671, Dept. NN
Princeton, NJ 08540
800/257–9445
800/792–8333
Free catalog

La Shack
19 The Plaza, Dept. NN
Locust Valley, NY 11560
800/645–3524
516/671–1091
Free catalog

Laughing Bear Batik Co.
PO Box 732, Dept. NN
Woodstock, NY 12498
914/679–7650
Free catalog

Laura Ashley
Mail Order Dept., 55 Triangle Blvd.,
   Dept. NN
Carlstadt, NJ 07072
$3 catalog

Laura Copenhaver Industries
Rosemont, Box 149, Dept. NN
Marion, VA 24354
703/783–4663
Free catalog

Laura Furlong Designs
PO Box 25, Dept. NN
Jenner, CA 95450
Free catalog

Laura Todd Cookies
29 Powell St., Dept. NN
San Francisco, CA 94102–2811
800/233–2929
415/986–2929
Free catalog

Lee Kee
65 Peking Rd., Dept. NN
Kowloon, HONG KONG
No catalog

Lee's Fruit Co.
PO Box 450, Dept. NN
Leesburg, FL 32748
904/753–2064
Free catalog

Le Jardin du Gourmet
Dept. NN
West Danville, VT 05873
$.25 catalog

Leon R. Horsted
Rte. 2, Dept. NN
Waunakee, WI 53597
SASE catalog

Les Filatures de Paris
75 Rue Lecourbe, Dept. NN
Paris 75015, FRANCE
Free catalog

Le Tricoteur
Pitronnerie Rd. Estate, St. Peter Port,
   Dept. NN
Channel Islands, ENGLAND
Free catalog

Lewis Marketing
Rte. 1, Box 299, Dept. NN
Weiser, ID 83672
208/549–0806
No catalog

Li-Lac Chocolates
120 Christopher St., Dept. NN
New York, NY10014
212/242–7374
Free catalog

Life Tools Co-op
401 N. Clay St., Dept. NN
Green Bay, WI 54301
414/432–7399
$1 catalog

Limericks Linens Ltd.
117 Victoria Ave., Dept. NN
Southend on Sea SS2 6EL, ENGLAND
Free catalog

Lisa Norman Lingerie Etc.
1134 Montana Ave., Dept. NN
Santa Monica, CA 90403
213/451–2026
Free catalog

Lismore Hosiery Co.
334 Grand St., Dept. NN
New York, NY 10002
212/674–3440
No catalog

Loden Frey
Maffeistrasse 7–9, 8000, Dept. NN
Munich 1, GERMANY
Free catalog

Lotions & Potions
2225 W. Mountain View #6, Dept. NN
Phoenix, AZ 85021
602/944–6642
Free catalog

Lundberg Farm
PO Box 369, Dept. NN
Richvale, CA 95974
916/882–4551
Free catalog

Macy-Havrda
47 Riverside Ave., Dept. NN
Westport, CT 06880
Free catalog

Mairtun Standun Teo
Spidal, Dept. NN
County Galway, IRELAND
Free catalog

**The Mannings Handweaving
School & Supply Center**
RD 2, Dept. NN
East Berlin, PA 17316
800/233–7166
717/624–2223
Free catalog

Marni's Soakers
PO Box 918, Dept. NN
Penngrove, CA 94951
Free catalog

Mary Green Enterprises
456 Lake St., Dept. NN
San Francisco, CA 94118
415/386–3131
Free catalog

Mathers
PO Box 70, Dept. NN
Westminister, MD 21157
301/876–1203
$1.50 catalog

Matthews 1812 House
PO Box 15, Whitcomb Hill Rd.,
Dept. NN
Cornwall Bridge, CT 06754
203/672–6449
Free catalog

Maytag Dairy Farms
PO Box 806, Dept. NN
Newton, IA 50208
800/247–2458
515/792–1133
Free catalog

Meadowbrook Herbs & Things
Whispering Pines Rd., Dept. NN
Wyoming, RI 02898
401/539–7212
$1 catalog

Memphremagog Heat Exchangers
PO Box 456, Dept. NN
Newport, VT 05855
802/334–5412
Free catalog

Merry Gardens
Dept. NN
Camden, ME 04843
$1 catalog

Milan Laboratory
57 Spring St., Dept. NN
New York, NY 10012
212/226–4780
$3 catalog

Milton York
Milton York Bldg., Dept. NN
Long Beach, WA 98631
206/642–4466
Free catalog

Misty Morning Farm
2220 W. Sisson Rd., Dept. NN
Hastings, MI 49058
616/765–3023
$1 catalog

Mitsubishi Electric Sales America
3030 E. Victoria St., Dept. NN
Rancho Dominguez, CA 90221
Free catalog

Moffat Woolens
Benmar, Moffat, Dept. NN
Dumfriesshire DG10 9EP, SCOTLAND
Free catalog

Monaghans
15/17 Grafton Arcade, Dept. NN
Dublin 2, IRELAND
Free catalog

Monarch Trading Co.
170 W. Dayton, Harbor Sq., Dept. NN
Edmonds, WA 98020
800/367–6002
Free catalog

Moonflower
1502 Eureka Canyon Rd., Dept. NN
Corralitos, CA 95076
408/722–8505
Free catalog

Moonflower Birthing Supply
8593 Hwy. 172, Dept. NN
Ignacio, CA 81137
303/884–2383
Free catalog

Moravian Sugar Crisp Co.
Rte. 2, Dept. NN
Clemmons, NC 27012
919/764–1402
Free catalog

Morningland Dairy
Rte. 1, Box 188B, Dept. NN
Mountain View, MO 65548
417/469–3817
417/469–2974
Free catalog

Mothers Work
PO Box 40121, Dept. NN
Philadelphia, PA 19106
215/625–9259
Free catalog

Motherwear
PO Box 20572, Dept. NN
Denver, CO 80220
303/377–0647
Free catalog

Mountain Craft Shop
American Ridge Rd., Rte. 1, Dept. NN
New Martinsville, WV 26155
304/455–3570
Free catalog

Mountain Toy Makers
PO Box 51, Dept. NN
Long Lake, NY 12847
518/624–6175
$.50 catalog

Mrs. Appleyard's Kitchen
Maple Lane, Box 685, Dept. NN
Newport, VT 05855
800/343–0837
Free catalog

Muileann Beag A' Chrotail
Old School House, Camus Chros,
Dept. NN
Isle of Skye IV43 8QR SCOTLAND
$1 catalog

Nandi Naturals
PO Box 2719, Dept. NN
Petaluma, CA 94953
707/763–0888
Free catalog

The Nappi Co.
101 Dow Ave., Dept. NN
Franconia, NH 03580
603/823–5365
Free catalog

Natural Child
PO Box 1107, Dept. NN
Burns, OR 97720–0186
Free catalog

Natural Fantasy
8200 Oak Ave., Dept. NN
Ben Lomond, CA 95005
408/336–5073
Free catalog

Natural Fiber Fabric Club
521 Fifth Ave., Dept. NN
New York, NY 10175
$10 catalog

Natural Visions
PO Box 1042, Dept. NN
Chapel Hill, NC 27514
Free catalog

Nature de France
145 Hudson St., Dept. NN
New York, NY 10013
212/925–2670
Free catalog

Nature Food Centres
1 Nature's Way, Dept. NN
Wilmington, MA 01887
800/752–0132
617/657–5000
Free catalog

Nature's Herb Co.
281 Ellis St., Dept. NN
San Francisco, CA 94102
Free catalog

Nature's Little Shoes
PO Box 355, Dept. NN
Norcross, GA 30091
404/448–5995
$.25 catalog

Nauvoo Cheese Co.
Wells & Young Sts., Dept. NN
Nauvoo, IL 62354
217/453–2214
Free catalog

Nevalite Products
PO Box 829, Dept. NN
Corte Madera, CA 94925
No catalog

New Age Creations
219 Carl St., Dept. NN
San Francisco, CA 94117
415/564–6785
Free catalog

New England Cheesemaking Supply Co.
PO Box 85, Dept. NN
Ashfield, MA 01330
Free catalog

New Moon
PO Box 714, Dept. NN
Cambridge, MA 02139
800/343–4019
$2 catalog

New World Distiller Corp.
PO Box 476, Dept. NN
Gravette, AR 72736
501/787–6100
Free catalog

New Zealand Lambskins
PO Box 132, Dept. NN
Albion, CA 95410
707/937–4248
Free catalog

Nichols Garden Nursery
1190 N. Pacific Hwy., Dept. NN
Albany, OR 97321
503/928–9280
Free catalog

Nigra Enterprises
5699 Kanan #123, Dept. NN
Agoura Hills, CA 91301
818/889–6877
Free catalog

Nikko Natural Fabrics
PO Box 71, Dept. NN
Kamuela, HI 96743
808/885–7661
Free catalog

Nizhonie Fabrics
PO Box 729, Dept. NN
Cortez, CO 81321
303/565–7079
SASE catalog

Norm Thompson
PO Box 3999, Dept. NN
Portland, OR 97208
800/547–1160
503/644–2666
Free catalog

Northern Lights Imports
PO Box 143, Dept. NN
Cambria, CA 93428
805/927–8285
Free catalog

Northwest Futon Co.
PO Box 14952, Dept. NN
Portland, OR 97214
503/242–0057
Free catalog

Norton Candle & Handiwork House
1836 Country Store Village, Dept. NN
Wilmington, VT 05363
Free catalog

Nutricology
2336C Stanwell Circle, Dept. NN
Concord, CA 94520
415/685–1228
Free catalog

Nu Vita Food Co.
7524 SW Macadam, Dept. NN
Portland, OR 97219
Free catalog

The Old-Fashioned Milk Paint Co.
PO Box 222, Dept. NN
Groton, MA 04150
617/448–6336
Free catalog

Old Mill of Guilford
1340 N.C. 68 North, Dept. NN
Oak Ridge, NC 27310
919/643–4783
Free catalog

Old Mill Yarn
PO Box 8, Dept. NN
Eaton Rapids, MI 48827
517/663–2711
SASE catalog

The Oriental Rug Co.
PO Box 917, Dept. NN
Lima, OH 45802
Free catalog

Orkney Handknits
7 King St., Dept. NN
Kirkwall, Orkney, SCOTLAND
Free catalog

Orvis
31 River Rd., Dept. NN
Manchester, VT 05254
802/362–1300
Free catalog

Outer Banks Pine Products
PO Box 9003, Dept. NN
Lester, PA 19113
215/534–1234
Free catalog

Overland Sheepskin Co.
PO. Box 588, Dept. NN
Taos, NM 87571
800/247–8035
515/472–8480
Free catalog

P.E.R. Corp.
Box 64526, Dept. NN
Garland TX 75206
214/272–9118
Free catalog

Pace Industries
710 Woodlawn Dr., Dept. NN
Thousand Oaks, CA 91360
805/496–6224
Free catalog

Pascalite
PO Box 104, Dept. NN
Worland, WY 82401
307/347–3872
No catalog

Patagonia
PO Box 150, Dept. NN
Ventura, CA 93002
805/643–8616
Free catalog

Pathway
5415 Cedar Lane, Dept. NN
Bethesda, MD 20814
301/530–1112
No catalog

Patti Collins Canvas Products
16C Madrona, Dept. NN
Mill Valley, CA 94941
415/388–4934
Free catalog

Paul's Grains
Rte. 1, Box 76, Dept. NN
Laurel, IA 50141
515/476–3373
Free catalog

Paula Simmons
PO Box 12, Dept. NN
Suquamish, WA 98392
Free catalog

Peace Seeds
1130 Tethrow Rd., Dept. NN
Williams, OR 97544
Free catalog

Peach Blossom Futon
3808 Rosecrans, Dept. NN
San Diego, CA 92110
619/274–3401
Free catalog

Peerless Imported Rugs
3028 N. Lincoln Ave., Dept. NN
Chicago, IL 60657
312/472–4848
Free catalog

Pembroke Squares
8 Pembroke Sq., Dept. NN
London W8 6PA, ENGLAND
$1 catalog

The Pendleton Shop
PO Box 233, Dept. NN
Sedona, AZ 86336
602/282–3671
Free catalog

Penn Herb Co.
603 N. Second St., Dept. NN
Philadelphia, PA 19123–3098
800/523–9971
$1 catalog

The Peruvian Connection
Canaan Farm, Dept. NN
Tonganoxoe, KS 66086
800/228–2606
Free catalog

Peter M. Philhower
PO Box 475, Dept. NN
Frasier Park, CA 93225
No catalog

Piaffe
1500 Broadway, Dept. NN
New York, NY 10036
800/847–4173
212/869–3320
Free catalog

Pitlochry Knitwear Co.
PO Box 8, East Kilbride, Dept. NN
Glasgow G74 5QZ, SCOTLAND
$1 catalog

Pollyanna
The Old Coppermill, Dept. NN,
Coppermill Ln.
London SW17 OBN, ENGLAND
Free catalog

Poppy Singer-Sayada
714 N. Tioga St., Dept. NN
Ithaca, NY 14850
$1 catalog

Port Canvas Co.
PO Box H, Dept. NN
Kennebunkport, ME 04046
207/967–5570
Free catalog

Powers' Country Store
Rte. 120 P103, Dept. NN
Cornish, NH 03746
603/675–2666
Free catalog

Pratesi
381 Park Ave. South, Dept. NN
New York, NY 10016
Free catalog

Precious Times
PO Box 902, Dept. NN
Meadow Vista, CA 95722
Free catalog

Pure Kid
189 Huntington St., Dept. NN
Carroll Gardens, NY 11231
$2 catalog

Pure Planet Products
1025 N. 48th St., Dept. NN
Phoenix, AZ 85008
602/267–1000
$.25 catalog

Pure Water
3725 Touzalin Ave., Dept. NN
Lincoln, NE 68506
402/467–2577
Free catalog

PUTAMAYO
149 Wooster St., Dept. NN
New York, NY 10012
212/982–0775
$2 catalog

The Puzzle People
22719 Tree Farm Rd., Dept. NN
Colfax, CA 95713
916/637–4823
Free catalog

Q-Dot Corp.
701 N. First St., Dept. NN
Garland, TX 75040
214/487–1130
Free catalog

Queen Bee Gardens
1863 Lane 11 1/2, Dept. NN
Lovell, WY 82431
307/548–2543
Free catalog

NONTOXIC & NATURAL

Quiet Meadow Farm
8 Quiet Meadow Lane, Dept. NN
Mapleton, UT 84663
Free catalog

Quiltessence
133 Eldridge St., Dept. NN
New York, NY 10002
212/226–1060
$1 catalog

R. S. Duncan & Co.
Falcon Mills, Dept. NN
Bartle Lane, Bradford
West Yorkshire BD7 4QJ, ENGLAND
$1 catalog

R. Watson Hogg
Auchterarder, Dept. NN
Perthshire EH44 6HP, SCOTLAND
Free catalog

Ram Island Farm Herbs
Ram Island Farm, Dept. NN
Cape Elizabeth, ME 04107
207/799–0011
Free catalog

Rammagerdin of Reykjavik
h.f., Hafnarstr. 19, PO Box 751–121,
   Dept. NN
Reykjavik, ICELAND
Free catalog

Ramshead
3060 Kerner Blvd., Dept. NN
San Rafael, CA 94901
415/457–7180
415/457–2772
Free catalog

Ramus International
1208 Fourth St., Dept. NN
San Rafael, CA 94901
415/459–1313
Free catalog

Ras Distributors
16108 Malcom Dr., Dept. NN
Laurel, MD 20707
301/725–5326
Free catalog

Rebecca Lang
Cape Blance, Box 748, Dept. NN
Port Orford, OR 97465
503/348–2562
Free catalog

Red River Menstrual Pads
PO Box 486, Dept. NN
Huntsville, AR 72740
SASE catalog

Redwood City Seed Co.
PO Box 361, Dept. NN
Redwood City, CA 94064
415/325–7333
$.50 catalog

Reekie's of Grasmere
Old Coach House, Dept. NN
Stock Rd., Grasmere
Westmorland, ENGLAND
$1 catalog

Richman Co.
2627 Piner Rd., Dept. NN
Santa Rosa, CA 95401
Free catalog

Richters
Goodwood, Dept. NN
Ontario LOC 1AO, CANADA
$2 catalog

Riehs & Riehs
PO Box 157 Glenfield Rd., Dept. NN
Sewickley, PA 15143
412/741–2659
Free catalog

Romanes & Paterson
Edinburgh Woollen Mill, Langholm,
   Dept. NN
Dumfriesshire DG13, OBR, SCOTLAND
Free catalog

Romni Wools & Fibers
3779 West 10th Ave., Dept. NN
Vancouver BC V6R 2G5, CANADA
$1 catalog

Royal Silk
Royal Silk Plaza, Dept. NN
45 E. Madison Ave.
Clifton, NJ 07011
800/22–ROYAL
Free catalog

Ruggedwear
PO Box 336, Dept. NN
Narragansett, RI 02882
401/789–4115
Free catalog

Russell's Quilt Co.
4032 Tweedy Blvd., Dept. NN
South Gate, CA 90280
213/569–1512
Free catalog

RVP/The Health Savings Center
33 Bell St., Dept. NN
Valley Stream, NY 11582
800/645–2978
516/561–8137
Free catalog

S. & C. Huber, Accoutrements
82 Plants Dam Rd., Dept. NN
East Lyme, CT 06333
203/739–0772
$1 catalog

Safe Haven
PO Box 384, Dept. NN
Jacumba, CA 92034
619/766–4063
Free catalog

Saint Laurie Ltd.
84 Fifth Ave., 6th Fl., Dept. NN
New York, NY 10011
212/242–2530
800/221–8660
Free catalog

The Sandy Mush Herb Nursery
Rte. 2, Surrett Cove Rd., Dept. NN
Leicester, NC 28748
704/683–2014
$2 catalog

Santa Cruz Mattress & Upholstery Co.
923 Water St., Dept. NN
Santa Cruz, CA 95062
408/426–5073
Free catalog

Sara Fermi Clothing
25 Gwyoir, Dept. NN
Cambridge CB1 2LG, ENGLAND
Free catalog

Scandia Down Shops
1546 California St., Dept. NN
San Francisco, CA 94109
415/928–5111
Free catalog

Scientific Glass Co.
113 Phoenix NW, Dept. NN
Albuquerque, NM 87107
800/841–9803
502/345–7321
Free catalog

Scope Natural Fibers
3576 Stacy Circle, Dept. NN
Lumberton, NC 28358
919/738–8897
Free catalog

The Scottish Lion
Dept. NN
North Conway, NH 03860
800/258–0370
603/356–6381
$2 catalog

Scottish Products
24 E. 60th St., Dept. NN
New York, NY 10022
212/755–9656
Free catalog

Seabon Scandinavian Imports
54 East 54th St., Dept. NN
New York, NY 10022
212/755–0422
Free catalog

Sears
Call 800/44-SEARS for local information
$2 catalog

Sermoneta
740 Madison Ave., Dept. NN
New York, NY 10021
212/744–6551
$3 catalog

Shaker Workshops
PO Box 1028, Dept. NN
Concord, CA 01742
617/646–8985
$.50 catalog

Shaker Workshops West
5 Inverness Way, Dept. NN
Inverness, CA 94937
415/669–7256
$2.50 catalog

Shama Imports
PO Box 2900, Dept. NN
Farmington Hills, MI 48018
313/553–0261
Free catalog

The Sharper Image
680 Davis St., Dept. NN
San Francisco, CA 94111
800/344–4444
$2 catalog

The Sheepskin Co.
86–07 Eliot Ave., Dept. NN
Rego Park, NY 11374
212/793–9583
$1 catalog

Shelburne Farms
Dept. NN
Shelburne, VT 05482
802/985–3222
Free catalog

Shiloh Farms
White Oak Rd., Dept. NN
Martindale, PA 17549
717/354–4936
Free catalog

Shiloh Farms Cotton Collections
PO Box 97, Dept. NN
Sulphur Springs, AR 72768
800/643–3574
Free catalog

Sickafus Sheepskins
Intersection Rtes. 183 & 78, Dept. NN
Strausstown, PA 19559
215/488–1782
Free catalog

Simple Pleasures
2628 Parkwood Dr., Dept. NN
Columbia, SC 29204
803/799–8594
Free catalog

Simply Divine Designs
714 Patterson Ave., Dept. NN
Austin, TX 78703
512/444–5546
Free catalog

Sivad Bioresearch
28003 John Rd., Dept. NN
Madison Heights, MI 48071
800/521–5957
313/548–6420
Free catalog

Sleep & Dream
PO Box 430, Dept. NN
Gainesville, FL 32602
904/377–1335
Free catalog

Smoot Honey Co.
PO Box 171, Dept. NN
Power, MT 59468
406/463–2227
Free catalog

The Soap Opera
38 Miller Ave., Dept. NN
Mill Valley, CA 94941
415/381–0965
Free catalog

Solviva
12 Grove St., Dept. NN
Boston, MA 02114
617/720–0686
Free catalog

Southern Mobile Industries
PO Box 360, Dept. NN
Bay Minette, AL 36507
205/937–2690
Free catalog

Space Beds
1300 17th St., Dept. NN
San Francisco, CA 94107
415/552–8616
Free catalog

Sparks Enterprises
PO Box 412, Dept. NN
Cedar City, UT 84720
801/586–2346
Free catalog

Special Foods
9207 Shotgun Ct., Dept. NN
Springfield, VA 22153
703/644–0991
Free catalog

Springwell Dispensers
PO Box 8180, Dept. NN
Atlanta, GA 30306
404/874–0858
Free catalog

St. Patrick's Down
St. Patrick's Mill, Dept. NN
Douglas, Cork, Ireland
Free catalog

Starr Organic Produce
PO Box 561502, Dept. NN
S. Miami, FL 33256
305/856–7135
Free catalog

Stavros Kouyoumoutzakis
166 Kalokerinou Ave., Dept. NN
Iraklion, Crete, GREECE
Free catalog

Stokes Seeds
737 Main St., Box 548, Dept. NN
Buffalo, NY 14240
Free catalog

Strand Surplus Senter
2202 Strand, Dept. NN
Galveston, TX 77550
800/231–6000
713/762–7397
Free catalog

Straw into Gold
3006 San Pablo Ave., Dept. NN
Berkeley, CA 94702
415/548–5247
Free catalog

Sugar's Kitchen
PO Box 41886, Dept. NN
Tucson, AZ 85717
602/299–6027
Free catalog

Sugarbush Farms
RFD D, Dept. NN
Woodstock, VT 05091
802/457–1757
Free catalog

Sunburst Biorganics
838 Merrick Rd., Dept. NN
Baldwin, NY 11510
516/623–8478
800/645–8448
Free catalog

Sunflower Studio
2851 Rd. B ½, Dept. NN
Grand Junction, CO 81503
303/242–3883
$2.50 catalog

Sunnybrook Farms Nursery
PO Box 6, Dept. NN
Chesterland, OH 44026
216/729–7232
$1 catalog

Sureway Trading Enterprises
826 Pine Ave., Suites 5 & 6, Dept. NN
Niagra Falls, NY 14301
416/596–1887
416/596–8899
Free catalog

Suzanne Pierette
337 N. Crescent Heights Blvd.,
Dept. NN
Los Angeles, CA 90048
213/655–6052
Free catalog

Swaine Adeney Brigg
185 Piccadilly, Dept. NN
London W1V OHA, ENGLAND
Free catalog

Swanson Health Products
PO Box 2803, Dept. NN
Fargo, ND 58108
800/437–4148
Free catalog

Sweater Market
15 Frederkisberggade, DK 1459,
Dept. NN
Copenhagen, DENMARK
Free catalog

Taylor's Herb Gardens
1535 Lone Oak Rd., Dept. NN
Vista, CA 92083
714/727–3485
Free catalog

Teel Mountain Farm
Rte. 1, Box 130, Dept. NN
Stanardsville, VA 22973
804/985–7746
Free catalog

Tender Touch
PO Box 26605, Dept. NN
Denver, CO 80226
303/988–5280
Free catalog

Testfabrics
PO Drawer O, Dept. NN
Middlesex, NJ 08846
201/469–6446
Free catalog

Teuscher Chocolates of Switzerland
25 E. 61st St., Dept. NN
New York, NY 10021
212/751–8482
Free catalog

Thos. Moser Cabinetmakers
Cobb's Bridge Rd., Dept. NN
New Gloucester, ME 04260
207/926–4446
$3 catalog

Thousand Island Apiaries
RD 2, Box 212, Dept. NN
Clayton, NY 13624
315/654–2741
Free catalog

Tibetan Self-Help Refugee Center
65 Ghandi Rd., Dept. NN
Darjeeling, INDIA
Free catalog

Timber Crest Farms
4791 Dry Creek Rd., Dept. NN
Healdsburg, CA 95448
707/433–8251
$1.50 catalog

Trefriw Woolen Mills
Trefriw, Gwynedd, Dept. NN
North Wales LL27 ONQ, UK
Free catalog

Tryon Toymakers
Rte. 3, Box 148, Dept. NN
Campobello, SC 29322
803/457–2017
Free catalog

Tully Toys
4606 Warrenton Rd., Dept. NN
Vicksburg, MS 39180
601/638–1724
Free catalog

U.S. Health Club
Dept. NN
Yonkers, NY 10701
800/431–2186
Free catalog

Una O'Neill Designs
30 Oakley Park, Dept. NN
Blackrock, Dublin, Ireland
Free catalog

Uncle Sam Umbrella Shop
161 W. 57th St., Dept. NN
New York, NY 10019
212/582–1977
Free catalog

Utex Trading Enterprises
710 9th St., Suite 5, Dept. NN
Niagra Falls, NY 14301
716/282–4887
Free catalog

Valentine's Cosmopolitan Confections
1112 4th St., Dept. NN
San Rafael, CA 94901
415/456–3262
Free catalog

Valley Cove Ranch
PO Box 603, Dept. NN
Springville, CA 93265
209/539–2710
Free catalog

Vermont Bean Seed Co.
Garden Lane, Dept. NN
Bomoseen, VT 05732
802/265–3323
Free catalog

Vermont Country Store
Dept. NN
Weston, VT 05161
802/824–6932
Free catalog

Victoria's Secret
PO Box 16589, Dept. NN
Columbus, OH 43216
800/821–0001
614/276–3131
Free catalog

Victory Shirt Company
345 Madison Ave., Dept. NN
New York, NY 10017
212/687–6375
Free catalog

Visions
PO Box 850, Dept. NN
Menlo Park, CA 94025
Free catalog

Vita Green Farms
217 Escondido Ave., Dept. NN
Vista, CA 92083
619/724–2163
$2 catalog

Vitaline Formulas
PO Box 6757, Dept. NN
Incline Village, NV 89450
800/648–4755
Free catalog

Vitamin Specialties Co.
5521 25 Wayne Ave., Dept. NN
Philadelphia, PA 19144
800/523–3658
215/848–3800
Free catalog

Vita-Mix Corp.
8615 Usher Rd., Dept. NN
Cleveland, OH 44138–2199
800/848–2649
Free catalog

W. Atlee Burpee Co.
300 Park Ave., Dept. NN
Warminster, PA 18974
215/674–4900
Free catalog

Walnut Acres
Dept NN
Penns Creek, PA 17862
717/837–0601
Free catalog

Walpole Woodworkers
767 East St., Dept. NN
Walpole, MA 02081
800/343–6948
$1 catalog

Walter Drake
Drake Bldg., Dept. NN
Colorado Springs, CO 80940
303/596–3854
Free catalog

Warm Things
180 Paul Dr., Dept. NN
San Rafael, CA 94903
415/472–2154
Free catalog

Water Witch
PO Box 329, Dept. NN
Castine, ME 04421
207/326–4884
$1 catalog

Webb Metals
411 Colony Rd., Dept. NN
Myers Flat, CA 95554
707/943–3517
Free catalog

Wee Care
380 Juanita Rd., Dept. NN
Boulder Creek, CA 95006
Free catalog

Weleda
PO Box 769, Dept. NN
Spring Valley, NY 10977
914/352–6145
Free catalog

Well-Sweep Herb Farm
317 Mount Bethel Rd., Dept. NN
Port Murray, NJ 07865
201/852–5390
Free catalog

Western Natural Products
PO Box 284, Dept. NN
S. Pasadena, CA 91030
Free catalog

**The Western Reserve Antique
Furniture Kit**
PO Box 206A, Dept. NN
Bath, OH 44210
$1 catalog

West Wind Farm
Rte. 1, Box 67, Dept. NN
Sheridan, OR 97378
503/843–3492
Free catalog

The White House
51–52 New Bond St., Dept. NN
London W1Y OBY, ENGLAND
Free catalog

The White Pine Co.
2038 Pennsylvania Ave., Dept. NN
Madison, WI 53704
800/356–5310
608/241–2225
Free catalog

Whole Earth Access
2990 7th St., Dept. NN
Berkeley, CA 94710
415/845–3000
$5 catalog

Wholesome Paks
4919 W. 43rd Ave., Dept. NN
Denver, CO 80212
303/477–0881
$.50 catalog

Wide World Games
3527 West SR 37, Box 450, Dept. NN
Delaware, OH 43015
614/369–9631
Free catalog

Wide World of Herbs
11 St. Catherine East, Dept. NN
Montreal, Quebec H2X IK3, CANADA
Free catalog

Williams & Foltz
1816 4th St., Dept. NN
Berkeley, CA 94710
415/644–2022
Free catalog

Williams-Sonoma
PO Box 7456, Dept. NN
San Francisco, CA 94120–7456
415/652–9007
Free catalog

Winter Creek Farms
Rte. 7, Box 174, Dept. NN
Columbia, MO 65202
Free catalog

Wish Poultry
PO Box 362, Dept. NN
Prairie City, OR 97869
503/820–3509
Free catalog

Wolfe's Neck Farm
RR 1, Box 71, Dept. NN
Freeport, ME 04082
207/865–4469
Free catalog

Wondercraft
1 Constitution St., Dept. NN
Bristol, RI 02809
401/253–2030
Free catalog

Wood's Cider Jelly
RFD 2, Box 266, Dept. NN
Springfield, VT 05156
802/263–5547
Free catalog

Woodcraft Supply Corp.
41 Atlantic Ave., Box 4000, Dept. NN
Woburn, MA 01888
800/225–1153
617/935–9278
Free catalog

The Wooden Spoon
Rte. 6, Dept. NN
Mahopac, NY 10041
800/431–2207
Free catalog

Woodsedge Wools
PO Box 275, Dept. NN
Stockton, NJ 08559
609/397–2212
$1 catalog

Wooldrest USA
PO Box 58946, Dept. NN
Seattle, WA 98188
206/575–1811
Free catalog

Woolies
413 Shrader, Dept. NN
San Francisco, CA 94117
415/221–8556
Free catalog

World Wide Games
PO Box 450, Dept. NN
Delaware, OH 43015
614/369–9631
Free catalog

Wrap Arounds
Rte. 3, Box 117, Dept. NN
Floyd, VA 24091
703/745–2472
Free catalog

Xhaxhi
239 Wickenden St., Dept. NN
Providence, RI 02903
401/351–7616
Free catalog

Yellow Bird Crafts
PO Box 785, Dept. NN
Northampton, MA 01060
413/586–2740
$2 catalog

Yield House
Dept. NN
North Conway, NH 03860
800/258–4720
800/552–0320
$1 catalog

Zimmerman Chair Shop
1486 Colebrook Rd., Dept. NN
Lebanon, PA 17042
Free catalog

Directory Two

MANUFACTURERS, IMPORTERS, AND DISTRIBUTORS

A. B. Ramlösa, Hälsobrunn, Sweden
A. Giurlani & Bro, France
A. V. Olsson Trading Co., Scarsdale, NY
A & F Pears / DEP Corp., Los Angeles, CA
A & R Scott, Cupar, Fife, Scotland
Aapri Cosmetics, Boston, MA
Abracadabra, Guerneville, CA
Abundant Earth Herb Co., San Diego, CA
ACS Communications, Scotts Valley, CA
ACS-Hoval, Wood Dale, IL
Adamba Imports International, Brooklyn, NY
Adams Foods, Tacoma, WA
Adams Natural Beverage Co., Calistoga, CA
Adam's Olive Ranch, Strathmore, CA
Adolph Coors Co., Golden, CO
Ahmad's Peelu, Chicago, IL
Aireox Research Corp., Riverside, CA
Airwick Industries, Carlstadt, NJ
Albino Garcia y Fco., Mexico
Alfalfa-Omega Express, Oakland, CA
Alive Polarity Distributors, Murrieta, CA
All-Clad Metal Crafters, Canonsburg, PA
Allermed Corp., Dallas, TX
All-One-God-Faith, Escondido, CA
All Ways Natural Industries, Brooklyn, NY
Almay, New York, NY
Alta-Dena, City of Industry, CA

Alvita Products Co., Huntington Beach, CA
A-M Bakeries, Sanger, CA
American Home Foods, New York, NY
American Kefir Corp., New York, NY
American Licorice Co., San Francisco, CA
American Maple Products Corp., Newport, VT
AMF/CUNO, Menden, CT
Amsnack, Stockton, CA
Amway Corp., Ada, MI
Ananda Products, Oklahoma City, OK
Anheuser-Busch, St. Louis, MO
Apollinaris Brunnen, A.G., W. Germany
Applegate Spring Water Co., Applegate, CA
Arden Organics, Asheville, NC
Arrowhead Mills, Hereford, TX
A Sante, Calistoga, CA
Associated Mills, Chicago, IL
A T & T, Morristown, NJ
Attar Bazaar, Santa Fe, NM
Aubrey Organics, Tampa, FL
Ault Foods, Delta, Ontario, Canada
Au Natural, Santa Fe, NM
Aura Cacia, Weaverville, CA
Aura Enterprises, Los Angeles, CA
Autumn-Harp, Bristol, VT
Avery Label, Azuza, CA
Barbara Jo Ranch Products, Sebastopol, CA
Barbara's Bakery, Novato, CA
Bare Escentuals, Los Gatos, CA

Barth Vitamin Corp., Valley Stream, NY
Bartons Candy Corp., Brooklyn, NY
Bates, New York, NY
Bauman Family, Sagramacksville, PA
Beh Housewares Corp., New York, NY
Belle Maison, Lafayette, CA
Bendicks (Mayfair) Ltd., England
Bentley Springs Farm, Canada
Bernard Jensen Products, Solana Beach, CA
Berner International Corp., Woburn, MA
Bertolli America, San Francisco, CA
Bickford Laboratories Co., Akron, OH
Biobottoms, Petaluma, CA
Bio-Familia, Switzerland
Bioforce A.G., Switzerland
Bioforce of America, Plainview, NY
Bio-Nutritional Products, Harrison, NY
The Birkett Mills, Penn Yan, NY
Blairex Labs, Evansville, IN
Body Love, Petaluma, CA
Boles & Co., Foster City, CA
Bolinas Foods, Bolinas, CA
Borden Co., Columbus, OH
Boyd Wilson International, Castro Valley, CA
Boyle-Midway, New York, NY
Bremner Biscuit Co., Franklin Park, IL
Brigittine Monks, Woodside, CA
Brio, Osby, Sweden
Brookstone Co., Peterborough, NH
Brown Cow Farm, Newfield, NY
Bruce Hardwood Floors, Dallas, TX
C. M. Products, Lake Zurich, IL
Caesar Cardini Foods, Culver City, CA
California & Washington Co., Burlingame, CA
Calistoga Mineral Water Co., Calistoga, CA
Camp Plessisville, Canada
Campbell Soup Co., Camden, NJ
Canandaigua Wine Co., Canandaigua, NY
Cannon, Cannon, NY
Carlson, Arlington Valley, IL
Carme, Novato, CA
Carnation Co., Los Angeles, CA
Carr's of Carlisle, Great Britan
The Carter's Ink Co., Waltham, MA
Casablanca Food, San Pedro, CA
Cascade Continental Foods, San Francisco, CA

Cascadian Farms, Rockport, WA
Caswell-Massey Co., New York, NY
Celestial Seasonings, Boulder, CO
Certainteed, Valley Forge, PA
Cheeseborough-Ponds, Greenwich, CN
Chenti Products, Union City, CA
The Cherry Tree, Sonoma, CA
Chicago Dietetic Supply, La Grange, IL
Chico-San, Chico, CA
Chico Soda Works, Chico, CA
Chocolat Poulain S.A., France
Church & Dwight Co., Piscataway, NJ
Clinique Labs, New York, NY
The Clipper Tea & Produce Co., England
Coast Filtration, Brea, CA
The Coca-Cola Co., Houston, TX
Cold Spring Brewing Co., Cold Spring, MN
Colgate-Palmolive, New York, NY
Colin Ingram, Sebastopol, CA
Colonial Garden Kitchens, Valley Stream, NY
Color Tile Supermart, Fort Worth, TX
Columbia Data Products, Columbia, MD
Colvada Date Co., Coachella, CA
Conagra, Omaha, NE
Continental Culture Specialists, Glendale, CA
Continental Mills, Kent, WA
Cook Flavoring Co., Napa, CA
The Cookie Co., St. Augustine, FL
Cooper Laboratories, Wayne, NJ
CooperVision Pharmaceuticals, San Germain, Puerto Rico
Copper Brite, Los Angeles, CA
Corning Glass Works, Corning, NY
Corr's Beverage Co., Chicago, IL
Country Comfort, Guerneville, CA
Country House, Truckee, CA
Country Sausage & Meat, Santa Barbara, CA
Crabtree & Evelyn, Woodstock Hill, CT
Crown Zellerbach Corp., San Francisco, CA
Crystal Geyser Water Co., Calistoga, CA
Cuisinarts, Greenwich, CT
Curds & Whey, Oakland, CA
Cycles, San Jose, CA
Dacopa Foods/California Natural Products, Manteca, CA
Dalco, Oakland, CA
Dannon Co., Long Island City, NY

Dap, Dayton, OH

Data Terminals & Communications, Campbell, CA

D-Con Co./Sterling Drug, Montvale, NJ

DeBoles Nutrition Foods, Garden City Park, NY

Deer Garden Foods, Santa Cruz, CA

Del Monte Corp., San Francisco, CA

Dennison Manufacturing Co., Framingham, MA

Denny Co., Caldwell, OH

Des Champs Laboratories, E. Hanover, NJ

Desert Essence Cosmetics/Jojoba Products, Topanga, CA

Desert Rose Salsa Co., Tucson, AZ

Dessaux Fils, France

Dick's Country Smoked Meats, Petaluma, CA

Dolefam Corp., Washington, DC

Dorothy Gray, New York, NY

Double Rainbow, San Francisco, CA

Dowman Products, Long Beach, CA

Doxsee Food Corp., Baltimore, MD

Dr. R. Hauschka Cosmetics, Wyoming, RI

Droste/H. Hamstra & Co., West Caldwell, NJ

Druide, Canada

Duram Un-Coffee Co., N. Hollywood, CA

Durastill, Kansas City, MO

E. L. Foust Co., Elmhurst, IL

E & J Gallo Winery, Modesto, CA

Early California Industries, Los Angeles, CA

Earthe Tones, San Francisco, CA

Earthen Joys, Astoria, OR

East Earth Herb, Florence, OR

East Wind Community, Tecumseh, MO

Eaton-Allen Corp., Brooklyn, NY

Eberhard Faber, Wilkes-Barre, PA

Economics Laboratory, St. Paul, MN

Eden Foods, Clinton, MI

Edner Corp., Redwood City, CA

Edward & Sons, Union, NJ

Elam Mills/National Bakers Service, Broadview, IL

Elfa Ab, Sweden

El Mar Corp., Carson, CA

El Molino Mills, City of Industry, CA

Ener-G Foods, Seattle, WA

Ente Fiuggi S.P.A., Italy

Environmental Purification Systems, Danville, CA

Erewhon of California, Los Angeles, CA

Escondido Mills, Escondido, CA

The Estee Corp., Parsippany, NJ

Everything Natural, Los Angeles, CA

E-Z-Est Products Co., Oakland, CA

F. L. Wilson Co., Parson, KS

Fabercastell, Newark, NJ

Farm Foods, Summertown, TN

Farnam Companies, Omaha, NE

Far West Trail Cooks Assn., Fullerton, CA

Faultless Starch/Bon Ami Co., Kansas City, MO

Fearn Soya Foods/Richard Foods Corp., Melrose Park, IL

Fieldcrest Mills, New York, NY

Finnfoods, Cresskiu, NJ

Firehouse No. 1 BBQ Restaurant, San Francisco, CA

Fisher Pen Co., Boulder City, NV

Floyd & Ila, Oakland, CA

Fox Run Craftsmen, Ivyland, PA

Fox's Biscuits, England

Frey Vineyards, Redwood Valley, CA

Frito-Lay, Dallas, TX

Fr. Kaiser, GmbH., W. Germany

Frusen Gladje, Sweden

Fuchs Zahnpflege, W. Germany

Fumakilla, Japan

G. S. Pepper Co., Sacramento, CA

G. Herleman Brewing Co., La Crosse, WI

G. Raden & Sons, Seattle, WA

Gailstyn—Suiton, S. Plainfield, NJ

Garden of Eatin', Los Angeles, CA

Gathering Winds Natural Foods, Ithaca, NY

Gelato Primo, San Rafael, CA

General Foods, White Plains, NY

General Mills, Minneapolis, MN

Genesee, Rochester, NY

Georgia Pacific Corp., Portland, OR

Gerber Products Co., Fremont, MI

Gerolsteiner Sprudel/GMBH & Co., W. Germany

Ghirardelli Chocolate Co., San Leandro, CA

Gides Nu-Life, Long Beach, CA

Gillette Co./Paper-Mate Division, Boston, MA

Glenn Foods, Wantagh, NY

Gloucester, Franklin, MA
Godiva Chocolatier, Reading, PA
Golden California Co., Valencia, CA
Golden Grain Macaroni Co., San Leandro, CA
Golden Lotus, Englewood, CO
Golden Temple Bakery, Eugene, OR
Golden Temple Natural Products, Tucson, AZ
Goldrush Ent., S. San Francisco, CA
Good Stuff Bakery, Los Angeles, CA
The Good Time Spice Couple Co., Tiburon, CA
Gourmet France, Los Angeles, CA
Gourmet Resources International, New York, NY
Granny Goose Foods, Oakland, CA
Granny's Old-Fashioned Products, Pasadena, CA
Great Lakes Beverage Corp., Bronx, NY
Great Waters of France, Greenwich, CT
Green Foods Corp., Carson, CA
Green Valley Marketing, Montclair, CA
Grid Systems Corp., Mountain View, CA
Grocery Store Products, Oakland, CA
Guittard Chocolate Co., Burlingame, CA
H. Corne Chocolatier, Belgium
H. Coturri & Sons, Glen Ellen, CA
H. F. Staples & Co., Merrimack, NH
H. J. Heinz Co., Pittsburg, PA
Haagen-Dazs, New York, NY
Hain Pure Food Co., Los Angeles, CA
Halgren's, Ontario, CA
H & J Foods, Los Angeles, CA
Hansen Foods, La Mirada, CA
Harmony Farms, La Crescenta, CA
Hawaiian Pacific Wholesalers, Honolulu, HI
Hawaiian Plantations, Honolulu, HI
Head Shampoo, Los Angeles, CA
Health Foods, Des Plaines, IL
Health Valley Natural Foods, Montebello, CA
Healthway, S. San Francisco, CA
Heather Isle Kitchen, New York, NY
Heinke's, Paradise, CA
Helix Corp., Boulder, CO
Heritage House of California, Norco, CA
Heritage Products, Virginia Beach, VA
Hershey's Chocolate Co., Hershey, PA
Heublein, Farmington, CT
Hobart Corp., Troy, OH
Holistic Prods Corp., E. Rutherford, NJ

Holland Honey Co., Holland, MI
Hollywood Health Foods, Los Angeles, CA
Honey Hill Farms Cultured Specialties, Antioch, CA
Honey Pure Corp., Herndon, VA
Hopping Bottling Co., Sunnyvale, CA
Hot Cha Cha, Austin, TX
House of Quality Herbs, Woodland Hills, CA
Hunt-Wesson Foods, Fullerton, CA
I. Rokeach & Sons, Farmingdale, NJ
Ida Grae/Nature's Colors, Mill Valley, CA
Illustrator, Windsor, CT
Imperial-Vienna, W. Germany
Indian Earth, Beverly Hills, CA
Infinity Herbal Products, Canada
Inofood Corp., Merrill, WI
Interbake Foods, Richmond, VA
International Multifoods, Minneapolis, MN
International Protein Industries, Smithtown, NY
Itoya, Santa Monica, CA
J. Paterson & Son, Scotland
J. B. Williams Co./Toiletries Division, Cranford, NJ
J. M. Smucker Co., Orrville, OH
J. P. Stevens, New York, NY
J. T. Eaton Co., Twisburg, OH
Jacob Leinekugel Brewing, Chippewa Falls, WI
Jake's Products, Laguna Beach, CA
Jason Natural Cosmetics, Venice, CA
Jimaino Ranches, San Luis Obispo, CA
John Ritzenthaler Co., W. Conshohochen, PA
John Wagner & Sons, Ivyland, PA
John Woods Products, Suamice, WI
Johnson & Johnson, New Brunswick, NJ
Jojoba Farms, Novato, CA
Jokari/US, Dallas, TX
Jones Dairy Farm, Ft. Atkinson, WI
Jory Farm, Stockton, CA
The Joseph Dixon Crucible Co., Jersey City, NJ
Joseph Walker/Strathspey Bakery, Aberlour, Scotland
Joy of Health, Austin, TX
Judyth's Mountain, San Jose, CA
Justin Matthew, San Francisco, CA

Kal, Canoga Park, CA
Katreen Foods, Los Angeles, CA
Kelley Energy Systems, Waterbury, CT
Kellogg Co., Battle Creek, MI
Kenner Products, Cincinnati, OH
Kentile Floors, Chicago, IL
Kidco, Bensenville, IL
Kidde, Bronx, NY
Kikkoman Corp., Tokyo, Japan
Kimberly-Clark Corp., Neinah, WI
Kings Inn Farm, Langdon, NH
Kiss My Face, New Paltz, NY
Klein & Trumbly, Santa Cruz, CA
Knudsen Corp., Los Angeles, CA
Koolau Distributors, Kaneohe, HI
Koppers Co./Forest Products Division, Pittsburgh, PA
Kozlowski Farms, Forestville, CA
Kraft, Glenview, IL
Lakewood, Miami, FL
L & A Juice Co., Downey, CA
Las Montañas Winery, Napa, CA
La Taste Forcalquier, France
Latrobe Brewing Co., Latrobe, PA
Lea & Perrins, Fair Lawn, NJ
Lesney Product Corp., Moonachie, NJ
Le Vision Care Products, New City, NY
Libby, McNeil & Libby, Chicago, IL
Lifeline Natural Soaps, San Francisco, CA
Lifestream Natural Foods, Canada
Linden's Elf Works, Chapel Hill, NC
Lindt & Sprungli, Switzerland
Little Chemical Co., Portland, OR
Living Lightly, San Francisco, CA
Loanda Products, Novato, CA
Loma Linda Foods, Riverside, CA
L-Tec, San Rafael, CA
Ludford Fruit Products, Los Angeles, CA
Lundberg Farm, Richvale, CA
M. J. McDonald Juice Co., Sebastopol, CA
M. K. Health Food Distributors, Cypress, CA
M. W. Armstrong-Lindsay, CA
Macy-Havrda Co., Westport, CT
Magic Gardens, Los Angeles, CA
Magic Lotion, Fort Bragg, CA
Magic Mountain Herb Tea Co., Petaluma, CA
Malabar Formulas, Cypress, CA
Malt-O-Meal Co., Minneapolis, MN
M&M-Mars/Mars, Hackettstown, NJ
Manitou Corp., Manitou Springs, CO

Manna Milling Co., Mountlake Terrace, WA
The Maple Sugar Producers of Quebec, Canada
Marantha Natural Foods, Ashland, OR
Marie Vega & Associates, Hollywood, CA
Marie's Quality Dressings, Woodland, CA
Marin Food Specialties, Byron, CA
Market Square Food Co., Highland Park, IL
Marley Hodgson, Norwalk, CT
Marsdel, Everett, WA
Marsh Industries, Los Angeles, CA
Martex, Spartanburg, SC
Martins Bakery, San Francisco, CA
Masonite Corp., Chicago, IL
Mattel, Hawthorne, CA
Max Factor, Hollywood, CA
McConnell's Fine Ice Creams of Santa Barbara, Santa Barbara, CA
McCormick & Co., Baltimore, MD
Meadowbrook Herbs & Things, Wyoming, RI
Memphremagog Heat Exchangers, Newport, VT
Mendocino Juicers, Willits, CA
Mendocino Mineral Water, Mendocino, CA
Mexi-Snax, Hayward, CA
Mikasa, Japan
Mill Creek Natural Products, Rolling Hills, CA
Mille Lacs Maple Co., Onamia, MN
Mitoku Co., Japan
Mitsubishi Electric Industrial Products, Rancho Dominguez, CA
Mitsubishi Pencil Co., Japan
Modern Products, Milwaukee, WI
Moravian Sugar Crisp Co., Clemmons, NC
Morehouse Foods, Emeryville, CA
Mortell Co., Kankakelt, IL
Mother Earth Enterprises/Pure Sales, Corona, CA
Mountain High Products, Englewood, CO
Mountain Valley Water, Hot Springs, AK
Mrs. Gooch's Ranch Markets, Los Angeles, CA
Mt. Madonna Natural Juices, Watsonville, CA

Multi Pure Drinking Water Systems, N. Hollywood, CA
Mystic Lake Dairy, Redmond, WA
Nabisco, E. Hanover, NJ
Nalley's Fine Foods, Tacoma, WA
Naturade Products, Paramount, CA
Natural & Kosher Foods, Los Angeles, CA
Naturally Vitamin Supplements, Scottsdale, AZ
Natural Nectar Products Corp., Culver City, CA
Natural Protein Products, Hayward, CA
Nature Cosmetics, Beverly Hills, CA
Nature de France, New York, NY
Nature's Best, Torrance, CA
Nature's Gate Herbal Cosmetics, Chatsworth, CA
Nature's Organics Plus, Paramus, NJ
Nature's Plus, Farmingdale, NY
Nellson Candies, Los Angeles, CA
Neo-Life Co. of America, Hayward, CA
NEOPC, Leominster, MA
Neutrogena Corp., Los Angeles, CA
New Age Creations, San Francisco, CA
Newman's Own, Westport, CT
New Oakland Food Co., Oakland, CA
New Planet, Cotati, CA
NF Factors, Concord, CA
Nick Sciabica & Sons, Modesto, CA
Non-Linear Systems, Solana Beach, CA
Norganic Foods, Anaheim, CA
NS Khalsa Co., Salem, OR
Nutricology, Concord, CA
Nutritional Food Products, Mecca, CA
O. Kavli A/S, Norway
Oak Valley Herb Farm, Camptonville, CA
Oakite, Berkeley Heights, NJ
Odlum, Ireland
Okidata, Mt. Laurel, NJ
The Old-Fashioned Milk Paint Co., Groton, MA
Old Ranchers Co, Upland, CA
O'Natural, Los Angeles, CA
Orchid Paper Products, La Palma, CA
Oregon Dairy Goats, Junction City, OR
Orelia West, San Francisco, CA
Organic Milling Co., Los Angeles, CA
Original New York Seltzer, New York, NY
Orjene Co., New York, NY
Oroweat Foods Co., Greenwich, CT
Ortega Mexican Foods, Oxnard, CA

Ortho Pharmaceutical Corp.
Pabst Brewing Co., Milwaukee, WI
Pace Foods, San Antonio, TX
Pace Industries, Thousand Oaks, CA
Palm Springs Perfume & Cosmetics Laboratory, Palm Springs, CA
Panda, Finland
Para Laboratories, Hempstead, NY
Parastar, Salt Lake City, UT
Parsley Patch Pure Spices, Santa Rosa, CA
Paul de Sousa's Co., Banning, CA
Pearl Brewing Co., San Antonio, TX
PeggyJane's Special Products, Laguna Beach, CA
Pel-Freeze Rabbit Meat, Rogers, AK
Penn Herb Co., Philadelphia, PA
Pentel of America, Torrance, CA
Pepperidge Farm, Norwalk, CT
Pet, St. Louis, MO
Peter Paul Cadbury, Naugatuck, CT
Peterstaler Mineralquellen/Huber GMBH & Co. KG, W. Germany
Pet Snack Foods, Anaheim, CA
Pilot Corp. of America, Port Chester, NY
Pineyhill Vineyards, Calistoga, CA
Pionier-Reformprodukte AG, Switzerland
Playskool/Milton Bradley, Chicago, IL
Plus Products, Irvine, CA
Pompadour, Dusseldorf, W. Germany
Popsicle Industries, Englewood, NJ
The Postilion, Fon du Lac, WI
Pratesi, New York, NY
Pre de Provence, Canoga Park, CA
Prince Matchabelli, New York, NY
Procter & Gamble, Cincinnati, OH
Progresso Quality Foods, Ogden Food Products, Rochelle Park, NJ
Provender Kitchen Soap, Mt. Vernon, NY
P-Shine, Los Angeles, CA
Pure Body Creations, Londonderry, VT
Pure Sales, Newport Beach, CA
Pure Water, Lincoln, NE
Purex Corp., Lakewood, CA
Q-Dot Corp., Garland, TX
Quaker Oats Co., Chicago, IL
R. T. French Co., Rochester, NY
R. W. Knudsen & Sons, Chico, CA
Rachel Perry, Canoga Park, CA
Ragu Foods, Rochester, NY
Rainbow Henna Corp., New York, NY
Ralston-Purina, St. Louis, MO

The Real Aloe Co., Simi Valley, CA
Revere Copper & Brass, Clinton, IL
Richmaid Ice Cream Co., Lodi, CA
Richter Bros., Carlstadt, NJ
Ricola, Switzerland
Riehs & Riehs, Sewickly, PA
RJR Foods, San Francisco, CA
Robbies, Altadena, CA
Robinson Foods, Fairfield, IA
Rock Island Foods, Ignacio, CA
Rocky Mountain Ocean, Boulder, CO
Roman Meal Co., Tacoma, WA
Rombouts Coffee & Coffee Filter
    Marketing Co., Huntington, NY
Ross Chemical Co./Henkel Corp.,
    Detroit, MI
Royal Hawaiian Beverage & Water,
    Honolulu, HI
The Rumford Co., Terre Haute, IN
S. A. des Eaux Minerales d'Evian,
    France
S. Martinelli & Co., Watsonville, CA
Sabertooth, Rail Road Flat, CA
Safe-T Pacific Co., Redwood City, CA
Safeway Stores, Oakland, CA
Salad King, Westport, CT
Salus of America, Stowe, VT
S & W Fine Foods, San Mateo, CA
San Francisco Herb & Natural Food Co./
    Nature's Way Products, Provo, UT
San Pellegrino S.P.A., Italy
Sand-Oh-Sha, Grand Lake, CO
Sanford Corp., Bellwood, IL
Sangemini International, New Haven,
    CT
Sansel, New York, NY
Sanyo, Japan
Satori Products, Fremont, CA
Scarborough Fair, Wilton, NH
Schiff Bio-Food Products, Moonachie,
    NJ
Scientific Consulting, Concord, CA
Scientific Glass Co,. Albuquerque, NM
Scott Paper, Philadelphia, PA
Sea-N-Earth Distributor, New York, NY
Sears, Roebuck & Co., Chicago, IL
Sebastopol Co-Operative Cannery,
    Sebastopol, CA
Seelect, Chatsworth, CA
Select Origins, New York, NY
Seligco Food Corp., New York, NY
Seneca Foods Corp., Marion, NY
Sessu-Haarentferner-Kosmetik,
    W. Germany

Seven-Up Co., St. Louis, MO
Shady Maple Farms, Plainville, CA
Shaffer, Clarke & Co., Greenwich, CT
Shamitoff Foods, Redwood City, CA
Shasta Beverages, Hayward, CA
Shelton's Turkey Ranch, Pomona, CA
Shikai Products, Santa Rosa, CA
Shiloh Farms, Sulphur Springs, AK
Sierra Nevada Brewing Co., Chico, CA
Sigma Pharmaceutical Corp., New York,
    NY
Simple Soap, England
Small World Toys, Taiwan
Societe Generale de Grandes Sources
    d'Eaux, Contrexevelle, France
Societe Generale des Aux Minerales de
    Vittel, France
Soken Trading Co., Sausalito, CA
Solaray, Ogden, UT
Solgar Co., Lynbrook, NY
Sona Food Products Co., Los Alamitos,
    CA
Sonoma Mission Inn, Boyes Hot Springs
Sorbee International, Philadelphia, PA
Sorrell Ridge Farm, Rollingham NB,
    Canada
Source Naturals, Santa Cruz, CA
Specialty Beverages, Glendora, CA
Specialty Brands, San Francisco, CA
Spring Tree Corp., Brattleboro, VT
Springfield Creamery, Springfield, OR
Standard Milling Co., Kansas City, MO
Star & Crescent, Sacramento, CA
Stearns & Foster Co., Cincinnati, OH
Stone-Buhr Milling Co., Seattle, WA
The Stroh Brewing Co., Detroit, MI
Sugar Ripe Farms, San Jose, CA
Sunburst Farms Natural Foods, Goleta,
    CA
Sunfield Foods, Hayward, CA
Sunkist Growers, Ontario, CA
Sun-Ray Industries, Baltimore, MD
Sunshine Biscuits, New York, NY
Sunshine Scented Oils, Los Angeles, CA
Sunspire Natural Foods, San Leandro,
    CA
Sunstar, Newport Beach, CA
Swan Pencil Co., New York, NY
Swiss Gold, Philadelphia, PA
Sydnor Research Associates, Berkeley,
    CA
Tampax, Lake Success, NY
Tartufo Italgelateria, San Gabriel, CA
Tastebud Delight Co., Oakland, CA

Tenneco West, Bakersfield, CA
Terra Nova, Ojai, CA
Teva Natural Foods, Mill Valley, CA
Texas Best, Houston, TX
Thomas J. Lipton, Inc., Englewood Cliff, NJ
3M, St. Paul, MN
Tima Brand, Beverly Hills, CA
Timbercrest Farms, Healdsburg, CA
Tomorrow Food Products, Los Angeles, CA
Tom's of Maine, Kennebunk, ME
Tomy Corp., Carson, CA
Trader Vic's Food Products, Emeryville, CA
Traditional Medicinals, Santa Rosa, CA
Trans-India Products, Santa Rosa, CA
Tree of Life, St. Augustine, FL
Tree Top, Selah, WA
Tres Chocolat, Oakland, CA
Trinity Sun Bars, Westlake, OR
Tropical Soap Co., Dallas, TX
Twin Lab, Ronkonkoma, NY
Two Ducks, Laguna Beach, CA
Uncle Ben's, Houston, TX
Uncle Goose Alphabet Blocks, Grand Rapids, MI
Uni-Pac Labs
United Grocers, Richmond, CA
United States Borax & Chemical Corp., Los Angeles, CA
Universal Co-Operatives, Minneapolis, MN
Ushida of America Corp., Woodside, NY
US Mills, Omaha, NE
Ventre Packing Co., Syracuse, NY
Ventura Coastal Corp., Ventura, CA
Vera Products, Taos, NM
Vermont Country Maple, Jericho Center, VT

Veronique Raskin, San Francisco, CA
Vichy Springs Mineral Water Corp., Ukiah, CA
Vita-Mix Corp., Cleveland, OH
Viva Vera, Garland, TX
W. M. Thompson Co., Carson, CA
Wagner Health Food Products, Bellwood, IL
Walnut Acres, Penns Creek, PA
Wamsutta, New York, NY
W & R Jacob & Co., England
Wasa Ry-King, Stamford, CT
Weetabix of Canada Ltd., Ontario, Canada
Weleda, Spring Valley, NY
West Coast Growers & Packers, Selma, CA
Westbrae Natural Foods, Emeryville, CA
Westpoint Pepperell, Westpoint, GA
White King, Los Angeles, CA
Whittier Wood Products, Eugene, OR
Whole Earth, England
Willamette Mills, Eugene, OR
Willert Home Products, St. Louis, MO
William Escott's, San Marino, CA
William G. Bell Co., E. Weymouth, MA
Windflower Herbals, Columbia, CA
Winthrop Laboratories/Sterling Drug, New York, NY
Woltra Co., New York, NY
Woodkrafter Kits, Yarmouth, ME
Yahtae Farm, Mt. Angel, OR
Yasutomo & Co., San Francisco, CA
Yoplait USA, Minneapolis, MN
Young's Drug Products Corp., Piscataway, NJ
Young's Rubber Corp., Trenton, NJ
Z. I. Caudry, France
Zuckerraffinerie Tangermunde/Bahlsen of North America, Woodside, NY

BIBLIOGRAPHY

Banik, Dr. Allen E. *Your Water and Your Health*. Rev. ed. New Canaan, CT: Keats Publishing, 1981.

Barrett, Susan. "Diapers: The Ecological Issue." *Mothering*, Summer 1983.

Billman, Alice. *Guidelines: A Compilation of Products and Resources for the Chemically Sensitive*. Dallas: Human Ecology Research Foundation/SW, 1981.

Bommersbach, Jane. "The Case against NutraSweet." *Westword*, 25 January 1983.

Brandt, Pam. "A Henna Head Trip." *Ms.*, May 1983.

Brobeck, Stephen, and Averyt, Anne C. *The Product Safety Book: The Ultimate Consumer Guide to Product Hazards*. New York: E. P. Dutton, 1983.

Brody, Jane. "The Health Benefits of Not Eating Meat." *San Francisco Chronicle*, 8 December 1983.

Brown, Michael. *Laying Waste—The Poisoning of America by Toxic Chemicals*. New York: Pocket Books, 1981.

Buchman, Dian Dincin. *The Complete Herbal Guide to Natural Health & Beauty*. Garden City, NY: Doubleday & Co., 1973.

Calabrese, Edward. *Pollutants and High-Risk Groups*. New York: John Wiley, 1978.

California State Department of Consumer Affairs. *Clean Your Room! A Compendium Describing a Wide Variety of Indoor Pollutants and Their Health Effects, and Containing Sage Advice to Both Householders and Statespersons in the Matter of Cleaning Up*. Sacramento: California State Department of Consumer Affairs, February 1982.

Claire, R. *French Vegetarian Cosmetics*. San Francisco: Strawberry Hill Press, 1979.

Conry, Tom. *Consumer's Guide to Cosmetics*. Garden City, NY: Anchor Press/ Doubleday, 1980.

Consumer Reports. "Are Hair Dyes Safe?" August 1979.

Consumer Reports. "It's Natural! It's Organic! Or is it?" July 1980.

Consumer Reports. "Menstrual Tampons and Pads." March 1978.

Consumer Reports. "The Selling of H_2O." September 1980.

Consumer Reports. "Water Filters." February 1983.

Consumers Union. *Consumer Reports Buying Guide*. Mt. Vernon, NY: 1981, 1982, and 1983.

Cronin, Etain, *Contact Dermatitis*. Edinburgh: Churchill Livingstone, 1980.

Federal Register. United States Dept. of Health, Education, and Welfare, Food and Drug Administration. "Bottled Water," Part 3, Vol. 38, No. 226, Monday, 26 November 1973.

Fisher, Alexander A. *Contact Dermatitis*. Philadelphia: Lea & Febiger, 1973.

Freydberg, Nicholas, Ph.D., and Gortner, Willis A., Ph.D. *The Food Additives Book*. New York: Bantam Books, 1982.

Fritsch, Albert J., ed. *The Household Pollutants Guide*. Garden City, NY: Anchor Press/Doubleday, 1978.

Golos, N., et al. *Coping with Your Allergies*. New York: Simon & Schuster, 1979.

Gosselin, R. E., et al. *Clinical Toxicology of Commercial Products*. 4th ed. Baltimore: The Williams & Wilkins Co., 1976.

Grae, Ida, *Nature's Colors—Dyes from Plants*. New York: Macmillan Publishing Co., 1974.

Hawley, G. G., ed. *The Condensed Chemical Dictionary*. New York: Van Nostrand Reinhold, 1981.

Higgenbotham, P., and Pinkham, M. E. *Mary Ellen's Best of Helpful Hints*. New York: Warner Books, 1979.

Hunter, Beatrice Trum. *Beatrice Trum Hunter's Additive Book*. New Canaan, CT: Keats Publishing, 1980

Hunter, Beatrice Trum. *Consumer Beware! Your Food and What's Been Done to It*. New York: Simon & Schuster, 1971.

Jakubowski, W., and Hoff, J. C. *Waterborne Transmission of Giardiasis*. Cincinnati: Environmental Protection Agency, 1979.

Keough, Carol. *Water Fit to Drink*. Emmaus, PA: Rodale Press, 1981.

King, J. Gordon. "Air for Living." *Respiratory Care*, Vol. 18, No. 2, March-April 1973.

Krochmal, Connie. *A Guide to Natural Cosmetics*. Springville, VT: Thornwood Books, 1973.

Lafavore, Michael. "Clean Air Indoors." *Rodale's New Shelter*, May/June, 1982.

Lappé, Frances Moore. *Diet for a Small Planet*. New York: Friends of the Earth/Ballantine Books, 1971.

Lehmann, P. "More than You Ever Thought You Would Know about Food Additives." *FDA Consumer*, United States Dept. of Health, Education, and Welfare, April-June 1979.

Lipske, Michael. *Chemical Additives in Booze*. Washington, DC: Center for Science in the Public Interest, 1982.

Ludeman, K., and Henderson, L. *Do-It-Yourself Allergy Analysis Handbook*. New Canaan, CT: Keats Publishing, 1979.

Makower, Joel. *Office Hazards*. Washington, DC: Tilden Press, 1981.

Manufacturing Chemists Association, *Food Additives: What They Are, How They Are Used*, 1961.

Mauro, Elizabeth. "Inside Body Care." *Whole Life Times*, March 1983.

Marsch, A. *Beauty Recipes from Natural Foods*. New York: Sterling Publishing Co., 1974.

McAdoo, Maisie. "Birth Control." *Ms.*, May 1983.

McEntire, Patricia. *Mommy, I'm Hungry.* Sacramento: Cougar Books, 1982.

McGraw-Hill Encyclopedia of Food, Agriculture, and Nutrition. 4th ed., New York: McGraw-Hill, 1977.

National Research Council/National Academy of Science. *Indoor Pollutants.* Washington, DC: National Academy Press, 1981.

Nussdorf, M. R., and Nussdorf, S. B. *Dress For Health.* Harrisburg, PA: Stackpole Books, 1980.

Oetzel, Mary E. "Build For Health." *The Human Ecologist,* No. 21, Spring 1983.

Peterson, Iver. "Pollution: The Problem of Heating with Wood." *San Francisco Chronicle,* 7 December 1983.

Pfeiffer, M.D.; Guy, O.; and Nikel, Casimir M. *The Household Environment and Chronic Illness: Guidelines for Constructing and Maintaining a Less Polluted Residence.* Springfield, IL: Charles C. Thomas, 1980.

Randolph, T. G. *Human Ecology and Susceptibility to the Chemical Environment.* Springfield, IL: Charles C. Thomas, 1962.

Regenstein, Lewis. *America the Poisoned.* Washington, DC: Acropolis Books, 1982.

Rinzler, Carol Ann. *The Consumer's Brand-Name Guide to Household Products.* New York: Lippencott and Crowell, 1980.

Robertson, Laurel, et al. *Laurel's Kitchen.* Petaluma, CA: Nilgiri Press, 1976.

Rohé, Fred. *The Complete Book of Natural Foods.* Boulder: Shambhala, 1983.

Rose, Jeanne. *Kitchen Cosmetics.* Los Angeles: Panjandrum Books, 1978.

Rozyne, Michael. "Organic Foods: How Can You Be Sure?" *Whole Life Times,* August 1983.

Saifer, Phyllis, M.D., and Zellerbach. Merla. *Detox.* Los Angeles: Tarcher, 1984.

Samuels, Mike, M.D., and Bennett, Hal Zina. *Well Body, Well Earth: The Sierra Club Environmental Health Sourcebook.* San Francisco: Sierra Club Books, 1983.

Sequoia, Anna. *The Complete Catalog of Mail-Order Kits.* New York: Rawson, Wade Publishers, 1981.

Shepard, Robin. "Color Your Hair . . . Naturally!" *The Mother Earth News,* March/April 1982.

Stark, N. *The Formula Book.* New York: Avon.

Swezey, Kenneth M. *Formulas, Methods, Tips & Data for Home & Workshop.* New York: Popular Science Publishing Co., 1969.

Tortora, P. G. *Understanding Textiles.* New York: Macmillan, 1978.

Twenty Mule Team Borax: The Magic Crystal. Los Angeles: United States Borax & Chemical Corp.

United States Dept. of Health, Education, and Welfare. *Milk Ordinance and Code; 1953 Recommendations of Public Health Service.* PHS Publication #229. Washington, DC: U.S. Government Printing Office, 1953.

United States Dept. of Health, Education, and Welfare. *Milk Ordinance and Code, 1965 Recommendations of Public Health Service.* PHS Publication #229. Washington, DC: U.S. Government Printing Office, 1965.

United States Office of the Federal Register. *Code of Federal Regulations.* Washington, DC: U.S. Government Printing Office, 1981.

United States Statutes at Large. *Safe Drinking Water Act,* Vol 88 Pt 2, Public Law 93-523. Washington, DC: U.S. Government Printing Office, 1976.

Wallace, Dan, ed. *The Natural Formula Book for Home & Yard.* Emmaus, PA: Rodale Press, 1982.

Waters, Enoc P. *FDA Consumer.* "What about Bottled Water?" May 1974.

Weiss, G., ed. *Hazardous Chemicals Data Book.* Park Ridge, NJ: Noyes Data Corporation, 1980.

Whole Foods Magazine. *Natural Foods Guide.* Berkeley: And/Or Press, 1979.

Winter, R. *A Consumer Dictionary of Cosmetic Ingredients.* New York: Crown Publishers, 1978.

Winter, R. *A Consumer Dictionary of Food Additives.* New York: Crown Publishers, 1978.

Wylie, Harriet. *420 Ways to Clean Everything.* New York: Harmony Books, 1979.

Yiamouyiannis, John, PhD. *Lifesavers Guide to Fluoridation.* Delaware, OH: The Safe Water Foundation, 1982.

Young, R. J. "Benzene in Consumer Products." *Science,* 13 Jan 1978.

Zamm, Alfred V. *Why Your House May Endanger Your Health.* New York: Simon & Schuster, 1980.

Zimmerman, David R. *The Essential Guide to Nonprescription Drugs.* New York: Harper & Row, 1983.